Poetry, Painting, Park
Goethe and Claude Lorrain

LEGENDA

LEGENDA is the Modern Humanities Research Association's book imprint for new research in the Humanities. Founded in 1995 by Malcolm Bowie and others within the University of Oxford, Legenda has always been a collaborative publishing enterprise, directly governed by scholars. The Modern Humanities Research Association (MHRA) joined this collaboration in 1998, became half-owner in 2004, in partnership with Maney Publishing and then Routledge, and has since 2016 been sole owner. Titles range from medieval texts to contemporary cinema and form a widely comparative view of the modern humanities, including works on Arabic, Catalan, English, French, German, Greek, Italian, Portuguese, Russian, Spanish, and Yiddish literature. Editorial boards and committees of more than 60 leading academic specialists work in collaboration with bodies such as the Society for French Studies, the British Comparative Literature Association and the Association of Hispanists of Great Britain & Ireland.

The MHRA encourages and promotes advanced study and research in the field of the modern humanities, especially modern European languages and literature, including English, and also cinema. It aims to break down the barriers between scholars working in different disciplines and to maintain the unity of humanistic scholarship. The Association fulfils this purpose through the publication of journals, bibliographies, monographs, critical editions, and the MHRA Style Guide, and by making grants in support of research. Membership is open to all who work in the Humanities, whether independent or in a University post, and the participation of younger colleagues entering the field is especially welcomed.

ALSO PUBLISHED BY THE ASSOCIATION

Critical Texts
Tudor and Stuart Translations • New Translations • European Translations
MHRA Library of Medieval Welsh Literature

MHRA Bibliographies
Publications of the Modern Humanities Research Association

The Annual Bibliography of English Language & Literature
Austrian Studies
Modern Language Review
Portuguese Studies
The Slavonic and East European Review
Working Papers in the Humanities
The Yearbook of English Studies

www.mhra.org.uk
www.legendabooks.com

GERMANIC LITERATURES

Editorial Committee
Chair: Professor Ritchie Robertson (University of Oxford)
Dr Barbara Burns (Glasgow University)
Professor Jane Fenoulhet (University College London)
Professor Anne Fuchs (University College Dublin)
Dr Jakob Stougaard-Nielsen (University College London)
Professor Annette Volfing (University of Oxford)
Professor Susanne Kord (University College London)
Professor John Zilcosky (University of Toronto)

Germanic Literatures includes monographs and essay collections on literature originally written not only in German, but also in Dutch and the Scandinavian languages. Within the German-speaking area, it seeks also to publish studies of other national literatures such as those of Austria and Switzerland. The chronological scope of the series extends from the early Middle Ages down to the present day.

APPEARING IN THIS SERIES

1. *Yvan Goll: The Thwarted Pursuit of the Whole*, by Robert Vilain
2. *Sebald's Bachelors: Queer Resistance and the Unconforming Life*, by Helen Finch
3. *Goethe's Visual World*, by Pamela Currie
4. *German Narratives of Belonging: Writing Generation and Place in the Twenty-First Century*, by Linda Shortt
5. *The Very Late Goethe: Self-Consciousness and the Art of Ageing*, by Charlotte Lee
6. *Women, Emancipation and the German Novel 1871-1910: Protest Fiction in its Cultural Context*, by Charlotte Woodford
7. *Goethe's Poetry and the Philosophy of Nature: Gott und Welt 1798–1827*, by Regina Sachers
8. *Fontane and Cultural Mediation: Translation and Reception in Nineteenth-Century German Literature*, edited by Ritchie Robertson and Michael White
9. *Metamorphosis in Modern German Literature: Transforming Bodies, Identities and Affects*, by Tara Beaney
10. *Comedy and Trauma in Germany and Austria after 1945: The Inner Side of Mourning*, by Stephanie Bird
11. *E.T.A. Hoffmann's Orient: Romantic Aesthetics and the German Imagination*, by Joanna Neilly
12. *Structures of Subjugation in Dutch Literature*, by Judit Gera

Managing Editor
Dr Graham Nelson, 41 Wellington Square, Oxford OX1 2JF, UK
www.legendabooks.com

Poetry, Painting, Park

Goethe and Claude Lorrain

Franz R. Kempf

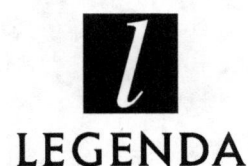

Germanic Literatures 22
Modern Humanities Research Association
2020

Published by Legenda
an imprint of the Modern Humanities Research Association
Salisbury House, Station Road, Cambridge CB1 2LA

ISBN 978-1-78188-410-2 (HB)
ISBN 978-1-78188-413-3 (PB)

First published 2020

All rights reserved. No part of this publication may be reproduced or disseminated or transmitted in any form or by any means, electronic, mechanical, photocopying, recording or otherwise, or stored in any retrieval system, or otherwise used in any manner whatsoever without written permission of the copyright owner, except in accordance with the provisions of the Copyright, Designs and Patents Act 1988, or under the terms of a licence permitting restricted copying issued in the UK by the Copyright Licensing Agency Ltd, Saffron House, 6–10 Kirby Street, London EC1N 8TS, *England, or in the USA by the Copyright Clearance Center, 222 Rosewood Drive, Danvers MA 01923. Application for the written permission of the copyright owner to reproduce any part of this publication must be made by email to legenda@mhra.org.uk.*

Disclaimer: Statements of fact and opinion contained in this book are those of the author and not of the editors or the Modern Humanities Research Association. The publisher makes no representation, express or implied, in respect of the accuracy of the material in this book and cannot accept any legal responsibility or liability for any errors or omissions that may be made.

Trademark notice: Product or corporate names may be trademarks or registered trademarks, and are used only for identification and explanation without intent to infringe.

© *Modern Humanities Research Association 2020*

Copy-Editor: Dr Alastair Matthews

CONTENTS

Acknowledgements   ix
Note on References and Translations   x
List of Illustrations   xi
Introduction   1

1   Nature, Art, Experience, Idea: Exploring Goethe's Aesthetics of Landscape Painting   14
     1.1   *Natura et Ars*   16
     1.2   A Practitioner's View: Jakob Philipp Hackert   18
     1.3   Landscape with a Bridge (Ponte Molle): Hackert and Lorrain   29
     1.4   Renaissance Landscape Painting and *Torquato Tasso*   36

2   The Poetry of Art Criticism: Goethe's 1772 Review of Lorrain   49
     2.1   The Rhetoric of Landscape Painting   53
     2.2   Lorrain as Ekphrasis   57
     2.3   Salomon Gessner: Painter and Poet of Pastorals   63
     2.4   *Ut Pictura Poesis*: Goethe's Challenge to Lessing   68
     2.5   Lorrain's Aesthetics of Dynamic Oppositions   72
     2.6   Storytelling as Landscape Painting: Goethe's Idyll 'Der Wandrer'   75

3   Italy: Landscape as Nature and Art   89
     3.1   Seeing through the Haze: Primeval Landscape, or *Urlandschaft*   91
     3.2   Goethe and Hackert Visit Lorrain in the Palazzo Colonna   97
     3.3   'Einfache Nachahmung der Natur, Manier, Styl' as a Theory of Landscape Painting   101
     3.4   Lorrain in Six Lines and One Monologue: *Nausikaa* and Faust's Arcadia   111
     3.5   *Natura et Ars* as Comedy: 'Amor ein Landschaftsmaler'   124

4   Painting into Poetry into Park: Lorrain and Goethe as English Gardeners   136
     4.1   James Thomson's Lorrainian Landscapes   140
     4.2   Lorrain, the Beautiful, the Sublime, and the Picturesque: Edmund Burke and Uvedale Price   142
     4.3   Alexander Pope: Gardener and Poet   145
     4.4   Through the Claude Glass: Lorrain's Protean Art   149
     4.5   Gardening is Painting: Horace Walpole's Essay *On Modern Gardening*   154
     4.6   Goethe: Gardener and Poet   155

4.7	The English Garden: A Testing Ground for the Nature–Art Dilemma	162
4.8	Counterfeit Eden: Goethe's Critique of the English Garden in *Die Wahlverwandtschaften* and in *Faust*	166

5 Light — Eye — Colour: The Metamorphosis of Landscape Painting   181

5.1	Mediterranean Colours	183
5.2	Goethe's *Zur Farbenlehre* and Lorrain's *Landscape with Tobias and the Angel* (1663)	185
5.3	The Eye: Perception and Production	193
5.4	Jacob van Ruisdael and Peter Paul Rubens: Lorrains of the North	199
5.5	Faust: Poet and Painter of Landscapes	209

Appendix: Goethe's Lorrain Collection   222

References   226

Index   242

ACKNOWLEDGEMENTS

I owe a debt of gratitude to Ritchie Robertson, who never wavered in his support of this project and whose advice was invaluable. I also owe much to Alastair Matthews's editorial acumen, and to Graham Nelson's managerial savvy.

F. R. K., New York, October 2019

NOTE ON
REFERENCES AND TRANSLATIONS

The following abbreviations are used:

CtO	Goethe, 'Contributions to Optics', trans. by Eleanor C. Merry, in Maria Schindler and Eleanor C. Merry, *Pure Colour*, 3 vols (London: New Culture Publications, 1946), III: *Extracts from Goethe's Scientific Work*, pp. 1–42
CV	Johann Peter Eckermann, *Conversations with Goethe*, trans. by John Oxenford (New York: Da Capo Press, 1998)
CW	*Goethe's Collected Works*, ed. by Victor Lange and others, 12 vols (Princeton: Princeton University Press, 1995)
FA	Goethe, *Sämtliche Werke*, ed. by Dieter Borchmeyer and others, 40 vols (Frankfurt a.M.: Deutscher Klassiker Verlag, 1985–2013)
GoA	*Goethe on Art*, trans. by John Gage (Berkeley: University of California Press, 1980)
GW	*Goethe-Wörterbuch* (Stuttgart: Kohlhammer, 1978–)
MRD	Marcel Roethlisberger, *Claude Lorrain: The Drawings*, 2 vols (New Haven: Yale University Press, 1961)
MRP	Marcel Roethlisberger, *Claude Lorrain: The Paintings*, 2 vols (New Haven: Yale University Press, 1961)
WED	Goethe, *West–Eastern Divan*, trans. by Edward Dowden (London: Dent, 1914)
WMT	*Wilhelm Meister's Travels* [1st edn, 1821], trans. by Thomas Carlyle (Columbia, SC: Camden House, 1991)

Goethe's *Faust* and *Torquato Tasso* are quoted by line number only, following the German version; line numbers may differ slightly in the English text. German quotations are from *FA*, VII.1 (*Faust*), and *FA*, V (*Tasso*); English quotations are from *CW*, II (*Faust*), and *CW*, VIII (*Tasso*).

Lorrain's works are cited according to Marcel Roethlisberger's catalogues raisonnés (MRP and MRD above). Following the convention in Lorrain scholarship, each painting is also accompanied by its number in Lorrain's own record of completed paintings, the *Liber Veritatis* (*LV*). Note that Roethlisberger identifies Lorrain paintings not in the *Liber Veritatis* with 'no.' (instead of '*LV*").

Translations are my own unless otherwise indicated here or in the text and notes. For the purposes of the argument, the analyses of individual passages sometimes tease out the meanings (literal and otherwise) of German words and expressions by means of English renditions that differ from the quoted translations.

LIST OF ILLUSTRATIONS

❖

FIG. I.1. Lorrain, *Pastoral with the Arch of Constantine*. Kunsthaus Zürich; donated by the Holenia Trust in memory of Joseph H. Hirshhorn, 1996/© Kunsthaus Zürich

FIG. I.2. Lorrain, *Coast View* [*An Artist Studying from Nature*]. Cincinnati Art Museum, Cincinnati, Ohio/© USA Gift of Mary Hanna — Bridgeman Images

FIG. I.3. Lorrain, *Seaport with the Embarkation of St Ursula*. National Gallery, London/© National Gallery — Art Resource, NY

FIG. I.4. Lorrain, *Landscape with Abraham Expelling Hagar and Ishmael*. Alte Pinakothek; Bayerische Staatsgemäldesammlungen, Munich/© Blauel Gnamm — Artothek

FIG. I.5. Lorrain, *Landscape with Psyche outside the Palace of Amor* [*The Enchanted Castle*]. National Gallery, London/© National Gallery — Bridgeman Images

FIG. 1.1. Lorrain, *The Herdsman*. National Gallery of Art, Washington, DC/© Courtesy National Gallery of Art, Washington

FIG. 1.2. Lorrain, *A View of the Campagna from Tivoli*. Royal Collection Trust/© Her Majesty Queen Elizabeth II — 2019

FIG. 1.3. Hackert, *View of the Tiber Valley with the Sabine Mountains*. Private Collection, USA/© Sotheby's, London; 6 July 2011, lot 70.

FIG. 1.4. Lorrain, *Pastoral Landscape with the Ponte Molle*. Birmingham Museum and Art Gallery, Birmingham, UK/© Birmingham Museums Trust — 1955P111

FIG. 1.5. Lorrain, *Landscape with Erminia and the Shepherd*. Holkham Hall, Wells-next-the Sea, Norfolk/© The Earl of Leicester and the Trustess of the Holkham Estate — Bridgeman Images

FIG. 1.6. Circle of Annibale Carracci, *Erminia*. National Gallery, London/© National Gallery — Art Resource, NY

FIG. 2.1. Mason, *The Landing of Aeneas in Italy: The Allegorical Morning of the Roman Empire*. Royal Academy of Arts, London/© Royal Academy of Arts, London — Prudence Cuming Associates Limited

FIG. 2.2. Woollett, *Roman Edifices in Ruins: The Allegorical Evening of the Roman Empire*. Royal Academy of Arts, London/© Royal Academy of Arts, London — Prudence Cuming Associates Limited

FIG. 2.3. Byrne, *Evening*. Royal Academy of Arts, London/© Royal Academy of Arts, London — Prudence Cuming Associates Limited

FIG. 2.4. Mason, *Sun Setting*. Royal Academy of Arts, London/© Royal Academy of Arts, London — Prudence Cuming Associates Limited

FIG. 2.5. Catel, *Gulf of Naples* [Pozzuoli]. Germanisches Nationalmuseum, Nürnberg; Leihgabe Kunstsammlungen der Stadt Nürnberg/© J. Musolf

FIG. 3.1. Kniep, *Bocca di Capri*. Klassik Stiftung Weimar, Museen: 27998/© Angelika Kittel

FIG. 3.2. Goethe, *Bucht und Kastell bei Neapel* [Bay and Castle near Naples]. Klassik Stiftung Weimar, Museen: 210521

FIG. 3.3. Lorrain, *Seaport with the Embarkation of Ulysses from the Phaeacians*. Musée du Louvre, Paris/© RMN-Grand Palais — Thierry Le Mage — Art Resource, NY

FIG. 3.4. Lorrain, *Coast View with Acis and Galatea*. Gemäldegalerie Alte Meister, Staatliche Kunstsammlungen, Dresden; © bpk Bildagentur — Ursula Maria Hoffmann — Art Resource, NY

FIG. 3.5. Lorrain, *Landscape with Dancing Figures* [*The Mill*]. Galleria Doria Pamphilj, Rome/© Luisa Ricciarini — Bridgeman Images

FIG. 4.1. Lorrain, *View of Tivoli at Sunset*. The Fine Arts Museums of San Francisco; gift of the Samuel H. Kress Foundation, 61.44.31

FIG. 4.2. Nicholson, *Rural Scenery at Stourhead*. British Museum, London/© Trustees of the British Museum

FIG. 4.3. Lorrain, *Coast View of Delphi with a Procession*. Trust Doria Pamphilj; Archivio Doria Pamphilj/© 2018 ADP s.r.l.

FIG. 4.4. Contemporary view of Stourhead. <http://geographic.org.uk/p/484205>/© Chris Downer

FIG. 4.5. Turner, *Pope's Villa at Twickenham*. Private collection/© Sotheby's, London; 9 July 2008, lot 91

FIG. 4.6. Gilpin, view of Castle Acre. Royal Academy of Arts, London/© Royal Academy of Arts, London — Prudence Cuming Associates Limited

FIG. 4.7. Knight, plate 1. British Museum, London/© Trustees of the British Museum

FIG. 4.8. Knight, plate 2. British Museum, London/© Trustees of the British Museum

FIG. 4.9. Goethe, *Roman House*. Klassik Stiftung Weimar, Museen: 212535/© Angelika Kittel

FIG. 4.10. Repton, sketches from *Red Book 65*. Red Book 65; private collection, Wales/© André Rogger

FIG. 4.11. Lorrain, *Landscape with Narcissus and Echo*. National Gallery, London/© National Gallery — Art Resource, NY

FIG. 5.1. *The Aldobrandini Wedding*. Biblioteca Apostolica Vaticana, Vatican City/© Vatican Museums

FIG. 5.2. Lorrain, *Landscape with Tobias and the Angel* [*Evening*]. The State Hermitage Museum, St Petersburg/© The State Hermitage Museum — Svetlana Suetova

FIG. 5.3. Ruisdael, *Waterfall with Castle on a Mountain*. Gemäldegalerie Alte Meister, Staatliche Kunstsammlungen, Dresden/© bpk Bildagentur — Elke Estel — Art Resource, NY

FIG. 5.4. Ruisdael, *The Monastery*. Gemäldegalerie Alte Meister, Staatliche Kunstsammlungen, Dresden/© bpk Bildagentur — Hans-Peter Klut — Art Resource, NY

FIG. 5.5. Ruisdael, *The Jewish Cemetery*. Gemäldegalerie Alte Meister, Staatliche Kunstsammlungen, Dresden/© bpk Bildagentur — Elke Estel, Hans-Peter Klut — Art Resource, NY

FIG. 5.6. Rubens, *The Peasants' Return from the Fields*. Gallerie degli Uffizi, Florence/© Gabinetto Fotografico

FIG. 5.7. Goethe, *Aesculap-Tempel in der Villa Borghese im Mondschein* [The Temple of Aesculapius at the Villa Borghese in Moonlight]. Klassik Stiftung Weimar, Museen: 210564/© Olaf Mokansky

FIG. 5.8. Lorrain, *Landscape with St Mary of Cervello*. Museo del Prado, Madrid/© Photographic Archive Museo Nacional del Prado

FIG. 5.9. Lorrain, *Landscape with St Onuphrius*. Museo del Prado, Madrid/© Photographic Archive Museo Nacional del Prado

FIG. A.1. Lorrain, *Reconciliation of Cephalus and Procris* (c. 1645). Klassik Stiftung Weimar, Museen: 27832/© Olaf Mokansky

FIG. A.2. Lorrain, *Pastoral Landscape* [with Shepherd Playing the Flute] (no date). Klassik Stiftung Weimar, Museen: 28935/© Renno

INTRODUCTION

As the first comprehensive consideration of Goethe and Lorrain across the three sister arts, this study fills a lacuna in Goethe scholarship. Although this book is intended for scholars of literature, philosophy, and art history, as well as specialists in the history and theory of aesthetics, landscape painting, and horticulture, my argument is largely aesthetic: it draws from exemplary readings of Goethe's landscape poetry and links these readings via analogy to Lorrain's landscape paintings. The power to summon up an image of nature relies on a particular set of poetic means and a particular poietic disposition. The differentiation is crucial to our understanding of artistic creation, in the sense that 'poetic' relates to means and product, and 'poietic' to mood and process. In a conversation on drawings (5 July 1827) with his amanuensis, Johann Peter Eckermann (1792–1854), Goethe describes the moment of artistic creation in which the purity of the artist's mind coalesces with the deftness of the artist's practice to reveal, and to enable the observer's revelry in, the poietic mood: a masterly drawing

> gives not only, in its purity, the mental intention of the artist but also brings immediately before us the mood of his mind at the moment of creation. In every stroke [...] we perceive the great clearness and quiet serene resolution in the mind of the artist; and this beneficial mood is extended to us while we contemplate the work. (*CV*, p. 210; *FA*, XXXIX, 248)

While this pictorial aesthetics in a nutshell is not explicitly about Lorrain, the epithet 'heiter' [serene], as we shall see, *is* Goethe's mark of distinction for Lorrain. When Goethe avers that the drawing is 'purely objective', he adds matter to mind, mood, and method, which when interwoven form a beautiful whole. The passage ends with Goethe contrasting poetry and painting by tying the aesthetics of production to those of effect: a painting 'speaks to us in a very decided manner', while a poem 'makes a far more vague impression — exciting in each hearer different emotions' (*CV*, p. 210; *FA*, XXXIX, 248–49). Complementing the complexity of aesthetics with that of hermeneutics — the reader's interpretive latitude vs the spectator's vicarious partaking in the producer's mood and the product's meaning — Goethe maps out the terrain of our exploration.[1]

Insofar as landscape is pictorial visualization, it is man's poetic imagination that informs and enables his relationship to 'nature', and it is (visual and verbal) poetry that weaves its golden thread through seemingly dissimilar manifestations of art. Likewise, the poetic is the link to the English landscape park; that is, verbal, painterly, and horticultural mediums evoke a shared visual perception, experience, and idea of 'nature'.[2]

In Tom Stoppard's play *Arcadia* (1993), Hannah Jarvis, the 'anti-Romantic' scholar specializing in horticulture and literature from 1750 to 1834, ridicules the notion that the English Garden originated in England: 'English landscape was invented by gardeners imitating foreign painters who were evoking classical authors. The whole thing was brought home in the luggage from the grand tour [...] Capability Brown doing Claude, who was doing Virgil. Arcadia!'.[3] Given the time period of her expertise, Jarvis could have equally cited Goethe as an example of someone who, from 1786 to 1788, went on a *Bildungsreise* through Italy in search of the cultural legacy of Antiquity and the Renaissance and who, uniquely so, 'did' all three arts.

As a landscape architect, he redesigned Weimar's Ilmpark to be an English Garden, the style initiated by England's master 'gardener', Lancelot 'Capability' Brown (1716–1783), including an expanse of meadows dotted with clumps of trees, gently contoured hillsides, serpentine paths, and, perched atop a hillock offering extensive vistas, a Renaissance villa called the Roman House. Officially registered in Rome as a 'pittore', he sketched and painted more than four hundred landscapes in Italy alone,[4] inspired by his experience of Mediterranean 'nature' and its pictorial correlative, the paintings of Claude Gellée (c. 1600–1682).[5] Gellée was born in Alsace-Lorraine — hence his adopted name 'Claude Lorrain' — and settled in Rome in 1627 to become Europe's most celebrated landscape painter and, taken possession of by the English (over fifty of his paintings were in England by 1750),[6] the father of the English Garden. A lifelong admirer of Lorrain, Goethe owned twenty-two original etchings, two drawings, and a painting, the 'infinitely delightful' *Landscape with the Three Heliads Searching for the Dead Phaeton* (c. 1657; *LV*, 143).[7] Finally, to illustrate the quartet formed by Goethe, poetry, landscape, and Antiquity, one can think of his European bestseller, *Die Leiden des jungen Werthers* [The Sufferings of Young Werther] (1774), which echoes Homeric pastoral scenes, or Johann Heinrich Wilhelm Tischbein's painting, *Goethe in the Roman Campagna* (1787), which shows him as author of the 1789 blank-verse drama *Iphigenie auf Tauris* (pictorially illustrated on the frieze), 'doing' Euripides while reclining in a landscape vaguely alluding to Lorrain.[8]

Lorrain has created some of the most mesmerizing landscapes, traditionally characterized as pastoral, idyllic, Arcadian, or classicist. These epithets suggest, in terms of substance, innocence and bliss in bucolic nature, and in terms of style, a serene effect produced by the ingeniously devised combination of aerial perspective, low horizon, balanced proportion, and harmonious interplay of colour, light, and shade. *Pastoral with the Arch of Constantine* (1648), a painting rediscovered only in 1989, and now in the Kunsthaus Zürich,[9] serves as an example.

Yet Lorrain is far more complex and ambiguous. There are also his 'urban' scenes, some of them capriccios, that is, architectural fantasies of Rome, and seaports at sunrise or sunset.[10] For illustrative purposes, paintings such as *Seaport* (1637; *LV*, 14) or *Landscape with Rural Dance* (1637; *LV*, 13) readily come to mind. But most remarkable for our purposes is the 1639 painting *Coast View* (*LV*, 44).

The painting's better-known title, *An Artist Studying from Nature*,[11] raises the question that will guide this study — what links nature to art, imitation to invention? The animated discussion with his two companions in which the draughtsman

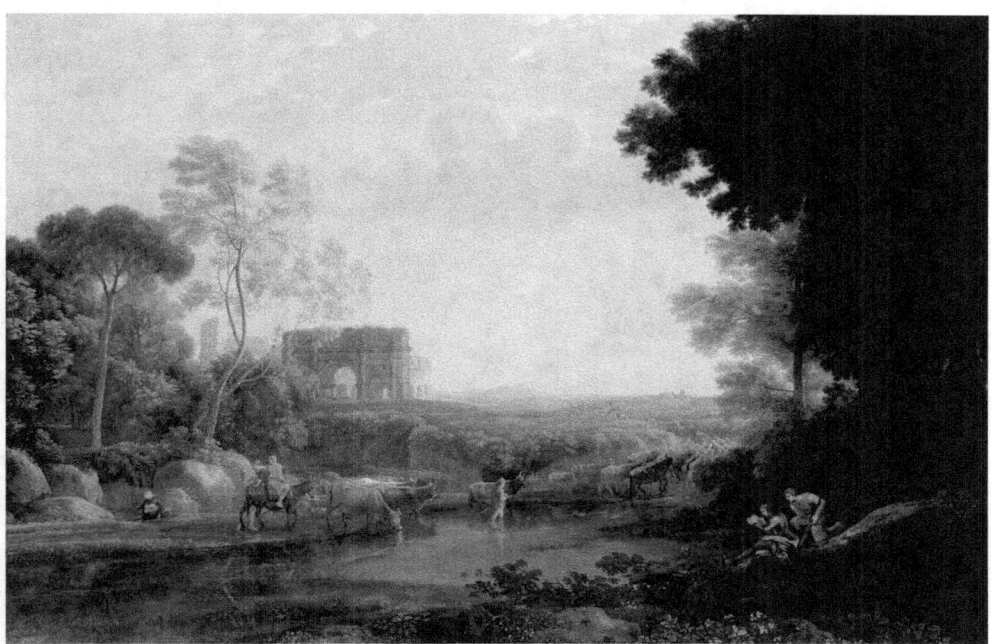

Fig. I.1. Lorrain, *Pastoral with the Arch of Constantine*. Kunsthaus Zürich; donated by the Holenia Trust in memory of Joseph H. Hirshhorn, 1996/© Kunsthaus Zürich

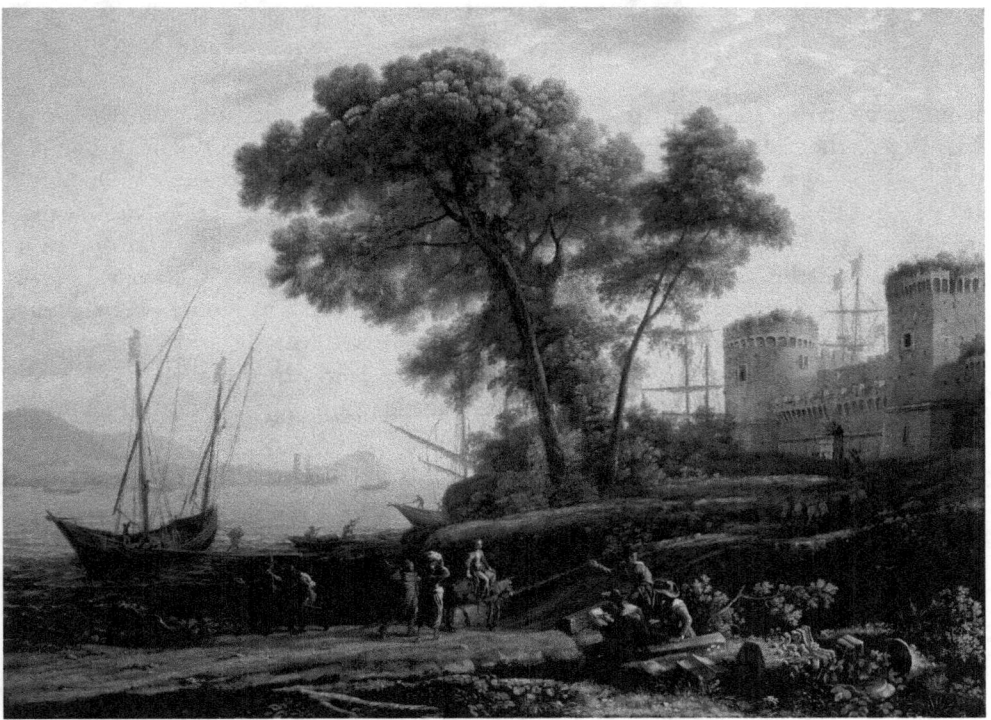

Fig. I.2. Lorrain, *Coast View [An Artist Studying from Nature]*. Cincinnati Art Museum, Cincinnati, Ohio/© USA Gift of Mary Hanna — Bridgeman Images

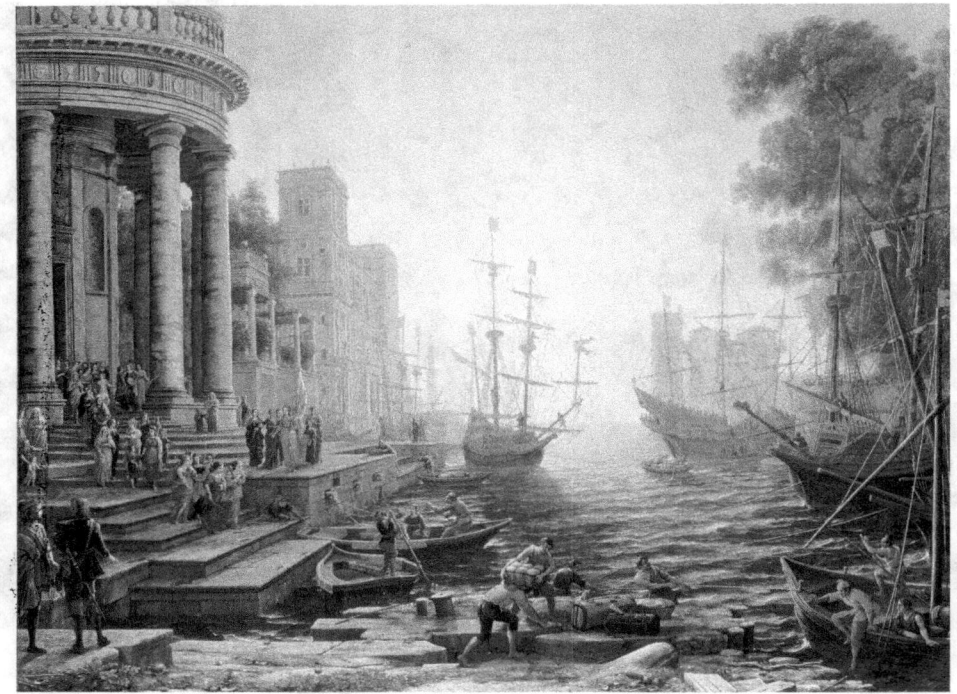

Fig. I.3. Lorrain, *Seaport with the Embarkation of St Ursula*.
National Gallery, London/© National Gallery — Art Resource, NY

seems engaged suggests that this question remains open to debate.[12] Goethe's own framing of the dichotomy in 'Über Wahrheit und Wahrscheinlichkeit der Kunstwerke: Ein Gespräch' [On Truth and Probability in Works of Art: A Dialogue] (1798) — as being between the 'Naturwahre' [truth of nature] and the 'Kunstwahre' [truth of art] (*FA*, XVIII, 504; *GoA*, p. 28) — offers a glimpse into the question's depths, while the breadth of the dispute is accentuated when we consider that Lorrain started out as a painter of large-scale ceiling frescoes in Roman Renaissance palazzos[13] and ended up inspiring a horticultural revolution.

As suffused with light as these sea-, city-, and landscapes may be, one easily overlooks how deeply fraught they often are with tension. There is the visual drama of time passing, evoked by the transitory light of sun rising or setting. But there is also the existential drama: the dewy innocence of pale morning strikes a stark contrast to the spectre of anguish conjured up by the prospect of exile, violence, death. Powerful examples of this 'mismatch' of style and substance can be seen in *Seaport with the Embarkation of St Ursula* (1641; *LV*, 54) or in *Landscape with Abraham Expelling Hagar and Ishmael* (1668; *LV*, 173).

Miniscule in size but monumental in meaning, the staffage figures are integral to Lorrain's pictorial *coincidentia oppositorum*, as is the tension between the meticulous detail of the foreground and the nebulous glow of the distance, or between the rectilinear geometry of architecture and the undulations of nature. Even when there

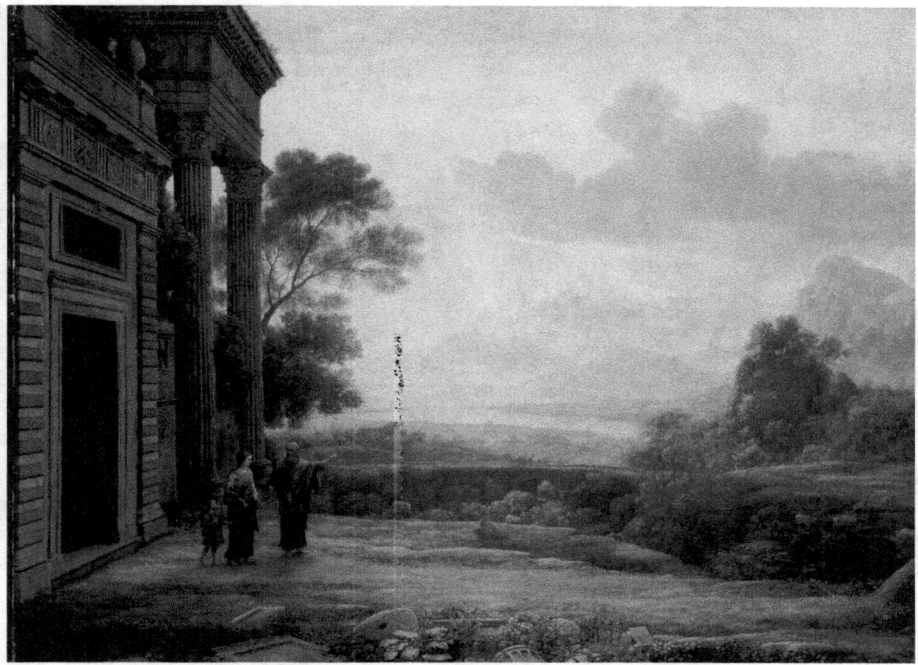

Fig. I.4. Lorrain, *Landscape with Abraham Expelling Hagar and Ishmael*. Alte Pinakothek; Bayerische Staatsgemäldesammlungen, Munich/© Blauel Gnamm — Artothek

is greater correspondence between motif, tone, and mood, Lorrain's distinctive style is 'oxymoronic', as captured by John Keats's ekphrastic rendering of *Landscape with Psyche outside the Palace of Amor* [*The Enchanted Castle*] (1664; *LV*, 162) (Fig. I.5) in these lines from 'Ode to a Nightingale': 'Charm'd magic casements, opening on the foam | Of perilous seas, in faery lands forlorn'.[14]

In notes for a posthumously published essay on landscape painting, Goethe asserts: 'Im Claude Lorrain erklärt sich die Natur für ewig' [In Claude Lorrain, nature proclaims herself to be eternal] (*FA*, XXII, 528). Although even the shortest account of the relationship between Goethe and Lorrain has to quote this aperçu, its illuminating and paradoxical implications have not been appreciated. A Goethean aperçu is less witty ingenuity and more epistemological paradigm — it is defined in the *Goethe-Wörterbuch* as 'a sudden perception of relations and principles' (*GW*, I, 766).[15] Part of the significance of this one, then, is that 'nature' is not just the subject of the sentence; beginning with Lorrain, 'nature' is the subject of landscape painting.[16] What is more, the odd reflexive construction also turns 'nature' into the object. As a public announcement, 'to proclaim' resonates with theatricality; and indeed, what Lorrain does more often than not is invite us to watch, even participate in, a play, especially in cityscapes such as *The Embarkation of St Ursula*, but also in dramatic landscapes such as *Abraham's Expulsion of Hagar and Ishmael*.

Insofar as 'nature' acts and is acted upon, she generates meaning from within but is also imbued with meaning from without. Personified as an actress, nature stages

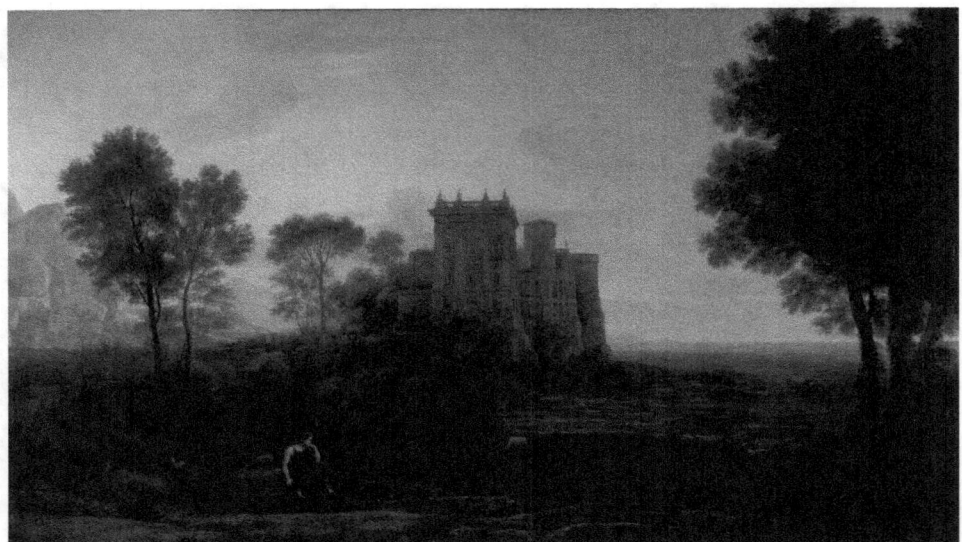

Fig. I.5. Lorrain, *Landscape with Psyche outside the Palace of Amor* [*The Enchanted Castle*]. National Gallery, London/© National Gallery — Bridgeman Images

herself as landscape confronting us, the spectators, with the tension between reality and illusion. We must add to this conundrum the fact that 'nature', for Goethe, is a dynamic concept; that is, nature is governed by the foundational principle of 'polarity' and 'intensification': 'Polarität ist in immerwährendem Anziehen und Abstoßen, Steigerung ist in immerstrebendem Aufsteigen' [Polarity is a state of constant attraction and repulsion, while intensification is a state of ever-striving ascent] (*FA*, xxv, 81; *CW*, xii, 6).[17] 'Eternal', on the other hand, evokes a stasis. If nature suggests the physical and the eternal suggests the spiritual, then by extension the aperçu also reflects the Enlightenment as the age of secularization where worldly objects are imbued with religious quality.

As *artists*, Goethe and Lorrain are kindred spirits because 'word and image', as Goethe puts it in two *Maximen und Reflexionen* from 1823, 'are correlates that perpetually seek each other', and 'he to whom nature begins to reveal her open secret' — or 'offenbares Geheimniß' in German — 'feels an irresistible longing for her most suitable exegete, art' (*FA*, xiii, 22, 24). Both word and image seem uniquely qualified to express the epistemological paradox of hiding and revealing the 'truth' inherent in the *et* of *natura et ars* (see Chapter 1) — in one way or another, our close readings will revolve around and probe this enigmatic yet fundamental Goethean paradox (*FA*, xxxiii, 459, 1027). Lorrain, however, is also a reluctant Muse for Goethe, less a model that he emulates and more a provocation with which he grapples, for, rather than celebrating the conceit of total artifice, Lorrain celebrates the possibilities engendered by the marriage of artistry with authenticity.

Goethe's statements on Lorrain range widely from critical commentaries to aesthetic reflections.[18] This randomness may explain to some degree the dearth of scholarship on Goethe and Lorrain.[19] Symptomatic is the lack of an entry on

Lorrain in the authoritative *Goethe-Handbuch* (originally published 1996–98). This void has now been filled by Ernst Osterkamp in the *Handbuch*'s third supplemental volume, *Kunst*, published in 2011.[20] While focusing on Goethe and the fine arts, it incorporates Lorrain into numerous discussions of Goethe's aesthetics — theoretical, practical, and political — chief among them a judiciously contextualized analysis of his writings on landscape painting by Steffen Egle.[21] Art-historical research on Lorrain and Goethe as draughtsman and painter respectively has been invaluable for our investigation, from fundamental works by Roethlisberger[22] and Femmel to exhibition catalogues and monographs.[23] Also notable here is research in the 1994 compendium *Goethe und die Kunst*, including the introductory essay 'Goethes Ideal', which features readings of Lorrain's *Landscape with Tobias and the Angel [Evening]* (1663; *LV*, 160) and *The Monastery* (c. 1650) by Jacob Isaackzoon van Ruisdael (c. 1628–1682).[24] The most detailed account of Goethe *and* Lorrain is to be found in Ernst Osterkamp's *Im Buchstabenbilde: Studien zum Verfahren Goethescher Bildbeschreibungen* (1991).

Osterkamp's focus on Goethe's method of describing Lorrain paintings is a masterly enquiry into the aesthetics of reception. We agree with Osterkamp's emphasis on 'the act of seeing' as well as his conclusion that this is an act of projection. But seeing, for Goethe, is also an act of production, and it is precisely in his poetic re-enactment of Lorrain that he overcomes the limitations of description. Instead of discerning, as Osterkamp does, 'deficits between description and painting', we focus on the new means of creation that Goethe gains. While benefiting from Osterkamp, this study breaks new ground in shifting the focus from description to ekphrasis.[25] To the 'lively perception', with which, according to Friedmar Apel, Goethe views the interrelation between art and nature and which involves 'mind, spirit, and sense',[26] we must add the poetic re-creation of a Lorrain painting or the poetic enactment of landscape after Lorrain. Even though this study opens up a new chapter in Goethe research, our Lorrainian readings acknowledge, evolve out of, and engage with previous research, albeit — given the latter's scope and focus — adopting as lens the multimedia aesthetics of landscape. Mindful of the fact that ekphrasis is an act of translation primarily concerned with fidelity to the original, which may or may not value the principle of beauty, the theoretical basis of this study's approach derives from Gottfried Boehm's musings on the 'show-don't-tell' character of a picture induced to 'speak' through ekphrasis. As a consequence, ekphrasis can rely on rhetoric to create beauty, *and* it can function as a mode of enquiry into beauty — a beauty that is vivid and dynamic.[27]

In a lifelong conversation with Lorrain, Goethe explores the dialectics between nature and art, imitation and invention, perception and cognition, subject and object. Goethe tries to understand Lorrain by enacting him, ekphrastically, as an experience and an idea. This tension is analogous to that intrinsic to 'landscape' and, by extension, to landscape painting and gardening. The enquiry remains open-ended because 'landscape' is a paradox: born of sublation, it negates and preserves both nature and art. 'Landscape', then, is an enquiry into the aesthetics of the probable, of the suspension of disbelief: the sublation is so 'dramatic' that we willingly accept its incredible 'reality' as believable.[28] The broader question that this project raises is the possibility of a shared, synthetic faculty that fuses — in the act of creating poetry, painting, and park — thought, feeling, and imagination, as well as potentially integrating subject and object in an aesthetics that circumvents Romantic and neoclassicist excesses.[29]

Different as they may be, the mediums of landscape painting, landscape poetry, and gardening all share a common denominator: each is a visual experience and a mode of enquiry in one. The aesthetic discovery and visualization of nature as landscape is consonant with the attempt to understand the world and our place within it. The three sister arts serve as mirrors for Goethe's self-understanding as an artist.

While striving to strike a balance between literary and art-historical analyses by including the examination of selected visual art by Lorrain and, in limited fashion, by Goethe, the close reading of relevant texts from Goethe's corpus of poetry and prose will preoccupy us throughout this study. Our aim is not to resolve the irresolvable, to reveal the 'open secret', as Goethe calls it repeatedly.[30] The aim, rather, is to trace their dialogue and listen in on their conversation. It is, and fundamentally so, through Goethe's poetry that we can enter into the specifics of their artistic affinity. Needless to say, the *sine qua non* of such a project is close reading, which necessitates that Goethe be cited in both English and German, and quoted generously.

Chapter 1 lays the groundwork by exploring the interrelation between nature and art as manifested in landscape painting. Goethe's own understanding will emerge, in the main, from his 'dialogue' with his mentor, Jakob Philipp Hackert (1737–1807), Europe's leading landscape painter in the eighteenth century. Lorrain's pioneering role in establishing the so-called 'classical' ('idyllic', 'ideal', 'idealized') landscape as an art-historical genre[31] comes to the fore in our discussion of Giovanni Battista Agucchi's *Instructions* (1602) for painting the Erminia story from Tasso's *Liberation of Jerusalem* (1581), and — hitherto unrecognized in Goethe scholarship — their relationship to Goethe's *Torquato Tasso* (1790) and Lorrain's pictorial rendering of this 'Arcadian' story in *Landscape with Erminia and the Shepherd* (1666; *LV*, 166). Crucially, Agucchi introduces into landscape painting the poetic principles of the real Tasso — namely, that the painter-poet, while grounded in 'the real', pursues 'the verisimilar' and expresses 'the marvellous', thus seeking to suspend the observer's disbelief and persuade him that what he sees is within the limits of the probable.

Chapter 2 examines Goethe's discovery of Lorrain in the form of engravings based on Lorrain's work and published in a *Collection of Prints Engraved after the Most Capital Paintings in England* (1772). Goethe's review of two of these engravings is discussed against the backdrop of contemporary aesthetic theory, especially the *ut pictura poesis* controversy surrounding the publication of Lessing's *Laocoön: An Essay on the Limits of Painting and Poetry* (1767). Pairing the pictorial and the poetic by reading Goethe's *Sturm und Drang* prose review as an ekphrastic poem makes the synergy that feeds Goethe's imagination almost palpable. Tapping into classical rhetoric to enhance the vividness of his language, Goethe transposes the copper engraving into a pictorial oratory, the 'still life' into a *tableau vivant*, thus emphasizing the theatricality of Lorrain's often stage-like scenic setups. Bringing the chapter to a close is a close reading of Goethe's idyll 'Der Wandrer' (1772). The versified idyll once again intertwines painting and poetry, for Goethe's inspiration — this is a new discovery in Goethe research — is a pair of Lorrain paintings whose engravings he encountered in the aforementioned collection.

Chapter 3 follows Goethe on his Grand Tour to Italy and Sicily from 1786 to 1788. Characterized by Goethe as a rebirth, his *Italienische Reise* [Italian Journey] — thus the title of his travelogue published in 1816–17 — offers him the chance to experience first-hand the 'South', including its light and landscapes, the art and architecture of 'Antiquity', and original paintings by Lorrain on display in Rome's famous palazzos. Sicily emerges as the crucible: not only does his drama fragment *Nausikaa* conjoin Mediterranean atmosphere, Homer's *Odyssey*, and Lorrain's *Seaport with the Embarkation of Ulysses from the Phaeacians* (1646; *LV*, 96); his discovery of the 'Urpflanze' [primordial plant] in Palermo's public gardens coincides with that of the 'primordial landscape' in Lorrain (*FA*, xv.1, 239; *CW*, vi, 181). Correlating painting and poem, this time *Coast View with Acis and Galatea* (1657; *LV*, 141) with Faust's 'Arkadien' — and *Landscape with Dancing Figures* [*The Mill*] (1648–49; *LV*, 113)[32] with the 1788 poem 'Amor ein Landschaftsmaler' [Amor as Landscape Painter] — Goethe explores, in a tragic and comedic mode, the feasibility and describability of such primordial landscapes, suspended as they are between loss and recovery (Faust's landscape), and the real and the imaginary (Amor's landscape). Goethe's characterization of Lorrain's creative practice opens up the possibility of reading his seminal essay 'Einfache Nachahmung der Natur, Manier, Styl' [Simple Imitation of Nature, Manner, and Style] (1789) as envisioning an ideal incorporation — and not, as is traditionally done, a hierarchically dogmatic demarcation — of diverse artistic dispositions and methods.

Growing out of my recent article on Goethe, *Kulturkritik*, and the English Garden, Chapter 4 expands our exploration of the sister arts by including the English landscape park. Taking our cue from Alexander Pope, who remarked in 1734 that 'all gardening is landscape painting',[33] a close reading of Pope's landscape poetry, along with that of James Thomson, explains that Lorrain's pioneering role in the horticultural revolution from the French Garden to the English Garden is, to a greater degree than has previously been assumed, a function of poetry's ekphrastic power to mediate his landscapes. Discussed alongside landscape poetry are 'landscape philosophy', particularly Edmund Burke's *A Philosophical Enquiry into the Origin of our Ideas of the Sublime and Beautiful* (1757), and theories of landscape gardening, such as Uvedale Price's *Essay on the Picturesque* (1796). Expanding Horace to include 'garden art', the notion of *ut pictura poesis et hortus* informs our analysis of Goethe's creative and critical appropriation of the English Garden model for his redesign of the park in Weimar, his novel *Die Wahlverwandtschaften* [Elective Affinities] (1809), and his *Faust II* (1832). Against the backdrop of the nature–art divide separating the English Garden from the French Garden, we show that

Goethe relies on Lorrain and his *Landscape with Narcissus and Echo* (1644; *LV*, 77) to question the utopian potential of the English Garden, that is, to question whether its reconciliation of nature and art provides a remedy for modern self-alienation. For Goethe, the English Garden's beautiful semblance is but a simulation of reality, a 'sham', to use Jarvis's expression.[34] A powerful literary manifestation is Faust's delusional creation of an English Garden at the end of *Faust II*.

The first portion of Chapter 5 focuses on Goethe's *Zur Farbenlehre* [Doctrine of Colours] (1810) and Lorrain's *Landscape with Tobias and the Angel* [*Evening*] (1663; *LV*, 160). We begin in Italy with Goethe's apprenticeship in 'seeing' — seeing, above all, the sun, which leads him to explore light as the source and catalyst for colour. Unlike Newton's prism-based conception of colour, Goethe's theory relies on the human eye as *the* apparatus of perception, maintaining that we are aesthetically equipped to *see* colour arise from the opposition of brightness and darkness. At work in the formation of colours are the dynamic principles of polarity (yellow calls forth purple) and of heightening (yellow intensifies to orange), and since 'the eye exhibits an exacting need for wholeness', it strives to encompass the entire colour circle (*CW*, XII, 178; *FA*, XXIII.1, 50). While Goethe never wavered in his predilection for the subdued and translucent colouring of the fresco — to wit, a copy of the ancient Roman *Aldobrandini Wedding* fresco took pride of place in the reception room of his Weimar residence — Lorrain's veiling of sharply contrasting colours and the softening of transitions coincides with Goethe's ideal of 'Harmoniespiel der Farben' [harmonious interplay of colours] (*FA*, XXIII.1, 774).

Our summation of Lorrain's significance for Goethe is based on the latter's exploration of a Northern landscape evolving out of his impressions of the Southern ur-landscape. The relevant texts include his 1816 essay on three paintings by Jacob van Ruisdael (c. 1628–1682), entitled 'Ruysdael als Dichter' [Ruisdael the Poet]; a lengthy conversation with Eckermann on Rubens's *Peasants' Return from the Fields* (c. 1640); and his final, and in many ways definitive, statement on Lorrain (also recorded by Eckermann) from 1829. Our analyses reveal the deep affinity between Lorrain and Goethe, at whose heart is a shared dynamics of nature and art, poetically and poietically. Finally, a similar metamorphosis seems to be at work in some of Faust's 'Northern' landscapes, as well as, after Faust's demise, in the playwright's mountain setting for the play's final scene. Among the discoveries of this study are two 'alpine' landscapes by Lorrain which must be added to Goethe's pictorial sources for this scene: *Landscape with St Mary of Cervello* (c. 1636; no. 218) and *Landscape with St Onuphrius* (c. 1636; no. 219).

In *Zur Farbenlehre*, Goethe describes what he calls an 'Urphänomen' [archetypal phenomenon], by which he means less an apprehensible object and more a process leading to a scientific epiphany:[35]

> Das was wir in der Erfahrung gewahr werden, sind [...] Fälle, welche sich mit einiger Aufmerksamkeit unter allgemeine empirische Rubriken bringen lassen. Diese subordinieren sich abermals unter wissenschaftliche Rubriken, welche weiter hinaufdeuten, wobei uns gewisse unerläßliche Bedingungen des Erscheinenden näher bekannt werden. Von nun an fügt sich alles nach und nach unter höhere Regeln und Gesetze, die sich aber nicht durch Worte und

> Hypothesen dem Verstande, sondern gleichfalls durch [...] Urphänomene dem Anschauenden offenbaren. (*FA*, XXIII.1, 80–81)
>
> [Events we become aware of through experience are simply those we can categorize empirically after some observation. These empirical categories may be further subsumed under scientific categories leading to even higher levels. In the process we become familiar with certain requisite conditions for what is manifesting itself. From this point everything gradually falls into place under higher principles and laws revealed not to our reason through words and hypotheses but to our intuitive perception through [...] *archetypal phenomena*.] (*CW*, XII, 194–95)

Never really separating — yet also never completely conjoining — nature, science, and art,[36] Goethe proceeds to present his theory of colour formation as one such archetypal phenomenon:

> Wir sehen auf der einen Seite das Licht, das Helle, auf der andern die Finsternis, das Dunkle, wir bringen die Trübe zwischen beide, und aus diesen Gegensätzen, mit Hilfe gedachter Vermittlung, entwickeln sich, gleichfalls in einem Gegensatz, die Farben, deuten aber alsbald, durch einen Wechselbezug, unmittelbar auf ein Gemeinsames wieder zurück. (*FA*, XXIII.1, 81)
>
> [On the one hand we see light or a bright object, on the other, darkness or a dark object. Between them we place turbidity and through this medium colours arise from the opposites; these colours, too, are opposites, although in their reciprocal relationship they lead directly back to a common unity.] (*CW*, XII, 195)

Shortly before his death in 1832, Goethe encapsulated his understanding of the archetypal phenomenon in the following formula:

> ideal als das letzte Erkennbare,
> real als erkannt,
> symbolisch, weil es alle Fälle begreift,
> identisch mit allen Fällen. (*FA*, XIII, 81)
>
> [ideal as the ultimate we can know,
> real as what we know,
> symbolic, because it includes all instances,
> identical with all instances.] (*CW*, XII, 303)

The thesis we would like to pursue is that, for Goethe, Lorrain is such an archetypal phenomenon. Goethe discovers what is real and ideal, particular and universal — that is, symbolic — in and through a process that strikingly resembles the dynamics of the archetypal phenomenon described here. In this process, Lorrain's landscape figures as the 'Urlandschaft' [primordial landscape] from which evolve all other landscapes.

Notes to the Introduction

1. For a similar reading of this passage from Eckermann's collection, see Worton, p. 175, in his introduction to the special issue of *Paragraph* on 'Painting and Narrative'.
2. Our indebtedness to Hagstrum's classic monograph of interart exploration will come to the fore repeatedly in this study. While relying on her expertise in the history of Horace's *ut pictura poesis*, as well as Pope's and Thomson's 'pictorialism', this study's focus on Goethe and Lorrain, and on the poetics and poiesis of landscape in poetry, painting, and park, goes beyond the scope of her monograph. Heeding her advice that a lack of art-historical expertise may lead to establishing merely 'fortuitous resemblances' between the three arts, we are confident that our 'ekphrastic' approach provides a systematic argument for an interart aesthetics (Hagstrum, pp. xvi–xvii).
3. Stoppard, p. 25.
4. See Femmel, II: *Italienische Reise 1786 bis 1788: Die Landschaften*.
5. For convenient online access to Lorrain's works (all of the paintings and a selection of the drawings), see the Delphi Classics e-book *Masters of Arts — Claude Lorrain*. For a succinct introduction to Lorrain's work, see Lagerlöf, pp. 73–94.
6. See Manwaring, p. 63; cf. Watkins and Cowell, pp. 127–28.
7. See the Appendix. Purchased by Goethe in 1797, the painting is no longer considered a genuine Lorrain. See *FA*, XXXI, 417, 996–97 (cf. MRP, I, 342); Femmel, ed., pp. 227, 229. On Goethe as an avid collector of French paintings and drawings, including Lorrain, see Mildenberger, 'Goethe and French Drawing'.
8. On Tischbein's painting and *Iphigenia*, see Moore, pp. 32–35; Bisanz.
9. The corresponding drawing in *LV* is no. 115, but, in 1961, Roethlisberger could only identify a modified painted version from 1651, entitled *Pastoral Caprice with the Arch of Constantine* (MRP, I, 287–90, II, 203).
10. Cf. Sapir; Beaven; Bergmann, pp. 87–97. For an extended reading of a port scene, see Lagerlöf's exemplary analysis of *Seaport with Ulysses Restituting Chryseis to her Father Chryses* (1644; *LV*, 80), pp. 224–31. Cf. Russell, pp. 148–49, on the same painting.
11. See Russell, pp. 136–37.
12. On the incorporation and the function of the artist figure in Lorrain, see 'Der Zeichner in der Landschaft', in Bergmann, pp. 9–16. Note the artist motif in Figure 1.1.
13. For a description and prints, see MRP, I, 89–91, II, 5–11.
14. Keats, p. 287, ll. 69–70. For details on this painting and its source, the story of Amor and Psyche from the *Metamorphoses* or the *Golden Ass* of Apuleius, see Russell, pp. 177–79; Wine, pp. 52–56, 86; Levey. Curiously, like Goethe for his own first ekphrastic encounter with Lorrain (see Chapter 2), Keats used an engraving of the original painting (see Pace, 'Claude the Enchanted', p. 734).
15. On Goethe's aperçus as an aesthetic-philosophical paradigm of knowledge acquisition, see Hoffmann, esp. pp. 253–67.
16. Cf. Trunz, pp. 191–92.
17. For a detailed discussion of this principle in Goethe's thought, see Tantillo, *Will to Create*, esp. ch. 1–2.
18. Documented extensively in Femmel, ed., pp. 88, 204–366.
19. In addition to Osterkamp's handbook entry cited below, see Petz, 'Lorrain'; Lenz; Trunz; Loehneysen, pp. 239–42, 261–66, 276–82, 286; Varenne; Koetschau; Gerstenberg, 'Goethe und die italienische Landschaft', pp. 641–47.
20. Osterkamp, 'Lorrain', pp. 513–16.
21. Egle.
22. See also Roethlisberger's 'Claude Lorrain Revisited', his latest update to the four-volume catalogue raisonné of paintings and drawings.
23. See, for instance, Russell; Sonnabend and Whiteley; Lagerlöf; Langdon; Daniel; Schade, ed.; Maisak, *Goethe: Zeichnungen*; Bergmann and Berndt; Münz.
24. Petz, 'Lorrain', 'Ruisdael'.
25. Osterkamp, Im Buchstabenbilde, p. 2. Despite some inevitable overlaps with his own readings

of relevant Goethe commentaries on Lorrain and, closely related, on Jakob van Ruisdael (see esp. pp. 37–52, 326–28, 339–56), the scope of Osterkamp's monograph transcends the genre of landscape painting. With regard to the latter, this study differs from Osterkamp in that it shows that Goethe's ekphrastic enactment of landscape and landscape painting overcomes what Osterkamp suggests is a kind of aphasia — culminating in a self-critical 'renunciation of description' — vis-à-vis Lorrain's pictorial representation of an 'immanent space of refuge' and 'earthly space of fulfilment' (e.g. pp. 320, 341, 349). Toni Bernhart's otherwise useful 2007 survey of recent scholarship on Goethe's aesthetics and theory of art is misleading when it (p. 165) adds 'ekphrasis' to the title of Osterkamp's study, for he (Osterkamp) seems disinclined to engage the poiesis of Goethe's 'descriptive' landscapes.

26. Apel, pp. 571–72.
27. See Boehm, pp. 31–36.
28. See Chapter 1 for elaboration on Samuel Taylor Coleridge's principle of the 'suspension of disbelief'.
29. Cf. Pfotenhauer, 'Weimar Classicism'.
30. In addition to the earlier quotation, see e.g. *CW*, I, 159; *FA*, II, 498.
31. The most recent comprehensive study of the genre is Lagerlöf. Relevant among older scholarship are Gerstenberg's monographs, Lorrain and Landschaftsmalerei (one on the history, the other on the typology of the genre), and the standard introduction by Clark, pp. 67–85; probably the most useful and informative recent introduction is Ditner, pp. 147–54. For the distinction made within the landscape aesthetics of the Italian Renaissance between the sixteenth-century 'conceptual' approach, represented by Dosso Dossi (c. 1489–1542) and the seventeenth-century 'visual' approach, exemplified by Lorrain's 'ideal landscape', see Gombrich, 'Renaissance Artistic Theory'.
32. Cf. Ziolkowski, 'Ich und die Vögel', pp. 248–53.
33. Spence, I, 109.
34. Stoppard, p. 27.
35. On the 'Urphänomen', see the succinct and comprehensive discussion in Hennigfeld, which has been of great benefit for this study.
36. See, for instance, Helbig, pp. 58–59, who argues that the dynamic reciprocity of subject and object underlying Goethe's scientific research is open-ended, manifesting itself metaphorically in nature's 'open secret'. For Goethe, this oxymoron is the core of man's aesthetic relationship to nature.

CHAPTER 1

Nature, Art, Experience, Idea: Exploring Goethe's Aesthetics of Landscape Painting

As a genre of art history, landscape painting can be divided into 'heroic' and 'ideal'. While the heroic landscape is associated with Nicholas Poussin (1594–1665), in whose works the grandeur of nature and the nobility of man mirror each other — think of *The Crossing of the Red Sea* (1633–34) — the ideal landscape is the domain of Claude Lorrain.[1] A working definition of the ideal landscape reads:

> A type of landscape painting developed at the beginning of the seventeenth century in Italy, in which nature is depicted as it ought to be, rather than as it is. In this idealized state, it is used as the setting for subjects from classical antiquity or the Bible. The compositions of such pictures, populated by small-scale figures, are balanced, with a carefully staged recession into the far distance.[2]

Additionally, 'the features of which it is composed must be chosen from nature, as poetic diction is chosen from ordinary speech, for their elegance, their ancient associations, and their faculty of harmonious combination. *Ut pictura poesis.*'[3] With the evocation of Horace's dictum from his *Ars Poetica* that painting and poetry are alike,[4] we have precipitously reached the heart of our enquiry.

Landscape painting is a medium, an aesthetic representation of 'land' or nature. More so, it is the aesthetic discovery and visualization of nature as landscape.[5] Landscape painting is *Weltanschauung*, literally and metaphorically. Viewing the world means trying to understand it *and* our place within it. The verb 'anschauen', according to the *Goethe-Wörterbuch*, has both sensory and spiritual properties in that it ranges from 'look at', 'perceive', 'contemplate', and 'imagine' to 'intuit an essence' (GW, I, 656–60). Landscape painting is an act of physical and intellectual appropriation — a process enacted by what Goethe calls the 'Auge des Leibes' [bodily eye], the organ of sight and perception, and the 'Auge des Geistes' [spiritual eye], the organ of mental imaging and intuition.[6] Landscape painting is a visual, emotional, and intellectual experience. It is the aggregation of physiology and theology transformed into art. Landscape painting is affect in its threefold sense: it is impact, response, and make-believe. Landscape painting is a reciprocal relationship between subject and object, a conversation between self and other, spirited, potentially delightful, even rapturous, subliminally erotic. Landscape painting is like a text created with visual means based on a reading of nature. That text may be prosaic or poetic, allegorical or symbolic. Landscape painting is part reality, part shaper of reality, and part metaphor for reality.

Admittedly, these are bold assertions. Yet they sound less far-fetched when we listen to Werther, the eponymous hero of Goethe's best-selling novel *Die Leiden des jungen Werthers*:

> Eine wunderbare Heiterkeit hat meine ganze Seele eingenommen, gleich den süßen Frühlingsmorgen, die ich mit ganzem Herzen genieße. Ich bin allein, und freue mich meines Lebens in dieser Gegend die für solche Seelen geschaffen ist wie die meine. Ich bin so glücklich, mein Bester, so ganz in dem Gefühle von ruhigem Daseyn versunken, daß meine Kunst darunter leidet. Ich könnte jetzt nicht zeichnen, nicht einen Strich, und bin nie ein größerer Mahler gewesen als in diesen Augenblicken. Wenn das liebe Thal um mich dampft, und die hohe Sonne an der Oberfläche der undurchdringlichen Finsterniß meines Waldes ruht, und nur einzelne Strahlen sich in das innere Heiligthum stehlen, ich dann im hohen Grase am fallenden Bache liege, und näher an der Erde tausend mannichfaltige Gräschen mir merkwürdig werden; wenn ich das Wimmeln der kleinen Welt zwischen Halmen, die unzähligen, unergründlichen Gestalten der Würmchen, der Mückchen, näher an meinem Herzen fühle, und fühle die Gegenwart des Allmächtigen der uns in ewiger Wonne schwebend trägt und erhält; mein Freund! wenn's dann um meine Augen dämmert, und die Welt um mich her und der Himmel ganz in meiner Seele ruhn wie die Gestalt einer Geliebten; dann sehne ich mich oft und denke: ach könntest du das wieder ausdrücken, könntest dem Papiere das einhauchen, was so voll, so warm in dir lebt, daß es würde der Spiegel deiner Seele, wie deine Seele ist der Spiegel des unendlichen Gottes! — Mein Freund — Aber ich gehe darüber zu Grunde, ich erliege der Gewalt der Herrlichkeit dieser Erscheinungen. (*FA*, VIII, 15)

> [A wonderful serenity has taken possession of my entire soul, like these sweet spring mornings which I enjoy with all my heart. I am alone and feel the joy of life in this spot, which was created for souls like mine. I am so happy, my dear friend, so absorbed in the exquisite sense of tranquil existence, that I neglect my art. I could not draw at all now, not a single line, and yet I feel that I was never a greater painter than in such moments as these. When the lovely valley teems with mist around me, and the high sun strikes the impenetrable foliage of my trees, and but a few rays steal into the inner sanctuary, I lie in the tall grass by the trickling stream and notice a thousand familiar things; when I hear the humming of the little world among the stalks, and am near the countless indescribable forms of the worms and insects, then I feel the presence of the Almighty Who created us in His own image, and the breath of that universal love which sustains us, as we float in an eternity of bliss; and then, my friend, when the world grows dim before my eyes, and earth and sky seem to dwell in my soul and absorb its power, like the form of a beloved — then I often think with longing, Oh, if only I could express it, could breathe unto paper all that lives so full and warm within me, that it might become the mirror of my soul, as my soul is the mirror of the infinite God! O my friend — but it will destroy me — I shall perish under the splendor of these visions!] (*CW*, XI, 6)

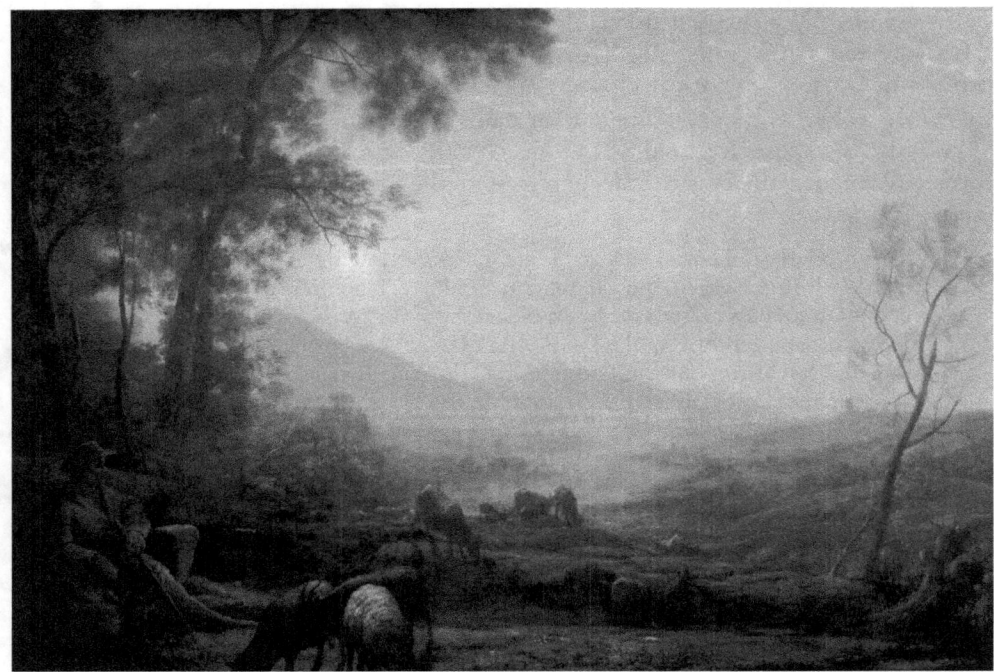

FIG. 1.1. Lorrain, *The Herdsman*. National Gallery of Art, Washington, DC/ © Courtesy National Gallery of Art, Washington

Alas, Werther fails as a landscape painter, for instead of conversing with nature he soliloquizes.[7] Outside of the novel's context, the soliloquy reads like an ekphrastic poem of a painting by Lorrain, whom Goethe discovered and began to comment on at the time of writing *Werther*. Resonating with Wertherian echoes is, for instance, the pastoral landscape known as *The Herdsman* (n.d.; no. 348).[8]

1.1. Natura et Ars

From 1635 to 1636, Lorrain decided to assemble a continuous record of his paintings through drawings, which he called the *Liber Veritatis*. Meant to safeguard the originals against widespread copying, the catalogue had grown to 195 paintings by the time of his death in 1682. In 1777, a copy of this sketchbook appeared in London as *Liber Veritatis; or, A Collection of Two Hundred Prints, After the Original Designs of Claude le Lorrain [...] Executed by Richard Earlom*. Goethe frequently borrowed the Weimar court library's copy of this collection to regale visitors and dinner guests, among them Eckermann.[9] In one of his conversations with Goethe, dated 13 April 1829, he records Goethe's remark that the book 'might as well be styled *Liber Naturæ et Artis* — for here we find nature and art in the highest state and fairest union' (*CV*, p. 328; *FA*, XXXIX, 356). By changing the original title, Goethe makes clear that Lorrain and landscape painting are about truth, nature, and art, and that Lorrain interrelates the three in exceptional fashion. This aperçu raises questions that will preoccupy us throughout this study, from the (im)possibility of defining 'nature' and 'art' to the (im)possibility of defining the 'and' — that is, the relation between the two. Mindful of the aperçu's conceptual complexity and ambiguity, we hypothesize that the 'and', while additive in certain respects, is mainly sublative in the Hegelian sense, implying not just a dialectical relationship but one fraught with tensions. And while 'additive' suggests harmony, 'dialectical' suggests paradox: a coincidence of opposites. As we shall see, the oxymoron is ubiquitously used to verbally articulate the pictorial tension; however, it also helps remind us that the core terms of our subject — 'landscape painting' and 'landscape' (literally, to 'give shape to land') — are already oxymoronic. The nature-cum-art correlation embeds Lorrain not only in theories of landscape painting during Goethe's lifetime — as exemplified by Christian Ludwig Hagedorn's *Observations on Painting* (1762), Carl Ludwig Fernow's 'On Landscape Painting' (1808), or Carl Gustav Carus's *Nine Letters on Landscape Painting* (1824)[10] — but also in eighteenth-century aesthetics; Karl Philipp Moritz (1756–93), Goethe's art-theoretical soulmate in Rome, supports our thesis with his tellingly titled treatise *Über die bildende Nachahmung des Schönen* [On the Formative Imitation of the Beautiful] (1788). To this we can add the fact that Goethe's own drawing practice is marked, as Petra Maisak argues, by the 'gegenseitige Durchdringung' [interpenetration] and the 'Wechselspiel' [reciprocity] of nature and art.[11]

In a comment about 'das Landschaftliche' [scenery] in another talk with Eckermann (18 January 1827), Goethe brings poetry and poiesis into the discussion:

> Because my early drawing of landscapes, and my later studies in natural science, led me to constant close observation, I have gradually learned Nature by heart to the minutest details — so that, when I need anything as a poet, it is at my command; and I cannot easily sin against truth. (*CV*, p. 156; *FA*, XXXIX, 211)

Here, Goethe relates his kinship with Lorrain not only to the fact that he was a landscapist himself, but also to the fact that the painter and the poet are united in that they both must know 'reality' to 'the minutest detail' in order to reproduce it in such a way as to reveal 'truth'. With the words 'fehlen' [to sin] and 'Gebot' [command], Goethe links poiesis to 'religion' and the artist to the Creator — in the fervent lingo of the *Sturm und Drang*, his drawings *are* 'Stosgebete' [quick prayers] with which to 'worship nature and art, God and the artists'.[12] While being 'in command' of nature seems to tip the balance in the nature–art relationship toward art, the end of Goethe's comment leaves the question open, or indeed paradoxical, for he says that the Swiss landscape in Schiller's play *Wilhelm Tell* (1804) 'possessed reality' even though he had never observed Swiss nature first-hand (*CV*, p. 156; *FA*, XXXIX, 211).[13]

Etymologically, 'landscape' is of German origin and denotes 'shaped land', a combination of uncultivated and cultivated terrain.[14] W. J. T. Mitchell captures the term's multilayered intrinsic tension: 'Landscape is a natural scene mediated by culture. It is both a represented and a presented space, both a signifier and a signified, both frame and what a frame contains, [...] both a real place and its simulacrum'.[15]

Mediation conditioned by culture begins with perception, that is, what (in) land we see, how we see land, and how we create a mental image derived from land. Perception is, as E. H. Gombrich pointed out in *Art and Illusion* (1960), not neutral: 'The innocent eye is a myth. [...] All thinking is sorting, classifying. All perceiving relates to expectations and therefore to comparisons.'[16] Expectations and comparisons presuppose criteria, aesthetic criteria, which tend to be fraught with hierarchies. Yet not all of our responses to land and landscape are 'constructionist' in Gombrich's sense: natural scenery can elicit a spontaneous or even instinctive reaction of, say, fear and wonder, excitement and serenity. Goethe, as we shall see shortly and throughout this study, grapples with the relationship between visual fact and imaginative construction.[17] He may waver in where exactly nature ends and art begins, but he always considers them as engaged in dialogic interaction. Thus, Goethe would argue, unlike E. Allen McCormick in 1976 and Stephen Bending in 2017 (to cite but two examples), landscape is not just in the mind; it is also out there, and in its pictorial or verbal manifestations it *is* mutual exchange between art and nature. In short, landscape as art *is* self- and other-expression in one.[18] Goethe puts it epistemologically in his 1820 admission 'Bedenken und Ergebung' [Doubt and Resignation]: 'Our intellect cannot think something as united when the senses present it as separate, and thus the conflict between what is grasped as experience and what is formed as idea remains forever unresolved'; for instance, Goethe explains, what in experience 'is bound by space and time' can be conceived 'in idea as both simultaneous and sequential' (*CW*, XII, 33; *FA*, XXIV, 449–50). As a bridge between experience and idea, between nature and art, landscape *is* this conflict — and so too is, the difference in medium notwithstanding, landscape poetry.

To map out the territory of this study further,[19] we want to bring into sharper relief Goethe's understanding of landscape painting. To do so is a difficult task given the lack, on Goethe's part, of a conclusive definition.[20] This lack is incomprehensible considering that he drew and painted landscapes throughout his life — numbering, in fact, close to six thousand individual works. The paradox of this situation may signal that landscape painting, for Goethe, is less a genre and more a creative process, a medium for visualizing a relationship between man and nature. Analogizing nature and art, as Goethe so often does, we might say that both nature and art are projects, improvisations, in the process of being formed, or rather, performed.[21]

1.2. A Practitioner's View: Jakob Philipp Hackert

While in Italy in the mid-1780s, Goethe studied landscape painting under the tutelage of Jakob Philipp Hackert. 'I was out there [in Tivoli] with Mr. Hackert', writes Goethe on 16 June 1787, 'who is incredibly expert at copying nature and immediately giving form to his drawings. I have learned much from him in these few days' (*CW*, VI, 278; *FA*, XV.1, 376). Shortly before, when visiting Hackert in Naples on 15 March 1787, Goethe ties Hackert's comments to his ambivalence vis-à-vis his own aptitude for landscape painting: 'He [Hackert] is tolerant of my weakness for insisting first of all on precision in drawing and then on sureness and clarity in aerial perspective', adding that Hackert says: 'You have talent [...] stay with me for eighteen months and you will produce something that will please you' (*CW*, VI, 169; *FA*, XV.1, 223). As officially appointed court painter of Ferdinand I of the Two Sicilies, Hackert had established himself at the time as the century's pre-eminent painter of Italianate landscapes.[22] Hackert owned, at one point, four paintings by Lorrain and continued making, on commission, copies of Lorrain into the 1780s, including a replica of *Landscape with Dancing Figures* (1648), widely known as *The Mill* (*LV*, 113), which may have served as an inspiration for Goethe's poem 'Amor ein Landschaftsmaler'.[23]

Goethe held him in high esteem and compiled, at the behest of Hackert, who provided relevant documents, his biography, *Philipp Hackert: Biographische Skizze, meist nach dessen eigenen Aussagen entworfen* [Philipp Hackert: Biographical Sketch, Mostly Based on his Own Statements] (1811).[24] In it, Goethe highlights Hackert's status in the history of landscape painting by tying him to Lorrain and the need for 'mimetic' sketches to create a painting that evokes a true and beautiful whole:

> So wichtig und durchaus notwendig es für den Künstler überhaupt ist, den Gegenstand seines Werks nach der Natur selbst zu studieren, so wenig war es damals in Rom üblich, nach der Natur zu zeichnen; am wenigsten aber dachte man daran, eine etwas große Zeichnung nach der Natur zu entwerfen und auszuführen. Man hatte solche solide Studien der Landschaft, seit den Zeiten der Niederländer und *Claude Lorrains*, vernachlässigt, weil man nicht einsah, daß dieser Weg eben so gut zum Wahren, als zum Großen und Schönen führt. Die von Frankreich pensionierten Maler in Rom hatten wohl mitunter manche Teile eines schönen Ganzen, unvollständig, auf einem Duodezblättchen, nach der Natur skizziert, und sie wunderten sich nun allgemein, als sie die beyden Hackert [Philipp und sein Bruder Georg] mit großen Portefeuilles auf dem Lande umherziehen, mit der Feder ganz fertige Umrisse zeichnen, aber wohl gar ausgeführte Zeichnungen in Wasserfarbe, und selbst Gemälde, ganz nach der Natur vollenden sahn. (*FA*, XIX, 425)

> [Although it is important and necessary for the artist to study his subject from nature, it was not usual to draw from nature in Rome in that time; and even less did one think of outlining sketches and executing large-scale designs from nature. These studies of the landscape had been neglected since the time of the Dutch and of *Claude Lorrain*, since artists did not realize how this approach could lead to truth, as well as to the great and beautiful. In Rome, the painters who received pensions from the French Academy made partial sketches of a beautiful whole, incomplete, in a small format, from nature; and they marvelled when they saw the two Hackerts [Philipp and his brother Georg] roaming the countryside with large folios, drawing complete outlines in ink, or finishing watercolour drawings and even paintings entirely from nature.]

What is crucial here is the phrase 'from nature' (we might also translate it as 'in imitation of nature'), which he uses five times with six different verbs: 'to study', 'to draw', 'to outline', 'to execute', 'to make sketches', and 'to complete'. If we associate 'to outline' with 'sketch', 'watercolour' with 'to execute', 'to finish' with 'complete', and add 'truth', 'great', 'beautiful', and 'beautiful whole', we find in this statement a theory of landscape painting in nuce.[25] In the most abstract sense, the theory is based on the assumption that landscape is a representation of the relationship between man and nature, whereas man is the seeing subject and nature is that which is perceived. Fed by the imagination, landscape painting sensualizes this relationship. Converted into imagery, the relationship becomes 'anschaulich' [intuitively graspable]. More specifically, applied even to 'studying' a 'subject' as it appears, not *is* in nature, the term 'after' indicates that man's relationship to nature is indirect; in fact, the verbs used generally make clear that nature is experienced 'aesthetically'.[26] This understanding of the relationship implies that natural beauty and pictorial beauty exist as 'aesthetic appearance' only, and thus only as a function of perception, for beauty exists neither in nature as such nor solely as a manifestation of projection.[27] Similarly, although 'great' resonates with different emotions in the experiencing subject, it too is a function of perception, especially when we associate it with the Kantian understanding of the 'Erhabene' [sublime] as an effect of nature — and not something materially *in* nature as such (Burke's pre-Kantian definition of the sublime). Finally, the activities expressed in the verbs form a blueprint for opening up an 'approach' — note how cautiously Goethe avoids using the verb 'to achieve' — to interrelate the parts so as to constitute a 'beautiful whole'. If nature presents herself to the subject as a whole, then the subject, relying on his perception, lifts his own aesthetically circumscribed whole out of nature; it is, as Max Friedländer puts it, as if the painting were 'nature's face', with its own physiognomy, its own distinctive character, its own essence or 'truth'.[28] What Goethe means by 'truth' is difficult to assess; it may be related to verisimilitude, as in perspectival truth, or a kind of philosophical truth, or the creative energy operative in the relational aesthetics of self and nature, sensualization and reflection, imitation and intimation.

Among the documents that Goethe received are three theoretical letters in which Hackert lays out — in response to a request made by Goethe — his thoughts 'on landscape painting'. In the biography, Goethe published them without substantive revisions, thus suggesting that they — Goethe's more protean view notwithstanding — reflect both Hackert's and Goethe's aesthetics of landscape painting.[29] However, in the pages that follow, we will quote Hackert's original letters to gain an accurate understanding of his thinking about the art at which he is considered to be unequalled in the eighteenth century.[30] To bring Lorrain, who left no theoretical writings, into the discussion, we will use accounts pertinent to his artistic practice from his first biographers, Joachim von Sandrart (1606–88) and Filippo Baldinucci (1629–97).[31] Art historians of the baroque period, they both knew Lorrain personally. Sandrart, a painter himself, accompanied Lorrain to the Roman countryside, where they painted together 'from life [and] from nature itself' (MRP, I, 48).[32]

Right at the outset, Hackert answers the question broached above regarding the land suitable for landscape in lapidary fashion: 'Italy', the 'magnificent Italian prospects' (pp. 108, 110). A key term in the vocabulary of landscape painting, 'Aussicht' [prospect] has, according to the *Goethe-Wörterbuch*, visual, formative, and emotional properties. In the plainest sense, it is a pleasing vista, it is what the painter looks at, what makes an impression on his mind (*GW*, I, 242–43). Yet this initial visual resonance quickly becomes — if it is not already — aesthetically and affectively circumscribed because it involves a frame, a spatial layout, a depth, and an arrangement of objects and staffage, not to mention delight. (Genre-specifically, 'Aussicht', as we shall soon see, also denotes a naturalistic depiction of a city- or landscape.) 'Groß', again following the *Goethe-Wörterbuch* (IV, 485–86, 488–89), interrelates perception and reception in the visual, aural, and mental experience of the awe-inspiring height, depth, width, and sound of a natural scene and its attendant feelings of wonder and fear, greatness and smallness — an experience commonly associated with the 'sublime'. Hackert was familiar with the 'naturalistic' notion of the sublime — as opposed to the 'rhetorical' sublime (see Chapter 2 below) — through Johann Georg Sulzer's widely consulted *General Theory of the Fine Arts* (1771–74), but he related it to his experience of Swiss Alpine nature, which he characterized as 'für[ch]terlich Schönn' [fearsomely beautiful], rather than to Italy.[33]

Continuing to delineate 'Italy', Hackert avers that it has 'the most beautiful objects for landscape painting where, as one can justifiably say, nature has ripened to perfection' (p. 108). As we know from his voluminous *oeuvre*, 'perfect' for Hackert is the Italian countryside from the Roman Campagna to Magna Graecia, i.e. the coastal areas of southern Italy with their remnants of Hellenic civilization around the Gulf of Naples and Sicily.[34] As for Lorrain, while studying for two years with Gottfried Wals in Naples, his 'Italy', as Sandrart specifies, was 'the open country in Tivoli, Frascati, Subiaco, and other places such as S. Benedetto', with 'the mountains, grottoes, valleys, and deserted places, the terrible cascades of the Tiber, the temple of the Sibyl, and the like' as favourite motifs (MRP, I, 51; Sandrart, I.3, 71).

Yet 'Italy' is not just a geographical location; it is also an aesthetic concept. Goethe speaks of Italy as 'a world made for landscape painters', using painterly concepts to differentiate 'the compendious and small-scale' Lake Albano region from the 'magnificent and more sweeping' vistas around Naples and Catania.[35] By characterizing beauty as 'volkomene Reife' [perfect ripeness], Hackert interrelates the physical and the spiritual, full natural growth and well-proportioned and well-rounded development. In sum, with the epithets 'most beautiful' and 'ripe', 'Italy' as land and landscape is already 'aesthetic' before it is art.[36]

To illustrate Goethe's and Hackert's 'theory' of landscape art so far, an aptly complementary 'practice' of landscape art may be found in Lorrain's painting *A View of the Campagna from Tivoli* (1645; LV, 89) (Fig. 1.2).

'Extraordinary pleasure' is offered by landscapes, Hackert continues, 'where great deeds [or] events in history took place' — examples would be his *Destruction of the Turkish Fleet in the Battle of Chesme* (1771)[37] and *The Eruption of Mount Vesuvius in 1774* (1774) — or 'where famous men lived', such as at 'Horace's Villa at Licenza near Tivoli' (pp. 120–21).[38] While landscape is a real place, it is also a metaphorical place, gaining significance from the various meanings attached to the site by history or literature; this is pivotal for understanding the development of landscape painting from historical to heroic-idyllic during the sixteenth and seventeenth centuries in Italy. Moreover, as we shall see, the workings and the imagery of Lorrain's paintings often relate to the outside, to literary sources like the Bible, Virgil, or Ovid.

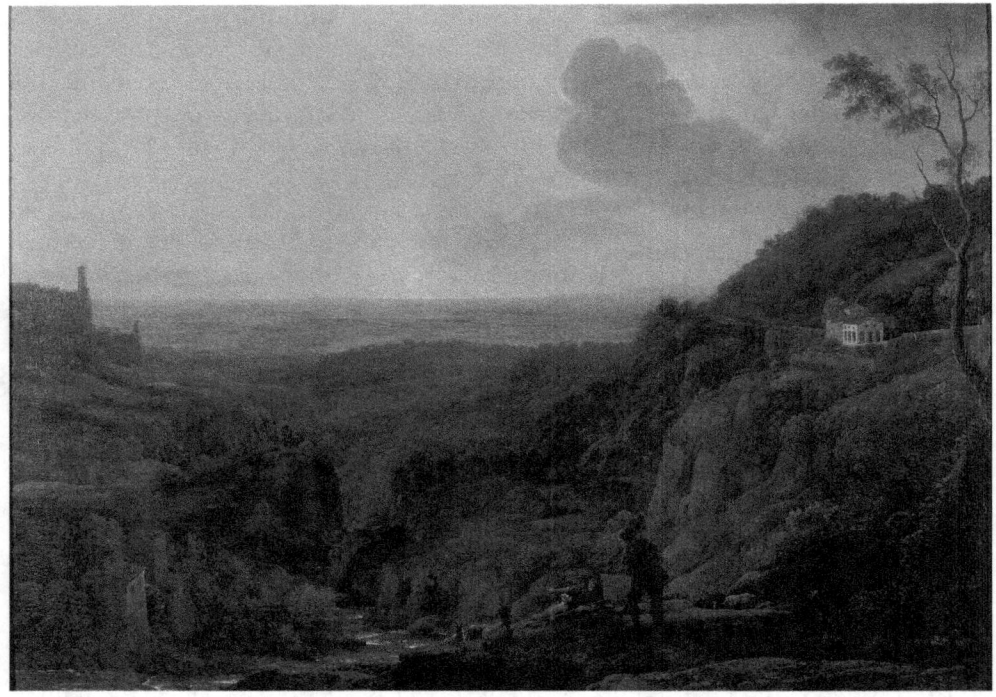

Fig. 1.2. Lorrain, *A View of the Campagna from Tivoli*. Royal Collection Trust/ © Her Majesty Queen Elizabeth II — 2019

While 'Italian prospects' feature ancient civilization in the form of classical architecture (both ruined and recreated), Hackert is wary of depicting manifestations of contemporary cultivation:

> Nahe bey die Städte findet man Kultur aber keine Mahlerische Gegenstände für den Landschafter [...] Angebautes Land ist fruchtbar, würcklich, aber nicht schön für den Landschafter [...] diese Natur: zu sehr gekimmet, [...] jeweniger die Gegenden Kultiviert sind je mahlerischer sind sie. (pp. 108–09)

> [Near the towns, the landscapist finds culture but no picturesque objects [...] cultivated land is fruitful, real, but not beautiful for the landscapist [...] this nature has been planed too much [...] the less cultivated an area the more picturesque it is.]

'Malerisch' [pictorial or picturesque], carries multiple meanings in Goethe's time. The *Goethe-Wörterbuch* (v, 1398–99) evidences its use to differentiate painting and drawing from the plastic arts and architecture. 'Malerisch' refers to subject matter (natural views and objects) that lends itself to pictorial representations which the observer considers pleasing, appealing, delightful, or captivating; more specifically, sights that stimulate the imagination. 'Malerisch' entails the aesthetic means and principles of painting, such as view, colour, light, and composition — in other words, the delineation of space, both horizontal and vertical, by means of contours, the tectonic layering of space into foreground, middle ground, and background, as well as linear and aerial perspective. A core concept in the grammar of landscape painting, 'aerial' or 'atmospheric perspective' — or 'Haltung' and 'Fernung' in Goethe's and Hackert's painterly vocabularies respectively — entails creating an illusion of depth by reducing the distinctness and colour of objects; that is, the more distant an object is, the paler and bluer it appears.[39] In regard to Lorrain's compositional and atmospheric practice, Sandrart states that, while out in the field, Lorrain devoted himself to painting 'the view from the middle to the greatest distance, fading away towards the horizon and the sky' (MRP, 1, 48).[40] Although the vanishing point is a distinguishing feature of Lorrain, it is a function of the hallmark of his 'perspective', the low horizon. Baldinucci elaborates:

> He placed the vanishing point where he pleased; but he used to divide the height of the picture into five parts, the horizon — that is the axis of the visual rays — being the second from the bottom; fixing then the vanishing point on this line, he took a thread, and pinning it on the point, turned it round over the picture, circumscribing it completely in that circle; fixing then the distance in that point where his horizon cut the circle. And he used the same procedure in drawing the view from nature, there observing the horizon so much that by the Flemish he was surnamed Orizzonte. (MRP, 1, 61–62)

This perspectival geometry has two major implications: first, by placing the horizon line at two-fifths of the painting's height, Lorrain gains the space needed for the elaborate spectacle of light and mist; second, excepting buildings, sets of parallels begin from within the painting's frame and converge at the vanishing point — which coincides with the oculus, the viewer's vantage point — 'thus giving the viewer the sense that he sees before him a total structure, complete and self-contained'.[41] As a consequence, the foreground's prominence for the dramatic staging of the staffage figures is diminished; unlike Poussin, Lorrain embeds his figures in the landscape as a whole, leaving the focus on nature as the protagonist intact.

As an epithet for the artist's eye, 'malerisches Auge' expresses the painter's instinctive aptitude and ability, his talent and flair for landscape painting. As an epithet for the artist's intellect, 'malerischer Verstand' characterizes his diligent attention to and study of physical details. And, as an epithet for effect, 'malerische Wirkung' characterizes the painter's emotional response to the strikingly beautiful landscape — a feeling of pleasure, of delight filled with wonder and enchantment, which he, in turn, elicits in the observer by capturing dramatic beauty and giving it life on canvas.

The empiricist in Hackert expounds upon what he calls the 'mechanics of the art' of landscape painting (p. 116). 'Being knowledgeable in the science of mathematics' (p. 109) equips the landscape painter with the necessary know-how to accurately and effectively render architectural objects and, in the area of optics, the physics and behaviour of light as well as perspective, be it linear or aerial. The painter must also be a chemist to skilfully handle chromatic issues (e.g. pigments, colour mixing, hue, tone), a geologist to differentiate between various 'calcareous sediments' and 'volcanic rocks', and a botanist to faithfully depict trees (pp. 110, 113, 115, 121). Trees are Hackert's hobby horse. His Linnaeus-like taxonomy features three classes: the chestnut with 'longish leaves', the oak with 'serrated leaves', and the poplar with 'round leaves' (pp. 110–11).[42] For good measure, he adds that 'the contour alone must show what kind of a tree it is', allowing 'the botanist [to] recognize [it] right away' (pp. 111, 113). How can, Hackert asks, a 'mere study of a tree [become] a landscape'? His answer shows that insisting on accurate and truthful signs does not make his theory a manual for simplistic mimesis. If the painter wants 'to create a whole', the naturalistic signs must be integrated in order to signify beauty, for land to be landscape:

> Nichts gefält mehr so wohl in der Natur als Zeichnung und Gemählde als ein Schöner Baum, mit einige Felsen Steine oder Andre Bäume in Mittel Grunde etwas Fernung macht es ein Schöne Landschaft wo der Baum am Ersten Brilliret. (p. 113)

> [Nothing pleases more both in nature and in a sketch or a painting than a beautiful tree, with a few rocks and other trees in the middle ground and a partial view into the distance, it makes for a beautiful landscape with a bright and radiant tree to catch sight of first.]

Given Lorrain's importance for the English Garden, it is noteworthy that Sandrart, even in 1675, is using the trees in landscape painting as an argument against the formality of the Renaissance or baroque gardens when he says that 'they ought not be round on top as if shorn nor plane or pointed and should sway and bend with ease'. Rather than characterizing their compositional function as providing a rigid skeletal framework, he sees trees as 'the muscles of the landscape' whose dynamic strength Lorrain captures so 'life-like' that it is 'as if they rustled and swayed in the breeze'. Similarly to Hackert, Sandrart underscores the trees' importance by calling for 'a beautiful natural science' for their portrayal, thus, as with perspective, conjoining knowledge *and* aesthetics.[43]

Weighing science, or rather technology, against art, Hackert rejects widespread use of the camera obscura, for it 'bends and elongates the contours' and 'darkens everything' so that

> in der Ferne und Mittel Grundt Vermißet man den Schönen Silberthon, der mit den Luft thon der so Schön in der Natur herschet. Es ist als wie ein leichter Flor Übergezogen, ein gewißer Rauch thon, den viele Künstler Speck thon nennen. (p. 109)

> [one misses in the distance and in the middle ground the beautiful pearly tone which glitters in the air and suffuses all of nature. It is as if a translucent gauze had been stretched across, a faint haze of smoke which many artists call greasy lustre.]

So far, in Hackert's theory of landscape painting, 'beautiful' is a concept that partakes of nature and art, of the source material and the execution, as well as the reception. It applies to the botany of a tree, the inverse relation between optical size and distance, and the optics of light. But this is only, in Hackert's jargon, the 'mathematical' aspect of 'beautiful'. 'Beautiful' is very much an aesthetic concept that defies definition; its elusiveness can only be captured metaphorically, and then only in an oscillating series of similes. For instance, the distinctive atmospheric luminance of the Mediterranean sky is, in tone, like 'silver' or, literally, like 'smoke' or 'bacon' or 'blubber'. When it comes to 'beautiful' as an aesthetic quality of landscape painting, the visual outdoes the verbal.

In other words, while Hackert comes across as a naturalistic empiricist, he makes clear that 'to imitate' is a function of 'art and taste' (p. 110), of 'refined taste and feeling' (p. 108). The eighteenth century's debate on 'Geschmack', or taste, is too complex to recount in detail here; suffice it to say that Hackert seems to align himself with Kant's notion of taste as a matter of judgement, the capacity to differentiate — on an intellectual and emotional level — between objects and notions that 'wohlgefallen' [please] and 'miszfallen' [displease] (*GW*, v, 3930). To wit, Hackert drives home that in landscape painting, 'grand nature pleases', while 'small things displease'. Another reason for rejecting the camera obscura is that it scales down the 'magnificent' in nature and an overabundance of small objects creates 'disorder'. Many of them, taste dictates, must be 'left out' in order to 'bring out the true illusion of the object' (p. 110). Taste assures that imitation does not 'alter the truth of nature' and imbues the imitated objects with the 'character of truth and beauty' (p. 108). Notable here is the reciprocity of beauty and truth, and Hackert's insistence that the artist's ability to 'select natural beauties' demonstrates 'taste' (p. 111) might itself be an echo of Giovan Pietro Bellori's influential aesthetic credo that only the selective artist can 'unite the truth with the verisimilitude of things that appear before the eye', thus bringing out the 'Idea' of perfection from its gestation 'in his soul'.[44]

Hackert's 'taste' entails negotiating extremes — say, grand and small. The result of this negotiation may please visually, but it is not free of friction. The borders between pleasure and displeasure, order and disorder, truth and fiction (illusion) seem porous. If landscape painting is not a genre but a medium, it is one that integrates nature, art, experience, and idea into a whole whose beauty thrives on harmonies *and* tensions. Only thus can the *pas de deux* of exact imitation of the minutiae of leaves and indistinct intimation of infinite distance become a source of 'Wohlgefallen', or delight. Remarkably akin to choreography, taste emerges as a basic concept in the art of landscape painting. It has intellectual properties insofar as it provides a measure for selecting, designing, and ordering. But it also has emotional properties insofar as its ultimate aim is the kindling of pleasure, even rapture, bliss.

'So wohl bey nachahmung der Natur als Componirte Baume Muß Alles schön und lachend oder freundlich und lieblich seyn' [As with the imitation of nature so with the composition of trees everything must be beautiful and smiling or friendly and pleasant] (p. 111). Applicable to both nature and art, the epithets 'smiling' and 'pleasant' carry vital connotations. Relevant for our purposes is that 'lachen' relates to light, specifically nature's beauty radiating forth as, for instance, in Goethe's poem 'Mailied' (1771): 'Wie lacht die Flur' [How the fields laugh] (*FA*, 1, 287). Metaphorically, 'lachen' also relates to mood, both as a property and effect, in which case the corresponding adjective's connotations range from 'cheerful' to 'serene'. When Hackert uses 'lieblich', he is consciously tapping into the lengthy literary tradition of the *locus amoenus*, or pleasant place, evoking an Arcadian landscape reminiscent of Eden — Horace's villa, mentioned above, must have struck Hackert as a *locus amoenus* par excellence, inspiring the series *Ten Views from Horace's Villa* (1780).[45] Reminiscent of the polyvalent 'malerisch', the quasi-oxymoronic term brings together — and holds in tension — landscape's fundamental opposites, be it the physical and the spiritual, or the optical and the ontological.

Although the *locus amoenus* is a landscape of the mind, Hackert emphasizes — both in terms of production and reception — the prominence of the senses vis-à-vis the intellect. 'Everything in painting is sensuous' (p. 111), he says at one point, and in light of further comments, 'sensuous' may very well imply 'sensual'. For instance: 'Die Neuheit des Objekts Reitzet zu sehr und macht neue Lust und Liebe die Natur nach zu Ahmen' [The novelty of the object acts as such a charm that it stirs new desire and love to imitate nature] (p. 114). While it is possible to read the second clause as 'to feel like and be fond of imitating nature', the wording of the first clause imbues 'desire' and 'love' with undeniable sensuality. According to the Grimms' *Deutsches Wörterbuch*, the verb 'reizen' ranges in meaning from teasing and captivating the imagination to stimulating a refined sensibility and sublimated desire (XIV, 794–95). Hackert's language, then, betrays nature's allure as a temptress as well as landscape painting's subliminal eroticism. To be sure, Hackert's emphasis on the emotional impact of a landscape painting on the observer, which in turn mirrors the painter's emotional response to nature, is just that — a refined sensitivity to natural and aesthetic stimuli. However, there is also the suggestion of landscape (both in reality and on canvas) as a subdued erotic experience. How does the landscape painter respond to 'nature that allures' (p. 114)? He 'listens' to her 'secretly' and 'intently'. Repeatedly, Hackert uses the rather peculiar term 'belauschen', which, in addition to the sensate activity just alluded to, also carries a significance involving the intellect — namely, 'to reconnoitre' or 'to spy'. It is as if nature were hiding a secret that, by eavesdropping, could be unveiled. If nature were to disclose her secret, it would only be at an auspicious moment: 'Er muß die Natur wohl belauschen in welchen Licht sie den besten Efeckt macht, es sey früe Morgens oder etwas Später, gegen Abend, oder bey untergehender Sonne' [He has to observe nature furtively and carefully to find out in which light she presents herself most advantageously, be it early morning, or somewhat later, toward evening, or at sundown] (p. 114).

The erotic push-and-pull between artist and nature seems to replicate self–other relationships, with nature, vaguely veiled as 'woman', cast as the other. To be sure, while the male gaze implies a monodirectional look, 'belauschen' relates to the sense of hearing, harking, therefore, back to the idea of landscape as dialogue, a notion that has ontological implications, for, in Mikel Dufrenne's words, 'nature speaks to me and I hear her [...], and she, by speaking to me about herself, speaks to me about myself'.[46] The more Hackert elaborates on a landscape's powerful expressiveness, the more we realize the reciprocal complexity of the resonance within us. That is, even though I may project my self onto the landscape, the landscape also projects her self onto me and, in the process, enriches me by expanding my horizons, emotionally, intellectually.[47] While art, to abstract further from Hackert's treatment, helps cultivate our appreciation, enjoyment, and understanding of nature, art never *is* nature, just as nature never *is* art — this is the conundrum of equivalence inherent to the nature-and-art formula.

In Hackert's final landscape letter, there is a passage he calls 'Vom Morahlischen in der Landschaft' [On the Morals in Landscape] (p. 120). Just as Goethe uses 'moral' to describe the effects of colours in *Zur Farbenlehre* ('Sinnlich-Sittliche Wirkung der Farbe' [Sensory-Moral Effect of Colour]; *FA*, XXIII.1, 247; *CW*, XII, 278), 'morahlisch', here, is not to be understood in the ethical sense but rather as referring to emotions of the mind, the mind's capacity to receive stimuli from — or be affected by — the landscape. Hackert writes:

> Die Menschen fühlen so wenig die Schönheit der Natur als daß Gemählde welches sie vorstellet, und ofte in der wahren Würckung die Natur sehr wahr vorstellet. In dir Landschaft herschet nicht allein die Elusion und wahre nachahmung und Kunst, sondern es ist ofte mit Mohrahl verbunden. Viele Gegenden Gefallen Vorzüglich bloß aus Mohrahlischen Umständen ob sie gleich nicht die Schönsten sind, weil andere Ideen des Zuschauers sich damit verbinden. (p. 120)
>
> [People rarely feel the beauty of nature or of a painting which represents it, even when [the painting], as is often the case, faithfully imitates nature in its true effect. A landscape is not just illusion and truthful imitation and art; it often goes hand-in-hand with the effects on the mind. Many landscapes please extraordinarily for moral reasons, even if they are not the most beautiful, because the observer associates with them different ideas.]

Hackert's reflections here are remarkable for several reasons. Within the span of two sentences he sets up an analogy between nature and art, beauty and truth, and men's emotional and intellectual responses. In the same breath, he also problematizes this analogy: the fuller the manifestation of beauty, the more incomplete men's emotional engagement; the more incomplete the manifestation of beauty, the fuller men's intellectual response. The equation of 'natural verisimilitude' and 'artistic truth' is open to doubt, for there is a third variable — illusion — that is of equal value in the aesthetics of reception, perspicaciously enumerated by the connecting and separating 'and'. As he continues, he elevates men's 'frame of mind' even further, matching mind and mimesis in their function within the process of reception, relativizing notions of beauty and 'idealized landscape':

> Es komt viel auf die Gemüts beschaffenheit an, [...] ob eine Schöne Landschaft mehr oder weniger eindruck auf uns macht, Öfters Mittel Mäßige Schöne Gegenden die wahr vorgestellet sein, machen aus Morahlischen Ursachen mehr Eindruck als ein Idial Schöne Landschaft. (p. 120)
>
> [Much depends on the disposition of the mind, [...] whether we find a beautiful landscape more or less impressive; often moderately beautiful landscapes which are faithfully depicted impress us more than a beautifully idealized landscape.]

The level of self-reflexivity on Hackert's part is astonishing given that, with his emphasis on 'morals', he undermines his distinctive style as an artist, the painting of ideal landscapes. Tied to mind and mimesis is memory: 'Anschauen einer solchen Gegend Erweckt in ihm vergangene angenehme Umstände seiner Freunde und viele Neue Ideen, kurz er fühlt sich in dem Augenblick glücklich' [Observing and contemplating such a landscape brings to life past pleasant circumstances involving friends as well as new ideas. In short, at that very moment, one feels happy] (p. 120). Just as 'anschauen' establishes a tension between intuition and cognition, so 'emotional' access to the past opens up a 'rational' horizon on the future, a kind of multivalent understanding suggested by 'many new ideas'. A landscape's effect on the mind, be it in nature or on canvas, is a generative experience: the initial feelings of heightened emotions are followed by a rush of thought. This complex tension inherent in landscape is existential: pictorial thinking implies an enjoyable and satisfied state of being, even if the fulfilment lasts but a moment. Yet, for Hackert, landscape is also an invitation to enter nature and prolong the moment, to, Faust-like, 'tarry a while' (l. 11,582): 'Eine Schöne Gegend [...] Erregt [...] den Wunsch Spaziren zu gehen, in der Einsamkeit sich selbst überlaßen seine Eigene Ideen nach zu hangen' [A beautiful landscape [...] awakens [...] the wish to go for a stroll, to become absorbed in oneself in the solitude and to give oneself up to one's own thoughts] (p. 120). A landscape is beautiful when it is experienced as so real that the observer feels invited to saunter around in it; at the same time, it is experienced as so unreal that it makes possible the observer's conscious entry into the preconscious mind, a lucid dreaming. Aroused by the painting's immediacy — 'as though it were happening before our eyes' — the observer's body and mind begin to wander; this is a notion redolent of Longinus's rhetorical sublime, in which the Roman landscape painters of the seventeenth century are steeped. Since the 'genius' cult of the *Sturm und Drang* movement is interwoven with this rhetorical tradition, we will elaborate on it when we discuss Goethe's comments on Lorrain in the early 1770s in the next chapter.

Hackert's idea that a beautiful landscape makes accessible a state of reverie seems to echo Rousseau's *Reveries of a Solitary Walker* (1782). Rousseau, a dedicated botanist like Hackert — and Goethe — sought images that could mirror the experience of rift or rupture and fill it with a constructed reality on the frontier of dreaming that kindles new understanding. The effect of landscape on the mind is dreamlike, associative, drifting. The paradox is that it constitutes these effects and enacts them using elements taken from reality. As we averred above, an image, like a word, is indeed part of reality, a shaper of reality, and a metaphor for reality. And, just as grammar arranges words, composition arranges images. In both cases, it is the arrangement that produces the meaning. Semiotically speaking, the signifiers, be they concrete (e.g. trees) or abstract (e.g. grandeur), are communicated through images. Translation between signifier and image relies on a code that is culturally constructed: heroic or Arcadian-idyllic. Triggering ideas in our mind, the code stabilizes meaning but does not fix it. Hackert writes: 'Since everything in painting is sensuous, none of our idealizations are possible that are not more or less given by nature; even though we often believe ideas to be new, they originate from known objects' (p. 111). To observe, contemplate, and paint a landscape is a process of assuring the self, an opportunity for the self to relate to the world, to bind with it. As long as the world has not become landscape, it has not materialized; as long as the painter has not become a painting, he does not exist.

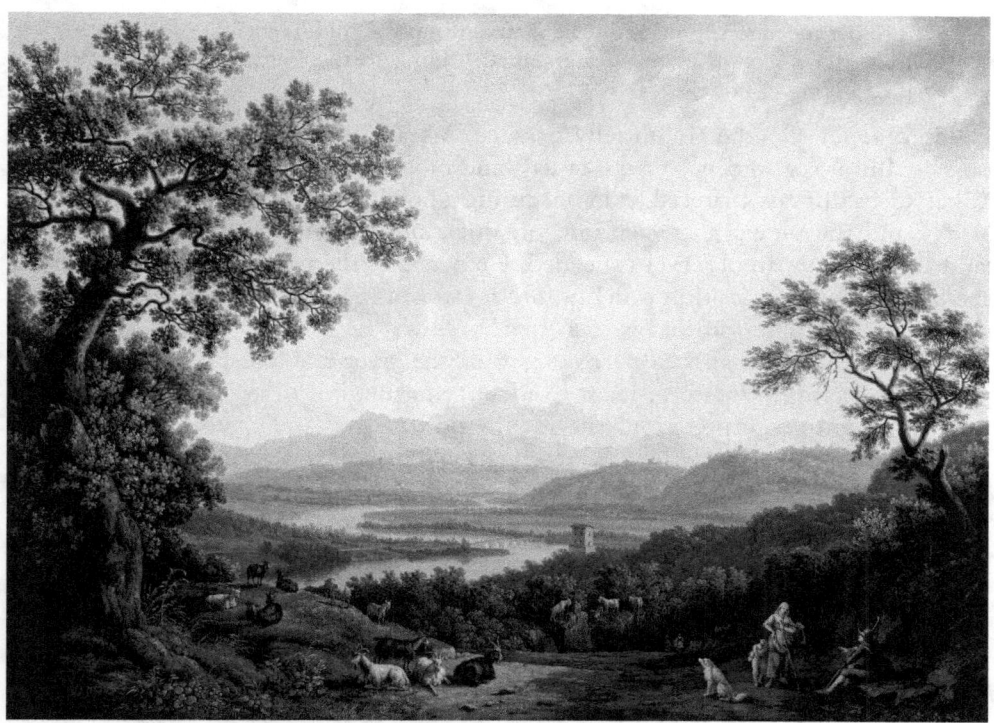

Fig. 1.3. Hackert, *View of the Tiber Valley with the Sabine Mountains*. Private Collection, USA/© Sotheby's, London; 6 July 2011, lot 70.

1.3. Landscape with a Bridge (Ponte Molle): Hackert and Lorrain

To complement Hackert's theory of landscape painting, and to give Goethe a direct voice in the dialogue between the two — a conversation that we will rejoin when they debate Lorrain in the Palazzo Colonna in Rome in the autumn of 1787 — we draw here upon Goethe's review of a Hackert painting for the *Jenaische Allgemeine Literatur-Zeitung* [Jena General Literary Journal] in 1804, and on some of his most relevant reflections on landscape drawing and painting in general.[48]

While the actual painting has been lost, the similar *Blick auf den Tiber und Monti Sabini* [View of the Tiber Valley with the Sabine Mountains] (1799) is used here to highlight similarities and differences between Hackert and Goethe.[49]

In the review, Goethe emphasizes his intimate familiarity with the 'land' behind the 'landscape', writing that Hackert gives us

> von der Höhe der *Villa Madama* herunter, die Aussicht über einen Teil der *Campagna di Roma* nach den Gebirgen des Sabinerlandes hin, welche im Schimmer des Abendlichts glühen; man sieht den Tiberstrom mit mannigfaltigen Wendungen die Ebene durchfließen, im Mittelgrund *Ponte Mole*, nebst einem Stück der geraden, zur ehemaligen *Porta Flamina*, jetzt del *Popolo* führenden Straße. (*FA*, XVIII, 929)

> [a view from the Villa Madama of part of the Campagna below, in the direction of the Sabine mountains, which are aglow in the evening light. One can see

> the Tiber meandering through the plain and, in the middle ground, the Ponte Molle and a section of the straight road leading to the Porta Flaminia, now called Porta del Popolo.] (*CW*, III, 68)

Landscape, for Goethe, is initially a space, a tract of land consisting of natural objects. But it is also time, a time of day, and motion, a meandering body of water. What keeps this raw material from becoming a hotchpotch of natural features is (the artist's and the viewer's) perception, organization, and interpretation. To present land as landscape, an observer is needed. He occupies the point of view from which the land is seen. Its position is delineated as 'from the height', and it offers a 'view' that is 'partial'. The framing is such that it allows the view to widen 'toward the mountain range' but also to narrow toward the river and the plain. Seeing, as a process of stratifying nature, leads to identifying natural objects by name, which in turn leads to interpretation: the recognition of the land's geography (e.g. the Roman Campagna) and the characterization of the land's atmosphere (sunset). What merely *is*, land, begins to *mean*, landscape. With the perception of a man-made object, the bridge — cultivation in its physical manifestation as architecture — comes into (the) view, followed by a second manifestation, the road. While the wild and the cultivated coexist side-by-side — note the pictorial and verbal analogy encapsulated in 'bridge' and correlated in the pairing of 'meandering' and 'straight', 'flow' and 'direct' — interpretation extends to history, juxtaposing the movement of the land, the flowing river, with the movement of the landscape, from the past, 'former', to the present, 'now'. Add to this the movement of the setting sun and the movement toward and through the Porta, and land and landscape evoke a mood of transitoriness and nostalgia, and a memory — of entering Rome through the Porta del Popolo in 1786.

The reciprocity of land and landscape is multifaceted and complex. The glue, if you will, that links experience, idea, and emotion is a fourth, equally significant aspect of this complexity — namely, the aesthetic — as indicated by the compositional concept of the 'middle ground'. Just as 'view' implies selection, a hierarchy of features based on aesthetic grounds, so too does the intricate mix of visual facts and imaginative construction:

> Gemälden, welche [wie dieses von Hackert], treu nach der Natur gemalte Aussichten darstellen, würde großes Unrecht wiederfahren, wenn man sie nach dem Maßstabe beurteilen wollte, den der höchste Begriff von der Landschafts-malerei dem Kunstrichter an die Hand gibt. Im Allgemeinen gehören sie freilich mit zu diesem Fache, machen aber eine untergeordnete Art desselben aus. Wenn der Landschaftmaler, im edelsten Sinne, sich landschaftlicher Formen mit Freiheit bedient, um sein Gedicht darzustellen, und alle Springfedern der Kunst in Bewegung setzt, um durch Ton, Farbe, Beleuchtung, Anordnung u.s.w. ein schönes Ganzes zu erzielen: so unterwirft sich hingegen der Maler von Aussichten den Bedingungen gewissenhafter Treue, er behält keine andere Freiheit, als allenfalls die Wahl des Standpunkts und der Tageszeit, hat aber auch die übernommenen Pflichten erfüllt, sobald alle in seinem Gesichtskreis gelegenen Gegenstände mit möglichster Wahrheit dargestellt sind. (*FA*, XVIII, 930)

[A great injustice would be done to paintings like [this one by Hackert], which represent scenic settings in close imitation of nature, if they were to be judged by the lofty criteria used by the art critic to evaluate landscape paintings. Generally speaking, scenic pictures do belong to that category, but they constitute a subcategory. The landscape painter in the truest sense treats his subject matter freely in order to create his own poetic version of reality, calling upon all the resources of art to arrive at the beautiful whole through tone, colour, light, composition, and so forth. The painter of scenic settings, on the other hand, must adhere scrupulously to reality, his only freedom being the choice of vantage point and time of day. Furthermore, he has fulfilled his artistic obligation as soon as he has presented as realistically as possible all objects within his range of vision.] (*CW*, III, 69)

Goethe's denial of the validity of 'unjust' critical criteria is but a rhetorical ploy. He sets up a hierarchy by distinguishing the painter of landscapes from 'the painter of prospects'. To add to the hierarchy, he characterizes the landscapist's creation as a 'poem', a term he uses to separate imaginative depiction from realistic depiction, that is, 'invention' from 'imitation' (*GW*, III, 1196). The identification of 'painting' with 'poem' in the *Goethe-Wörterbuch* recalls Horace's dictum of *ut pictura poesis*. Both the scenist and the landscapist enjoy artistic freedom, the former in the choice of point of view and time of day, the latter — so Goethe emphasizes — in the topography, the shaping and layout of contours. Yet these freedoms are not without limits. The scenist's duty is to render the 'reality' that he sees with his eyes as faithfully as possible; the landscapist relies on sight too, but, fuelled by creativity's 'Springfeder', or spiritual energy, uses his mind to transpose 'reality' by means of composition, colour, tone, and light.

In regard to means, Goethe is more specific, both in praise and criticism:

Mittelgrund und Ferne, so weit die Ebene reicht, können hier [...] für beinahe unverbesserlich gelten; die Hügel bei *Aqua acetosa* sind wunderbar schön ausgeführt, mit wohlbeobachteter Übereinstimmung des Tons; und gleichwohl könnte ein jeder derselben für sich allein ein kleines herrliches Gemälde vorstellen. Die entfernteren hohen Gebirge scheinen etwas zu Lackrot gefärbt, und gegen den mit Sonnenschein übergossenen Mittelgrund haben die Farben der nächsten Gegenstände nicht Glanz und Schimmer genug. (*FA*, XVIII, 931)

[Middle ground and background, as far as the plain extends, can [...] be considered almost faultless. The hills near Acquacetosa are executed beautifully, with well-observed harmony of tone, so that each is virtually a magnificent painting in itself. The redness of the high mountains in the distance is a shade too bright, and compared to the sun-drenched middle ground, the colours of the adjacent objects are somewhat lackluster.] (*CW*, III, 69–70)

While Goethe applauds Hackert for his execution of tectonic layering and tonal harmony of the planes receding from middle ground to background, culminating in the characterization of each space as a little 'magnificent painting in itself', it is precisely this latter praise, introduced in the German by the ominous 'gleichwohl', that betrays the 'fault': the incomplete correlation of the particulars fails to evoke 'beautiful wholeness'. Goethe also finds fault with the 'distance' beyond the 'plain' and the middle ground. His doubts concern Hackert's use of colour and light. The

Goethe-Wörterbuch lists 'lackrot' [lacquered red] as a synonym for 'karmesinrot' [carmine] (v, 909), which Goethe identifies at one point in *Zur Farbenlehre* as 'Pfirsichblütfarbe' [peach-blossom colour] (*FA*, XXIII.1, 108; *CW*, XII, 209), which in its silvery-pinkish shade would aptly characterize Hackert's colouring of mountains and sky in the distance — were it not for Goethe finding it insufficiently pale to satisfy the demands of the aerial perspective. 'Lacquer' relates the shiny reddish coating to light, specifically to the gleaming atmospheric haze which warms and softens objects and colours. When Goethe bemoans the starkness of contrasts in the middle ground, the implication is that Hackert's uneven distribution of light, his inadequate handling of the *sfumato*, impedes the evocation of beauty and totality. Goethe's conflicted view of Hackert stems from the gap he perceived between process and product. Hackert succeeded in transmitting optical reality, technically and compositionally, but failed to transpose it imaginatively and expressively, thus producing an aesthetically pleasing but non-auratic painting. Goethe disparaged, as we will see in the next chapter, the maxim that Hackert followed — namely, the maxim popularized by his art-theoretical friend Sulzer, who stated in his *General Theory of the Fine Arts* that the artist's goal is to imitate and embellish nature.[50]

Goethe's conclusion is another exercise in indirect directness: 'Wir bemerken eben, daß unsere Wünsche sich über die Grenzen der höhern, dichterischen Landschaftsmalerei verlieren' [We just now realize that our objections go beyond what we should expect of paintings of scenic settings, and that we are straying into the higher realm of poetic landscape painting] (*FA*, XVIII, 931; *CW*, III, 69). The juxtaposition of 'prospect painting' and 'landscape painting' — the former implicitly characterized as 'prosaic', the latter as 'poetic' — recurs in an essay of 1817, in which Goethe bemoans how Hackert's 'enticing model' of prospect painting has led to a 'growing neglect of free poetic creation' (*FA*, XX, 110).[51] As we shall see, the juxtaposition raises a question at the heart of this study.

On his Italian journey, while sailing through the Strait of Messina on 13 May 1787, with Charybdis and Scylla coming into sight, Goethe elaborates on this aesthetic conundrum:

> Man hat sich bei Gelegenheit beider, in der Natur so weit aus einander stehenden, von dem Dichter so nah zusammengerückten Merkwürdigkeiten, über die Fabelei der Poeten beschwert und nicht bedacht, daß die Einbildungskraft aller Menschen durchaus Gegenstände, wenn sie sich solche bedeutend vorstellen will, höher als breit imaginiert und dadurch dem Bilde mehr Charakter, Ernst und Würde verschafft. Tausendmal habe ich klagen hören, daß ein durch Erzählung gekannter Gegenstand in der Gegenwart nicht mehr befriedige, die Ursache hievon ist immer dieselbe: Einbildung und Gegenwart verhalten sich wie Poesie und Prosa, jene wird die Gegenstände mächtig und steil denken, diese sich immer in die Fläche verbreiten. Landschaftsmaler des sechszehnten Jahrhunderts gegen die unsrigen gehalten, geben das auffallendste Beispiel. Eine Zeichnung von Jodocus Momper, neben einem Kniepschen Contour würden den ganzen Kontrast sichtbar machen. (*FA*, XV.1, 335–36)

> [People have seized upon these two curiosities, spaced so far apart in nature and moved so closely together in literature, to complain about the wild imagination

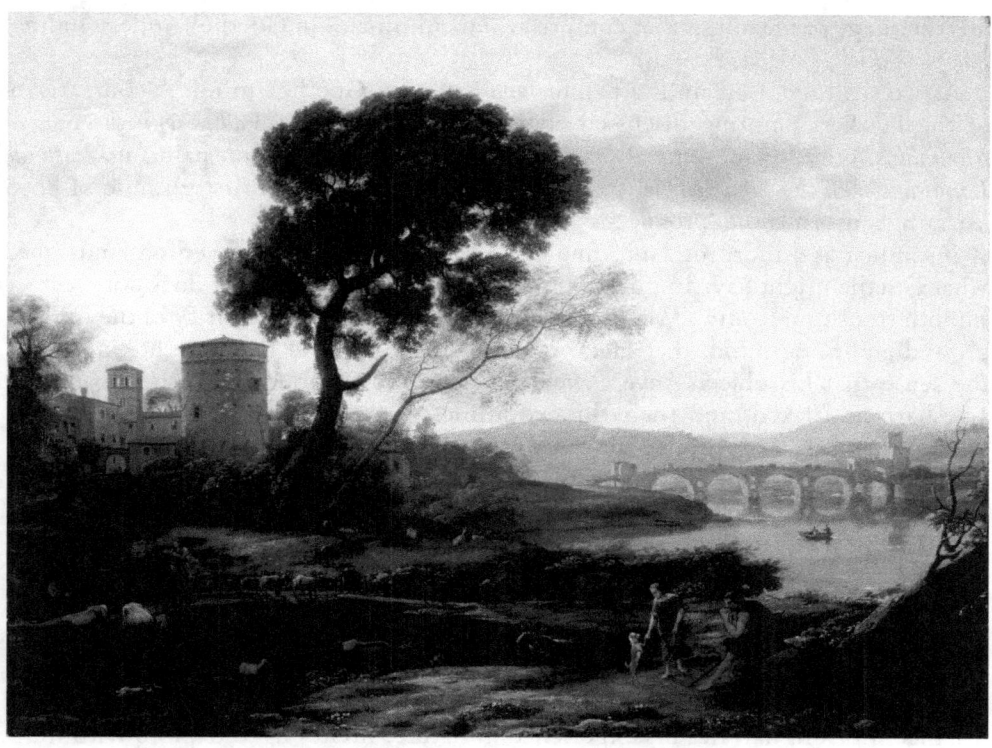

Fig. 1.4. Lorrain, *Pastoral Landscape with the Ponte Molle*. Birmingham Museum and Art Gallery, Birmingham, UK/© Birmingham Museums Trust — 1955P111

of poets. They have not taken into consideration that when human fantasy wants to think of things as being significant, it always imagines them as larger than life, and thus provides the image with more character, gravity, and dignity. I have heard the complaint a thousand times that something known from a story is always disappointing in reality. The reason for this is ever the same: imagination and reality correspond to each other as do poetry and prose; the former will conceive of things as mighty and steep, the latter will always spread them out flat. Landscape painters of the sixteenth century, compared to ours, offer the most striking example. A drawing by Jodocus Momper next to one of Kniep's outlines would make the whole contrast evident.][52] (*CW*, VI, 249)

At first blush, Goethe's comment reads as poetic license, giving the imagination free reign over optical reality. But underneath the tone of indignation and provocation is the clear conviction that the imagination is inextricably bound up with negotiating the contrast between art and nature for the sake of 'representing' what is 'significant'. Used here as a synonym for 'poetic', 'significant' is a fundamental concept in Goethe's aesthetics. Its range of meanings in the *Goethe-Wörterbuch* corresponds to its diverse meanings in Goethe's observation: 'to signify' is interrelated with 'to intimate' and 'to intuit', 'characteristic' with 'unique' and 'peculiar', 'larger' with 'mighty', 'dignified' with 'sublime', and 'solemn' with 'profound' and 'essential' —

it is the range of meanings that comprises and culminates in Goethe's understanding of 'symbolic' (*GW*, II, 154–56).

As we shall see, Lorrain is a painter *and* a poet in Goethe's mind. A comparison of the Hackert painting discussed above, *View of the Tiber Valley with the Sabine Mountains*, with a panoramically and motivically related Lorrain painting, *Pastoral Landscape with the Ponte Molle* (1645; *LV*, 90) (Fig. 1.4) offers a first glimpse of how Lorrain transcends the 'prosaic'.[53]

Insomuch as a morning landscape can be compared with an evening landscape, what Goethe might have in mind is, in boldest terms, that Hackert does not create a smooth transition from the vaporous background to the crystal clarity of the middle ground and foreground; that Hackert's light is the light of the Enlightenment, in the sense that his objects have a well-polished gleam about them, their contours are sharp and fixed, and their this-worldliness is explicit; that Hackert's colours are too 'lustrous' and 'motley' to meet Goethe's ideal of a harmonious interplay of softly transitioning colours;[54] and that Hackert's reliance on mathematics and the natural sciences results in an earthen solidity akin to consonants and a transparency that is plain and univocal. Lorrain, on the other hand, has the ethereal quality of vowels and an insubstantial translucence that is equivocal and mysterious; suffuses the whole scene in dim refulgence and veils it in an indefinite allusiveness; and lets his objects emerge from the diffuse background but leaves them shrouded in an obscurity that dematerializes their corporeality, infusing in them an air of changeability and incompletion. Hackert stages a display of nature, keeps us at a distance; Lorrain narrates his experience in nature, invites us to explore with him. Lorrain darkens nature in order to enchant it; Hackert illuminates it in order to grasp it mentally. Yet, paradoxically, Lorrain's landscape appears probable, while Hackert's provokes disbelief. Hackert synthesizes, Lorrain sublates. In retrospect, a passage in Goethe's novel *Wilhelm Meisters Wanderjahre* [Wilhelm Meister's Travels] (1821) can be read as alluding to the difference between his mentor and his muse.[55] On Lago Maggiore in northern Italy, Wilhelm, after discussing landscape painting with a painter he has recently got to know, observes:

> Verdächtig waren ihm von jeher Nachbildungen Italienischer Gegenden gewesen; der Himmel schien ihm zu blau, der violette Ton reizender Fernen zwar höchst lieblich doch unwahr und das mancherlei frische Grün doch gar zu bunt; nun verschmolz er aber mit seinem neuen Freunde aufs innigste, und lernte […] mit dessen Augen die Welt zu sehen, und indem die Natur das offenbare Geheimnis ihrer Schönheit entfaltete, mußte man nach Kunst als der würdigsten Auslegerin unbezwingliche Sehnsucht empfinden. (*FA*, X, 132)
>
> [Hitherto all copies of Italian scenery had seemed suspicious; the sky, he thought, was too blue; the violet tone of those charming distances was lovely but untrue; and the abundant fresh green too bright and gay: but now he united in his inmost perceptions with his new friend; and learned […] to look at the Earth with that friend's eyes; and while Nature unfolded the open secret of her beauty, he could not but feel an irresistible attraction to Art, as towards her most fit expositor.] (*WMT*, p. 196)

Not only is the 'open secret' an oxymoronic leitmotif in Goethe's aesthetic vocabulary that is also, as we shall see, applicable to Lorrain; his art also achieves the hermeneutic function he seeks.

More specifically, in Goethe's outline and draft of his history of landscape painting, on which he worked intermittently between 1814 and 1829 (without finishing it),[56] he intended to trace landscape painting's emancipation from the predominance of history painting, with Lorrain representing the pinnacle of this development:

> Von Claude Lorrain, der nun ganz ins Freye, Ferne, Heitere, Ländliche, Feenhaft-architectonische sich ergeht, ist nur zu sagen, daß er ans letzte einer freyen Kunstäußerung in diesem Fache [der Landschaftsmalerei] gelangt ist. Jedermann kennt seine Werke, jeder Künstler strebt ihm nach, und jeder fühlt mehr oder weniger, daß er ihm den Vorzug lassen muß. (FA, XXII, 534)

> [All there is to say about Claude Lorrain, who indulges himself luxuriously in [rendering] the open, distant, serene, pastoral, fairy-like architectural, is that he achieved the utmost in terms of a free artistic expression in the area [of landscape painting]. Everyone knows his works, every artist tries to emulate him, and everyone is more or less resigned to granting him pride of place.]

Crucial for Goethe's art-historical argument here is that, with the expression 'indulges himself luxuriously' — 'sich ganz ergehen in', or literally 'to walk straight out into' — 'nature' is no longer background, as it is in history painting, but foreground, no longer in the supporting role but the lead. What is equally crucial is that Lorrain's 'landscape' has natural, spiritual, and affective properties, and that his 'magic realism' can only be captured by oxymoron. One last crucial point is tied to language, too: with the repetition 'ins Freye'/'freyen', Goethe in the German analogizes nature and art insofar as, in boldest strokes, the former characterizes 'content', the latter 'form'. The Introduction already cited Goethe's statement that 'in Claude Lorrain nature proclaims herself to be eternal'; the essay, in which nature figures not as object but as subject, continues with a reversal in the sense that nature in 'heroic' landscape painting becomes subservient to the high-minded ideals of the genre. Goethe names the 'Poussins' — that is, Nicolas Poussin and his pupil and brother-in-law, Gaspard Dughet (1615–75), known as Gaspard Poussin — as examples who 'guide her [nature] to the solemn, lofty, the so-called heroic' (FA, XXII, 528). While both Lorrain and the Poussins 'inspire successors', Goethe contends that after Lorrain the history of landscape painting ends on a downward trajectory by 'eventually lapsing into portrait-like landscapes', that is, topographical land- and cityscapes (FA, XXII, 528). To mark the transition from the landscapist to the vedutist, he juxtaposes the 'ideal' with the 'real', the 'atmospheric' with the 'topographic', the 'freye Kunstäußerung' [free artistic expression] with the 'strenge Manier' [strict manner] — think of Paul Bril's vedute of Flanders, or Canaletto's vedute of Venice, or Paolo Panini's capriccios, whose ingenious assemblages of actual architecture and topography may occupy a middle ground between — to use Goethe's epithets — 'delightful', 'serene', and 'clear', 'painstaking attention to detail' (FA, XXII, 526, 527, 529, 531, 534). 'Serene' is used three times in the drafts on landscape painting, and is exclusively reserved for Lorrain. According to the *Goethe-*

Wörterbuch, its spectrum ranges from the material to the spiritual, as characterized by words that encompass both, such as 'bright', 'tranquil', 'reflective', 'empyrean', or 'radiant'; 'serene' is identified, not least, as we shall see, as a horticultural and chromatic effect (*GW*, IV, 849–50). Goethe distinguishes Hackert's 'clear, rigorous manner' from Lorrain's 'Ausbreitung über eine heitere Welt, Zartheit, Wirkung der atmosphärischen Erscheinungen aufs Gemüth' [unfolding across a serene world, airiness, affect of atmospheric phenomena on the soul] (*FA*, XXII, 530, 531).

1.4. Renaissance Landscape Painting and *Torquato Tasso*

The following investigation of 'landscape' in Goethe's drama *Torquato Tasso* will provide a sense of this study's method and scope. Begun in 1780, Goethe reworked a partial prose version in blank verse on his trip to Sicily in 1787. Loosely based on the life of the Italian Renaissance poet Torquato Tasso, its central conflict between art and politics unfolds against the backdrop of Renaissance villa culture outside Ferrara.[57] It comes as little surprise, then, that the opening scene transports us into a Lorrainian world, a sun-filled spring day in the villa's garden, with the two female leads dressed as shepherdesses weaving wreaths with which they crown busts of Virgil and Ariosto. Leonora greets the awakening spring:

> Ja es umgibt uns eine neue Welt!
> Der Schatten dieser immergrünen Bäume
> Wird schon erfreulich. Schon erquickt uns wieder
> Das Rauschen dieser Brunnen, schwankend wiegen
> Im Morgenwinde sich die jungen Zweige.
> Die Blumen von den Beeten schauen uns
> Mit ihren Kinderaugen freundlich an.
> Der Gärtner deckt getrost das Winterhaus
> Schon der Zitronen und Orangen ab,
> Der blaue Himmel ruhet über uns
> Und an dem Horizonte löst der Schnee
> Der fernen Berge sich in leisen Duft. (ll. 28–39)

> [Yes, a whole new world surrounds us here!
> The shade alone of these old evergreens
> Delights the senses. Then the splashing of
> These fountains quickens us. The young boughs glitter,
> And sway in response to the morning breeze.
> These flowers with friendly, trustful children's eyes
> From beds and borders seem to look at us.
> Confident, too, the gardener is removing
> Covers from orange and from lemon trees.
> A blue and limpid sky rests over us,
> And on the horizon's distant mountain tops
> Into faint haze the late snow dissolves.] (trans. modified)

This 'new' world is a thoroughly Southern, bucolic world, and the last three lines in particular reverberate with, indeed quote from, as we shall see, not just the *Italienische Reise* but also Goethe's 'Sicilian' drama fragment *Nausikaa*. What is more, the peculiar atmosphere evoked in the poem, 'haze', seems to correspond to the experience of Mediterranean 'nature' *and* its visualization in a Lorrain painting: 'Hovering over the ground all day', writes Goethe in his *Italienische Reise* in 1787, 'is a haze which is familiar to us only from the paintings and drawings of Claude Lorrain; but in nature the phenomenon is rarely seen as beautifully as here' (*CW*, VI, 142; *FA*, XV.1, 186).

The insurmountable dilemma that dooms Tasso, the protagonist, is encapsulated in his — the artist's — motto, 'erlaubt ist was gefällt' [What pleases, is allowed], and society's motto, 'erlaubt ist was sich ziemt' [What's fitting, is allowed] (ll. 994, 1006). Tasso derives his credo from the Golden Age, the Arcadian pastoral paradise, a tradition that harks back to Hesiod and was reborn during the Renaissance in, for instance, the real Tasso's idyll *Aminta* (1573). In fact, in the lines quoted below, Goethe paraphrases a passage from *Aminta*, including the first maxim just cited (the second is from Giovanni Battista Guarini's *Aminta* parody, *Il pastor fido* (1590)). The Princess warns him that his devotion to the pursuit of this ideal alienates him from society:

> Auf diesem Wege werden wir wohl nie
> Gesellschaft finden, Tasso! Dieser Pfad
> Verleitet uns durch einsames Gebüsch
> Durch stille Täler fortzuwandern; mehr
> Und mehr verwöhnt sich das Gemüt, und strebt
> Die goldne Zeit, die ihm von außen mangelt,
> In seinem Innern wieder herzustellen,
> So wenig der Versuch gelingen will. (ll. 970–77)
>
> [Tasso, that way, I am sure, we'll never find
> Companionship! That way of yours must lead us
> To ramble on through solitary copses,
> Through silent valleys; more and more our feelings
> Grow pampered, spoilt, for ever they'll be striving
> Inwardly to restore that golden age
> Which outwardly they cannot find, though never
> That effort succeeded, or can succeed.]

In Chapter 2, we will discuss Goethe's pastoral idyll 'Der Wandrer' (1774), whose protagonist 'literally' sets out to find, as it were, his Golden Age. Now, Goethe tells us, through the poet Tasso, that it can only be recreated in and through language:

> O welches Wort spricht meine Fürstin aus!
> Die goldne Zeit wohin ist sie geflohn?
> Nach der sich jedes Herz vergebens sehnt!
> Da auf der freien Erde Menschen sich
> Wie frohe Herden im Genuß verbreiteten;
> Da ein uralter Baum auf bunter Wiese
> Dem Hirten und der Hirtin Schatten gab,
> Ein jüngeres Gebüsch die zarten Zweige
> Um sehnsuchtsvolle Liebe traulich schlang;
> Wo klar und still auf immer reinem Sande
> Der weiche Fluß die Nymphe sanft umfing;

Wo in dem Grase die gescheuchte Schlange
Unschädlich sich verlor, der kühne Faun
Vom tapfern Jüngling bald bestraft entfloh;
Wo jeder Vogel in der freien Luft
Und jedes Thier durch Berg und Thäler schweifend
Zum Menschen sprach: erlaubt ist was gefällt. (ll. 978–94)

[A powerful word you've spoken, my Princess.
The golden age, what has become of it,
That for which every heart still longs in vain?
When on a free earth human beings roamed
Like happy herds, to pasture on delight;
When a most ancient tree on flowery meadow
Cast shade for shepherds and for shepherdesses,
A younger shrub entwined with delicate boughs
Languishing love, as though in league with it;
Where clear and still on sand forever pure,
Gently the lissome river clasped the nymph;
Where in the grass a snake, surprised and startled,
Harmlessly vanished, and the fearless faun,
Soon punished by a young man bolder, fled;
Where every bird in unrestricted air
And every beast that rambled hill and valley
Said to our kind: What pleases, is allowed.]

From the grove with a shady tree on a flowering meadow to the pure water of a spring or brook, from the shepherds in a state of repose to the birds singing in the clear sky, from roving freely to loving committedly — Tasso weaves the main motifs into his evocation of the Golden Age. The Princess considers it as times gone by:

Mein Freund, die goldne Zeit ist wohl vorbei:
Allein die Guten bringen sie zurück;
Und soll ich dir gestehen wie ich denke,
Die goldne Zeit, womit der Dichter uns
Zu schmeicheln pflegt, die schöne Zeit, sie war,
So scheint es mir, so wenig als sie ist,
Und war sie je, so war sie nur gewiß
Wie sie uns immer wieder werden kann.
Noch treffen sich verwandte Herzen an
Und teilen den Genuß der schönen Welt;
Nur in dem Wahlspruch ändert sich, mein Freund,
Ein einzig Wort: erlaubt ist was sich ziemt. (ll. 995–1006)

[My friend, I think, that golden age, is over;
Only consummate goodness brings it back.
And if I may confess to you what I think:
That golden age with which the poets like
To flatter us, that beautiful age no more
Existed ever than it now exists;
And if it did, I'm sure it was none other
Than that which ever again we can make ours.

Still hearts that are akin can find each other
To share the enjoyment of our lovely world;
The only change, my friend, is in the motto,
A single word: What's fitting, is allowed.]

Apart from their different worldviews, the Princess relates the notion of the Golden Age to time, while Tasso relates it to space, signified unmistakably by the adverb 'wohin', and the repeated 'da' and 'wo'. What they agree on is the power of poetry, and specifically, in Tasso's case, of ekphrastic poetry. For the 'space' where he locates the Golden Age is in a pastoral Lorrain, which feeds his ekphrastic imagination to a fundamental degree.[58]

In line with Lorrain's oxymoronic or tensional aggregation of diverse elements, polarities abound: man and woman, human and animal, earth and water, mountain and valley, wild and tamed, old and young, lust and love, Christian and pagan. These diverse elements are integrated into a kind of creation myth that culminates in a secular Garden of Eden, from which not man but the devil is exiled. The integration results in a 'whole' suggested by the circular movement from 'human being' to 'human being' in the first and last lines respectively. Integrated into the whole are not just the polarities already mentioned but also the juxtaposition of sense and sensibility, ranging through the senses from sight ('flowery', 'clear') and touch ('gentle', 'lissome') to hearing ('still') and feeling ('languishing', 'happy', 'intimate' [traulich]), and on to the spiritual ('free', 'unrestricted') which links 'earth' to 'air', that is, sky or heaven, and reverberates in the maxim 'pleases'. As self-evident as the reciprocal coordination of various faculties and the 'connections' that Goethe deems so indispensable to his notion of the 'whole' are, the integrative balance is nonetheless precarious. This is strikingly illustrated by the ambiguous meaning of the morpheme 'schlang' [wound [itself round]], which is used, on the one hand, in the German words for 'snake' and, on the other, in 'embraced'. Through the lens of ekphrasis, the term 'golden age' is ambiguous, too, in that 'golden' is philosophical and pictorial, denoting a time of bliss, epitomized for our purposes by Poussin's painting *Et in Arcadia Ego* (1637–38), and a 'light' — namely, the radiance of the sun that suffuses so many of Lorrain's paintings. The polyvalence of 'golden' is important because the sun as such is not an explicit pictorial element. But it is not in Lorrain either: even if technically not present, the sun's light emanates from a vanishing point beyond the horizon, creating an interplay of light and shadow. The sun's light is also suggested in the brightly coloured meadow, and in the iridescent luminosity of the river. The application of Lorrainian procedures does not end with the weaving of diverse elements into an Arcadian whole. Painting and language are interrelated in the way Goethe (the lyric 'I') looks at this Arcadian landscape. The initial question of 'wohin' is followed by five different answers, which reveal the same structure: subordinating conjunction (i.e. 'da' or 'wo'), subject, and predicate. Underlying the creative process is a question–answer pattern that brings with it a verb-final subordinate syntax in German (more on this in a moment). Analogizing the pictorial and the verbal, the singular question corresponds to the position from which the painter observes the scenery, while the multiple answers correspond to the various movements of the eye. From this point of view, the landscape radiates outward. The local detail of the description is designed to show just how far toward the horizon the perimeter of the scenery extends. The eye embarks on a journey through receding planes, establishing foreground, middle ground, and background: the pastoral staffage and the tree, the ancient figures and the meandering river, the mountains in the distance and the birds in the haze above. The quasi-anaphoric 'da'–'wo' lines arrange the landscape into five main bands, or more specifically into two six-line segments, the first comprising the foreground, the second encompassing both middle ground *and* background (which ends with the mountains forming the horizon). Eye movement and depth-perception are correlative: the faster the eye travels, the more the depth extends. An additional line offers a view into the vast and distant sky. While the twofold 'da' segment allows the eye to focus on a close-up, the tripling of 'wo' sections, and the enjambments in the second 'wo' portion, suggest increasingly rapid movements of the eye across the various planes and into the ever-expanding depths. Syntactical and visual means interlock in a dynamics of enticement and repose, for the tension created by separating the predicate from the subject draws the eye into the plane but also arrests it once the verb is reached. Coming to rest as it completes, verbally, the subject–verb logic and, visually, the plane, the eye establishes connections between the objects and the ideas they represent. Similarly, after the enjambments, the pace of the sentence slackens — signalled by the extra unstressed syllable in the penultimate line (the '-end' in 'schweifend' [roaming]) — forming the transition from the sensual language of the description to the sententious language of the motto. It is not just the 'bodily eye' that scans the actual landscape but also the 'mental eye' that, as it scans the diversity for unity, establishes meaning. Guided by the painterly principle of aerial perspective — literally suggested by the term 'air' — it reaches the farthest distance, the birds in the sky above the horizon. Emulating the push and pull of Lorrain's sun, the ekphrastic eye returns to where the viewing began, the 'human being' who now, as the switch in verb tense indicates, no longer exists in the past but in the present — in the presence, that is, of pictorial pleasure.

If *Torquato Tasso* is a meditation on poetry, it is tied rather directly to the pastoral tradition. When the Princess praises Tasso for how deeply his love poetry moves his readers, he singles out the powerful manifestations of love in his epic poem *The Liberation of Jerusalem* (1581), among them the unrequited love between Tancred and Erminia. When, in Goethe's play, the Princess tells Tasso that love's 'holy song [...] draws us on, and on, we listen to it, | We listen and we think we understand', until finally this song 'wins us over', the source of her enchantment is likely lyrical (ll. 1108, 1111–14, trans. modified). Tasso, however, interprets her praise 'pictorially': he speaks of the 'heaven you open up for me', and sees 'light' and 'endless happiness | Gloriously pour on me in golden rays' (ll. 1115–18).

But the link between Tasso, poetry, and painting is much more pronounced than what meets the ear and eye. In the seventeenth century, *The Liberation of Jerusalem* offered about fifty artists a feast of scenes, the majority pastoral not martial, for pictorial representations, among them Poussin's *Tancred and Erminia* (*c.* 1634) and, as shown here, Lorrain's *Landscape with Erminia and the Shepherd* (1666; *LV*, 166).

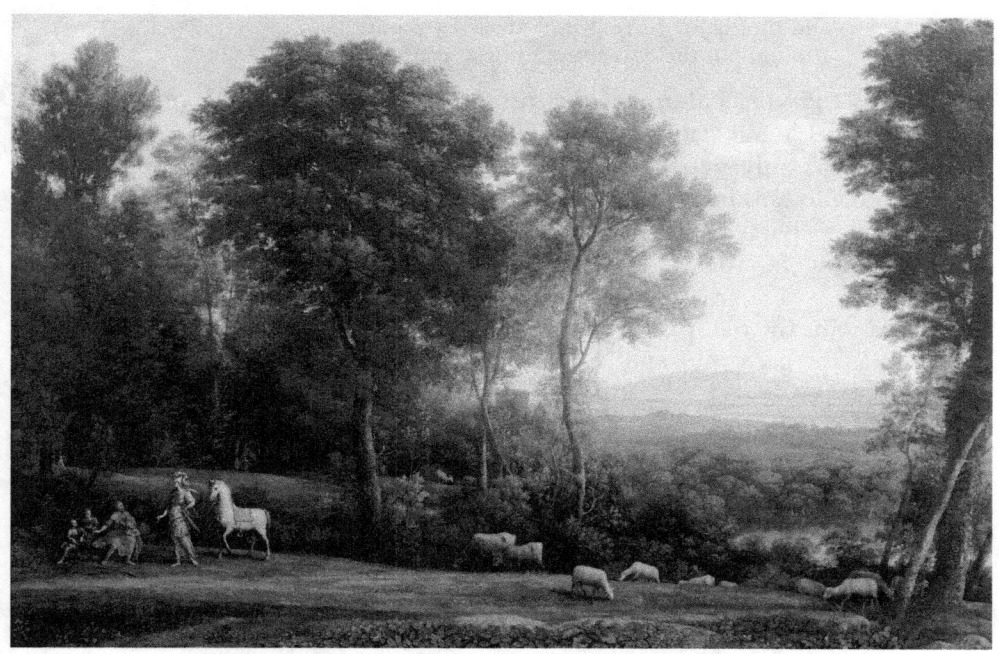

Fig. 1.5. Lorrain, *Landscape with Erminia and the Shepherd*.
Holkham Hall, Wells-next-the Sea, Norfolk/© The Earl of Leicester and the
Trustess of the Holkham Estate — Bridgeman Images

Following Tasso's description in Canto VII, Lorrain paints the encounter between the Saracen Princess Erminia and the shepherd and his sons.[59] She has fled from the Crusaders' camp in search of the wounded Tancred, her love. Pursued by enemy soldiers, she seeks shelter in the remote countryside with the shepherd's family. After falling asleep on the banks, 'where Jordan's crystal waters pour' (Tasso, *Liberation*, VII. 3, p. 120), she awakes to 'the river murmur' as 'the birds | with merry chirping greet the whitening dawn' (VII. 5, p. 121). From the nearby grove, she hears 'a simple pastoral air | mixed with rude notes on woodland whistles played', and as she approaches,

> She sees an old man in the pleasant shade,
> braiding (his flock close by) some basket thing
> and listening while three striplings play and sing. (VII. 6, p. 121)

In the ensuing dialogue, the old shepherd tells Erminia that in this 'fair dwelling-place' his 'kin and flock from prey | and spite are safe', and

> [...] no rout
> of soldiers ever comes here, nor has Mars
> as yet disturbed this far place with his jars. (VII. 8, p. 121)

Earlier in his life, he says, he left his 'native soil [...] thinking herding base',

> and lived in Memphis, and there found a place
> even in the palace retinue of the king;

> and though my care was gardens, by report
> I found out the corruptions of the court. (VII. 12, p. 122)

As much as the villa culture of Renaissance Italy with its juxtaposition of city and country, its 'renunciation of the life of the city and advocacy of rural retreat', underlies Tasso's only, but pronouncedly, bucolic scene in his drama about the First Crusade, he also taps into ancient literature, such as Ovid's account of the Golden Age, Horace's 'Beatus ille' (second Epode), or Virgil's 'O fortunatus nimium' (second Georgic) in order to evoke an Arcadia that culminates, visually, in Lorrain's painting.[60]

Erminia joins the old man in the 'bliss' and 'contentment' of his 'pleasant place', dons a 'peasant garment', and 'leads the flock to pasture' (VII. 15, 18, p. 123). There,

> [...] while her young lambs lie stretched at ease
> in mottled shade [...]
> into the bar of beech and laurel trees
> she carves her love's [Tancred's] name in a thousand ways,
> and the strange tale of her adversities. (VII. 19, p. 123)

The evergreen laurel not only locates this Arcadia in the Mediterranean but also makes it a realm where nature, poetry, and painting (if Erminia's calligraphic etching qualifies as such) are, spurred on by 'Cupid', conjoined.

Elaborating in such detail on reverberations of Tasso's poetic evocation of Arcadia in Goethe is imperative because the beginnings of what came to be known in the nineteenth century as the 'ideal landscape' are not just tied to Tasso but, of course, to Lorrain. Commissioning in 1602 a painting of Erminia's encounter with the old shepherd, Monsignor Giovanni Battista Agucchi (1570–1632) handed the painter Ludovico Carracci (1555–1619) *Impresa per dipingere l'historia d'Erminia* [Instructions for the Painting of the Erminia Story].[61] The *Impresa* is a translation of a literary *locus amoenus* into a pictorial *locus amoenus*; it is also a transmutation in the sense that exposition transforms into evocation, allegory into symbol. 'Painting the story of Erminia', as Agucchi puts it in the title, means that the painting is not about a static scene but a narration of events. For Agucchi, the painter is a storyteller who straddles fact and fiction, imitation and intimation. What is more, and crucially so for the history of landscape painting, the story *is* nature herself.

For a man of letters with appointments in the Papal States, Agucchi's visual, or rather painterly, awareness is striking. His eye literally scans the canvas for the appropriate arrangement of elements, beginning at the top with a 'sweeping prospect', followed by fortified buildings and soldiers in the distance, finally reaching the canvas's 'lowest section' with the River Jordan and its 'pellucid water', and, lining it, 'fresh, green meadows' with 'small bushes and trees here and there' (p. 107). Repeatedly using the verb 'to compose' [formare], he continues his set-up, this time starting with the foreground. He sees the old shepherd reclining 'in the shade of one of the trees', then, 'in the plane above' him (i.e. the middle ground), 'part of the herd of sheep and goats', and, 'above the herd', the small house or hut of the shepherd's family. As Agucchi's eye travels to the background or, in his words, through 'the remaining space [...] to the circumference of the horizon, it delights in the perspective of a beautiful, charming landscape composed with mountains, hills, valleys, and planes'. Finally, the image of the 'birds hovering in the air beyond the trees next to the river' completes this landscape as 'a place of tranquillity, a blissful Arcadia' (p. 108).

Even though Agucchi's theory of landscape painting is inspired by the pastoral tradition in literature (from Theocritus to Tasso) — which in itself is interwoven with Roman and Renaissance villa culture[62] — what is of greatest consequence for the history of landscape painting is the originality of his pictorial thinking. What should be obvious by now is that nature is not a coulisse for some heroic action. Rather, she takes centre stage. She is the protagonist. Accordingly, the staffage plays a minor role. Agucchi writes: 'Against the size of the [landscape's] space and the distances the staffage need to be small' (p. 108). Tellingly, the paintings' titles reflect this compositional hierarchy. Take, for instance, Paolo Veronese's history painting, *The Family of Darius before Alexander* (c. 1565), where the title identifies the historical significance of event and personage — the only painting, by the way, that Goethe mentions while in Venice during his Italian journey in 1786, praising Veronese for his 'great artistry' in the distribution of 'light and shadow' and the 'wise alternation of local colours' (*CW*, VI, 73; *FA*, XV.1, 92). In landscape painting, the titles reflect the division into 'heroic', with figures prominently occupying the foreground, such as *Erminia Takes Refuge with the Shepherds* (early seventeenth century) by an artist from the circle of Annibale Carracci (1560–1609), and the 'idyllic', where nature takes precedence over event and person, as in Lorrain's *Landscape with Erminia and the Shepherd*. (We shall return to these two versions of the Erminia story below.)

However, in Agucchi's pictorial thinking, the figures' small size does not imply insignificance, for in satisfying the 'stipulations of our charming story, the more the figures give rise to action and effect, the more they must be executed with great care and refined technique' (p. 108). The figures' function is tied to the notion of the painting as a story, which imbues the landscape with an epic or narrative quality with the aim of affecting the observer. Agucchi's *Impresa* agrees and disagrees with Tasso's poetics set forth in *Discourses on the Heroic Poem* (1594). Agucchi insists that the painter follow the principle of 'the real' or 'the true' [il vero], that is, in our context, be truthful to nature and use her as the model — as opposed to Tasso, who calls on the poet to imitate history. However, of outmost consequence for the genre of landscape painting is that Agucchi, like Tasso, emphasizes the need to follow the principle of 'verisimilitude' [il verosimile].[63] The verisimilar delights the observer with the 'semblance of truth', enticing him to suspend his disbelief, that is, persuading him that what he sees is within the limits of the likely, that it is, in short, probable. Temporarily to 'suppose real' what seems incredible requires 'visual faith', the analogue of the 'poetic faith' which Coleridge posits (when coining the term 'suspension of disbelief' in 1817) as necessary for 'transferring from our inward nature a human interest and a semblance of truth sufficient to procure for [the unnatural] shadows of imagination that willing suspension of disbelief for the moment, which constitutes poetic faith'.[64] Analogizing poetry and painting, or

Tasso and Lorrain, is not far-fetched, considering that Tasso likened the image-creating poet to a 'speaking painter' who moves the reader to wonder. The interplay, or indeed interdependence, of imitation and invention, of 'the real' [il vero] and 'the marvellous' [il meraviglioso] is very much in line with Goethe's assessment of Lorrain. This, in turn, explains why Lorrain is so pertinent to Goethe's aesthetics of landscape painting, indeed to his aesthetics in general. For Lorrain, to be verisimilar and to express the marvellous is to engender in the observer a sense of wonder, an amazed delight in — and a contemplative curiosity about — the beauty of a landscape. In his *Claude: The Poetic Landscape* (1994), Humphrey Wine writes that Lorrain's *Erminia* is both 'episodic' and 'evocative', and that this triggers 'two quite different types of reaction in the viewer: the pleasure of recognising the particular part of the story and the afterglow of the pastoral associations with which Claude invested it'.[65]

The *Erminia* of the circle of Annibale Carracci (shown in Figure 1.6), on the other hand, is, in Wine's estimation, 'a painter's automatic response to [Tasso's] text', that is, more (or even purely) 'episodic' than 'evocative'. In terms of Agucchi's ekphrastic reading of Tasso's text, this means that the Carracci *Erminia* is too literal a translation for the 'marvellous' to take effect — just as 'nature' is not the sole model for a classical landscape painting.

At the end of the play, Goethe's Tasso falls to pieces, overcome by an experience of self-alienation in the presumably most wholesome of landscape settings, Italian

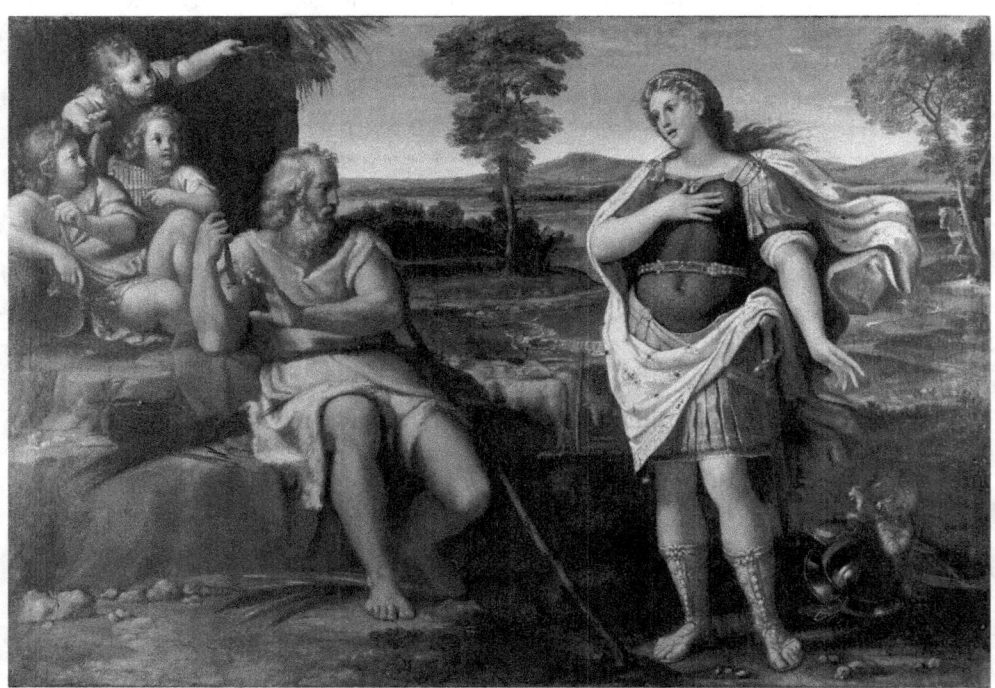

FIG. 1.6. Circle of Annibale Carracci, *Erminia*. National Gallery, London/ © National Gallery — Art Resource, NY

Renaissance villa culture. The dream of Arcadia has indeed ended. He pins his last hope on becoming a gardener and caretaker in the Duke's 'most distant' estate:

> Wie will ich deine Bäume pflegen! die Zitronen
> Im Herbst mit Brettern und mit Ziegeln decken
> Und mit verbundnem Rohre wohl verwahren!
> Es sollen schöne Blumen in den Beeten
> Die breiten Wurzeln schlagen, rein und zierlich
> Soll jeder Gang und jedes Fleckchen sein.
> Und laßt mir auch die Sorge des Palastes!
> Ich will zur rechten Zeit die Fenster öffnen
> Daß Feuchtigkeit nicht den Gemälden schade. (ll. 3198–3206)

> [How I will tend your trees! In autumn cover
> The lemon trees with boards and brick them in,
> With canes and rushes keep them safe from harm!
> Beautiful plants in flowerbeds shall put down
> Their struggling roots; and every avenue,
> Each polt, each bower be charming and well trimmed.
> And leave to me the palace's maintenance too!
> At the right time I'll have the windows open.
> So that no dampness shall impair the paintings.]

Anachronism aside, it would be counter-intuitive not to imagine that at least one of the paintings is a Lorrain. Given his quasi-mythical stature as the father of the English Garden, and since Goethe and his fictional alter egos dabbled in gardening, we will revisit the motif extensively, including its ancient variant, Arcadia. Before we do this, however, we visit Goethe in Frankfurt where he, in 1772, as a twenty-three-year-old *Sturm und Drang* genius, first encountered Lorrain.

Notes to Chapter 1

1. Cf. Andrews, *Landscape and Western Art*, pp. 92–103.
2. Clarke.
3. Clark, p. 67.
4. As Hagstrum, p. 9, points out in her archaeology of the maxim, Horace says that some poems may 'please us only once' while others can 'bear repeated readings'. Similarly, one painting may please us only from a distance in a darkened gallery, while another requires sustained examination in a brightly lit environment. Rather than meaning what it says, namely 'as a painting, so also a poem', Hagstrum suggests that the maxim implies 'as sometimes in painting, so occasionally in poetry'. For a detailed discussion of the dictum's source material, see Trimpi.
5. Ritter, p. 151.
6. Cf. Tantillo, *Will to Create*, pp. 37–47; Förster.
7. Cf. Grave, 'Diesseits und jenseits der Landschaft', pp. 434–38, who argues that Werther, experientially immersed as he is in nature, lacks the distance required for landscape to be perceived and painted.
8. On the changing views on the authenticity of this Lorrain, see Roethlisberger (MRP, I, 536); Russell, p. 331.
9. Library records show the following borrowing dates: 28 March 1802–12 June 1804, 7 October 1806–20 February 1807, and 9 April 1829–19 September 1829; see Keudell, nos. 277, 459, 1981.
10. For the most recent critical overviews of the theoretical debates, see Noll, who covers landscape treatises (and the varying estimations of Lorrain in them) from Gerard de Lairesse's

Groot Schilderboeck (1707) to Carl Ludwig Fernow's 'Über die Landschaftsmalerei' (1808), and Bätschmann's introduction to the English edition of Carus's *Nine Letters on Landscape Painting*. For Hagedorn, nature and art are distinct, not, as for Goethe, interdependent entities: 'What do I need landscapes for when I can see them in nature?' (quoted in Greif, 'Verschwinden', p. 408). For him, Lorrain's landscapes are essentially daydreams, as are those of his Dutch disciple, Jan Both (see Greif, 'Verschwinden', pp. 403–04). Fernow's and Carus's 'Romantic' theories lie beyond the scope of the present study, as does Goethe's conflicted relationship with them and 'Romantic' landscape painting itself, especially Caspar David Friedrich (see Bätschmann; Büttner; Grave, 'Illusion'; Greif, 'Jenseits von Arkadien'); for Carus's conflicted position between Friedrich and Goethe, see Scholl.

11. Maisak, *Goethe: Zeichnungen*, p. 22.
12. Letter to Ferdinand Kobell, 5 February 1781 (*FA*, XXIX, 327).
13. Cf. Femmel, VII: *Die Zeugnisse*, p. 121.
14. Interestingly, the *OED Online* lists 'lant-shape' as a term used in the early sixteenth century (<http://www.oed.com/view/Entry/105515> [accessed 6 September 2019]).
15. Mitchell, p. 5.
16. Gombrich, *Art and Illusion*, pp. 298, 301.
17. Cf. the 'Landschaft' entry in the *Goethe-Wörterbuch*, V, 940–42.
18. The critical literature seems divided on this issue. For instance, from a more general perspective, Bending, 'Literature and Landscape', argues in favour of the landscape of the mind, as does, focusing on Goethe, McCormick, '*Poema Pictura Loquens*' and 'Young Goethe in the Landscape', while Schulze Altcappenberg, p. 100, argues for both the 'tension between ideal and reality' and the 'reconciliation of idea and experience' in Goethe's theory and praxis of landscape art.
19. Offering a broader perspective, but illuminating for the task at hand, are the 'theories' of landscape and landscape painting elaborated upon in the salient critical literature, see Noll and others, eds, and Smuda, ed. (essay collections); Busch, ed. (handbook); Andrews, *Landscape and Western Art* (monograph).
20. The closest Goethe comes to a definition, according to Egle, pp. 281–82, is Hackert's 'naturalist classicism'; however, as exemplary as Hackert is in this regard, Goethe's attempts at defining landscape painting are marked, conceptually, by 'breaks' and, perceptually, by 'inconsistencies' (Egle, p. 279).
21. See Smuda, pp. 51, 54.
22. Cf. Werche.
23. See Hackert, pp. 122, 155, 298, 394. The poem will be discussed in Chapter 3.
24. See Weidner, *Jakob Philipp Hackert*, 'Philipp Hackert'. On Goethe and Hackert, see Mildenberger, '"Die Hackertsche klare, strenge Manier"'; Miller, '"Die Regeln des großen Stils"', 'Der Dichter als Landschaftsmaler'.
25. Cf. Fehrenbach. On the importance of 'the whole' as a crucial notion in Goethe philology, see the summary by Bernhart, pp. 180–82.
26. Taking a broader view than the landscapist's lens, Stephenson, p. 53, writes that, for Goethe, 'aesthetic experience [...] is the indirect way by means of which Idea and Experience converge', and that only 'inter-faculty testing of the products of imagination' can 'achieve 'truth' and 'wholeness'.
27. Smuda, p. 45, quoting Eduard von Hartmann and Friedrich Theodor Vischer.
28. Quoted in Smuda, p. 50.
29. Cf. Trunz, pp. 158–59.
30. Hackert's handwritten letters, kept at the Goethe–Schiller Archive in Weimar, are quoted from Maul's edition, p. 108; subsequent citations from this edition are given as page numbers in parentheses in the text. Although Hackert's German is flawed, it is important to listen to his voice for its authenticity and expressiveness. For a broader analysis of the letters than we can offer here, see Miller, '"Über die Kunst ist es ein ander Ding"'. On Goethe's editorial work, see Weidner, 'Philipp Hackert', pp. 401–02; Nutt-Kofoth.
31. Both Sandrart and Baldinucci are quoted — where possible, in the case of the former — using Roethlisberger's translations in the first volume of his critical catalogue of Lorrain's paintings

(MRP, I, 47–62). References to the German original of Sandrart's multivolume compendium are provided in the notes.
32. Sandrart, II.3, 332.
33. Letter of 28 July 1779 (Hackert, pp. 44, 282–83); cf. Weidner, *Jakob Philipp Hackert*, pp. 83–88, 94, 356–60.
34. See Stolzenburg, 'Hackert in Rom', 'Hackert in Paestum und Sizilien'; Prange.
35. Letter to Karl Ludwig von Knebel, 21 December 1787 (*FA*, xxx, 363).
36. Cf. Flach, p. 22; Smuda, p. 46.
37. To be sure, Chesme Bay is in the Aegean Sea, but Hackert based his painting on a miniature re-enactment of the famous naval battle in the harbour of Livorno.
38. For prints and critical commentaries on these paintings, see the catalogue raisonné of Nordhoff and Reimer, I, 117, II, 24–25 (Chesme), I, 121, II, 37–38 (Vesuvius), I, 138–43, II, 60–66 (Horace's villa).
39. Cf. e.g. *Zur Farbenlehre* (*FA*, XXIII.1, 271–72; *CW*, XII, 290).
40. Sandrart, II.3, 332.
41. Ditner, p. 152; cf. MRP, I, 62 n. 33.
42. Cf. Mildenberger, 'Baumporträts'.
43. The quotations in this paragraph are from Sandrart, I.3, 71. Sandrart's discussion of trees is not in Roethlisberger, so I have provided my own translation.
44. Long regarded as a doctrine of a Winckelmannian ideal of classicist beauty, Bellori's 'Idea of the Painter, Sculptor and Architect' appeared in 1672 as the introduction to his *Lives of the Modern Painters, Sculptors and Architects*, pp. 57–65 (pp. 58, 60). Of interest to us is that his 'Idea' is now seen more as an explication of his new mode of art-historical writing as practised in the *Lives*: self-conscious ekphrastic analyses of works of the visual arts aimed at freeing them from any taint of mechanical exercise and raising them to the level of the liberal arts by '*Idea*-lizing' (that is, intellectualizing) them (see Montanari). Also of interest to us is the fact that his ekphrastic art history accords with Giovanni Battista Agucchi (1570–1632), whom we will discuss extensively below. On the 'incompatibility' of Bellori's theory and Lorrain's work, see Lagerlöf, pp. 189–93.
45. See Nordhoff and Reimer, I, 138–43, II, 60–66; Stolzenburg, 'Zehn Aussichten'.
46. Quoted in Smuda, p. 51.
47. Cf. Smuda, pp. 59, 61.
48. The copious but widely scattered observations are painstakingly collected in Femmel, VII: *Die Zeugnisse*.
49. The painting is in a private collection (see Hackert, p. 742). At the behest of Carl August, Goethe acquired two paintings with Italian subjects from Hackert. While they have been identified as *Arnotal bei Florenz* [The Arno Valley near Florence] and *Blick auf den Tiber und die Milvische Brücke* [View of the Tiber and the Milvian Bridge], both disappeared in 1945 (cf. Nordhoff and Reimer, where they are listed as nos. 315 and 314). The correspondence between Goethe and Hackert makes it more than plausible that the *Blick auf den Tiber und Monti Sabini* and the painting reviewed by Goethe are similar. Hackert is explicit about the prospect and some of its details: 'Ponte Molle as seen from the Villa Madame [*sic*], with the aerial perspective of the Sabine countryside [...] a tall chestnut tree and goats in the foreground'; he is also frank about his practice of 'producing' paintings from a vast stock of 'sketches after nature' and of 'copying' existing paintings on demand, including the two sent to Weimar: 'will make copies for Mr [Francis Edward] Acton' (pp. 91, 93).
50. See Miller, 'Der Dichter ein Landschaftsmaler', pp. 392–96, 407. For a comprehensive exposition of Goethe and Hackert's relationship, see Miller, '"Die Regeln des großen Stils"'. For a contrasting view of Goethe's estimation of Hackert, see Mildenberger, '"Die Hackertsche klare, strenge Manier"'; Egle, pp. 281–82.
51. Cf. Beitl, p. 16.
52. The 'Landschaftszeichner' Christoph Heinrich Kniep accompanied Goethe to Sicily and to sights around Naples; for more on Kniep and a discussion of one of his 'outlines', see Chapter 3. Goethe owned engravings by Joos[t] de Momper the Younger (1564–1635), the Flemish landscape painter with a predilection for mountainous settings; see Schuchardt, pp. 245–56.

53. A fact-based, art-historical survey of the relationship between Hackert and Lorrain is provided by Weidner, *Jakob Philipp Hackert*, pp. 95–103.
54. In his brief analysis of the painting, Gowing, p. 95, specifies the peculiar colour scheme as follows: 'Toward the horizon the lightly clouded sky is citron yellow. Against it, at the skyline, there is a neutral greenish-blue, with the clear grey of a hill in front. Nearer, a bank shines yellow-green, showing an affinity to the sky; it is crossed by the warm shadow of the bridge, edged thickly with gold where it catches the transverse light.'
55. Cf. Pfotenhauer, 'Farbe', p. 192.
56. On the genesis and art-historical context of this 'history', its roots in the Italian journey, Goethe's visits to galleries and his collections of art works, and his lifelong study of the genre (and Lorrain's prominent role in it), see Trunz's meticulously edited and annotated edition; cf. also Büttner, who reads the fragments as aiming at presenting an alternative to the Romantic model exemplified by Karl Friedrich Schinkel (1781–1841).
57. Cf. Benes; Andrews, *Landscape and Western Art*, pp. 53–67.
58. On the Golden Age and Lorrain, see Pace, ' "Golden Age" '. See also, with an eye on Tasso and Lorrain, Lagerlöf, pp. 166–76.
59. Cf. Russell, pp. 182–83; Wine, p. 89.
60. Pace, ' "Free from Business" ', pp. 158, 161.
61. Original reprinted in Whitfield, pp. 218–20. For the passage (and its translation into German by Doris Müller-Ziem and Marina Neri) of Agucchi's ekphrasis of Tasso's Arcadian landscape, see Busch, ed., pp. 106–08. The following quotations are from Busch, with page numbers in parentheses in the text. For a critical edition of extant texts of the tract in Italian, and an exposition of Agucchi's art theory, see Mahon, pp. 109–54, 231–75. Cf. also Lagerlöf, pp. 21, 50.
62. See Pace, ' "Free from Business" '; Cantor.
63. Whitfield, pp. 223–24; Busch, ed., p. 109.
64. Coleridge, II, 5–6. In regard to the ideal landscape in painting, cf. Lagerlöf, pp. 134–41.
65. Wine, p. 37.

CHAPTER 2

❖

The Poetry of Art Criticism: Goethe's 1772 Review of Lorrain

Goethe's earliest writing on Lorrain is a review of two engravings after his works, one by James Mason (1710–80), the other by William Woollett (1735–85), commonly known in the 1770s as *The Landing of Aeneas in Italy: The Allegorical Morning of the Roman Empire* and *Roman Edifices in Ruins: The Allegorical Evening of the Roman Empire*. Here are the two prints that Goethe actually *saw* in volume II of the *Collection of Prints Engraved after the Most Capital Paintings in England* (1772).

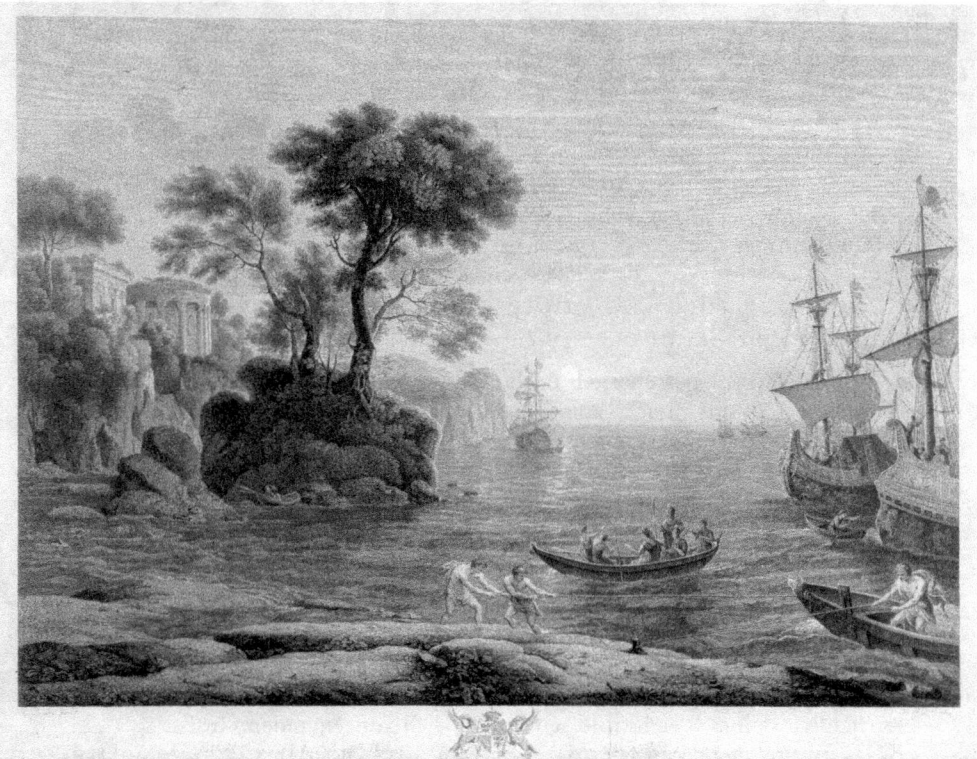

FIG. 2.1. Mason, *The Landing of Aeneas in Italy: The Allegorical Morning of the Roman Empire*. Royal Academy of Arts, London/© Royal Academy of Arts, London — Prudence Cuming Associates Limited

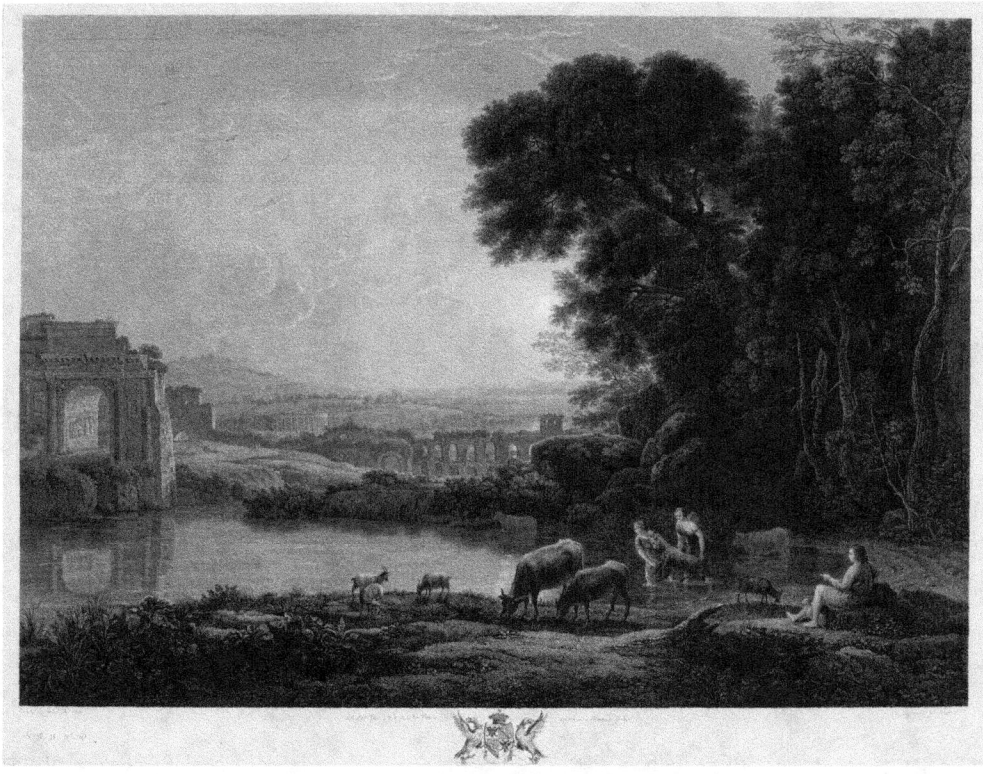

Fig. 2.2. Woollett, *Roman Edifices in Ruins: The Allegorical Evening of the Roman Empire*. Royal Academy of Arts, London/ © Royal Academy of Arts, London — Prudence Cuming Associates Limited

The review was published in a twice-weekly journal of reviews, the *Frankfurter Gelehrte Anzeigen* [Frankfurt Literary Advertiser], in 1772:

> 59. 60. Zwei Landschaften nach *Claude Lorrain*. Kinder des wärmsten poetischen Gefühls, reich an Gedanken, Ahndungen und paradiesischen Blicken. Das erste, gestochen von *Mason*, ein *Morgen*. Hier landet eine Flotte, von der Morgensonne, die überm Horizont noch im Nebel dämmert, angeblickt, an den Küsten des glücklichsten Weltteils; hier hauchen Felsen und Büsche in jugendlicher Schönheit ihren Morgenatem um einen Tempel edelster Baukunst, ein Zeichen edelster Bewohner. Wer bist du? der landet? an den Küsten, die, von Göttern geliebt und geschützt, in untadeliger Natur aufblühen, kommst du mit deinen Heeren, Feind oder Gast des edlen Volkes? Es ist *Aeneas*, freundliche Winde von den Göttern führen dich in den Busen Italiens. Heil dir, Held! werde die Ahndung wahr! der heilige Morgen verkündet einen Tag der Klarheit, der hohen Sonne, sei er dir Vorbote der Herrlichkeit deines Reichs und seiner taggleich aufsteigenden Größe.
>
> Das zweite! herabgestiegen ist die Sonne, vollendet ihr Taglauf, sinkt in Nebel, und dämmert über Ruinen in weiter Gegend. Nacht wird zur Seite hier der Felsenwald, die Schafe stehn und schauen nach dem Heimweg, und mühsam zwingen diese Mädchen die Ziege zum Bade im Teich. Zusammengestürzt

bist du Reich, zertrümmert deine Triumphbogen, zerfallen deine Paläste, mit Sträuchen verwachsen und düster, und über deiner öden Grabstätte dämmert Nebel im sinkenden Sonnenglanz. (*FA*, XVIII, 68–69)

[59. 60. Two Landscapes after *Claude Lorrain*. The product of the warmest poetic feeling, rich in thought, destiny and paradisal prospects. The first, engraved by Mason, a morning. Here on the coast of the happiest region of the world, a fleet of ships is landing, watched by the sun, which still gleams palely in the mist above the horizon. Here rocks and bushes breathe the morning air in youthful beauty, about the temple of the noblest architecture, the sign of noble inhabitants. Who are you, landing on these coasts beloved and protected by the gods and blooming with irreproachable nature? Do you bring your armies as the enemy, or the guests of this noble people? It is Aeneas, and the friendly winds of the gods are blowing you into the bosom of Italy. Hail to you, hero! Know your destiny! the divine morning announces a clear day, and may the high sun be the prophet of the magnificence of your empire, and its daily increasing greatness!

The second! The sun has set; her course completed, she sinks into the mist and gleams fitfully over a broad prospect of ruins. Night waits beside the rocky forest; the sheep stand looking at their homeward way, and the girls have some difficulty in driving their goats to water in the pond. Empire, you have fallen, your triumphal arches are in ruins, your palaces collapsed and overgrown with bushes, shrouded in gloom, and in your deserted cemeteries the mist glows palely in the sinking sun.] (*GoA*, p. 216, trans. modified)

The review appears under the heading 'English Copper Engravings'. With the seemingly inconspicuous term 'Kupferstiche', Goethe not only draws attention to the *means* of the (mechanical) reproduction and dissemination of paintings in the pre-lithographic age but also situates us in the midst of an aesthetic-hermeneutical debate with wide-ranging implications.[1] This matters because what he saw was neither the original paintings nor the original colours, but black-and-white reproductions. While Goethe came to appreciate Lorrain in colour later on — *Zur Farbenlehre*, as we shall see, is unthinkable without Lorrain — most of his exposure to Lorrain's work was through black-and-white engravings or etchings. In fact, he owned more than twenty original Lorrain etchings and numerous prints of Lorrain originals by others (see the Appendix). In Goethe's time there was a considerable market for prints, and Goethe was always augmenting his collection.[2]

Goethe had learned and practiced engraving while a student in Leipzig around 1770, and, strikingly, right from the start, as he relates in his autobiography *Aus meinem Leben: Dichtung und Wahrheit* [From my Life: Poetry and Truth] (1811–33), the visual kindles the verbal:

Die mancherlei Gegenstände, welche ich von den Künstlern behandelt sah, erweckten das poetische Talent in mir, und wie man ja wohl ein Kupfer zu einem Gedicht macht, so machte ich nun Gedichte zu den Kupfern und Zeichnungen, indem ich mir die darauf vorgestellten Personen in ihrem vorhergehenden und nachfolgenden Zustande zu vergegenwärtigen, bald auch ein kleines Lied, das ihnen wohl geziemt hätte, zu dichten wußte, und so mich gewöhnte, die Künste in Verbindung mit einander zu betrachten. (*FA*, XIV, 342)

[The many subjects which I saw treated by the artists awoke my poetic talent, and just as one makes a copperplate engraving for a poem, so I made poems for these engravings and drawings. I could visualize the personages depicted in them as they had been before and would be afterwards, could compose a little song to suit them, and so trained myself to view the arts in combination with each other.] (*CW*, IV, 236)

With his differentiation between the poem's vivid diachronic dramatization of a subject and, by implication, the painting's static synchronic depiction, Goethe hints at, as we shall see in a moment, Lessing's demarcation of the arts in his *Laokoon; oder, Über die Grenzen der Malerei und Poesie* [Laocoön: An Essay on the Limits of Painting and Poetry] (1766). Yet, with his insistence on the interrelatedness of the arts, and specifically that (as will be shown) the dynamic is not necessarily opposed to the pictorial, he simultaneously voices his opposition to Lessing. More importantly, for Goethe, the analogy between painting and poetry is both rhetorical and lyrical, with the imagination involving both eye and ear in its verbal 'actualization' of the stimulus engendered by the visual work of art. Before we take Goethe up on his cross-art conversion by reading the prose review as an ekphrastic poem, we shall explore his interart translation. In 1770, two years before the review, he wrote in his notebook, the *Ephemerides*: 'a copper engraving is like a translation; one has to translate into thoughts that which is best in it in order to feel the spirit of the original' (*FA*, XXVIII, 191). Somehow, Antiquity and Rome already loom over the first encounter between Goethe and Lorrain, for the occasion of Goethe's comment derives from engraved copies of original artwork on ancient Rome by Jean Barbault (1718–62). Of immediate concern for our purposes is the need for 'translation', which Goethe seems to understand as a hermeneutical task in order to intuit and cognize the 'spirit' of the original. 'To feel the spirit of the original' is, to say the least, sheer provocation on Goethe's part. Not only has he never seen the originals, but if he had, he might have realized that their order was actually the reverse: *Pastoral Landscape with the Arch of Titus* (1644; *LV*, 82) and *Seacoast with the Landing of Aeneas in Latium* (1650; *LV*, 122). As Marcel Roethlisberger, the doyen of Lorrain scholarship, tells us: 'In both works the sun occupies precisely the same place', but 'the landscape has a slightly orange sky, whereas the blue is more predominant in the coastal view, suggesting evening' (*MRP*, I, 233). Reflecting mainly the Lorrain reception in England of the eighteenth and nineteenth centuries, the two paintings 'were called the Decline and the Rise of the Roman Empire, and their atmospheres were wrongly characterized as evening and morning, respectively' (*MRP*, I, 233). Unmistakably, then, Goethe's first encounter with Lorrain amounts to a kind of art-historical Rohrschach test; what we are called upon to interpret is what Goethe reads into the engravings, what he sees and how he sees Lorrain, what image Lorrain engenders in his mind. As the following shows, Lorrain is not just an invitation to think and wonder and poetize; he is a state of mind, landscape as a state of mind transposed into poetry. And it is through poetry that Goethe, so to speak, fashions Lorrain into a figure of speech, vocalizes him as an emotion, deepens him into myth, and raises him into symbol. The intriguing question is, of course, whether this landscape of the mind is just Goethe's, or whether his creative appropriation transcends the subjective and reveals something about Lorrain's art as such.

The correlation of thought and emotion in the comment on the engravings hints at the perceived aesthetics of Lorrain's art, which Goethe tries, in his pithy introduction, to encapsulate by characterizing it as crafted from 'warmest feelings' and 'rich thoughts', while also bringing intuition and cognition into the discussion with the enigmatic, and essentially untranslatable, 'Ahndung'.[3] The term is as idiosyncratic as Goethe's *Sturm und Drang* aesthetics. It ranges in meaning from intuitive apprehension of some higher order to a formative impulse active in 'Einbildungskraft', the constructive power of the mind, and on to 'Einfühlungsvermögen', the capacity to respond emotionally to, or be affected by, objects in nature and art (*GW*, I, 296–302). It encapsulates a process of cognition that involves thought, sensation, and imagination. To complicate matters, the second time Goethe uses 'Ahndung' in the review, it suggests 'destiny' (as in the translation cited above) or 'prophecy', while Mephistopheles ironizes Faust's 'Ahndung' as (sexualized) 'lofty intuition' (l. 3291). Paying heed to the oxymoronic quality of Goethe's aesthetics and epistemology, an appropriate English equivalent for 'Ahndung' would seem to be 'hazy realization'.

Finally, and crucially, the word 'poetic' also appears in the introduction, leading one to wonder whether the 'translator' is not better served by poetry, rather than expository writing, to 'feel' its spirit and to transmute its 'poetry' into thought.

2.1. The Rhetoric of Landscape Painting

The *Ephemerides*, Goethe's commonplace book of the early 1770s, attest to his familiarity not only with Horace's concept of *ut pictura poesis*, mainly through an annotated edition of the *Ars Poetica*, but also with rhetoric on a broader scale. Indeed, Goethe's creative appropriation of the rhetorical tradition was such that a case can be made for reading his review as ekphrasis, the rhetorical device that aims at relating one artistic medium to another, or, in this case, recreating a painting in and through poetry. Goethe's recourse to rhetoric in order to articulate the inspiration with which Lorrain affected him — and which he would like to impart upon his audience through the vivid poetic enactment of the painting's scenery and plot — is part of his Faustian quest for identity and signature as a poet. If, in its juxtaposition of spiritedness and dispiritedness, the Lorrain review reflects this struggle, then Lorrain serves as a foil for Goethe's oscillation between the major poetic currents marking the *Sturm und Drang* period of German literature around 1770, namely between the mania of a panegyric to nature's exuberance in the vein of Friedrich Gottlieb Klopstock (1724–1803) and the melancholia of an elegy on nature's evanescence as practiced by Edward Young (1683–1765) — both of which are stupendously articulated in Werther's lyrical prose.

As Olaf Kramer's authoritative study makes clear, Goethe's preoccupation with the rhetorical tradition runs deep: in addition to Horace, he studied Cicero at the university in Leipzig, excerpted Cicero and Quintilian in the *Ephemerides*, and corresponded with family on Longinus.[4] His tribute — in his essay 'Von deutscher Baukunst' [On German Architecture] (1773) — to Erwin Steinbach, architect of the Strasbourg cathedral, is a rhetorical tour de force with the aim of invoking the sublime and the genius's godliness, including the apostrophe 'Hail to you, youth!' (*GoA*, p. 111; *FA*, XVIII, 118), which occurs in modified form — 'Hail to you, hero!' — in the Lorrain review. As Kramer shows, rhetoric was important for Goethe for reasons other than just figures of speech or style (*elocutio*). Important for his aesthetics is rhetoric's *natura–ars* model.[5] While Goethe employs conventional rhetorical devices (e.g. *exclamatio*, parallelism, climax, *amplificatio*, hyperbole), the evidence reveals an aesthetic trinity of poiesis, poetics, and persuasion. Key among the rhetorical concepts that illustrate this point and illuminate the Lorrain review is, for instance, *affectatio*:

> Will he [the hearer] weep when the speaker's eyes are dry? [...] The first thing, then, is that those feelings should be strong in us which we want to be strong in the judge, and that we should ourselves be moved before we try to move others. (Quintilian, VI. 2. 27–28)

The act of affecting and being affected goes hand-in-hand with *evidentia*: 'The speaker stimulates by his animation and kindles our emotions not just by a representation of things but by their reality' (Quintilian, X. 1. 16).[6] *Evidentia*'s act of stimulating visualization in the listener through vivid description is an act of mental imaging. Quintilian writes:

> It is a great virtue to express our subject clearly and in such a way that it seems to be actually seen. A speech [should go] further than the ears, and [the story should not] merely be told, without their being brought out and displayed to [the] mind's eye. (VIII. 3. 62)

Inexplicably, with the exception of Bernhard Scholz and Eckart Förster, Goethe scholarship fails to acknowledge that Goethe's critical distinction between the 'outer eye' and the 'inner eye' — which, to put it boldly, defines him as an 'Augenmensch' [ocular person],[7] if not, indeed, a Renaissance man — derives from his immersion in the rhetorical tradition.[8] Take, for instance, this comment on the physiologist Caspar Friedrich Wolff, who

> setzt als Grundmaxime aller seiner Forschungen: daß man nichts annehmen, zugeben und behaupten könne, als was man mit Augen gesehen und andern jederzeit wieder vorzuzeigen imstande sei [...] Wie vortrefflich diese Methode auch sei, durch die er so viel geleistet hat; so dachte der treffliche Mann doch nicht, daß es ein Unterschied sei zwischen Sehen und Sehen, daß die Geistes-Augen mit den Augen des Leibes in stetem lebendigen Bunde zu wirken haben, weil man sonst in Gefahr gerät zu sehen und doch vorbeizusehen.[9] (*FA*, XXIV, 432)

> [adopted as the fundamental maxim for all of his research: that one must not assume, admit, or assert anything except what one sees with one's own eyes, and what one is always in a position to show to others [...]. However excellent this method may be that allowed him to achieve so much, it never occurred to the splendid man that there is a difference between seeing and seeing, and that

> the eyes of the mind always have to work in a living union with the eyes of the body, otherwise one runs the risk of seeing yet at the same time not seeing.] (trans. by Förster, p. 88)

Another instance is the seeing of colours, which Goethe understands as a process in which both the physical and the mental eyes actively (i.e. productively) participate (cf. *Zur Farbenlehre*, §242). Here, however, it is the distinction's relationship to ekphrasis that interests us. Scholz writes: 'The seeing of the "outer eye" [...] is restricted by the spatial and temporal limits of the here and now. By contrast', he continues, 'the "inner eye" [...] is entitled by memory and imagination to go beyond the limitations imposed by the outer eye',[10] as evidenced, according to Quintilian, by

> what the Greeks call *phantasiai* (let us [Romans] call them 'visions'), by which the images of absent things are presented to the mind in such a way that we seem actually to see them with our eyes and have them physically present to us.[11] (VI. 2. 29)

The *natura-et-ars* reciprocity originates in the rhetorical dynamic of innate talent and acquired skills, of emotional authenticity and artistic virtuosity. Regarding the latter dichotomy, Quintilian emphasizes the interplay of 'heart' and 'mind' when he advises that

> everything on which we intend to speak, every person and every question, and all the hopes and fears likely to be attendant on them, must be kept full before our view, and admitted as it were into our hearts, for it is strength of feeling, combined with energy of intellect, that renders us eloquent. (X. 7. 15)

The orator's *ingenium*, that is, his natural reservoir of creativity, exemplifies the former, for, according to Cicero, 'certain lively activities of the intelligence and the talents alike should be present, such as to be at once swift in invention, copious in exposition and embellishment, and steadfast and enduring in recollection' (*De Oratore*, I. 113).

The tension between *natura* and *ars* comes into play in the cardinal concept of the sublime. In his treatise *On the Sublime*, Longinus, whom Goethe studied avidly, and whose 'rhetorical' understanding was the most widespread before Burke's and Kant's 'natural' notions,[12] identifies five sources of the sublime. The first two are mainly inborn — namely, 'the power of grand conceptions' and the 'inspiration of vehement emotion' — while the other three come partly from art: 'figures of thought and figures of speech'; 'nobility of language', that is, 'the use of metaphor and elaborated diction'; and 'dignified and elevated word-arrangement' (Longinus, VIII.1, p. 181). Echoing Quintilian's mental image-making, Longinus maintains that 'grandeur' is 'very largely produced [...] by the use of "visualizations" ("*phantasiai*") [...] in passages where, inspired by strong emotions, you seem to see what you describe and bring it vividly before the eyes of your audience' (XV. 1, pp. 215–17). It is important to note that Longinus's emphasis on the artist's 'lofty thoughts' and on 'sublimity' as an 'echo' of the artist's 'noble mind' (IX. 1–2, p. 185) feeds the *Sturm und Drang* genius cult — as does his preference for literary models from

Antiquity whose 'grandeur' may be 'flawed' (rather than those whose 'triviality' is 'impeccable'), among them, foremost, Homer, but also Pindar, who 'seems to fire the whole landscape as he sweeps across it' (XXXIII. 1–5, pp. 267–71). Asserting that aspiring to the sublime trains the soul, which in turn pours itself into the work of art, Longinus's treatise is not only an enquiry into the sublime but also an ethical dissertation, since the sublime is the product of a 'noble spirit' (IX. 1–4, pp. 183–85). Goethe, as we shall see, speaks of Lorrain's 'schöne Seele' in precisely this Longinian way.

Since Longinus's sublime is not based on natural sources with which we have come to associate the sublime, it is in keeping with Longinus to read Goethe's Lorrain review as a rhetorical enactment of a sublime experience of art. However, Goethe expands the Longinian sublime by introducing 'nature' into the discussion, not in the sense of the sublime as an experience of nature's overwhelming grandeur (thus Burke and Kant, with the Alps as an example), but nature as a creative force to be emulated by the artist.[13] In the essay 'Die Natur: Fragment' (c. 1780), which reflects Goethe's natural credo at the time but was actually written by Georg Christoph Tobler, we read that there is 'everlasting life [...] growth, and movement' in nature, and even though 'she has few mainsprings to drive her [...] these never wind down; they are always at work, always varied' (*CW*, XII, 3–4; *FA*, XXV, 11–12). And, in another review written for the *Frankfurt Literary Advertiser*, Goethe draws a parallel between nature's creativity and the human genius: 'We firmly believe that the genius does not imitate nature but that he himself creates analogously to nature' (*FA*, XVIII, 61). The pattern underlying this dynamic naturalism is also an ideational naturalism that the creator, be he poet or painter, shares with the Creator, for it 'rests upon an idea which sets the pattern according to which God creates and works in nature, and nature in God, throughout eternity' (*CW*, XII, 33; *FA*, XXIV, 449).

The overlap of Longinus's sublime with the review's initial characterization of Lorrain's art is indeed striking. As the 'father' who procreates artistic offspring out of the 'warmest feeling' and 'rich thought', he seems to possess the inborn traits of Longinus's sublime artist, which he complements with acquired 'poetic' skills, that is, rhetorical devices, noble diction, and dignified style. While the term 'sublime' appears nowhere in Goethe's Lorrain review, he asserts in his programmatic hymn to the architect of the Strasbourg cathedral, 'Von deutscher Baukunst', that the 'erhaben' [sublime] art of a genius engenders 'Ahndungen', or hazy realizations, in the observer (*FA*, XVIII, 114). If we relate the epiphanic revelation of 'paradise' to Longinus's claim that 'a well-timed flash of sublimity shatters everything like a bolt of lightning' and 'inspires wonder' and 'amazes us' (I. 4, p. 163), then Goethe, Lorrain, and Longinus coalesce into a rhetorical triumvirate.

In the *Collection of Prints Engraved after the Most Capital Paintings in England*, Goethe found not only the two engravings after Lorrain discussed above but also an engraving of Lorrain's painting *Landscape with Mercury and Battus* (1654; *LV*, 131). This is important because it establishes a first-hand pictorial link between Goethe, Lorrain, and rhetoric. In her chapter ' "As though it were happening before our eyes": The Ideal Landscape and Rhetoric', Margaretha Lagerlöf points out that thirteen of Lorrain's works feature Mercury, the 'representative of the rhetorical and persuasive arts (and of lies and deception) in his confrontations with Apollo, the highest of all the personifications of art'.[14] Given Goethe's familiarity with mythology and rhetoric, he must have quickly realized that Lorrain had been nurtured in both traditions.

Lagerlöf expounds at length on the importance of rhetoric for landscape painting in seventeenth-century Rome. Basing much of her discussion on Longinus, she provides a set of incisive observations that will guide our analysis of Goethe's Lorrain review. She notes that, in Lorrain's time, 'rhetoric became the accepted model for both pictorial art and literature'; that landscape painting was deemed 'theatrical' in that it creates an 'illusion of immediacy' that not only draws the observer into the painted world but makes him 'a direct participant'; that, as 'myth', which itself employs rhetoric, 'enters the landscape, nature becomes imbued with human conceptions and attributes'; that, with the concept of the eye of the mind, 'the visual sense' becomes 'an instrument of thought'; and that rhetoric provides the means to render an impossible actuality possible through 'force of conviction'.[15]

2.2. Lorrain as Ekphrasis

Associated with rhetoric, and harking back to Homer's descriptions of pictures in the *Iliad* and *Odyssey*, ekphrasis, the quondam rhetorical device, evolves into a special literary genre that is more than just a verbal description of visual art.[16] For, to use Edward Hirsch's felicitous elucidation,

> ekphrastic modes inevitably address — and sometimes challenge — the great divide between spatial and temporal experience, eye and ear, visual and verbal mediums. They brave the mystery dividing the seen from the unseen, image from text. They teach us to look more closely. They dramatize with great intensity the actual experience of encounter. That is why the proper response to a work of visual art may well be an ode or an elegy, a meditative lyric, a lyrical meditation. (Hirsch)

Reading the review's prose as poetry shows that, on the one hand, the ekphrastic synergy enhances the impact of the original, and the illuminative liveliness brings to the fore the original's 'spirit'; on the other hand, it shows that, although the poem enhances the original, it takes on a life of its own precisely through the vividness of its poetic language. In the act of translation, Goethe functions as both creator and creation. When he says that 'word and image seek each other', an implied meaning is that, for him, each is a bridge between idea and experience — here, it is the word as ekphrasis and the image as painting.[17]

Here are, so to speak, the engravings as poems:

Das erste [Bild:] ein *Morgen*

Hier landet eine Flotte,
von der Morgensonne, die überm Horizont
noch im Nebel dämmert, angeblickt,
an den Küsten des glücklichsten Weltteils.

Hier hauchen Felsen und Büsche
in jugendlicher Schönheit ihren Morgenatem
um einen Tempel edelster Baukunst,
ein Zeichen edelster Bewohner.

Wer bist du? der landet?
an den Küsten, die,
von Göttern geliebt und geschützt
in untadeliger Natur aufblühen,
kommst du mit deinen Heeren,
Feind oder Gast des edlen Volkes?

Es ist *Aeneas*,
freundliche Winde von den Göttern
führen dich in den Busen Italiens.
Heil dir, Held!
werde die Ahndung wahr!

Der heilige Morgen verkündet
einen Tag der Klarheit, der hohen Sonne,
sei er dir Vorbote der Herrlichkeit
deines Reiches
und deiner taggleich aufsteigenden Größe.

Das zweite!

Herabgestiegen ist die Sonne,
vollendet ihr Taglauf,
sinkt in Nebel und dämmert über Ruinen
in weiter Gegend.

Nacht wird zur Seite hier der Felsenwald,
die Schafe stehn und
schauen nach dem Heimweg,
und mühsam zwingen diese Mädchen
die Ziege zum Bade im Teich.

Zusammengestürzt bist du Reich,
zertrümmert deine Triumphbogen,
Zerfallen deine Paläste,
mit Sträuchern verwachsen und düster,
und über deiner öden Grabstätte
dämmert Nebel im sinkenden Sonnenglanz.

[The first [picture:] a *morning*

Here, a fleet is landing
Greeted by the sun, above the horizon,
Gleaming as yet palely in the mist
On the coast of the happiest region of the world.

Here, rocks and bushes breathe
The morning air in youthful beauty
About a temple of the noblest architecture,
A sign of the noblest inhabitants.

Who are you, landing
On these coasts
Beloved and protected by the gods,
Bloomimg with irreproachable nature?
Do you bring your armies as the
Enemy or the guest of this noble people?

It is *Aeneas*,
The friendly winds of the gods
Are blowing you into the bosom of Italy.
Hail to you, hero!
May the prophecy become true!

The divine morning announces
A day of brightness and high sun,
May it be the herald of the magnificence
Of your empire,
And its day-like rising greatness.

The second!

The sun has set,
Her course completed,
She sinks into the mist and gleams
Fitfully over a broad prospect of ruins.

The rocky forest here on the side turns to night,
The sheep stand
Looking at their homeward way,
And the girls, with difficulty,
Force the goat to water in the pond.

Fallen have you, empire,
Ruined are your triumphal arches,
Collapsed your palaces,
Overgrown with bushes, gloomily,
And in your deserted graveyards,
The mist gleams palely in the sinking sun.]

The ekphrasis begins with a demonstrative 'here', as if the painting were enacting a scene right before the observer's eyes. Indeed, as 'here' marks the site where water meets land, it also prepares the stage for a dramatic action: we witness the landing of a fleet. Significantly, the landing coincides with the dawning of a new day and the solemn affirmation of utmost happiness: the personified 'morning sun' greets the fleet with rays of light brightening the mist on the horizon. Establishing an alliterative link between the opening 'here' and 'horizon', we arrive, tonally, at the second 'here', whose 'h' heralds the next action, indicated by the verb 'hauchen' [to breathe], thus fusing sound — 'h' is an aspirate — and meaning. 'Breathe' interweaves raw nature, 'rocks' and 'bushes', with high culture, not just in the choice of 'edel' [noble] and 'Baukunst' [architecture] and 'Bewohner' [residents], but also poetically supported by the repetition of the superlative 'noblest' and the alliterative 'b' which echoes back to the 'b' in 'Büsche' [bushes]. 'Breathe' personifies inanimate nature and at the same time breathes life into rather abstract designations of human spiritual and artistic objects, 'temple' and 'architecture', as well as a person's domicile, 'residence'. As we move from 'bushes' to 'inhabitants', time does not pass; there just seems to be a resonant moment of presence, for there is no 'ein-' or 'aus-' prefix denoting '*in-*' or '*ex*hale', which would indicate a cyclical notion of time. Instead, 'breathe' is tied to 'morning', 'youth', and 'beauty'.

With the twice-repeated 'here' introducing us, as it were, to a play, the observer now proceeds to bring one of the figures to life by means of an apostrophe, 'Who are you, landing?'. Especially with the use of this direct address, the painting has become a *tableau vivant* with 'real' characters. Notably, the interlocutory 'du' [you] establishes an emotional bond of familiarity, even intimacy. With the repetition and further modification of 'on these coasts', we learn that the human being embodied by the 'you' in the here and now is, and has been, an object of divine attention, 'beloved' and 'protected' by the gods.

That 'nature' blooms 'untadelig' [irreproachably] — an unusually abstract epithet for nature — further underscores the interrelatedness of the physical and the spiritual, of earth and heaven. Etymologically, 'untadelig' connotes exemplariness, and since 'adelig' is related to the already used 'edel' [noble], the natural, cultural, and human come together to form a unison of the highest order. In light of this image of an ideal world, the following question seems rhetorical, despite its alliterative allusion to war ('Heere' [armies]) and its ambivalence as to the role of the new arrival, 'friend' or 'guest'. Once again, the language is telling in that 'guest' interrupts the conventional juxtaposition of friend and foe, thus suggesting that the initial emotional apprehension vis-à-vis the 'Fremdling' [stranger] — this is the meaning of the Middle High German root of 'Gast' [guest] — will turn out to be as noble as the people at whose shores he arrives.

If the dilemma posed by the rhetorical question lingers, it is dispelled not only by the flash of an answer — corresponding as such to Longinus's understanding of the sublime — 'It is *Aeneas*', but also by the confirmation of 'friend' in the adjectival characterization ('friendly') of the god-sent winds that carry Aeneas to the 'bosom of Italy', with 'Busen' ranging in meaning from 'bay' and 'gulf' to 'chest' and 'breast' — the latter suggesting nourishment, care, and protection. If Italy offers the motherly element, it is Troy that provides the fatherly — note the redoubling continuation of 'h' — in the form of the 'hero' who is saluted as the saviour, 'Hail to you, hero!'. The prospect of a totality that is complete and salubrious is articulated as pathos-filled exhortations, 'May the prophecy become true!' and 'May it be the herald'. Intensified by erstwhile religious vocabulary, 'holy' and 'verkünden' [to announce], Goethe creates a secularized beatific vision of dawn, be it the birth of a new day or new empire. Noteworthy is, again, the alliteration of 'h', this time from 'heilige' [divine] to 'hohen' [high] and on to 'Herrlichkeit' [magnificence], establishing a tonal link between morning, sun, and empire, and leading crescendo-like to the apex of this ekphrasis — 'greatness'.

If the 'h' alliteration was the sonorous signature of the 'Rise', then the 'Fall' resounds with the repeated 'z'. To be sure, there is a faint echo of 'h', but in its first reccurrence it is linked to a downward movement, the setting of the sun, 'herab' [down], whereas the second 'h' introduces a tonal variation of 'here'. No longer beckoning the observer to look at, or enter, the bright scene unfolding centre-stage, it guides his gaze to the side of the stage, where the personified rocks no longer breathe morning air but change into 'night'. A similar contrast is evoked by the final reiteration of 'h' in 'homeward way'. The dynamics of Aeneas's epic journey and grandiose arrival at his newly discovered urban home pose a stark contrast to the inertia of the sheep eying their homeward path.

If, tonally, the 'h's erstwhile major key shifts into minor, then the alliterative 'z' — in German an affricate phoneme that combines a plosive with a fricative — borders on atonality. Inconspicuously announced as the 'zweite' [second] picture, two further iterations — 'zwingen' [to force] and 'Ziege' [goat] — lead up to a triplet of past participles that start with 'z' — 'zusammengestürzt' [collapsed], 'zertrümmert' [ruined or shattered], 'zerfallen' [crumbled] — and that, onomatopoetically, intone staccato bursts of sharp blows that lay waste to the 'empire', 'triumphal arches', and 'palaces'. Whereas in the first engraving the familiar forms of 'you' referenced creation and rise, they now relate to collapse and fall. The 'noblest architecture' is 'overgrown', with 'dark shrubs' or 'undergrowth' replacing the luxuriantly growing 'bushes'.

Relying once again on speech sounds, Goethe juxtaposes the 'Größe' [greatness] of the rising empire with the 'Grab' [tomb] of the declining empire, underpins the disparity with 'splendid' and 'desolate', and uses, to corroborate the contrast, sonic parallelism to suggest a visual and semantic antithesis: 'above the horizon' and 'above your graveyard'. To bring to the fore the inherent circularity of the two scenes, Goethe resorts once again to rhetoric with the chiastic or crosswise arrangement of 'mist gleams' and 'Gleams [...] mist' to paint in words the contrary dynamic: the sun rising and burning off the morning mist vs the sun sinking and vanishing into thickening evening mists. While the final alliteration in 'setting sun' [sinkende Sonne] turns dusk into a 'tone poem', the last word, 'Glanz', seems to suspend the downward movement in an ever-present 'glow' — note the use of the present participle, 'setting', that contrasts starkly with the previous quartet of past participles marking the finality of dusk and decline. What is crucial, then, is that, within and without, the two paintings as a pair mirror Goethe's notion of nature as a dynamic mixture of 'setting' and 'rising', of transformation and preservation. What is also crucial is that Goethe's understanding of nature ties in with Lorrain's understanding of art as reflected in the recurring creation of 'pendants'. Noting that the two paintings reviewed by Goethe 'have always been considered a pair', Roethlisberger explains: 'The notion of contrasting unity in the pairs is an extension of the principles governing each single composition, which forms an entity in itself but assumes its full meaning only in connection with the pendant' (MRP, I, 233, 27).

'Glanz', it would seem, is another key, yet multivalent, term in Goethe's poetic arsenal.[18] Here, as a visually manifest reflection of the sun, it symbolizes light, albeit not the shiny brightness heralding the arrival of Aeneas but the soft glow of twilight. Metaphorically, Aeneas's resplendent appearance in the 'high sun' seems to articulate an experience of the sublime, while the ruins that shimmer in the twilight seem to mirror a feeling of *Weltschmerz*. The poems' pronounced dialectic of the sun's bright and subdued light is curiously prescient in anticipating the dialectic occurring half a century later in *Faust II*, which begins with its eponymous hero waking up to the rising sun only to turn from its blinding light and toward its 'farbigen Abglanz' [many-hued reflection] in a rainbow arching over the horizon (l. 4727).

A hitherto unrecognized meaning of 'Glanz' can be gleaned from Goethe's preoccupation with Pindar at the time of the Lorrain review.[19] Pindar's eighth Pythian Ode, which furnishes a compelling corrective to Goethe's exuberant *Sturm und Drang* aesthetics (see below), seems to suggest that, if the poet understands 'Glanz' as the divine creative impulse that can turn the mania–melancholy dilemma into a dialectic, then a poem will gestate in his mind: 'Eintagswesen! Wer ist einer? Wer ist keiner? Eines Schattens Traum der Mensch. Aber wenn Glanz von Gott gegeben kommt, dann ist ein strahlendes Licht bei den Menschen und wonnige Zeit' [Creatures of a day! Who is someone? Who is no one? A dream of a shadow is man. | But whenever Zeus-given brightness comes, | a shining light rests upon men, and a gentle life] (German version quoted from Ponzi, p. 58; Pindar, Pythian Ode 8, ll. 95–97). In the midst of darkness, this 'brilliance', this sensation of light, is pure stimulation. Indeed, it is the interaction of *light* and *darkness* that brings forth painting and poetry and, as we shall explore, colour.

Pursuing the question of poiesis or creative production more specifically, we may ask ourselves who articulates the versified review and how can we characterize this voice. Even though there is no lyric 'I', the use of 'you' implies an interlocutor. This speaker is both an observer and a creator; together, they describe, narrate, converse — with Aeneas and the personified 'empire', and through them, dawn and dusk and the sun — and articulate their emotional response, which ranges from 'manic' in the first poem to 'melancholic' in the second.

What is more, this interlocutor does not only speak to, as it were, the paintings, but to an imagined listener. In and through the poetic language, he communicates his emotional, imaginative, and speculative response to the paintings. They affect him so deeply that they become an experience, in particular their theatrical and sublime qualities. To wit, for him, it feels as if Lorrain were staging a play before his eyes — the repeated 'here' is like an invitation to join him in the performance, with the architectural backdrop acting as props and the low horizon simulating a front-row view. From the outset, rhetorical language dramatizes his excitement about, and his arrested attention to, the events unfolding 'on stage'.

What we have witnessed so far in our reading of Goethe's reading of Lorrain is not only a deployment of rhetorical devices but a veritable poetic performance of ekphrasis. Inspired and stimulated by Lorrain, Goethe translates one medium (painting) into another (poetry), and in so doing connects Lorrain to an audience. Through the poems' rhetorical vividness, he highlights what is shown and what is happening in the paintings. The ekphrastic synergy 'translates' the copper engravings into pictorial oratory, a 'still life' into a *tableau vivant* pulsating with a range of reciprocities, be they emotional and intellectual, effulgent and gloomy, mythological and factual, static and dynamic, auditory and visual, lyrical and prosaic. As much as the ekphrasis takes on a life of its own through the vivid brilliance of its language, and mindful of the fact that we have glimpsed a pattern or essence, in order to speculate on how this translation should enable us to 'feel the spirit of the original', we need to contextualize Goethe's review in terms of his aesthetic beliefs and convictions of the early 1770s, as evidenced in his reviews of art and literature in the *Frankfurt Literary Advertiser*.

2.3. Salomon Gessner: Painter and Poet of Pastorals

Since the ekphrastic synergy presupposes the pairing of the pictorial and the poetic, it would seem worthwhile to consider a prominent painter and poet of the time, Salomon Gessner (1730–88), celebrated across Europe for his pastorals and idylls. Unlike Lessing, but similarly to Goethe (see Chapter 4 below), he was drawn to Thomson's 'descriptive poetry', or, to use his words, 'pictures', and praised them for their Lorrainian 'grace and amenity'. The admiration found expression in the echoes of two episodic narratives of the *Seasons* (Palemon and Lavinia, Celadon and Amelia) in his idylls *Daphnis* (1754) and *The Death of Abel* (1758),[20] and in the title vignettes he drew for each season when he oversaw the publication of the first German translation of the complete 1744 edition of the *Seasons* from 1757 to 1764.[21] In 1770, in 'A Letter from M. Gessner to M. Fueslin [...] on Landscape Painting',[22] Gessner indicated that, by using Lorrain as a model, he had trained his skills as a landscapist. What he learned from Lorrain was 'a happy choice of vistas, and a fine harmony of the grounds', as well as 'to imitate the verdure of the fields, the soft distances, and the admirable gradations, by the secret artifice of their shades'. In Lorrain, Gessner continues, he

> found dignity and truth united. Not a simple and servile imitation of nature, but a choice of the most sublime and interesting beauty. [...] Repose and amenity reign throughout all countries which the pencil of Lorrain has created.

> The mere view of his pictures, excites that sweet emotion, those delicious sensations, which a well chosen prospect has the power to produce in the mind. His fields are rich, without confusion; variegated, without disorder. Every object presents the idea of peace and prosperity. We continually behold a happy soil, that pours its bounteous gifts on the inhabitants; a sky, serene and bright, under which all things spring forth, and all things flourish.

Barely two months before the Lorrain review, in August 1772, Goethe had published an appraisal of Gessner's poetic idylls in the *Frankfurt Literary Advertiser*. The review is set up as a debate between an advocate and a detractor of Gessner's art.[23] The advocate speaks of Gessner's 'mastery', and defines it as Gessner having the

> empfindlichste Auge für die Schönheiten der Natur, das heißt für schöne *Massen*, *Formen* und *Farben* hat er reizende Gegenden durchwandelt, in seiner Einbildungskraft zusammen gesetzt, verschönert, und so standen paradiesische Landschaften vor seiner Seele [...] er schuf sich [...] Gestalten aus seiner schmachtenden Empfindung und erhöhten Phantasie, staffierte seine Gemälde damit aus, und so wurden seine Idyllen. Und in diesem Geiste lese man sie! und man wird über seine Meisterschaft erstaunen. (*FA*, XVIII, 47)

> [most sensitive eye for nature's beauties, that is, in search of beautiful *masses*, *forms*, and *colours*, he ambled through delightful rural areas, reassembled and beautified them in his imagination, and thus paradisal landscapes appeared before his soul [...] he created [...] figures from a yearning feeling and a heightened imagination, decked out his paintings with them, and thus his idylls came into being. And this is the spirit in which they should be read! And if one does so, one marvels at his mastery.]

The advocate grants Gessner the eye necessary for perceiving in nature elements that lend themselves to composing harmonious scenery, and the sensitivity and imagination required for creating the setting's inhabitants. The detractor counters:

> so trefflich das Detail sein mag [und] zu gewissen Zwecken wohl geordnet ist, so mißt ihr doch überall den Geist, der die Teile so verwebt, daß jeder ein wesentliches Stück vom Ganzen wird. Eben so wenig kann er Szene, Handlung und Empfindung verschmelzen. (*FA*, XVIII, 48)

> [the details may be well crafted [and], for certain purposes, well ordered, but everywhere one misses the mind that weaves them together in such a way that each becomes an essential part of the whole. In the same way, he is unable to blend scenery, action, and sentiment.]

The reassembly of which the advocate spoke seems to fall short of suggesting an ultimate 'purpose', that is, of rising to the level of symbolism, due to failed integration of the elements. Goethe does not speak of 'fusion' or 'synthesis', as one recent critic has it,[24] but of 'weaving together', of combining elements into a 'whole' without the loss of their 'essential' identity. In a poem called 'Antepirrhema', a term borrowed from ancient Greek comedy denoting a public address by the chorus, weaving can be read as a metaphor for creativity personified in archetypally dynamic principles:

Antepirrhema

So schauet mit bescheidnem Blick
Der ewigen Weberin Meisterstück,
Wie Ein Tritt tausend Fäden regt,
Die Schifflein hinüber herüber schießen,
Die Fäden sich begegnend fließen,
Ein Schlag tausend Verbindungen schlägt,
Das hat sie nicht zusammengebettelt,
Sie hat's von Ewigkeit angezettelt;
Damit der ewige Meistermann
Getrost den Einschlag werfen kann. (*FA*, II, 500–01)

[Antepirrhema

Thus view with unassuming eyes
The Weaver Woman's masterpiece:
One pedal shifts a thousand strands,
The shuttles back and forward flying,
Each fluent strand with each complying,
One stroke a thousand links commands;
No patchwork, this, of rag and tatter,
Since time began She plots the matter,
So may the Master, very deft,
Insert with confidence the weft.] (*CW*, I, 163)

Extrapolating the weaving metaphor to landscape painting, Goethe's is a warp-and-weft aesthetic: just as the shuttle interlaces warp and weft into a fabric, so the painter, in a process involving observation and imagination — the outer eye and the inner eye — interlaces distinct elements into a varied whole, creating a re-presentation that is both real and unreal, that both reveals and conceals. The verbal equivalent of the criss-crossing dynamic is the conjunction of contradictory terms, e.g. 'one' and 'thousand', 'back' and 'forth', 'momentary' and 'eternal', 'homogeneous' and 'multifarious' ('one pedal'/'one stroke', 'a thousand strands'/'a thousand links'), and 'female' and 'male' (note the 'Mann' [man] in the penultimate line). A metaphor for the unity and interpenetration of opposites, weaving is a key concept in Goethe's aesthetics (and epistemology),[25] one we will see at critical moments in this study, as in the late essay on the 'Lorrain of the North', the Dutch landscapist Jacob van Ruisdael.

If the interlacing of nature and art does not evolve from a dynamic of polarities, the result is an 'abstract', even 'repulsive', illusion. The detractor elaborates on this point when characterizing the figures as 'shadowy creatures' who interact neither with each other nor with the nature around them, as their language is 'cold' and their environment is 'artificial' (*FA*, XVIII, 48). Instead of leading us 'to the land of ideas', Gessner enchants us with what interests us 'only to a certain extent' and with 'dreamy pleasure' (*FA*, XVIII, 49). Little insight seems to emanate from a poiesis that flourishes on 'yearning sentiment' and 'extravagant fantasy' — both expressions insinuate insensible excess. Gessner's Arcadian idyll is not Platonic, that is, without a metaphysical focus; it is a vision of a 'sentimental' universe not structured by concepts. If we look for an example of poietic 'transcendence' in Goethe's well-known *Sturm und Drang* poems, 'Mailied' is particularly instructive because the force that brings forth spring also brings forth the poem, and, while the language enacts the reciprocity of the stimulating movement within and without the lyric 'I', it also carries the speaker beyond the empirical into the realm of art and beauty:

> O Lieb'! o Liebe!
> So golden-schön,
> Wie Morgenwolken
> Auf jenen Höhn!
> [...]
> O Mädchen, Mädchen,
> Wie lieb' ich dich!
> [...]
> Die du mir Jugend
> Und Freud' und Mut
> Zu neuen Liedern
> Und Tänzen gibst. (*FA*, I, 288)

> [O love, with a golden
> Glow you adorn
> The hilltops yonder
> Like mist in the morn.
> [...]
> Sweetheart, I love you
> [You]
> [...]
> Who give me youth's gladness
> And brace my mood
> New songs to be making,
> New dances to know.] (*CW*, I, 11–13)

Insofar as 'paradise' is a metaphor for this realm, it is important to contemplate its poietic significance. For, when Goethe applies the phrase 'paradisal landscapes appeared before his soul' to Gessner's poiesis, the implication is that the landscape becomes visible without a noticeable agent or cause, which runs counter to Goethe's conviction that the artist's 'soul' is both receptive and productive. The introduction to the Lorrain review is revealing, for with the modification 'paradisal sights', Goethe — echoing the rhetoric of *evidentia* — alludes to the mind's, or rather the eye's, active participation in the creative process.

If we return to the advocate's initial characterization of Gessner's 'mastery', we now begin to realize the irony of the praise: Gessner sees only nature's pleasing aspects, not her rawness, because he only seeks 'delightful' prospects, not to mention the fact that he 'wande*l*t' instead of 'wande*r*t': 'wandeln' [to amble] produces idylls, whereas 'wandern' [to ramble] produces 'Wandrers Sturmlied' [Wanderer's Storm-Song]. Or, as Goethe sums it up sarcastically in his review, Gessner's idyll *The Storm* 'is unbearable [...] Voltaire cannot have watched the storm on Lake Geneva more calmly in the mirror from his bed than the people [the figures in Gessner's idyll] on the rock around which the tempest raged' (*FA*, XVIII, 48). Insofar as Goethe insinuates that the mirror produces a mere likeness of nature, he participates in the eighteenth-century debate regarding the idyll, which comes under scrutiny for being little more than — albeit etymologically sanctioned (the Greek *eidyllion* translates as 'small picture') — a 'schöner Schein', a beautiful semblance.[26]

When we hear 'beautiful' for the third time in quick succession, we suspect that something is amiss; and indeed, to 'verschönern', that is to 'beautify', nature or impressions affected by nature in the poietic act is anathema for *Sturm und Drang* aesthetics. In a 1772 review of an essay extracted from Johann Georg Sulzer's *General Theory of the Fine Arts*, Goethe writes: 'He [Sulzer] wants to displace the vague *imitation of nature* with an equally vague principle: *the beautification of material objects*' (*FA*, XVIII, 97).

Denouncing both principles, in another review of the work of a Sulzer popularizer, Goethe states programmatically: 'Beauty exists merely in the mind which senses it', adding, for good measure, the example that even the 'monotony' of an infinite prospect is beautiful as long as we 'feel' it (*FA*, XVIII, 61). Equally programmatic is Goethe's statement on mimesis: 'Das Genie ahmt nicht der Natur nach, sondern schafft selbst wie die Natur' [The genius does not imitate nature but himself creates analogously to nature] (*FA*, XVIII, 61). That is, if it is imitation of nature, then imitation of the creative power of nature; or, in the breathless syntax of *Sturm und Drang*:

> Was wir von Natur sehn, ist Kraft, die Kraft verschlingt nichts gegenwärtig alles vorübergehend, tausend Keime zertreten jeden Augenblick tausend geboren, groß und bedeutend, mannigfaltig ins Unendliche; schön und häßlich, gut und bös, alles mit gleichem Rechte neben einander exisitierend. Und die *Kunst* ist gerade das Widerspiel, sie entspringt aus den Bemühungen des Individuums, sich gegen die zerstörende Kraft des Ganzen zu erhalten. (*FA*, XVIII, 99)
>
> [What we see of nature is power, the power devours nothing present, everything transitory, a thousand seeds crushed every moment a thousand born, great and significant, multifarious into eternity; beautiful and ugly, good and evil, everything existing equally next to each other. And *art* is precisely conflict; it emerges from the efforts of the individual to preserve itself against the destructive force of the whole.]

Art *thrives* on conflict and it *strives* for wholeness — and rhetoric, as we know from Goethe's Pindar comment, tames these energies until a 'composition' emerges that renders visible the underlying pattern. This could be considered the meaning of Goethe's aesthetic credo at the time, namely 'that the genius does not feel anything as beautiful that is not true and beautiful in nature' (*FA*, XVIII, 63).

The irony of Gessner's advocate culminates in his characterization of Gessner as a 'malender Dichter' [pictorial poet] or 'poetischer Maler' [verbal painter] and referencing Lessing as an opponent of such descriptive nature poetry while secretly agreeing with him on — as Lessing calls it — 'the conception of the whole'.[27]

2.4. *Ut Pictura Poesis*: Goethe's Challenge to Lessing

As noted above, the context in which Goethe makes the copper-engraving comment in the *Ephemerides* is in relation to Lessing's *Laocoön*.[28] Unable to see the original or a copy of the famous statue, Lessing had to rely on an engraving to present his argument that Horace's dictum, *ut pictura poesis*, had been misread and that painting and poetry were not alike. While appealing to the eye, Lessing argued, painting primarily describes shapes arranged in space. Poetry, on the other hand, while speaking to the ear, primarily narrates actions developed in time. The enthusiastic assessment of *Laocoön*'s impact that Goethe gives in *Poetry and Truth* — a 'beam of light' descending on him through 'gloomy clouds' — should be taken with a grain of salt (*CW*, IV, 238; *FA*, XIV, 345). The fact that, as they both admitted, the engraver 'distorted' (Goethe's word is 'verderben') the original did not keep them from creating a mental image of it — a landscape of the mind and a statue of the mind — or from drawing far-reaching aesthetic conclusions from doing so. On the other hand, Goethe did not share Lessing's disparagement of landscape painting as purely descriptive and its relegation to second rank in the hierarchy of the pictorial arts. As our enquiry will show, he was sceptical about Lessing's seemingly doctrinaire separation of painting and poetry, including the disconnection between eye and ear.

In *Laocoön*, Lessing cited the notorious gentian passage from Haller's 1729 poem 'Die Alpen' [The Alps][29] to prove that, no matter how vivid and faithful the descriptions of herbs and flowers may be, their sequential order vitiates the formation of 'an approximate idea of the whole!' (ch. 17, p. 86); or, in the vocabulary of the *Laocoön* theory:

> I do not deny to language altogether the power of depicting the corporeal whole according to its parts. [...] But I do deny it to language as the medium of poetry because the illusion, which is the principal object of poetry, is wanting in such verbal description of bodies. And this illusion, I say, must be wanting because the coexistent nature of a body comes into conflict with the consecutive nature of language, and although dissolving the former into the latter makes the division of the whole into its parts easier for us, the final reassembling of the parts into a whole is made extremely difficult and often even impossible. (ch. 17, p. 88)

Lessing adduces Homer's diachronic 'painting' of Achilles' shield as an example of 'transforming what is coexistent in [a] subject into what is consecutive, and thereby making the living picture of an action out of the tedious painting of an object' (ch. 18, p. 95). Given Goethe's ekphrastic practice, one cannot help but draw an analogy between him and Homer, for with his enactment of the dynamic interplay between the descriptive and the narrative, the synchronic and the diachronic, he lives up to realizing Lessing's illusion of beauty — but there is a decisive difference: Lessing speaks of 'harmony' (ch. 23, p. 121), Goethe of tension. To push the envelope of the Goethe–Homer analogy further, there is a passage in Lessing that sounds like a clairvoyant characterization of the congeniality between Goethe and Lorrain. Taking his cue from another Homer scene, Lessing explores the advantages and disadvantages of the poet and the painter in regard to the same subject matter. What can the poet do, Lessing asks, to match or surpass the painter who paints a particular 'moment [so] suggestive' that he creates the perfect 'illusion' of a 'visible object'? The poet, Lessing answers, avails himself of the 'liberty to extend his description over that which preceded and that which followed the single moment represented', thus 'showing not only what the [painter] shows, but also that which the [painter] must leave to the imagination', and he concludes:

> Only by means of this liberty and this power can the poet again raise himself to equality with the [painter]. Their works will appear most alike when their effect is equally vivid; but this is not so when the one does not impart to the soul through the ear more or less what the other can present to the eye. (ch. 19, p. 99)

Goethe, unsure of his true calling — only two decades later, toward the end of his Italian journey, would he give up his dream of becoming a painter — was likely intrigued by Lessing's hint at reconciliation between 'two equitable and friendly neighbors' (ch. 18, p. 91), or by his reference to Longinus (and Plutarch) when characterizing *evidentia*'s illusions as 'waking dreams' (ch. 14, pp. 74–75; p. 207 note b).[30] Even though he moved beyond Lessing's binary opposition, the mentor of the younger Goethe, Johann Gottfried Herder, argued similarly in his critique of *Laocoön* in the first of his *Critical Forests* (1769).[31] Herder claimed that *enargeia* (ancient Greek for Latin *evidentia*),[32] via the imagination and memory, has a dual function: it engages the soul in sensing the presence of coexistent objects, and it engages the soul in perceiving the whole comprised of sequentially arranged objects. 'Only if both aspects are considered together', Herder writes, 'can I say that the essence of poetry is force, which operates *out of space* (the objects to which it gives sensuous expression) and *in time* (through a succession of many parts forming one poetic whole)'. Operating '*in space*', *evidentia* engenders in the soul two types of 'intuitive cognition', Herder maintains. First, *enargeia*'s '*meaning*' resides not in its means, the 'words', but in it as creative energy. Second, 'presenting' objects 'visibly before the soul' or 'before the eyes of the imagination' produces a 'painterly reality'; or, as Herder concludes, 'the first essential aspect of poetry is really a *kind of painting, sensuous representation*'. Operating 'in time', *evidentia*, in as much as it is language, 'affects the soul *through* the rapidity, the coming and going of its representations' as well as 'through the alternation of different elements' and 'through the whole that it constructs in the sequence of time'. For Herder, the 'perfection' created by the simultaneity of sequentiality and wholeness 'energizes' a 'melodic reality' which makes 'poetry a music of the soul'. Our analysis of Goethe's ekphrastic practice suggests that Goethe follows Herder's aesthetics rather closely: his ekphrasis is akin to a poiesis and poetics of the soul; he relies on the animating power of the imagination and memory; his language is sensuous, intelligible, and lyrical; and he creates an illusion that oscillates between virtuality and actuality. When Herder characterizes his aesthetics as painterly and narrative, we can even argue for a link between painting and poetry (or indeed between Lorrain and Goethe) insofar as both are image and story in one.

Captivated by Herder's seemingly less doctrinaire 'theory', Goethe must have felt provoked by Lessing's argumentative strategy when he first cited James Thomson's *Seasons* (1726–30) as an example of bad 'descriptive poetry', only to use him later to make a point against landscape painting:

> There are even cases where the merit of the artist is greater when he has imitated nature by following the poet's imitation. The painter who produces a beautiful landscape from the description of a Thomson has done more than one who copies directly from nature. This is because the latter has his original model directly before him, while the former must first apply his imagination until he believes that he has it before him. The former creates something beautiful out of vivid and sensible impressions, the latter out of indefinite and weak images of arbitrary symbols. (ch. 11, p. 63, trans. modified)

Lessing makes forays into semiotics here when he understands the words employed by the poet to convey images as 'arbitrary' or 'artificial' signs because they have no natural connection with the image they conjure up, as opposed to the 'natural' signs of the painter — forms, figures, and colours (cf. ch. 17). The difference in means corresponds to a difference in perception: natural signs engender spontaneous, intuitive understanding and insight; arbitrary signs require intellectual decoding. If the painter gains an advantage by taking literature rather than nature as his model, then what about the poet who takes a landscape painting rather than nature as his model? If the poet–painter order were reversed, would not a logical quagmire of poetic disposition, perception, and means ensue that questions the viability of ekphrastic artistry?[33] Avoiding the corner that Lessing seems to have backed himself into with his aversion to landscape painting, yet inadvertently echoing Lessing, ekphrastic theory puts the conundrum this way:

> What is being described in ekphrasis is both miracle and mirage: a miracle because a sequence of actions filled with befores and afters such as language alone can trace seems frozen into an instant's vision, but a mirage because only the illusion of such an impossible picture can be suggested by the poem's words.[34]

This ties in with Hutchings's exemplary discussion of Thomson's poetic distinction against the backdrop of Lessing's *Laocoön*. Thomson insists that the work of art be plausible, and that this plausibility — evolving from the tension, not the separation, between natural and arbitrary signs — 'creates the power that stimulates the imagination'.[35] It is the kind of poety that is comparable to what Goethe strives for in his ekphrastic readings and enactments of Lorrain. It is interesting to note that, as uncompromising as Lessing is in regard to 'pictorial' representations of Laocoön, the only one that 'can serve well in place of an engraving' when publishing his essay is an ekphrastic rendering by Jacob Sadoletus (ch. 6, pp. 40–44; pp. 178–81 note b).

Irritating, too, for Goethe must have been Lessing's contention that, in terms of 'substance', the painter is limited to representing the 'visible', while the poet can evoke the 'invisible' (ch. 12, pp. 66–70; cf. ch. 15, pp. 76–77), and that, in terms of 'meaning', the painter's craft could only aspire to the allegorical, not the symbolic, as the poet's craft.³⁶ To counter, in a 1776 essay ostensibly on a statue of Marcus Aurelius by the French sculptor Etienne-Maurice Falconet, but actually a panegyric on Rembrandt's *Adoration of the Shepherds (with the Lamp)* (c. 1654), Goethe maintains that the visual artist's 'eye' penetrates the natural source material — be it the 'cobbler's shop', the 'face of his beloved', or the 'Antique' — until he discovers 'divine vibrations' and 'scarcely perceptible tones by means of which nature unites all objects into a whole' (*GoA*, p. 17; *FA*, XVIII, 176). Once again, Goethe analogizes nature and art and interrelates the particular and the universal. Vaguely identifying the universal as 'Schwingungen' [vibrations] and 'Töne' [tones], he reiterates that both nature and art communicate to the observer an underlying pulsating energy and induce a mood, that is, a feeling or a state of mind. The power of 'light' is here effect and affect; or, as Goethe insists with supreme verve:

> Warum ist die Natur immer schön? Überall schön? Überall bedeutend? Sprechend! Und der Marmor und Gyps warum will der Licht, besonder Licht haben? Ists nicht, weil die Natur sich ewig in sich bewegt, ewig neu erschafft und der Marmor, der belebteste, dasteht tot. Erst durch den Zauberstab der Beleuchtung zu retten von seiner Leblosigkeit. (*FA*, XVIII, 176)

> [Why is nature always beautiful, and beautiful everywhere? And meaningful everywhere? And eloquent? And with marble and plaster, why do they need such a special light? Isn't it because nature is continual movement, continually created afresh, and marble, the most lively material, is always dead matter? It can only be saved from its lifelessness by the magic wand of lighting.] (*GoA*, p. 17)

Thus, this curiously titled short piece, 'Nach Falkonet und über Falkonet' [According to Falconet and about Falconet], brings together salient points of Goethe's early visual aesthetics: light holding the physical and the metaphysical in 'vibrating' tension, its 'eloquence' creating meaning and a liveliness that can be perceived by the ear and the eye — such is the dual significance of 'tone', that is, mood or atmosphere and sound. It is an aesthetics that avoids extremes, for the 'tones' are 'soft' — later on, as already alluded to, Goethe, in reference to Lorrain, will replace 'soft' with 'serene'.

Returning to Lessing and mindful of the Falconet commentary, it comes as little surprise that Goethe, when he reminisces in *Poetry and Truth* about his visit to the collection of plaster casts in the Electoral Gallery at Mannheim, among them the Laocoön group, he is thrilled that they can be viewed 'in the most advantageous light by opening and closing the curtains' (*CW*, IV, 371, trans. modified; *FA*, XIV, 546).³⁷ It is not a surprise, either, that he takes issue with Lessing's bowdlerized notion of beauty, that is, that the Greeks understood that despair and pain had to be banished from the plastic (and visual) arts. In his *Laocoön* comment in the *Ephemerides*, Goethe wrote: 'The ancients [...] avoided not so much what was ugly as what was false', and continues: 'This is to me another proof that the excellence of the ancients is to be sought in something other than the creation of beauty.'³⁸ When the sea serpent bites Laocoön, he twitches so violently that he cannot scream; that is, his expression is neither true to Winckelmann's ideal ('noble simplicity, quiet grandeur') nor Lessing's ideal (the plastic arts need to mitigate violent passions and ugliness for the sake of beauty; ch. 23, p. 121), but it *is* true to nature. In February 1769, Goethe writes to Friederike Oeser, the daughter of his drawing teacher in Leipzig:

> Was an einem Gemälde am unerträglichsten ist, ist Unwahrheit [...] O, meine Freundinn, das Licht ist die Wahrheit, doch die Sonne ist nicht die Wahrheit, von der doch das Licht quilt. Die Nacht ist Unwahrheit. Und was ist Schönheit? Sie ist nicht Licht und nicht Nacht. Dämmerung; eine Gebuhrt von Wahrheit und Unwahrheit [...] ein Scheideweg so zweydeutig. (*FA*, XXVIII, 159–60)
>
> [What is most insufferable in a picture is untruth. [...] Oh! My friend, light is truth; yet the sun is not truth, although light flows from it. Night is untruth. And what is beauty? It is not light, and it is not night. Twilight, an offspring of truth and untruth [...] a crossroads, so ambiguous.]

As iconoclastic and contentious as this assertion sounds, it is nothing short of amazing that, with Goethe's discovery of Lorrain, this 'Ahndung' would become 'Anschauung', the 'hazy realization' a 'sensory pereception' or an 'intuition of essence'. The transition is foreshadowed in a statement about the impact of Goethe's drawing teacher, Adam Friedrich Oeser: 'He taught me that the ideal of beauty is simplicity and serenity'.[39]

2.5. Lorrain's Aesthetics of Dynamic Oppositions

It is only after close reading of the ekphrastic 'translation' of the copper engravings that the introduction of the review reveals itself as a pithy articulation of Goethe's aesthetics at the time: 'Zwei Landschaften nach *Claude Lorrain*. Kinder des wärmsten poetischen Gefühls, reich an Gedanken, Ahndungen und paradiesischen Blicken' [Two landscapes after *Claude Lorrain*. Children of the warmest poetic feeling, rich in thought, hazy realizations and paradisal prospects]. As we have seen, the seemingly lapidary judgement resonates with Longinus's understanding of the rhetorical sublime. The poems themselves bear out this claim, especially in their 'as if before your eyes' application of *evidentia* techniques. But if it is through poems that Goethe allows his aesthetic priorities to emerge, we need to probe deeper.

The very first word, 'two', draws immediate attention to the self-conscious choice to review an object of two parts that can be regarded as both separate (a morning and an evening) and connected (insofar as the sun evolves as the main actor, the energy driving the core dynamic of 'ascending' and 'descending' and advancing it along an ever-evolving time continuum).[40] Goethe sees the two paintings as pendants forming a 'lebendiges Ganzes' [living whole] — to borrow a term from his paean to the Strasbourg cathedral, a companion piece to the Lorrain review (*GoA*, p. 108; *FA*, XVIII, 116). As we have now learned from our analysis of Goethe's ekphrasis, this whole is not static — a fusion or synthesis would be static, that is, an achieved ideal — but dynamic. The dynamic manifests itself in the 'children' procreated out of 'emotion' and 'thought', a poietic process which generates 'hazy realizations' and 'paradisal prospects'.

As shown in the previous chapter, the term 'landscape' involves the aesthetic perception of rural scenery, that is, in boldest strokes, the stylized depiction of 'nature'. It is key at this point that, as 'landscape' is perceived and produced, rhetoric emerges as the means of, or even the prerequisite for, arranging nature, or perceptions of nature, in such a way that the instinctive urge to reflect, interpret, and seek patterns or archetypes in it becomes consciously pursuable.

The polyvalent 'Ahndung' requires no further discussion. With 'Blick' [view, sight, or vista], and its verbal form 'blicken' [to look or gaze], we enter the quintessential Goethean realm of the 'eye', which sees, perceives, discerns, and 'apprehends', and imagines and forms vistas of 'paradise'. Read as a political allegory, the *Morning* painting engenders a vision of Rome, with Aeneas as progenitor. But it could also be read as a 'geahndetes' [hazily realized] ideal of a living interplay between nature and art, with Aeneas-cum-Goethe as progenitor of a new kind of art modelled on Lorrain whose realization the speaker hopes to bring about with pathos-laden formulas.

While Gessner taps into 'delicate sensibilities' for his verbal painting, Goethe attests to Lorrain's 'warmest feeling' as a poietic source, which seems to reference the 'inner warmth' of 'Wandrers Sturmlied':

> Weh! Weh! Innre Wärme,
> Seelenwärme,
> Mittelpunkt!
> Glüh' entgegen
> Phöb'-Apollen;
> [...]
> Wie vom Gebirg' herab
> Kieselwetter ins Tal;
> Glühte deine Seel' Gefahren, Pindar!
> Mut. — Glühte? —
> Armes Herz!
> Dort auf dem Hügel,
> Himmlische Macht!
> Nur so viel Glut,
> Dort meine Hütte,
> Dorthin zu waten! (*FA*, II, 294–95)

> [Woe! Woe! Inner warmth!
> Soulwarmth,
> Midpoint!
> Glow toward
> Phoebus Apollo;
> [...]
> Into the dale from the mountain,
> Showers of hailstones,
> Did your soul glow, Pindar, against perils
> Courage. — Glow, did it?
> Poor heart,
> There on the hill,
> Heavenly power,

> Glow enough only,
> There my hut,
> To wade my way there!]
>   (*CW*, I, 21–23, trans. modified)

Insofar as, poietically speaking, this rhapsodic effusion of conflicted feelings and thoughts can make sense of the speaker's inner sun, the 'warmth of the soul' glows out toward the outer sun, Phoebus Apollo, vying for creative supremacy.[41] This is reminiscent of Prometheus, who, in the poem, forms man after his own image, and, in the drama, calls his statues 'my children'.[42] Relying solely on the excessive poietic energy of a heated heart generates a landscape that is, as evidenced by the last five lines, so raw and primeval that the lyric 'I' can only move in quasi-amphibian fashion ('waten' [to wade]). However, out of the diluvial depths rise a hill and a hut, illuminated by a flash of heavenly light. Rhetorically speaking, *natura* is, slightly but not negligibly, balanced by *ars*. Goethe's 'warmest poetic feeling' expresses the rhetorical dilemma underlying *Sturm und Drang* aesthetics in aphoristic fashion, for 'poetic' stands for *ars*. Even a cursory look at the *Goethe-Wörterbuch* indicates that the semantics of 'poetisch', or its German cousin 'dichterisch', is exhaustively comprehensive, indeed contradictory, ranging from 'fictional' (i.e. transcending naturalistic mimesis) to a conceptual *and* invigorating impulse that permeates a work of art, from the aesthetic representation of ideas and ideals to the capacity for a 'beseelte' [spirited] response to natural beauty and the ability to experience 'ästhetisches Wohlgefallen' [aesthetic pleasure] (II, 1184–85). However, what is crucial for our purposes is the distinction that, if 'warmest feeling' involves the imaginative power of the mind, then 'poetic' involves, as the *Goethe-Wörterbuch* tells us, the 'Gestaltungskraft', or formative power, of the mind (II, 1184–85).

What is probably most striking about Goethe's earliest response to Lorrain is not that the two engravings serve as an object with which to exercise the dynamics of the mania–melancholy polarity within the *Sturm und Drang* artist — poetically manifested in the review's panegyric and elegiac tones — but rather that Lorrain emerges as the model for an artist who holds art and nature in dynamic opposition. In the months immediately preceding his discovery of Lorrain, it was Pindar (or rather, Goethe's reading of Pindar) that pointed him in this aesthetic direction.[43] On 10 July 1772 he writes to Herder:

> Über ἐπικρστειν δυασθαι Worten Pindars ist mirs aufgegangen. Wenn du kühn im Wagen stehst, und vier neue Pferde wild unordentlich sich an deinen Zügeln bäumen, du ihre Kraft lenckst, den austretenden herbey, den aufbäumenden hinabpeitschest, und jagst und lenckst, und wendest, peitschest, hältst, und wieder ausjagst, biss alle sechzehn Füße in einem Trackt ans ziel tragen. Das ist Meisterschafft, ἐπικρατέω, Virtuosität.[44] (*FA*, XXVIII, 256)

> [It dawned on me when I was reading Pindar's words ἐπικρατέω δύναμαι. If you stand boldly in a chariot, with four fresh horses straining wildly at the reins, you steer their power with your whip, urging the straying one to go forward, the rearing one to calm down, and you drive and steer, change direction, whip, stop, and then drive them onward again, until all sixteen legs fall into step and carry you to your goal — that is mastery, ἐπικρατέω, virtuosity.]

The Greek terms 'δύναμαι' [be able, strong enough] and 'ἐπικρατέω' [rule over], quoted from Pindar's eighth Nemean Ode (ll. 4–5), and, in the same verses (not cited by Goethe), 'ἥμερος' [tame],⁴⁵ are metaphors for harnessing the poet's intoxication by rhetoric, analogous to the taming of the poet's intoxication by the pictorial. To wit, the blazingly hot 'Glut' in 'Wandrers Sturmlied' has become the palely gleaming 'Glanz' in (Goethe's reading of) Lorrain's painting. Is it plausible that Lorrain acted as a catalyst for Goethe's conviction that productive artistic activity can emerge from the conflict between a soaring imagination and a disciplined craft?

If it is possible to abstract a preliminary conclusion from Goethe's nascent affinity with Lorrain, then the following points seem to be pertinent. From the rhetorical dynamic between nature and art on the level of style, to the interplay of the physical and the metaphysical on the level of substance, Lorrain's consummate compositions are more about holding dialectical oppositions in tension than about fusing them into a synthesis. Simultaneously separating and connecting disparate objects without — say, 'goat', 'water', and 'Aeneas' — and dispositions within — say 'mania', 'lyrical', and 'melancholy' — Lorrain imbues his landscapes with a pulsating energy whose ultimate metaphorical representation is the sun. The cross-fertilization between light and darkness brings about a 'living whole' that feeds off the particular to evoke the universal, making his art both allegorical and symbolic.

2.6. Storytelling as Landscape Painting: Goethe's Idyll 'Der Wandrer'

As a fitting end to this chapter, we want to ask whether Goethe's first encounter with Lorrain left any traces in his poetic output. Far from raising the spectre of 'influence', this is about the poetics and hermeneutics of creative appropriation. The work in question here is Goethe's 1774 idyll 'Der Wandrer'.⁴⁶ In it, in the barest outlines, a wanderer seeking shade and water meets a peasant woman and her boy. As the sun starts to set, she leads him to her dwelling, a cottage, comprised partly from the stones of a crumbled temple. The scenery, and the exposure to the happy and prosperous coexistence of rusticity and Antiquity, engenders in the wanderer thoughts about the interplay of nature and art, and, as he bids farewell and sets off anew to Cumae on his quest, a vision of himself becoming integrated into such an idyllic life. Already noticeable is an inner connection to Lorrain: the interplay of 'wanderer' and 'cottage' corresponds to Aeneas coming home to Italy, or the shepherdesses driving home the sheep, or the sun's homecoming in the evening after wandering across the sky.

Can the 'Wandrer' then be read as an ekphrasis of an imagined Lorrain painting? In other words, is this a Lorrain 'landscape', and as such a 'child of the warmest poetic feeling, rich in thought, hazy realizations, and paradisal prospects'?

While Goethe may have been inspired by Gessner's 1772 idyll *Daphnis and Micon*,⁴⁷ in the second volume of *A Collection of Prints Engraved after the Most Capital Paintings in England*, in which Goethe found the two engravings he reviewed, he encountered six more prints after Lorrain. One was an engraving of Lorrain's 1644 *Pastoral Landscape* [*Landscape with a Temple of Bacchus*] (*LV*, 78), bearing the title

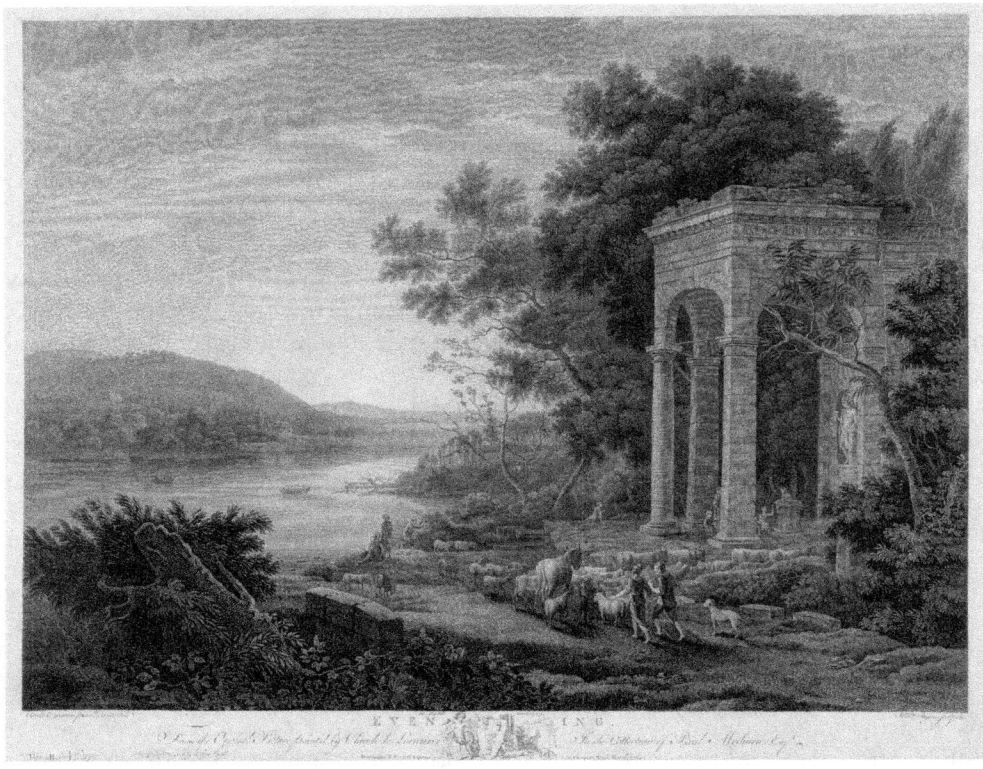

Fig. 2.3. Byrne, *Evening*. Royal Academy of Arts, London/
© Royal Academy of Arts, London — Prudence Cuming Associates Limited

Evening. Done by William Byrne (1743–1805), it shows herdsmen and cattle passing an overgrown portico that houses a statue of Bacchus and serves as a gathering point for the rural community and as a playground for their children, with the river glistening in the evening sun and reflecting the forms of mountains and hills before vanishing into the dim mists.

The other engraving, *Sun Setting* by James Mason, while identifying the original artist as 'Claudio Gilee Lorenese' in the lower left, may not be the work of Lorrain (no. 307).

Nevertheless, echoes of Lorrain include the tectonically layered composition of the landscape, stretching from the almost touchable riverbank in the foreground to the sun dipping behind the horizon in the far distance while still bathing much of the scene in a warm light, as well as the prominence and poignant placement of the trees — in the middle and, framing the scene, on the left and right. As our eye moves from foreground to middle ground and background, we see a peasant woman holding an infant and, barely discernible, a footpath meandering up to the ruins of an antique structure in the distance. Given Goethe's propensity for creative appropriation of visual-art sources,[48] one may ask whether Goethe, by means of his alter ego — the wanderer — inserts himself into the Lorrain landscape and thus

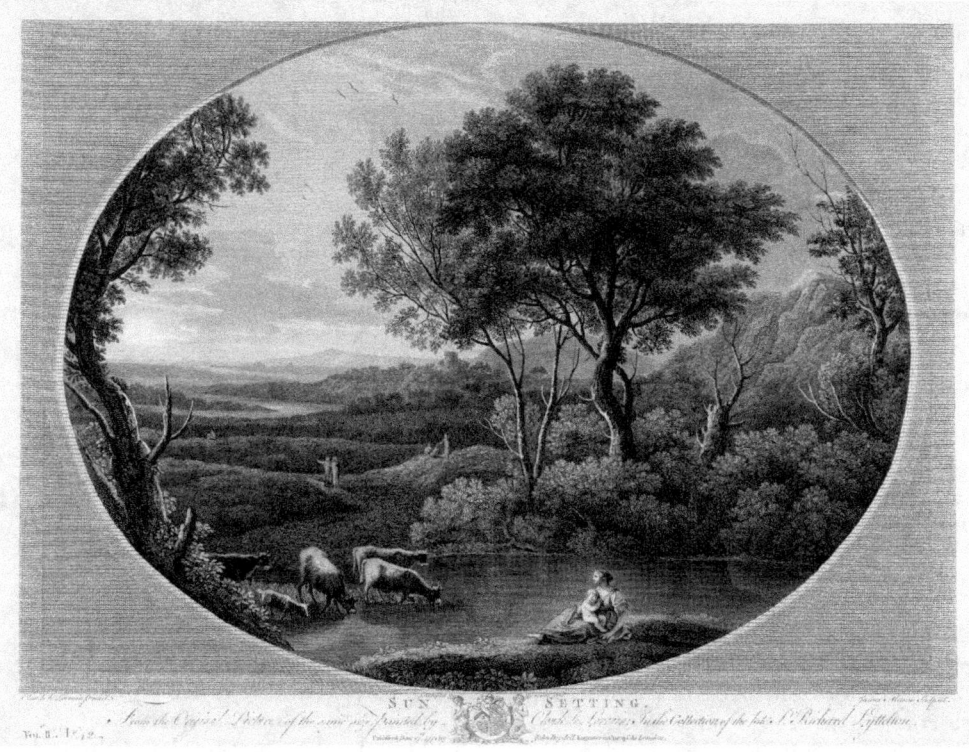

FIG. 2.4. Mason, *Sun Setting*. Royal Academy of Arts, London/
© Royal Academy of Arts, London — Prudence Cuming Associates Limited

not only animates the painting but also imbues it with ideas in his quest for the ur-landscape.

Der Wandrer

Wandrer
Gott segne dich junge Frau,
Und den säugenden Knaben
An deiner Brust!
Laß mich, an der Felsenwand hier
In des Ulmbaums Schatten
Meine Bürde werfen,
Neben dir ausruhn.

Frau
Welch Gewerbe treibt dich
Durch des Tages Hitze
Den sandigen Pfad her?
Bringst du Waren aus der Stadt
Im Land herum?
Lächelst Fremdling
Über meine Frage?

[The Wanderer

Wanderer
Young woman, may God bless thee,
Thee, and the sucking infant
Upon thy breast!
Let me, 'gainst this rocky wall,
Neath the elm-tree's shadow,
Lay aside my burden,
Near thee take my rest.

Woman
What vocation leads thee,
While the day is burning,
Up this dusty path?
Bring'st thou goods from out the town
Round the country?
Smil'st thou, stranger,
At my question?

Wandrer
Ich bringe keine Waren
Aus der Stadt.
Schwühl ist schwer der Abend
Zeige mir den Brunnen
Draus du trinkest,
Liebes junges Weib.

Frau
Hier den Felsenpfad hinauf!
Geh voran! Durchs Gebüsche
Geht der Pfad nach der Hütte,
Drin ich wohne
Zu dem Brunnen
Da ich trinke draus.

Wandrer
Spuren ordnender Menschenhand
Zwischen dem Gesträuch — !
Diese Steine hast du nicht gefügt
Reich hinstreuende Natur

Frau
Weiter 'nauf.

Wandrer
Von dem Moos gedeckt ein Architrav!
Ich erkenne dich. Bildender Geist,
Hast dein Siegel in den Stein geprägt.

Frau
Weiter Fremdling!

Wandrer
Eine Inschrift, über die ich trete!
Der Venus — und ihr übrigen
Seid verloschen,
Weggewandelt, ihr Gesellen,
Die ihr eures Meisters Andacht
Tausend Enkeln zeugen solltet.

Frau
Staunest Fremdling
Diese Stein an?
Droben sind der Steine viel
Um meine Hütte.

Wandrer
Droben?

Frau
Gleich zur Linken
Durchs Gebüsch hinan!
Hier!

Wanderer
From the town no goods
I bring.
Sultry's now the evening;
Show to me the fountain
Whence thou drinkest,
Woman young and kind!

Woman
Up the rocky pathway mount;
Go thou first! Across the thicket
Leads the pathway tow'rd the cottage
That I live in,
To the fountain
Whence I drink.

Wanderer
Signs of man's arranging hand
See I 'mid the trees!
Not by thee these stones were join'd,
Nature, who so freely scatterest!

Woman
Up, still up!

Wanderer
Lo, a mossy architrave is here!
I discern thee, fashioning spirit!
On the stone thou hast impress'd thy seal.

Woman
Onward, stranger!

Wanderer
Over an inscription am I treading!
To Venus — and ye are seen
No longer,
Are wander'd off, companions,
Who your master's true devotion
Should have shown to thousand grandsons!

Woman
At these stones, why
Start'st thou, stranger?
Many stones are lying yonder
Round my cottage.

Wanderer
Yonder?

Woman
Through the thicket,
Turning to the left,
Here!

Wandrer
Ihr Musen und Grazien.

Frau
Das ist meine Hütte!

Wandrer
Eines Tempels Trümmern!

Frau
Hier zur Seit hinab
Quillt der Brunnen
Da ich trinke draus.

Wandrer
Glühend webst du über deinem Grabe
Genius! Über dir
Ist zusammengestürzt
Dein Meisterstück
O du unsterblicher.

Frau
Wart! ich will ein
Schöpfgefäß dir holen.

Wandrer
Efeu hat deine schlanke
Götterbildung umkleidet!
Wie du emporstrebst
Aus dem Schutte
Säulenpaar!
Und du einsame Schwester dort
Wie ihr,
Düstres Moos auf dem heiligen Haupt,
Majestätisch traurend herabschaut
Auf die zertrümmerten
Zu euren Füßen
Eure Geschwister!
In des Brombeergesträuches Schatten
Deckt sie Schutt und Erde;
Und hohes Gras wankt drüber hin
Schätzest du so, Natur
Deines Meisterstücks Meisterstück?
Unempfindlich zertrümmerst
Du dein Heiligtum
Säst Disteln drein.

Frau
Wie der Knabe schläft!
Willst du in der Hütte ruhn
Fremdling willst du hier
Untern Pappelbaum dich setzen?
Hier ist's kühl! Nimm den Knaben,
Daß ich Wasser schöpfen hinabgeh.
Schlaf Lieber schlaf.

Wanderer
Ye Muses and ye Graces!

Woman
This, then, is my cottage.

Wanderer
'Tis a ruin'd temple!

Woman
Just below it, see,
Springs the fountain
Whence I drink.

Wanderer
Thou dost hover o'er thy grave,
All-glowing, Genius! while upon thee
Hath thy master-piece
Fallen crumbling,
Thou Immortal One!

Woman
Stay, a cup I'll fetch thee
Whence to drink.

Wanderer
Ivy circles thy slender
Form so graceful and godlike,
How ye rise on high
From the ruins,
Column-pair
And thou, their lonely sister yonder, —
How thou,
Dusky moss upon thy sacred head, —
Lookest down in mournful majesty
On thy brethren's figures
Lying scatter'd
At thy feet!
In the shadow of the bramble
Earth and rubbish veil them,
Lofty grass is waving o'er them
Is it thus thou, Nature! prizest
Thy great masterpiece's masterpiece?
Carelessly destroyest thou
Thine own sanctuary,
Sowing thistles there?

Woman
How the infant sleeps!
Wilt thou rest thee in the cottage,
Stranger? Wouldst thou rather
Sit beneath the poplar-tree?
Now 'tis cool! take thou the child
While I go and draw some water.
Sleep on, darling! sleep!

Wandrer
Süß ist deine Ruh.
Wie's, in himmlischer Gesundheit
                schwimmend
Ruhig atmet!
Du, geboren über Resten
Heiliger Vergangenheit
Ruh ihr Geist auf dir!
Welchen der umschwebt,
Wird in Götter selbstgefühl
Jedes Tags genießen.
Voller Keim blüh auf
Lieblich dämmernden Lenzens Schmuck
Scheinend vor deinen Gesellen!
Und welkt die Blütenhülle weg
Dann steig aus deinem Busen
Die volle Frucht, und reif der Sonn
                entgegen.

Frau
Gesegn' es Gott! — Und schläft er noch?
Ich habe nichts zum frischen Trunk
Als ein Stück Brot
Das ich dir bieten kann.

Wandrer
Ich danke dir.
Wie herrlich alles blüht umher
Und grünt.

Frau
Mein Mann wird bald
Nach Hause sein
Vom Feld; bleib Mann
Und iß mit uns
Das Abendbrot.

Wandrer
Ihr wohnet hier?

Frau
Hier zwischen das Gemäuer her
Die Hütte baute noch mein Vater
Aus Ziegeln und des Schuttes Steinen.
Hier wohnen wir.
Er gab mich einem Ackersmann
Und starb in unsern Armen.
Hast du geschlafen liebes Herz?
Wie er munter ist und spielen will!
Du Schelm.

Wandrer
Natur du ewig keimende,
Schaffst jeden zum Genuß des Lebens
Deine Kinder all

Wanderer
Sweet is thy repose!
How, with heaven-born health imbued,
Peacefully he slumbers!
Oh thou, born among the ruins
Spread by great antiquity,
On thee rest her spirit!
He whom it encircles
Will, in godlike consciousness,
Ev'ry day enjoy.
Full, of germ, unfold,
As the smiling springtime's fairest charm,
Outshining all thy fellows!
And when the blossom's husk is faded,
May the full fruit shoot forth
From out thy breast, and ripen in the
                sunshine.

Woman
God bless him! — Is he sleeping still?
To the fresh draught I nought can add,
Saving a crust of bread
For thee to eat.

Wanderer
I thank thee well.
How fair the verdure all around!
How green!

Woman
My husband soon
Will home return
From labor. Tarry, tarry man,
And with us eat
Our evening meal.

Wanderer
Is't here ye dwell?

Woman
Yonder, within those walls we live.
My father 'twas who built the cottage
Of tiles and stones from out the ruins.
'Tis here we dwell.
He gave me to a husbandman,
And in our arms expired. —
Hast thou been sleeping, dearest heart
How lively, and how full of play!
Sweet rogue!

Wanderer
Nature, thou ever budding one,
Thou formest each for life's enjoyments,
And, like a mother,

Hast mütterlich mit einem
Erbteil ausgestattet
Einer Hütte.
Hoch baut die Schwalb an Architrav
Unfühlend welchen Zierat
Sie verklebt,
Die Raup' umspinnt den goldnen Zweig
Zum Winterhaus für ihre Brut;
Und du flickst zwischen der Vergangenheit
Erhabne Trümmer
Für deine Bedürfnis
Eine Hütt', o Mensch
Genießest über Gräbern.
Leb wohl du glücklich Weib!

Frau
Du willst nicht bleiben!

Wandrer
Gott erhalt euch
Segn' euren Knaben!

Frau
Glück auf den Weg

Wandrer
Wohin führt mich der Weg
Dort übern Berg?

Frau
Nach Cuma.

Wandrer
Wie weit ists hin?

Frau
Drei Meilen gut.

Wandrer
Leb wohl!
O leite meinen Gang
Natur; den Fremdlingsreisetritt,
Den über Gräber
Heiliger Vergangenheit
Ich wandle;
Leit ihn zum Schutzort,
Vorm Nord geschützet,
Wo dem Mittagsstrahl
Ein Pappelwäldgen wehrt.
Und kehr ich dann
Am Abend heim
Zur Hütte vergoldet
Vom letzten Sonnenstrahl,
Laß mich empfangen solch ein Weib
Den Knaben auf dem Arm.
(FA, 1, 208–14)

All thy children dear,
Blessest with that sweet heritage,
A home.
The swallow builds the cornice round,
Unconscious of the beauties
She plasters up.
The caterpillar spins around the bough,
To make her brood a winter house;
And thou dost patch, between antiquity's
Most glorious relics,
For thy mean use,
Oh man, a humble cot, —
Enjoyest e'en mid tombs! —
Farewell, thou happy woman!

Woman
Thou wilt not stay, then?

Wanderer
May God preserve thee.
And bless the boy!

Woman
A happy journey!

Wanderer
Whither conducts the path
Across yon hill?

Woman
To Cuma.

Wanderer
How far from hence?

Woman
'Tis full three miles.

Wanderer
Farewell!
Oh Nature, guide me on my way!
The wandering stranger guide,
Who o'er the tombs
Of holy bygone times
Is passing,
To a kind sheltering place,
From North winds safe,
And where a poplar grove
Shuts out the noontide ray!
And when I come
Home to my cot
At evening,
Illumined by the setting sun,
Let me embrace a wife like this,
Her infant in her arms!]
(Bowring, trans., pp. 259–64)

The dialogic structure — typical of the idyllic genre, dating back to Antiquity — sets the stage for an oscillation between opposites that reverberates throughout the text. Among the varied oppositions that are held in tension, we find the back-and-forth between male and female, urban and rural, cultivated and natural, spiritual and concrete, past and present, morning and evening, elevated and vernacular.

The oscillation evolves out of the dialogue between the two voices — one male, learned, and reflective, the other female, untutored, and intuitive. The difference is reflected in their diction — his is noun-based, conceptual, stylized, hers is verb-based, concrete, colloquial — and their rhythm — his accentuated by three or four stresses per line, hers with a prose-like flow. This, from our perspective, troubling gendering of opposites expands into a sweeping cultural history involving broad conceptual frameworks, especially and significantly the opposition of art and nature. Initially, this opposition tends to seem binary: art manifests itself in the act of 'arranging', 'ordering', 'joining together', and 'fitting into', while nature's actions are characterized as chaotic: 'to scatter', 'to cover', or 'to overgrow'. Other binary oppositions include the contrast between the familial community and the wanderer's solitary foreignness, their stasis and his nomadism, on both a spatial and spiritual level: their man-made 'hut' or 'cottage' and his 'temple' built by the godlike 'Genius'.

Yet, on closer inspection, these binary oppositions seem more complex. In fact, Goethe's poetic handling of the language and imagery of the polarities suggests that they are charged by a dynamic reciprocity that holds the poles in tension. It is this peculiar kind of magnetism that makes this idyll an enactment of *evidentia*, for, before our inner eye, the juxtapositions, movements, and transformations transmute into a lived and animated 'reality', a kind of landscape of our minds.

Let us elaborate. Via the alliterative 'w' in 'Wandrer', 'Gewerbe', and 'Waren', the wanderer appears as a representative of city and commerce, while the woman personifies the countryside and the natural resource 'water'. Couching this juxtaposition in terms of trade suggests that the relation is one of exchange or interdependence, namely between a prelapsarian and a proto-industrial realm. As the contrast between the two evolves through their differing relation to, and 'use' of, 'antiquity', it diminishes and intensifies as they make their way to the well where the wanderer finally quenches his thirst. This is also the moment where the two poles seem to fuse when she switches from addressing him as 'stranger' to 'man', underscoring the increasing intimacy through the pleading repetition of 'stay', 'stay'. However, as the ambiguity of the language suggests, the 'intimacy' will not be consummated, that is, there is no synthesis, for she used 'Mann' only two lines earlier to reveal the imminent return of her 'husband' — which is but one of the reasons why the wanderer moves on.

As the wanderer leaves, his 'natural' eye and his 'cultivated' eye create an 'intuition' out of which a paradisal prospect evolves, a vision of salvation beyond the mountain, a destiny to which the sun-cum-sibyl draws him but also returns him: he leaves the idyll behind in order to return to the idyll. Elevating the oscillation to the level of myth — thus echoing his review of Lorrain — Goethe ends his idyll by alluding to the Sibyl of Cumae, the prophetess who partakes in, and stands apart from, two realms, precisely at the site where Aeneas descends to the sphere of the dead and ascends to the sphere of the living.[49]

To pursue our argument that what light does in Lorrain, language does in Goethe — namely, integrating diverse elements and forces without fusing them into a facile synthesis — we need only consider the string of words starting with the letter 'm' in order to 'see' the self-conscious composition of the idyllic world of the 'Wandrer'. 'Master' and 'masterpiece' signal the power of the mind to cultivate, to build artefacts, such as the temple; in related fashion, 'majestic' captures the effect of sublime beauty, such as the architrave, columns, and statues. 'Muse' obviously indicates the presence of divinely inspired art in this world. 'Moss' references the power of nature to grow and be fruitful. 'Gemäuer' suggests the 'Mauer' [wall] of the human-built artefact, the 'hut', which would not have been possible without repurposing the stones from the crumbled master's temple — a process suggested by the 'ge-' prefix which disrupts the harmony suggested by the 'm' sequence. 'Mensch' represents the human world in its physicality, with 'Mann' referencing 'husband' but also the 'male' acting as procreator and progenitor — and thus the family as the nucleus of communal life. 'Munter' [cheerful] characterizes contentedness based on frugality;.'Mittagsstrahl' [noontide ray] emphasizes the importance of the sun and its light. 'Me' suggests a grammatical awareness of seeing, or even need to see, oneself as an object. This is a remarkable departure from the contemporaneous poem 'Prometheus', which ends with 'ich' [I], thus celebrating the birth of the self-centered genius who creates in defiant rivalry with Zeus. As speculative as it is, one wonders whether Lorrain played a role in this development in Goethe's thinking.

Enhancing the complexity of the integrative power of language is the fact that the 'master' and the 'man' are not the only builders; that animals build their own 'house' or 'nest'; that there is also a spiritual fulfilment, one based on 'godlike self-awareness'; and that the bright midday light changes into the 'golden' glow of evening, suggesting the sun's perpetual motion and, by extension, the dynamic contrast between past and present — and future, in its millenarian manifestation of 'a thousand offspring'.

While the familiar form of address — be it the singular 'du' [you] or the plural 'ihr' [you] — sets up the dialogic interaction of separate entities, it is also the fulcrum of their connectedness, from 'to rest' to 'to ruin' or 'to shatter' and a terminological multitude in-between. No matter how separate, the connection is often established through alliterative sound patterns: 'Brust' [breast], 'Brunnen' [well]; 'Frau' [woman], 'Fremdling' [stranger]; 'Gräber' [graves], 'Grazien' [Graces]; 'Herz' [heart], 'Heiligtum' [sanctuary]; 'Knabe' [boy], 'Keim' [germ or shoot]; 'Mensch' [human], 'Muse'; 'reifen' [to ripen], 'ruhen' [to rest]; 'Schutt' [rubble], 'Schwester' [sister]; 'treiben' [to compel to move], 'trauern' [to mourn]; 'unenmpfindlich' [insensitive], 'unsterblich' [immortal]; 'Weib' [woman], 'Wort' [word]. What dialogue does in terms of structure — namely, to separate and connect — echo does in terms of sound. In a single stanza, the initial alliterative 'sh' sound in 'Schutt' [debris], 'Stein' [stone], 'starb' [died], 'schlafen' [to sleep], 'spielen' [to play], and 'Schelm' [rascal] interrelates such diverse concepts as rubble and rogue.

There seems to be no single element in this idyll that is not somehow in a reciprocal relationship with another element. Part of the nature–art interplay is that, although art repurposed nature in the past by hewing rock and imprinting its seal in the stone, nature repurposes art in the present by reclaiming the stone in order to build — an act of cultivation — its dwelling. The interplay between the human and the divine features the divine, 'godlike form', taking on human properties ('slender', 'to clothe' or 'to wrap around', 'sister'), whereas the human, the 'boy', aspires to realize himself in 'godlike self-awareness'. Yet another interplay involves life and death, not only in the human sphere (the infant and his grandfather) but also in the inanimate one — encapsulated in the oxymoronic phrase of 'aus des Schuttes Steinen' [debris serving as building blocks]. Closely related to this interplay is the reciprocity between the eternal and the transitory: nature is as 'eternal' as art is 'immortal', yet nature can also 'wither', and art can be 'erased' or 'expunged'. The use of assonance alerts us to the fundamental role of language in the principle of oscillation. There is the obvious contrast between the intellectual diction of the wanderer and the natural diction of the woman, but again we find a split within one and the same pole, for instance in the emotionally charged apostrophes to nature and art — reaching a delicate height in the wanderer's 'Ye Muses and ye Graces!' when he catches sight of the rough-hewn cottage, or exclamations such as 'How splendidly everything turns green and blossoms!', as opposed to cerebral formulations such as 'in the blackberry bush's shadow', or, with alliterative and assonant reinforcement, 'deines Meisterstücks Meisterstück' [thy masterpiece's masterpiece]. On the other hand, the woman seems to be affected by his elevated language, especially in the use of the literary genitive, 'droben sind der Steine viel' [many a stone is up there] and 'des Schuttes Steine' [the rubble's stones].

Rhetoric once again is used to transport the reader into the wanderer's conflicted mind and heart. The oxymorons 'mourning gloriously' and 'sublime ruins' serve this purpose in dramatic fashion, as do the occasional extensions of the oxymoron proper into pithily juxtapositional phrases such as 'dusky moss on the sacred head', 'thistles sown in the sanctuary', or 'you enjoy amid tombs'.

Distinctly reminiscent of Lorrain is the interplay of rising and falling, with the dynamic almost palpable, for as the cottage rises, the temple falls, just as the path to the well leads both 'upward' and 'downward' while the sun rises to the 'heat' of 'midday' and sets in the 'coolness' of 'evening'. There is another dimension to this interplay, for sun and man interact: while the fruit cultivated by man 'ripens toward the sun', the sun beams forth its 'evening light bathing man in gold'. This final image of the sinking sun reminds us of the 'glow' with which the Lorrain review ended.

'Golden' is the only colour in this otherwise black-and-white engraving in verse, and it can be no coincidence that it is applied to Lorrain's quintessential manifestation of light. It is used another time too, in the phrase 'golden branch', and as such it strikes us as both a visual echo of one of Lorrain's many sunlit branches, and another allusion to the *Aeneid*, the episode wherein the Cumaean Sibyl tells Aeneas to offer a 'golden bough' to Proserpina as a 'hallowed gift'.[50] Yet, since Goethe's Lorrain experience is in black-and-white, 'golden' must have been conjured up by his imagination as part of the landscape of the mind.

While addressed repeatedly as 'you', nature and art occupy a unique position in that, while present in their outward physicality, they are also present on the inside, as the inspiration for a dialogue with — and within — the lyric *and* reflective 'I'. That is to say, the wanderer observes nature and art with both the eyes of the body and those of the mind. We are drawn into this stream of consciousness witnessing, or rather participating in, a process of description, narration, and interpretation. We watch him, step-by-step, conjuring up a landscape of the mind. Strikingly, Lorrain's duality, articulated pictorially, has become Goethe's duality, articulated verbally.

Crucially, the 'I' repeatedly evokes some ultimate essence, an archetypal energy, calling it at one point a 'glowingly weaving spirit'. This spirit of creation 'schafft' just as nature 'schöpft' (both verbs mean 'to create', 'to produce'); that is, while creating in separate realms, 'schaffen' and 'schöpfen' mirror each other — 'schaffen' relates to 'temple', 'statue', 'pillar', 'architrave', 'inscription', and by extension to Antiquity and myth; 'schöpfen' [to draw water, to procreate] relates to the woman, who 'schöpft' water and a child. The multilayered imagery of creative energy would be imcomplete without an emotional apostrophe to 'budding nature', which for Goethe, as we now know, is an analogy for the gestating genius.

Our close reading shows that the common denominator between Lorrain and Goethe is a dynamic tension created by opposites. While it may be possible to argue that Lorrain and Goethe eventually resolve the tension in some kind of 'beautiful semblance', it is also possible to argue that the opposites act like magnets that attract and repel each other without ever becoming one. The site where painting and poetry interrelate is akin to a magnetic field that is, in the painting, suffused with light, in the poem, with the lyrical — just as 'divinity' suffuses a church. Reviewing a copper engraving after Caravaggio's *Three Apostles*, Goethe speaks of the juxtaposition of their 'triple manifoldedness', and their 'spiritual *association*' is suffused by a light-filled 'aerial' or 'atmospheric perspective', which he characterizes with the same vocabulary as in the Lorrain review — namely, 'dämmern' [to shimmer palely], and 'Hauch' [haze] — imbuing the engraving and the observer with 'tranquillity' or 'peace of mind' (*FA*, XVIII, 25). While this result suggests a fusion or synthesis of polarities, Goethe also argues for the tension between 'sentiment' and 'cognition' or, in yet another review, between 'feeling heart' and 'thinking mind' (*FA*, XVIII, 44). We may recall here Goethe's use of the oscillatory 'twilight' as a 'natural' metaphor for 'artistic truth'.

The multilayered oppositions reveal an archetypal pattern underlying the imagined landscape. Yet, despite its constructedness, the tensions between the oppositions make the landscape seem 'natural', in the *evidentia*-sense of 'real'. That is to say, we see it before our inner eye; or, as Rilke described in his short essay on the 'Wanderer', this poem is one of those that 'captivate' and 'excite' the reader. He continues: 'I could never resist the magic of this poem — and there is hardly any other place that I see so vividly before my inner eye as this one.' For Rilke, the oppositional framework is 'symbolic' because the particular duality of man and

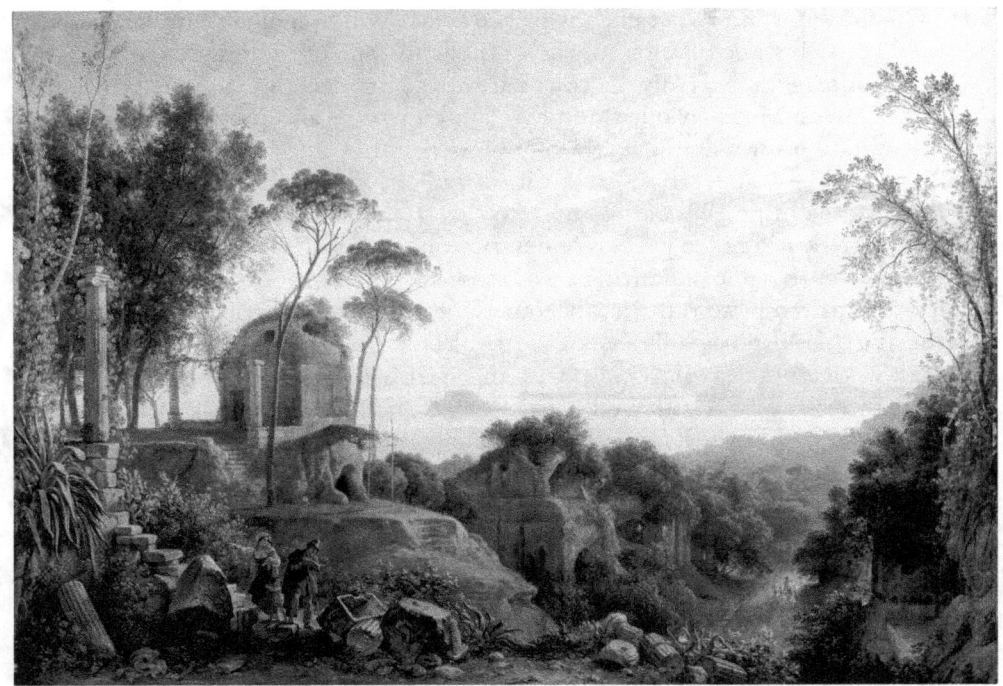

Fig. 2.5. Catel, *Gulf of Naples* [Pozzuoli]. Germanisches Nationalmuseum, Nürnberg; Leihgabe Kunstsammlungen der Stadt Nürnberg/© J. Musolf

woman invokes a universal duality of 'venturing forth' and 'lingering on', spatially and spiritually. The vivid imagery gives body and shape to Goethe's elusive feeling of 'longing for Antiquity' and Italy, with Lorrain's art beckoning to him — just as it did a century later to Nietzsche.[51] Franz Ludwig Catel (1778–1856), an acquaintance of Goethe, transmutes this longing, in a kind of reverse ekphrasis, into his own pictorial version of *ars et natura*. Echoing Lorrain's *Coast View with Apollo and the Cumaean Sibyl* (c. 1646; *LV*, 99),[52] the 1831 painting bears the title *The Gulf of Naples* [Pozzuoli][53] — one of Goethe's cherished destinations on his Italian journey, for which we embark in the following chapter.

Notes to Chapter 2

1. Cf. Traeger, pp. 130–31.
2. See Grave, 'Goethes Kunstsammlungen' and *Der 'ideale' Kunstkörper*, pp. 9–288.
3. In translating Goethe's programmatic *Sturm und Drang* essay 'Von deutscher Baukunst' [On German Architecture], Gage renders 'leise Ahndungen' as 'hinted understatements' (*GoA*, p. 107), while Gearey suppresses it altogether (*CW*, III, 6).
4. Goethe, *Briefe* (*FA*, XXVIII, 60–61, 192–95, 196–97, 722–27, 732–34), *Dichtung und Wahrheit* (*FA*, XIV, 281, 587; note that the English translation of this passage (*CW*, IV, 398) leaves out Quintilian); Kramer, pp. 74–90, 98–105, 119.
5. Kramer, pp. 73–80.
6. Excerpted by Goethe in *Ephemerides* (*FA*, XXVIII, 194; cf. 726).

7. See Fehrenbach, pp. 129–30, 132, who emphasizes that Goethe's 'seeing' is 'synaesthetic' and (more on this in Chapter 5 below) that the eye is both 'receptive' and 'productive', especially in regard to 'seeing' colours. For a problematization of the prevalent notion of Goethe as an 'ocular person', see Vaget.
8. While there is no entry on rhetoric in the *Goethe-Handbuch*, it does give a brief account of his 'education in rhetoric' (cf. Ueding).
9. On the function of the distinction in Goethe's epistemology and scientific approach, see Förster.
10. Scholz, p. 19.
11. On Goethe's visions, or 'vivid mental images', see Currie, pp. 5–17.
12. Kramer, pp. 69, 87, 117–32.
13. On Goethe's notion of the sublime, see Powers, 'Sublime'; on the broader discussion of the sublime before Kant, see Powers, 'Where are the Mountains?'.
14. Lagerlöf, pp. 133–34.
15. The quotations in this paragraph are from Lagerlöf, pp. 130, 137, 140, 130–32, 134–35.
16. For a 'Genealogy of Ekphrasis' in 'Homer, Virgil, and Dante', see Heffernan, pp. 9–45. For a discussion of (the limits of) the cross-fertilization of the visual and verbal, see M. Krieger; Boehm.
17. For a non-ekphrastic reading of Goethe's review, see Osterkamp, *Im Buchstabenbilde*, pp. 37–52.
18. Cf. *GW*, IV, 235–41.
19. See in particular the letter to Herder from 10 July 1772, in *FA*, XXVIII, 255–58, 774–76 (commentary). For diverging assessments of Pindar's importance for the young Goethe, see Reiff; Trevelyan, pp. 53–57, 76–83; Ponzi. Further sources are summarized by Collatz.
20. L. M. Price, p. 83.
21. See Jung, pp. 43–46.
22. Quotations here are from the letter in Gessner, pp. 133–34, 121, 125–27. For examples of Lorrainian echoes in Gessner's works, see Bircher and Weber, pp. 81, 87 (ideal landscapes), 91, 138–39 (tree studies), 144, 156 (light, colouring, mood).
23. Read as a dramatization of Goethe's own inner conflict vis-à-vis Gessner, the review offers a glimpse into Goethe's creative-critical appropriation of Gessner in his own work at the time, especially in *Werther* and, to be discussed below, in the idyll 'Der Wandrer' (cf. Delp). For Goethe's Gessnerian 'poetization' of his prose, cf. Hibberd (to whose examples we might add the Lorrain review discussed above).
24. Lütteken, pp. 191, 195.
25. See Fehrenbach, pp. 133–34.
26. Pabst, pp. 17, 24.
27. *Laocoön*, ch. 14, p. 87. All further citations from the *Laocoön* are given in parentheses in the text.
28. The following reading of *Laocoön* is based on McCormick's introduction and notes in his English translation, and on Kreikenbom; Fick, pp. 232–61; Barner and others, eds, pp. 235–47.
29. Haller, pp. 37–38, ll. 380–400.
30. Note that Lessing here argues for the superiority of 'poetic pictures' over 'material pictures', i.e. paintings. As we have seen, and will see again, in Goethe's mind, Lorrain's paintings *are* 'poetic' (unlike, for instance, Hackert's).
31. Quotations in this paragraph are from Herder, p. 140–41. The argument is based on Carrdus; M. Krieger, pp. 147–51, 217–18.
32. Both Herder and Lessing use *enargeia* for *evidentia*.
33. The Thomson statement in reverse would read something like this: 'The poet who makes a beautiful landscape from the pictorial representation of a Lorrain, does less than one who takes his image at first hand from nature. The latter, seeing his model before him, must by an effort of the imagination, turn it into a beautiful imitation using feeble, uncertain representations of arbitrary signs; the former, presented with a beautiful imitation, needs no imagination to make a beautiful picture from vivid, sensible impressions.'
34. M. Krieger, pp. xvi–xvii.

35. Hutchings, p. 46.
36. Against the backdrop of seventeenth- and eighteenth-century aesthetics, it is important to note here that in her *Persistence of Allegory*, Brown, p. 37, observes that Goethe's review 'reflects the shift' taking place at the time that 'gave the mimetic mode priority over the allegorical mode of representation'.
37. On the importance of Goethe's pre-Rome exposure to classical art in Mannheim, see Robson-Scott, pp. 31–34.
38. Trans. by Trevelyan, pp. 47–48; *FA*, XXVIII, 191–92.
39. Letter to Philipp Erasmus Reich, 20 February 1770, trans. by Robson-Scott, p. 28; *FA*, XXVIII, 183.
40. Thus anticipating Goethe's fundamental credo of 'Polarität' [polarity] and 'Steigerung' [intensification or heightening].
41. See Boyle, I: *The Poetry of Desire*, p. 159.
42. *FA*, I, 204, 330, IV, 408, 409, 416.
43. On this and the Pindar allusion in the following quotation, see Trevelyan, pp. 76–77. For a detailed analysis of Pindar and 'Wandrers Sturmlied', see Reiff and Jølle, who looks at the relationship through Goethe's translation of Pindar's fifth Olympian Ode.
44. See also *FA*, XXVIII, 776 (commentary).
45. See the Greek Word Study Tool for the Greek original of Pindar's eighth Nemean Ode, in the Perseus Digital Library <http://data.perseus.org/citations/urn:cts:greekLit:tlg0033.tlg003.perseus-grc1:8> [accessed 7 October 2017].
46. On this topos in Goethe's poetry, including 'Der Wandrer', see Willoughby. For a much broader perspective on the topos, cf. also Schrimpf; Kaiser, *Wanderer und Idylle*.
47. See Lütteken, p. 197.
48. Cf. e.g. 'Illustrations for Faust' (*FA*, VII.2, 1069, nos. 1–16).
49. See Virgil, VI. 300–744.
50. Virgil, VI. 162–70.
51. Rilke, pp. 283–84, 286; on Nietzsche and Lorrain, see Betram, pp. 213–22.
52. Cf. its 1665 pendant, *LV*, 164.
53. For the Lorrain connection, see Roethlisberger, ed., pp. 263–64. For readings of Goethe's poem in relation to Catel's painting, see Miller, *Wanderer*, pp. 9–35; Schuster.

CHAPTER 3

Italy: Landscape as Nature and Art

> Italien ohne Sicilien macht gar kein Bild in der Seele: hier ist der Schlüssel zu Allem.
> (from the *Italienische Reise*, 13 April 1787 (Palermo); *FA*, xv.1, 271)
>
> [Italy without Sicily forms no image in the soul; only here is the key to everything.] (*CW*, vi, 203)

On 25 January 1788, as Goethe's journey to Italy draws to a close, he sends a letter to Duke Carl August of Saxe-Weimar, who had made Goethe a member of his privy council, and who supported Goethe even during a two-year absence from administrative duties in the Duchy's government. To convince the Duke of the merits of his investment, Goethe dutifully lists the literary pieces he is preparing in order to complete the planned eight-volume *Collected Works* (on the occasion of his fortieth birthday in 1789). However, what Goethe emphasizes in this summary of his Grand Tour is the impact on him of exposure to nature and art:

> Als ich zuerst nach Rom kam, bemerckt ich bald daß ich von Kunst eigentlich gar nichts verstand und daß ich biß dahin nur den allgemeinen Abglanz der Natur in den Kunstwercken, bewundert und genossen hatte, hier that sich eine andre Natur, ein weiteres Feld der Kunst vor mir auf, ja ein Abgrund der Kunst, in den ich mit desto mehr Freude hineinschaute, als ich meinen Blick an die Abgründe der Natur gewöhnt hatte. Ich überließ mich gelassen den sinnlichen Eindrücken, so sah ich Rom, Neapel, Sicilien und kam auf Corpus Domini nach Rom zurück. Die großen Scenen der Natur hatten mein Gemüth ausgeweitet und alle Falten herausgeglättet, von der Würde der Landschafts Mahlerey hatte ich einen Begriff erlangt, ich sah Claude und Poussin mit andern Augen. (*FA*, xxx, 374–75)
>
> [When I first arrived in Rome I soon realized that I actually knew nothing about art and up to then had only been admiring and enjoying the general reflection of nature in works of art. Here another nature opened up, a broad field of art, in fact an abyss of art, which I peered into with the more pleasure because I had accustomed my eye to the abysses of nature. I calmly gave myself up to sense impressions, thus I saw Rome, Naples, Sicily, and came back

to Rome on Corpus Christi. The great scenes of nature had broadened my mind and smoothed away all its creases, I had gained an idea of the dignity of landscape painting, I saw Claude and Poussin with new eyes.] (Reed, ed. and trans., p. 138)

As described at length in his travelogue, the *Italienische Reise* (1816–17), what Goethe means in this excerpt by 'nature' is essentially the landscape of the Roman Campagna and the Mediterranean landscapes in Naples and Sicily.[1] While he mentions the plastic arts of Antiquity several paragraphs later, his focus here is on landscape painting, with Poussin and Lorrain as its representatives. To articulate the profundity of Southern nature and Southern landscape painting, Goethe compares it to looking into an 'abyss', a term he uses, according to the *Goethe-Wörterbuch*, for an experience whose depth is immeasurable and whose symbolism is inexhaustible (*GW*, I, 78–79). He also traces the development of a new way of seeing, involving sensation, 'sense impressions', and cognition, 'gained an idea', that is the prerequisite for a poiesis that moves away from 'imitation', 'reflection of nature', and toward 'creation' from the 'grand' and 'purified' image of nature imprinted on the 'soul'. To see and recreate nature in this fashion presupposes a 'calm' or 'serene' disposition. Goethe's summation culminates in the 'dignity of landscape painting', implying that there is an ethics to his 'Italian' aesthetics.

The letter to Carl August continues with Goethe describing extended trips to Tivoli, Frascati, and Castello, where he drafts and sketches landscapes sedulously, under the tutelage of painters like Philipp Hackert. It provides a glimpse into what might be called Goethe's Italian identity. No précis can do justice to his 'Bildungsreise', though. The experience affected him so profoundly as a person *and* a Renaissance man that he likened it to a 'Wiedergeburt', or rebirth.

Here are but the bare bones relevant for this study. When Goethe arrived in Rome on 29 October 1786, he registered under the pseudonym 'Filippo Miller, tedesco, pittore 32 <anni>' (*FA*, xv.2, 1248). The alias was more than just a cover to avoid being recognized as the best-selling author of *Die Leiden des jungen Werthers* or as the privy counsellor of a foreign potentate; it also pointed to Goethe's long-held conviction that his true identity was that of a painter and draughtsman. During eighteen months of continuous interaction with painters and extensive and intense study *and* practical training, he produced over four hundred sepia and ink-and-wash drawings, as well as numerous aquarelles.[2] While he takes pride in his formal and technical progress, in 'perspective and architecture and also in landscape composition' (*CW*, vi, 295; *FA*, xv.1, 398), he admits in February 1788 that he is essentially a dilettante: 'My thirst is quenched, I am on the right path as far as viewing and study are concerned', and so, in practice, 'it does not matter how much, or how little, I botch things' (*CW*, vi, 416; *FA*, xv.1, 554). After explicitly citing Angelika Kauffmann's praise 'that she knows few people in Rome who *see* better in art than I do', he concludes: 'The benefit that I shall have from my rather long stay in Rome is that I am giving up the practice of the visual arts [for] I was really born for literature' (*CW*, vi, 417; *FA*, xv.1, 556). To lend credence to his resolution, he lists literary works to be rewritten, expanded, or completed, among them the play *Torquato Tasso*, the Singspiel *Claudine von Villa Bella*, the novel *Wilhelm Meisters Lehrjahre*, and the poem 'Amor ein Landschaftsmaler', which will serve as our focus later in this chapter (*CW*, vi, 415–16, 417; *FA*, xv.1, 553–54, 556). When Goethe left Rome on 24 April 1788, he had with him 'the worthiest gift a host could have presented to me as a farewell', a sizable collection of original etchings by Claude Lorrain.³ While in Rome, in the many palazzos with their galleries, he had the opportunity to see around two dozen original paintings by Lorrain, such as *Landscape with the Father of Psyche Sacrificing at the Milesian Temple of Apollo* (1663; *LV*, 157) in the Palazzo Altieri, *Pastoral Landscape with Castel Gandolfo* (1639; *LV*, 35) in the Palazzo Barberini, *Parnassus* (1680; *LV*, 193) in the Palazzo Colonna, and *Landscape with Apollo Guarding the Herds of Admetus and Mercury Stealing Them* (1645; *LV*, 92) in the Galleria Doria Pamphilj.⁴

3.1. Seeing through the Haze: Primeval Landscape, or *Urlandschaft*

The first Lorrain entry in the *Italienische Reise* dates from 19 February 1787: 'Über der Erde schwebt ein Duft, des Tags über, den man nur aus Gemälden und Zeichnungen des Claude kennt, das Phänomen in der Natur aber nicht leicht so schön sieht als hier' [Hovering over the ground all day is a haze which is familiar to us only from the paintings and drawings of Claude Lorrain; but in nature the phenomenon is rarely seen as beautifully as here] (*FA*, xv.1, 186; *CW*, vi, 142). What is curious about this aspect of the Mediterranean light that Goethe tries to capture is that it manifests itself in three forms — the natural, the verbal, and the pictorial — without their beauty being determined by a hierarchy (except for the superior beauty of Southern nature as opposed to, say, Northern nature). Note also that Goethe does not relate the three comparatively, through the use of similes, for instance, but rather contiguously; that is, each 'medium' fulfils the need to articulate beauty. Landscape as nature and landscape as art, or landscape as experience and landscape as idea, are connected qua effect and separated qua vehicle. Consequently, and typical for Goethean perception, 'seeing' is both sensory, 'sieht', and cognitive, 'kennt'. Goethe's diction is striking in this regard, for the chiastic inversion of the first and second phrases, 'über der Erde' [over the ground] and 'des Tags über' [all day, literally 'the day over'], puts the emphasis on 'über' [over] and relates it to both space and time. By using this rhetorical device, Goethe implies that 'haze' is not just a visual but also a conceptual experience. Equally noteworthy is the observer's line of sight — neither foreground nor middle ground comes into view. Instead, Goethe's eye is drawn to, and captivated by, the light spreading over the horizon, the vanishing point of Lorrain's 'aerial perspective', the technique, so fundamental to his suggestion of depth, of modulating the brightness and distinctness of objects — the more distant, the paler and blurrier they are — to simulate changes effected by the 'Duft', or atmosphere. While these modulations may primarily involve tone or hue, with his explicit mention of 'drawings' Goethe underscores that the use of light and shade serves the same purpose. This is significant because, as a visual artist, Goethe saw himself first and foremost as a draughtsman, not a colourist.

It is not until his boat trip to Sicily that he bears witness to 'the mechanics of watercolour painting (*aquarelle*)', more for the purposes of 'shortening the long hours of the crossing' than artistic considerations (*CW*, VI, 188; *FA*, XV.1, 248). Much more important are the 'contours' of the landscape.[5] Goethe hired as his 'travel photographer' the German painter Christoph Heinrich Kniep (1755–1825), 'who draws with the greatest accuracy', to pictorially record their exploration of Sicily and 'sketch all the islands and coasts as they came into sight', while Goethe 'schematisiert', that is, sketches outlines (*CW*, VI, 188, 189; *FA*, XV.1, 248, 250). Before his discovery of colour while in Italy, Goethe's focus on contours and composition — whether for the purposes of framing or the layering of distance — is what links him to Winckelmann and the classicizing tendencies of the *disegno* school of the Italian Renaissance. Tellingly, Tischbein abandoned Goethe in Naples on learning that he could establish himself at the Neapolitan court as a *painter*, leaving behind Rome, where 'one is forced to draft'.[6] In light of our reading of the first Lorrain comment in Goethe's Italian travelogue, the final word, 'here', takes on several layers of meaning. Beyond signifying the obvious — 'in a naturally occurring atmospheric phenomenon observable in Rome' — it can be extended to include the sense of 'in and as a verbally and pictorially encoded or enacted natural atmospheric phenomenon'. With the 'here' tied to 'beautifully', Goethe hints at beauty as an effect resulting from a creative process that involves the 'plastic' and the 'experiential', or what Moritz encapsulated as 'formative imitation of the beautiful'. Goethe excerpted Moritz's essay, which evolved out of their intensive discussions, liberally in the *Italienische Reise*. Given Moritz's emphasis on painterly concerns such as contours, central perspective, and rays converging at a vanishing point as prerequisites for a 'self-contained' and 'internally coherent' work of art, one can argue that Lorrain served as a stimulus for the essay's neoclassical aesthetics.[7]

Lorrain is not Goethe's exclusive focus during his first stay in Rome; but, as he travels further south, his experience of the Mediterranean landscape in the Gulf of Naples and Sicily is inseparable from Lorrain. In fact, his most substantial Lorrain comment comes at the very moment he sets eyes on Sicily:

> Hat man sich nicht ringsum vom Meere umgeben gesehen, so hat man keinen Begriff von Welt und von seinem Verhältnis zur Welt. Als Landschaftszeichner hat mir diese große, simple Linie ganz neue Gedanken gegeben. [...] Mit keinen Worten ist die dunstige Klarheit auszudrücken die um die Küsten schwebte als wir am schönsten Nachmittage gegen Palermo anfuhren. Die Reinheit der Konture, die Weichheit des Ganzen, das Auseinanderweichen der Töne, die Harmonie von Himmel, Meer und Erde. Wer es gesehen hat der hat es auf sein ganzes Leben. Nun versteh' ich erst die Claude Lorrain und habe Hoffnung auch dereinst in Norden aus meiner Seele Schattenbilder dieser glücklichen Wohnung hervor zu bringen. Wäre nur alles Kleinliche so rein daraus weggewaschen als die Kleinlichkeit der Strohdächer aus meinen Zeichenbegriffen. Wir wollen sehen was diese Königin der Inseln tun kann.
> (*FA*, XV.1, 248–49)

[Whoever has not seen himself all surrounded by the sea can have no conception of the world and his relationship to the world. This grand, simple line has given me, as a sketcher of landscapes, entirely new ideas. [...] No words

can describe the misty transparency that hovered around the coasts as we sailed
up to Palermo on the most beautiful afternoon: the purity of the contours, the
softness of the prospect in toto, the gradations of the tones, the harmony of sky,
sea, and earth. To have seen it is to remember it for the rest of one's life. Now
at last I understand the paintings of Claude Lorrain, and can hope that I shall
be able, even someday in the north, to summon up mental images of this happy
domain. If only everything trivial were as thoroughly expunged from my mind
as the triviality of thatched roofs has been from my ideas about subjects suitable
for drawing. Let us see what this queen of islands can do.] (*CW*, VI, 187–88)

What reads at first sight like a recounting of the scenic beauties encountered by
Goethe on his passage from Naples to Palermo in the spring of 1787 turns out to be
a vivid expression of an experience of nature that is, even for a seasoned 'naturalist'
like Goethe, new and unique. As the curiously worded first clause reveals, the
experience is existential and, if you will, epistemological, for it is fundamentally
tied to the position of the observer vis-à-vis the observed. What is even more
curious is that the reflexive construction presents the observer as the one who both
sees and is seen, and that it is precisely this tension or reciprocity between subject
and object that engenders an understanding of nature and the self's place within
it. This new kind of interrelational perception generates a new kind of art, for the
subject, the 'sketcher of landscapes', sees the object, nature, as a 'grand, simple line';
what strikes Goethe's pictorial perception most is the outline, the profile of the
scenery before him. It is crucial to note that Goethe takes the epithets 'grand' and
'simple' both in their literal and metaphorical senses, with 'grand' suggesting both
spatial largeness and spiritual grandeur, while 'simple' evokes a reduction to a shape
both un-complex and essential.

Goethe learned to see while in Italy.[8] Although one can argue that in Rome
it was mainly art that he saw with fresh eyes, here in Sicily it was mainly nature.
However, as the beginning of our first excerpt from the *Italienische Reise* reveals,
one could also argue that nature and art are indistinguishable; that is, that Goethe
saw landscape in nature and on the canvas simultaneously. Thus, it would seem
that the 'new' ideas are a function of the tension between what is natural and
what is aesthetic in nature's 'Sein' [being] and 'Schein' [semblance] respectively.
The tension is such that Goethe suffers momentarily from aphasia, 'no words', an
expression that echoes the 'not seen' at the very beginning — as if 'to see' and 'to
put into words' or 'to write' were prerequisites for the landscape's very existence.
But it is not just that the world vanishes without the visual and the verbal, it is the
self that — only qua the visual and the verbal, as painter-cum-poet — ascertains its
existence and relationship with the world.

When Goethe finds words to interrelate the pictorial and the poetic, it is initially
an oxymoron, 'misty transparency', as well as a verb, 'to hover', that express the
tensioned quality of the sight. While a variant of 'misty transparency' will reoccur
in *Zur Farbenlehre* as 'Trübe' [murkiness], the turbid yet light-transmitting medium
that permeates the atmosphere, Goethe's first 'concrete' characterization of the
scenery concerns the 'contours' whose significance for his visual aesthetics is
underscored by 'purity', which implies more than 'clean' or 'distinct' — namely,

being uncontaminated by extraneous elements. As Goethe makes his way on to Sicily and becomes a kind of 'contour-ist' — colours virtually become an afterthought — the dialectic of art and nature takes on more layers of meaning. Playing itself out in the tension between 'contour' and 'mist', it is, epistemologically, as if *tekhne* ('art' in Greek) enables actual fixation while *physis* causes notional dissolution. Perceptively, it is as if the gaze 'took possession' or 'conquered' — terms Goethe indeed uses to describe sketching (*CW*, VI, 178, 179; *FA*, XV.1, 235, 237) — while the look holds re-presentation in abeyance. Pictorially, the dialectic of sketch and *sfumato* results in a waking dream. It is translucent in the imagination but opaque (a 'shadow image' or 'silhouette') in memory.

As we have seen the importance of 'das Ganze' before, it is no surprise that Goethe includes it among the criteria for the perfect landscape. Italy, or rather Sicily, adds another dimension: 'softness'. The Grimms' *Deutsches Wörterbuch* documents 'weich' [soft] as related to climate, especially wind, to the overall visual impression of a landscape, as when muted light softens stark silhouettes (XXVIII, 465) — recall the lines in Goethe's 1775 poem 'Auf dem See' [On the Lake]: 'Weiche Nebel trinken | Rings die türmende Ferne' [Soft mists drink the circled | Towering world afar] (*CW*, I, 41; *FA*, I, 169) — and, finally, to painting technique in the sense that 'weich malen' [to paint in muted colours] results in a blurring of contrasts and contours. 'Weich' reoccurs in the next characterization, now in verbal form, suggesting that there is movement in this landscape, that the perception is dynamic. While the *Goethe-Wörterbuch* defines 'auseinanderweichen' as the 'stufenweise Differenzierung der Farbtöne' [gradual differentiation of chromatic tones] (*GW*, I, 1135), Goethe avoids the word 'colour' altogether in order to emphasize that with 'tone' he does not mean the colours' brightness but the faintness of 'tint' and 'shade', as well as the general effect produced by their interplay.

Goethe caps his characterization of the scenery before him with 'the harmony of sky, sea, and earth'. The statement lends itself to illustrating — corroborated by the entry on 'harmony' in the *Goethe-Wörterbuch* (IV, 709–11) — Goethe's idea of perfection, namely amalgamating heterogeneous elements into an organic, well-proportioned, and coherent whole that may be, as here, of cosmic proportion. It is a concept he often applies, in the *Italienische Reise*, to architecture, particularly to Andrea Palladio (1508–80), and to painting, foremost to Paolo Veronese (1528–88), Leonardo da Vinci (1452–1519), Raphael (1489–1520), and — Lorrain. However aptly this synthesis fits Goethe's dialectic thinking, the imagery seems 'abstract' in its schematic listing, formulaic rather than optically concrete. While the triad of heaven, sea, and earth echoes the Bible, the more likely source is Homer, Goethe's Sicilian poet-companion, along with Lorrain, his painter-companion: recall Hephaistos's depiction of the three realms of the world at the heart of Achilles' shield, surrounded by Oceanus.[9] For Goethe, surrounded by water, the heaven–earth and earth–sea axes provide a certain amount of vertical and horizontal order and orientation.

> Was den Homer betrifft, ist mir wie eine Decke von den Augen gefallen. Die Beschreibungen, die Gleichnisse etc. kommen uns poetisch vor und sind doch unsäglich natürlich, aber freilich mit einer Reinheit gezeichnet, vor der man

erschrickt. [...] Nun ich alle diese Küsten und Vorgebirge, Golfe und Buchten, Inseln und Erdzungen, Felsen und Sandstreifen, buschige Hügel, sanfte Weiden, fruchtbare Felder, geschmückte Gärten, gepflegte Bäume, hängende Reben, Wolkenberge und immer heitere Ebenen, Klippen und Bänke und das alles umgebende Meer mit so vielen Abwechslungen und Mannigfaltigkeiten im Geiste gegenwärtig habe, nun ist mir erst die Odyssee ein lebendiges Wort. (17 May 1787; *FA*, xv.1, 345)

[With respect to Homer, it is as if scales had fallen from my eyes. The descriptions, the similes, etc., seem poetic and yet are inexpressibly natural, but drawn, to be sure, with warmth and purity that startle one. [...] Now that all these coasts and headlands, bays and inlets, islands and tongues, ornate gardens, well-tended trees, hanging grapevines, cloudy peaks and always sunny plains, reefs and shoals, and the all-encompassing sea with its many changes and variations are present in my mind, only now has the *Odyssey* become a living word for me.] (*CW*, vi, 256)

Replace 'Homer' with 'Lorrain', 'Odyssey' with 'landscape', and 'living word' with 'vivid picture', and the overlap of Sicily, Homer, and Lorrain — and by extension of nature and art — is palpable. We are now in a position to lay to rest the common misconception that Goethe sees 'Italy' through the lens of Lorrain or, for that matter, Homer.[10] That would be an act of mere projection. But the relationship is one of reciprocity, involving mirroring. Mirroring acknowledges projection but also engages reflection. The 'purity' of the painterly or poetic projection onto the natural — note that 'purity' is a concept shared by the comments on both Lorrain and Homer — 'silences' or 'startles' Goethe, who, jolted into reflection ('scales fall from the eyes' and 'now at last I understand'), realizes that nature breathes life into his artistic imagination and memory. To bring our discussion of 'harmony' to a close, it turns out to be an experience and an idea, with Lorrain (and Sicily and Homer) providing the connection between the two aspects.

If, indeed, as the travelogue entry suggests, Goethe has *not* 'understood' Lorrain, then what are we to make of the creative appropriation we have analysed so far, and why exactly is it that he can now claim to grasp Lorrain? Moreover, so far, he has been at no loss for words when expressing his emotive and self-reflective responses to two of Lorrain's paintings. On closer inspection, though, it is not a painting that causes the aphasia but, presumably, the painting's source, nature itself. It is Sicily, then, that induces Goethe to see beyond art and to 'absorb' nature, or rather, to place himself at the site where nature and art meet, which is also a site of cognition since its dynamic interplay enables improved understanding. It is in Sicily that Goethe sees in nature what, up to now, has (mainly) existed in his mind and as ekphrasis: the ideal of a landscape aglow with and energized by soft light, exuding an air of the vibrancy and tranquillity of a whole that is mosaic yet coherent. Not only do nature and art illuminate each other in the act of seeing, but an interdependence also connects perception and production, knowledge of nature and creation of art.

Unlike the 'image' that enters the panther's eye in Rilke's well-known poem, the 'image' that enters Goethe's 'soul' does not stop there but is stored as a resource for later 'production'. It is as if 'nature' impregnates the womb-like soul in which a landscape germinates and is carried to term. What emerges is a 'Schattenbild' [shadow image], which connotes, according to the Grimms' *Wörterbuch*, a likeness, a representation, a figment of the imagination (XIV, 2252–53); for Goethe, as we will see, the term comes from his technical vocabulary in *Zur Farbenlehre*. In the poietic context, however, it calls to mind 'umbra' [shade], and by extension the verb 'to adumbrate' as a synonym for 'to create'. What 'shadow image' evokes here is a landscape as an image cast like a shadow onto a canvas, a chiaroscuro representation showing shape and outline only, as in the silhouette of Lotte that Werther creates or in the 'contour', which is, for Goethe, the perceptual structure, the formal and tectonic basis with which the sketcher or painter of a landscape must begin — with the implication that both the silhouette and the contour evoke the essential features of the person or object depicted.

'Wohnung' [residence, abode] — for which the Grimms' *Wörterbuch* lists 'Himmelsstriche' [climes] or 'Gefilde' [realms] as figurative meanings — alludes to, in combination with the epithet 'happy' or 'blissful', 'pleasant climes' or, mythologically speaking, Elysian Fields (XXX, 1230–34). It is as if the Utopia that Goethe envisioned when reviewing the Lorrain engravings in 1772, 'paradisal prospects', has become a reality in the Sicilian scenery; yet, given the constant interplay between nature and art, the question persists as to whether it is nature that inspires art or art that prefigures (the perception of) nature. Intriguingly, Goethe, while interlocking 'North' and 'shadow', avoids locating the 'realm of bliss' explicitly in the 'South' or the 'Mediterranean'. Is the implication that, for Goethe, 'Sicily' — and, by extension, Lorrain's 'Sicilian' landscape — is both a phenomenon and an idea?

As seen above, Goethe ends his account of his first experience of Sicily with a statement that is both poetic and poietic: 'If only everything trivial were as thoroughly expunged from my mind as the triviality of thatched roofs has been from my ideas about subjects suitable for drawing.' In order for the soul to produce a 'mental image', it must be as 'pure' as the contour. In a purely composed landscape, there is no room for 'trivial' passages such as 'thatched roofs', because they contribute little meaning to the whole. 'Thatched roofs' are phenomenal but not ideational, particulars from which no general notion can be abstracted; or, as Goethe explains, albeit somewhat hyperbolically, in a statement about Homer but equally applicable to Lorrain as well: 'Diese hohen Kunstwerke sind zugleich als die höchsten Naturwerke von Menschen nach wahren und natürlichen Gesetzen hervorgebracht worden. Alles Willkürliche, Eingebildete fällt zusammen, da ist die Notwendigkeit, da ist Gott' [These sublime works of art are also the sublimest works of nature, created by men following true and natural laws. Everything arbitrary, everything imaginary crumbles away, there we have necessity, there we have God] (*FA*, XV.1, 424; *CW*, VI, 316). In order to analogize nature and art, the phenomenal and the noumenal, the act of creation becomes an act of removal, of peeling away the inconsequential, capricious, or fanciful. Goethe's aim is to distil the type from the individual, the exemplary from the idiosyncratic. What remains is an essence that Goethe can only allude to in 'religious' terms, identifying it as some ultimate origin, a correspondence between the natural and the artistic, an

'Urpflanze' [primal plant] and an 'Urlandschaft' [primal landscape]. It is in Sicily, in Palermo's public garden, that the idea of multitudinous botanical forms evolving out of one basic model begins to take root in Goethe's mind (*CW*, vi, 214; *FA*, xv.1, 286). Back in Naples he elaborates:

> With this model and the key to it an infinite number of plants can be invented, which must be logical, that is, if they do not exist, they *could* exist, and are not mere pictorial or poetic shadows and semblances, but have an inner truth and necessity. The same law will be applicable to every other living thing. (*CW*, vi, 256; *FA*, xv.1, 402)

Another 'living thing' is painting, and while Goethe identifies the 'leaf' as 'the true Proteus' of plant generation, we can surmise that he reads Lorrain as the primordial landscape from which a multitude of landscapes can be derived (*CW*, vi, 299; *FA*, xv.1, 402).

3.2. Goethe and Hackert Visit Lorrain in the Palazzo Colonna

Before we return to Sicily and discuss one such protean landscape, we accompany Goethe and Hackert to the Palazzo Colonna, 'where', Goethe writes, 'works by Poussin, Claude, and Salvator Rosa hang side by side' (*CW*, vi, 279; *FA*, xv.1, 377). At the time of the visit, 27 June 1787, Goethe had the opportunity to view and discuss seven Lorrain paintings: *Pastoral Landscape* (1641; *LV*, 56), *Pastoral Landscape with the Flight into Egypt* (1662; *LV*, 158), *Landscape with the Nymph Egeria Mourning over Numa* (1669; *LV*, 175), *View of Carthage with Dido, Aeneas, and their Suite Leaving for the Hunt* (1676; *LV*, 186), *Pastoral Landscape* (1677; *LV*, 190), *Parnassus* (1680; *LV*, 193), and *Parnassus with Minerva Visiting the Muses* (1680; *LV*, 195).[11] Hackert, Goethe remarks, 'said many good and well-considered things to me about these pictures' (*CW*, vi, 279; *FA*, xv.1, 377). Since he does not go into any detail, we must look elsewhere for a record of their conversation. It can be found in Hackert's letters on landscape painting, which we discussed in Chapter 1.[12] Recall that Hackert characterizes Poussin's and Dughet's landscapes as heroic by virtue of their 'grand', 'magnificent', and sublime style, that is, 'so terribly beautiful that they make you shudder' — unless the horrible is depicted 'from a bird's eye view', as in *Landscape with Abraham and Isaac Approaching the Place of Sacrifice* (c. 1665), in which case the response is 'pleasant' and 'delightful' (pp. 114–16).[13]

We also know from the Introduction that the *sine qua non* of landscape painting is intensive and extensive knowledge of nature — the expertise of a mathematician in regard to perspective, of a botanist in regard to trees, of a chemist in regard to colours. This is one of the reasons why Hackert considers Lorrain to be 'the greatest landscapist', for 'his diligence and genius and tireless studying' (p. 115). Another reason is that 'in terms of colouring, tone, and atmosphere no one', in Hackert's opinion, 'has attained the kind of perfection that he has' (p. 115), elaborating that Lorrain's

> vapeur in verschidne Tages Zeiten, so wohl in der Fernung als Luft is Außer ordentlich, man findet den Sanften Nebel des Morgens und die Ausdünstungen des Abens, nicht allein in der fernesten entfernung, sondern all Grade nach bis

> auf den Mittel Grund wo der Sanfte Nebel herschet, ohne local farben die die Natur zeiget, ohne detail zu alteriren sehr deutlich und macht den Zuschauer die Angenehmste Empfindung. (pp. 115–16)
>
> [haze is, at different times of day, both in far-off points and in the sky, extraordinary; one finds the soft mist of the morning and the water vapour of the evening not just in the farthest distance but also in minute gradations down to the middle ground, where the soft mist prevails and where nature shows, clearly and unmodified, her original colours, all of which evokes a feeling of utmost delight in the observer.]

'Perfection', in the master craftsman's sense of *tekhne*, does not mean flawlessness. Aiming for balance, Hackert writes that 'one could object that his perspective is incorrect, and one would wish in many instances that, with so many beautiful features, the lines of the horizontal divisions were more accurately drawn' (p. 115). Similarly balanced is his critique of Lorrain's chromatic technique: the

> trees in the foreground, even though they are grouped together beautifully, are often heavy; besides, in many instances, the earth green has darkened them into an indistinct black patch, so much so that no segment but only the silhouette remains visible. But since he used ultramarine blue, they are better preserved. (p. 116)

He tries to soften even his objection to Lorrain's skill in painting staffage — the human figures and cattle are generally 'rather mediocre' — by paraphrasing Lorrain's bon mot about adding staffage for free (p. 116). Behind Hackert's final reproach is his mantra of 'sketch first, paint second': if Lorrain 'had used sketches as a starting point and had more practice in what is called the mechanics of art, then his foregrounds would be as beautiful as his distant backgrounds and middle grounds' (p. 116).

While Hackert's critique is straightforward, his verdict has a polyvalence that is hard to translate. Lorrain, he writes, 'ist beständig Schön Reizen und gefält jemehr man seine Wercke Anschauet' [has an abiding beauty and charm, and the more one contemplates his works the more he pleases] (p. 116). Although Hackert's German is flawed, there is, in this clause, syntactically and visually, an arresting quality about the monolithic word 'Reizen': is it the plural of the noun 'Reiz', and thus suggesting, according to the Grimms' *Wörterbuch*, charm, delight, and allure? Or is it the capitalized verb 'reizen', and consequently ranging in meaning from teasing and captivating the imagination to stimulating a refined sensibility and a sublimated desire (XIV, 791–92, 794–98)? In short, Hackert's language betrays nature's allure as a temptress and Lorrain's subliminal eroticism. Is it too much of a stretch to argue that, during their visit to the Palazzo Colonna, Hackert and Goethe were not just 'contemplating' but 'gazing' at Lorrain's alluring beauties? To be sure, Hackert's emphasis on the emotional impact of Lorrain's art on the observer, which in turn mirrors Lorrain's emotional response to nature, is just that — a refined sensitivity to natural and aesthetic stimuli — but there is also the suggestion of landscape (in both reality and on canvas) as a subdued erotic experience. Witness this judgement on Lorrain: 'Sein Composition ist angenehm die Gruppirung der Verschidenen Bäumen Reizend über haupt siehet man das sein gefühl für die schöne Natur

Außerordentlich fein gewesen ist' [His composition is pleasant, the arrangement of different trees in groups is delightful; on the whole, one realizes that his feeling for beautiful nature was extraordinarily nuanced] (p. 116). Or this telling, and rhetorically subtle, objection to Poussin: 'Poussin is Einnehmend bey den Ersten Anschauen, so wie das Mer wen man es lange nicht gesehen hat, so fält seine Größe auf, man wird es in einigen Tagen sat, und siehet es mit Gleich Gültigkeit An' [Poussin is captivating at first sight, just as one is struck by the vastness of the sea after not seeing it for a long time, but looks at it with indifference because one is fed up with it within a few days] (p. 116).

Goethe sums up his discussion with Hackert at the Palazzo Colonna by drawing the following conclusion:

> Alles was er mir sagte hat meine Begriffe nicht geändert, sondern nur erweitert und bestimmt. Wenn man nun gleich wieder die Natur ansehn und wieder finden und lesen kann, was jene gefunden und mehr oder weniger nachgeahmt haben, das muß die Seele erweitern, reinigen und ihr zuletzt den höchsten anschauenden Begriff von Natur und Kunst geben. Ich will auch nicht mehr ruhen, bis mir nichts mehr Wort und Tradition, sondern lebendiger Begriff ist. (*FA*, xv.1, 377–78)

> [Everything he told me, instead of altering my concepts, merely expanded and defined them. If, then, one can immediately turn again to nature, and find and read again what those men found and more or less imitated, that surely has to expand the mind, purify it, and finally give it the highest intuitive concept of nature and art. I shall not rest until everything that is still merely words and tradition for me becomes a living concept.] (*CW*, vi, 279, trans. modified)

In terms of structure and wording, the back-and-forth between the personal 'I' and the impersonal 'one' is noteworthy because it not only establishes a correspondence between Goethe and Lorrain but also qualifies the statement as one of general import, an aesthetic maxim. This duality carries over into the 'auch' of the final statement in the German. Read as 'too' or 'likewise', it suggests, again, a point of identification; but it could be read as an emotionally charged modifying particle with the sense of 'indeed' or 'truly', indicating Goethe's resolve to follow in Lorrain's footsteps and pursue the same aesthetic ideal, leaving 'words and tradition' behind. By 'words', does he mean descriptive poetry? Or does he mean language that is too prosaic to convey experience? Or is it a more profound linguistic scepticism that Faust, too, strives to overcome (l. 385)? And does 'tradition', in turn, apply to art history and landscape painting before Lorrain? Is it an iconoclastic judgement on art that no longer stimulates or challenges, on soulless art? As we have seen before, the soul plays an important role in Goethe's notion of art. Finally, and notably, Goethe articulates his aesthetic maxim as a hypothetical, or even fictional, proposition — through the if–then construction — to make sure that he is suggesting an ideal.

Elaborating on this ideal, Lorrain is, once again, the authority to which Goethe makes recourse in order to illustrate and argue for a principle of landscape painting, even for the (visual) arts in general. What fascinates Goethe is the tension between truth of nature and truth of art. It evolves from a fourfold process through which the artist engages 'nature' — 'to look at' [ansehn], 'to find', 'to read', and 'to imitate', the latter modified by 'more or less'. The modification is, of course, the crux of the poietic process. It begins with the artist perceiving nature with his eyes and making discoveries through observation and contemplation. He then proceeds 'to read' or interpret the discoveries, and to extrapolate meaning from them. The last step in the 'more or less' process requires one not just to 'lesen' [read] but also '*verlesen*', that is, to sort, grade, select, and arrange systematically according to type, as well as to declutter by removing the unnecessary or, as discussed above, the 'trivial' and the 'arbitrary'. This process of purification, of turning the individual into the typical, the particular into the exemplary, 'expands and purifies the soul' and engenders in it the 'highest intuitive concept of nature and art'.

Goethe's understanding and use of 'anschauen' and 'begreifen' is complex and occasionally obscure. Outlined in the boldest strokes, they are mental processes aimed at interpretation, the apprehension of meaning, 'anschauen', and the comprehension of meaning, 'begreifen'. While apprehension relies more on the senses, the imagination, and feeling, comprehension relies more on the intellect and contemplation. But their boundaries are porous. They 'operate' at the site where nature and art, image and idea, sensory and symbolic meet without merging. Goethe's oxymoronic formula 'intuitive concept', or its synonym 'lively concept', reflects this contradictory conjunction. Thus, at the core of his conviction in the analogy of nature and art lies a paradox, and Lorrain exemplifies this paradox in 'supreme' fashion.

To give substance to Goethe's theorizing and to Lorrain's accomplishment, in a passage from the *Italienische Reise* (not directly related to Lorrain but relevant for our purposes), Goethe explains that 'the impression of the sublime, the beautiful [...] makes us uneasy, and we want to put our feelings, our perceptions, into words: but first, in order to do so, we would have to discern, penetrate, comprehend' (*CW*, vi, 440; *FA*, xv.1, 585). Admittedly, Goethe speaks here of his experience of being 'in the presence of ancient statues' in Rome, which, he quickly adds, is like being 'in the presence of nature' (*CW*, vi, 440; *FA*, xv.1, 585). Yet echoes of his experience of Lorrain are loud and clear, particularly since he has applied the categories of the sublime and the beautiful to Lorrain, too. While not identical with Goethe's 'Urphänomen', a 'kind of limit case of nature', such as the magnet or light,[14] the sublime and the beautiful are archetypes of Lorrain's primal landscape, which he, as we have shown, discovers in the presence of Sicilian nature. As such, this 'Urlandschaft' is the pictorial correlative of the 'Urpflanze', the leaf, which Goethe also discovers in Sicily: as he explicitly states, it is 'in intuition and concept' that he perceives the metamorphosis of plants — just as he discovers, we recall, 'polarity' and 'intensification', the two 'driving' or primal 'forces in all of nature' through 'intuitive perception' (*CW*, xii, 6; *FA*, xxv, 81). Another archetype that may serve as an example for Goethe's 'intuitive cognizing' is the symmetry he perceives in Lorrain. In a comment on Raphael, in which he interrelates the handling of space and symmetry with composition, as well as with nature and art, Goethe states:

> Selbst die herrlichen Bilder der Messe von Bolsena, der Befreiung des gefangenen Petrus, des Parnasses, wären ohne die wunderliche Beschränkung des Raumes nicht so unschätzbar geistreich zu denken. Eben so ist auch hier

in den Sibyllen die verheimlichte Symmetrie, worauf bei der Komposition alles ankommt, auf eine höchst geniale Weise obwaltend; denn wie in dem Organismus der Natur, so tut sich auch in der Kunst innerhalb der genausten Schranke die Vollkommenheit der Lebensäußerung kund. (*FA*, xv.1, 488–89)

[Even such magnificent pictures as the *Mass of Bolsena*, the *Freeing of the Captive St. Peter*, and the *Parnassus* could not be imagined as so inestimably ingenious without the curious limitation of space. Likewise, here too with *The Sibyls*, what predominates, in the most brilliant manner, is the concealed symmetry, the most essential factor in composition. For, in art as in natural organism, life manifests itself to perfection within the narrowest limits.] (*CW*, vi, 365–66)

Lorrain, unlike Raphael in the works in question, is not limited by the architectural frame provided for the frescoes but frames the space himself — with objects like buildings or trees — underpinning it with a symmetry both imitative and imaginative. 'Concealed symmetry' seems to suggest that art as construction is present but not visible, as it is, we recall, in Gessner and, at least in limited fashion, in Hackert. More importantly, 'concealed symmetry' seems to be one of Goethe's attempts at articulating that the essence intuitively perceived in nature can be imitated in art. That is, in boldest strokes, if the pre-Italian Goethe was preoccupied with emulating nature's creativity, the Italian Goethe sought to emulate, in practice and in theory, nature's essence.

3.3. 'Einfache Nachahmung der Natur, Manier, Styl' as a Theory of Landscape Painting

The essay 'Einfache Nachahmung der Natur, Manier, Styl' [Simple Imitation of Nature, Manner, and Style], which appeared in 1789, is Goethe's attempt at translating the artistic praxis of the Italian journey into an aesthetic theory.[15]

While Goethe discusses, without mentioning Lorrain, the place of landscape painting within his tripartite aesthetics, it is intriguing to speculate as to whether Lorrain fits into Goethe's stylistic scheme, and if so, where. Significantly, underlying the Italian connection between Lorrain and the essay is Goethe's use of 'artist', rather than 'poet', to accentuate the essay's focus on the visual arts and painting in particular. Goethe begins his typology of creative activity with imitation:

Wenn ein Künstler, bei dem man das natürliche Talent voraussetzen muß, in der frühesten Zeit, nachdem er nur einigermaßen Auge und Hand an Mustern geübt, sich an die Gegenstände der Natur wendete, mit Treue und Fleiß ihre Gestalten, ihre Farben, auf das genaueste nachahmte, sich gewissenhaft niemals von ihr entfernte, jedes Gemälde das er zu fertigen hätte wieder in ihrer Gegenwart anfinge und vollendete; ein solcher würde immer ein schätzenswerter Künstler sein; denn es könnte ihm nicht fehlen daß er in einem unglaublichen Grade *wahr* würde, daß seine Arbeiten sicher, kräftig und reich sein müßten. (*FA*, xviii, 225)

[If a naturally gifted artist, after practising his eye and hand somewhat with exemplars, soon turns to subjects in nature and copies her forms and colours exactly and conscientiously, truly, and diligently, and always beginning and ending in front of her, that artist will always be worthwhile, for it follows that he will be true to an incredible degree, and his works will be assured, powerful, and rich in variety.] (*GoA*, p. 21, trans. modified)

When Goethe illustrates 'simple imitation' with 'stilliegende Gegenstände' [immobile objects] as the subjects of still-life painting (*CW*, III, 71; *FA*, XVIII, 226), 'simple' seems to favour a type of pictorial representation where the painting coincides with nature to such an extent that the viewer tries to pick the flowers from the canvas. Yet 'simple' also hints at the possibility of a more complex mimesis. In fact, initially, it is not nature that is imitated, but art, paintings, that serve as models — this is, against the backdrop of Goethe's own career as a sketcher and painter, the implication of 'to practise that which is exemplary'. Paradoxically, then, imitating art is the first step for the successful imitator of nature. The next step for the painter is to turn his gaze toward nature; that is, the imitation of nature is a matter of perception, and thus not objective. Finally, the imitation must be executed with 'diligence', 'veridicality', 'utmost exactness', and 'conscientiousness' in maintaining propinquity to nature throughout the entire process.

The artist who follows these principles produces a work of art that is 'unbelievably *true*': it is 'assured', 'powerful', and 'rich'. According to the Grimms' *Wörterbuch* (XIV, 582–83, XVI, 723–24) and the *Goethe-Wörterbuch* (V, 680–82), 'assured' denotes 'skilled', 'with a sure or steady hand' in reference to ability, or 'sure' in regard to taste; 'rich' characterizes content as 'varied', 'rich in substance', or 'having a solid basis in reality'; 'strong' suggests 'clear and forceful', or 'expressive' with regard to effect. If these three characteristics are vital components of 'truth', then truth in the 'simple imitation of nature' is a function of technique and sensory perception.

Yet modifying 'true' with 'to an incredible degree' complicates the principle of verisimilitude. Is Goethe suggesting that simple imitation of nature results in a painting that is exceedingly true, a kind of heightened naturalism? Or is the sense of 'unglaublich' more like 'improbable', meaning that such a painting is unlikely to be true — i.e. the opposite of the previous sense of 'true'? Or does he have in mind, given that 'true' is conspicuously italicized, a yet to be defined 'aesthetic truth' such that a simple imitator, with his limited means, achieves a truth that is beyond belief? Even though Goethe sets out 'to give a clear indication' of what he means by simple imitation, the polyvalence of 'true' problematizes the notion of mimesis as a style of painting that aims at naturalistic depiction of the phenomena of a landscape as they are perceived and experienced. To this problematization we must add Goethe's unusual — for the purposes of an 'exact' definition of a technical term — wording, for the paragraph-length definition is one period, an elaborate if–then construction couched in the subjunctive mood. In other words, verisimilitude and truth become a matter of hypothesization, simple imitation of nature a matter of conjecture, if not faith — note Goethe's use of 'religious-moralistic' vocabulary: 'fidelity', 'conscientious', 'to sin', and 'unbelief'.[16] In short, Goethe advances and retracts simple imitation of nature as a 'creative' principle. Given the quasi-syllogistic, hypothetical reasoning, for poietic purposes, mimesis is both constitutive *and* regulative.

As conjectural a proposition as the first poietic principle may be, what is notably absent are the imaginative and the spiritual. These two are major components of the second principle, 'manner'. The 'mannerist'

> sieht eine Übereinstimmung vieler Gegenstände, die er nur in ein Bild bringen kann indem er das Einzelne aufopfert; es verdrießt ihn, der Natur ihre Buchstaben im Zeichnen nur gleichsam nachzubuchstabieren; er erfindet sich selbst eine *Weise*, macht sich selbst eine *Sprache*, um das, was er mit seiner Seele ergriffen, wieder nach seiner Art auszudrücken, einem Gegenstande den er öfters wiederholt hat eine eigne bezeichnende Form zu geben, ohne, wenn er ihn wiederholt, die Natur selbst vor sich zu haben, noch auch sich geradezu ihrer ganz lebhaft zu erinnern. (*FA*, XVIII, 226)

> [sees a harmony between objects which he can only introduce into a single picture by sacrificing the particular: he finds it tedious to spell out what it is in front of him according to the letter; he invents his own method, makes his own language to express what his spirit has grasped in its own way, to give an object which he has repeated often its own characteristic form, without having nature before him every time he repeats it, or without even recollecting it very vividly.] (*GoA*, p. 21)

Simple imitation 'vexes' the mannerist, for such mimesis is like an exercise in calligraphy. To 'imitate' is like 'spelling nature's letters'. As much as limited means constrain the artist, the craft-like rehearsal of nature's language is complemented by 'inventing'.[17] The mannerist invents his own 'language' and 'method'. 'Weise' has other connotations. It can also mean 'tune' or 'melody', so that 'Weise' implies both the process and the result of creation. Since a 'Weise' is a simple tune, it mirrors the simple imitation of Goethe's first poietic method, but deviates from it by means of its decidedly 'subjective' impulse. Just like 'true' before, 'Weise' is italicized, which is no coincidence, for 'weise' also means 'wise', suggesting that 'manner', too, is concerned with 'truth'. 'Weise', finally, implies 'composition', a principle, as we have seen time and again, at the core of Goethe's sketching theory, and indeed, as the *Goethe-Wörterbuch* tells us, a complementary aspect of 'invention' (*GW*, III, 277–79). 'To invent' includes 'irrational' and 'rational' aspects of the creative act. The phrase 'mit seiner Seele ergreifen' captures the reciprocity of sense and sensibility in the artist's response to nature. As subjective as this response may be — note the unusual reflexive constructions reinforced by the use of 'sich' and 'selbst' — the very same 'self' is also reserved for nature, thus holding the subjective and objective in tension. In terms of means, the mannerist 'generates out of his self a *language*' as a substitute for the 'letters' imposed on him by nature. This substitution of the 'material' by the 'sonorous' reoccurs in the mannerist's ideal: the 'concord of many objects [...] in one image'. If imitation's 'spelling' is additive, manner's 'bringing in tune' is synthetic. Significantly, Goethe makes recourse to music when verbalizing the painting's 'harmony'; that is to say, the successful mannerist produces a painting that, akin to a chorus unifying individual 'voices', creates an ethereal congruity of parts with one another and with the whole. In order to accomplish this 'whole', or as Goethe puts it, 'one image', the 'particular' must be 'sacrificed'. Inherent in the mannerist's language, be it visual or verbal, is a dialectic of order and expression, construction and invention.

With 'invent', Goethe harks back to the rhetorical tradition of *inventio*. Inventing the 'means' and 'method' to create an effective 'manner of his own' requires excogitation, which the mannerist can only engage in if he maintains — unlike the imitator who works in nature's 'presence' — his creative independence through spatial and temporal distance. But it is only a distancing, not an abandonment, as Goethe's awkward relativization of memory's role indicates.

For 'simple imitation', Goethe considered the still life the prime example; for 'manner', it is the landscape, precisely because it aims to invoke a 'large whole':

> Wir sehen daß diese Art der Nachahmung am geschicktesten bei Gegenständen angewendet wird, welche in einem großen Ganzen viele kleine subordinierte Gegenstände enthalten. Diese letztere müssen aufgeopfert werden, wenn der allgemeine Ausdruck des großen Gegenstandes erreicht werden soll, wie z.E. bei *Landschaften* der Fall ist, wo man ganz die Absicht verfehlen würde, wenn man sich ängstlich beim Einzelnen aufhalten, und den Begriff des Ganzen nicht vielmehr fest halten wollte. (*FA*, XVIII, 226–27)

> [We see that this sort of imitation is most appropriate to subjects which comprehend a large number of subordinate objects within a large whole: they must be sacrificed to the general expression of the subject at large, for example in landscapes where the whole point would be lost if we stayed timidly with the details rather than keeping the idea of the whole in the forefront of our minds.] (*GoA*, p. 22)

If the mannerist's art involves the deft sublation of a physical picture, 'object', and a mental picture, 'concept', so that its essential 'whole' can be experienced and comprehended, then 'landscape' — comprising both visual and verbal practices — is indeed an example of mannerist creativity. If manner is a language, or as here, the language of landscape, then Goethe shows us how this language works. With the exception of the 'whole', this is a verb-based language. The first verb group, consisting of to 'sacrifice', 'miss', and 'reach [for]', frame the picture, so to speak, by enacting the process of selection (winnowing) for the sake of attaining the goal. The second verb group enacts the process of composition — to 'contain' or 'consist of', to 'linger over' or 'occupy oneself with', and to 'grasp' or 'represent' are prefixed derivatives of the base verb 'to hold'.[18] That is to say, one verb functions as the compositional device for integrating that which is particular, multiple, and phenomenal and that which is universal, single, and noumenal into a likeness of *ex pluribus unum*.

If, in 'manner', Goethe tips the scale holding the subjective and the objective toward the former, in 'style', the order is reversed. The most obvious give-away is, grammatically speaking, the absence of a personal subject. Instead, 'art' becomes the subject. Yet, as a personified object, it retains the capacity to act:

> Gelangt die Kunst durch Nachahmung der Natur, durch Bemühung sich eine allgemeine Sprache zu machen, durch *genaues und tiefes Studium der Gegenstände selbst*, endlich dahin, daß sie die Eigenschaften der Dinge und die Art *wie* sie bestehen genau und immer genauer kennen lernt, daß sie die Reihe der Gestalten übersieht und die verschiedenen charakteristischen Formen neben einander zu stellen und nachzuahmen weiß: dann wird der *Styl* der höchste Grad wohin sie

gelangen kann; der Grad, wo sie sich den höchsten menschlichen Bemühungen gleichstellen darf. (*FA*, xviii, 227)

[If art succeeds in creating, through the imitation of nature, a general language, and if an *exact and in-depth study of objects* teaches it more and more precisely the characteristics of things, and how they subsist, so that it surveys the whole range of forms and can juxtapose and imitate various characteristic ones, then the highest level it can reach is style, the level on which it is equal to the highest achievement of man.] (*GoA*, p. 22, trans. modified)

Of the three creative principles, imitation of nature remains the common denominator. In contrast to simple imitation, where the 'most exact' imitation of natural features was required, now it is knowledge and understanding of nature — the '*exact and in-depth study of natural objects*' themselves — and grasping their characteristics and 'how they subsist'. 'Kennen lernen', according to the *Goethe-Wörterbuch*, ranges from the discovery and experience of something for the first time to seeking to comprehend fully its complexity and essence (*GW*, v, 338–39). It is not surprising, then, that Goethe complements it with 'characteristics', that which is typical or essential in a particular object, and 'how an object *is*', what its assembly and intrinsic nature consist of. Even though by itself the compound verb already implies process, Goethe emphasizes its perpetuity through the slightly awkward combination of positive and comparative: literally, 'precise and more and more precise'. Goethe's thinking is procedural, even operational here. The conditional structure of the paragraph, this time without the subjunctive (as in 'simple imitation'), is telling; but, even if Goethe's language is firmer, there is still the conditional and the conclusion. Style depends on 'reaching' or 'attaining' ('gelangen' is used twice) so as to achieve the 'highest' manifestation humanly possible — that is, not the highest per se. Style is an ideal that ceases to be the ideal if it is reached; style, therefore, is a matter of striving, or rather, striving itself.

The third condition that art strives to fulfil is — more literally translated — 'to survey the whole range of shapes and to juxtapose and imitate various characteristic forms'. Semantically, the two clauses are multivalent to the extreme. Both 'shape' and 'form' suggest the presence of raw material that is perceived, experienced, selected, and imitated. However, in contrast to 'simple imitation', the emphasis now lies on shaping and moulding, and in arranging the elements in a complex composition marked by divisions and coordinations. What is crucial here is the dynamics invoked by the verbs meaning 'to look out over' and 'to place side-by-side', with the former suggesting a panoramic view, a totality, and the latter a sequential view, a partition. The perception of wholeness and consistency — that is, the harmonizing agreement, or rather the dialogic interaction, between parts — is an aesthetic function of this dynamics. The dynamics applies to 'shape' and 'form', too — namely, the interdependence between the visually perceived, outward appearance and the conceptually apprehended, inner being, or 'das Wesen der Dinge' [the essence of things] (*FA*, xviii, 227; *GoA*, p. 23) — one of the dynamics that generates meaning, the moulding into a specific shape, especially as defined by a 'contour', where outward form and inner form are interdependent.

It is noteworthy that Goethe speaks again of 'language' as the vehicle for representing the 'object'. In 'simple imitation', the vehicle seemed to be charcoal and paint, contour and image, while in 'manner', Goethe already invoked language, albeit the artist's 'own', not, as now, art's 'general' language. That Goethe speaks of language is no surprise in light of his assertion that painting and poetry, composition and grammar, are analogous, as are the tensions and harmonies that give rise to meaning and mood. Against the backdrop of the essay under scrutiny, another analogy emerges — that language is a stylistic formula *and*, to borrow David Ditner's felicitous phrase, a 'natural and unaffected mode of expression that goes far beyond the labored dryness of a mere imitative exercise'.[19] But Goethe, the neoclassicist 'linguist', may have something else in mind here when he speaks of 'forming a language'. Recall also that Moritz calls his treatise on art's autonomy *Formative Imitation of the Beautiful*. Inventing a language would seem a prerequisite for making autonomous art, be it visual or verbal.

'It is easy to see that these three ways of producing works of art, presented separately here, are in fact precisely related and that the one shades into the other' (*GoA*, p. 22; *FA*, XVIII, 227). As Goethe contemplates the interrelation of the three creative activities, he makes recourse to the notion of familial relations to indicate the sharing of a common origin (imitation) and a common goal (style) or, by extension, attribute: art's unique capacity, *beautifully*, to imitate, and extract an essence from, nature. The natural scientist comes to the fore, again, when he makes recourse to chemistry by using the term 'sich verlaufen', or to 'dissolve' or 'disperse', to indicate that he views the relation not as a synthesis but as a colloid.

Goethe exemplifies the process of merging imitation imperceptibly with style. Using flowers as an example, he maintains that an imitator can perfect his imitation of a rose to such a 'high degree' that he comes close to intimating 'a clear concept of the beauty of the rose' (*GoA*, pp. 22–23; *FA*, XVIII, 227–28). Although this process involves 'laborious abstraction', it also paradoxically involves vivification. He describes the process as a metamorphosis from a still life into a *tableau vivant*, interweaving aesthetics with natural science and his 'Sicilian' discovery of the metamorphosis of plants.[20] Within a few lines, Goethe deploys a remarkable vocabulary of germination to illustrate the transformative vivification of the still life: 'pollination', 'new seed', 'fruit', 'thriving' or 'flourishing', and 'growth'. Undergoing 'successive development', the tableau comes alive, inducing the stylist to 'choose' from among the parts and consider their 'reciprocity' and 'influence' on the whole for the sake of an 'accurate representation' that 'astonishes' and 'enlightens'. This is the painterly imagination required to 'form a style' — note how Goethe avoids 'the style' (which is reserved for the ideal) or 'his style' (which would be the mannerist's) — in order to gain entry into the 'ante-chamber of style' [Vorhof des Styls] (*GoA*, p. 23; *FA*, XVIII, 228–29). Where the mannerist is concerned, Goethe, while maintaining that he uses the term 'in an elevated and respectable sense', insinuates that the mannerist is caught between the poles of imitation and style. If he engages the polarities dynamically — note the repeated use of the correlative comparative 'the more [...] the more' — the 'intensification' results at best in a 'higher' art, not the 'highest' that the striving for style promises to 'reach' (*GoA*, p. 23–24; *FA*, xviii, 229). Indeed, Goethe seems conflicted with regard to his estimation of the mannerist, for a mannerist unwilling to subject himself to the arduous transformative process of the imitator-cum-stylist 'expresses only the striking and the dazzling' (*GoA*, p. 23; *FA*, xviii, 228–29). As we are well aware by now, the sole focus on the particular is anathema to Goethe's aesthetics. If we apply this qualification to landscape painting, and recall that he presents landscape painting as the mannerist's domain but cautions that 'the whole point would be lost if we stayed timidly with the details rather than keeping the idea of the whole in the forefront of our minds', we might think of Goethe's veiled critique of Hackert. If, on the other hand, we recall that Goethe used the superlative 'highest' to describe the level that Lorrain's art has 'reached', we might apply the following summary of the imitator-cum-stylist to Lorrain:

> Je treuer, sorgfältiger, reiner [er] zu Werke gehet, je ruhiger [er] das, was [er] erblickt, empfindet, je gelassener [er] es nachahmt, je mehr [er] sich dabei zu *denken* gewöhnt, das heißt, jemehr [er] das Ähnliche zu vergleichen, das Unähnliche von einander abzusondern, und einzelne Gegenstände unter allgemeine Begriffe zu ordnen lernet: desto würdiger wird [er] sich machen die Schwelle des Heiligtums selbst zu betreten. (*FA*, xviii, 229)
>
> [The more honestly, carefully and neatly [he] goes about it, the more calmly [he] feels what [he] sees, the more deliberately [he] imitates it, the more [he] is in the habit of reflecting, that is of comparing the similar and distinguishing the dissimilar, and of subsuming individual objects under general concepts, the more worthy [he] makes [himself] able to cross the threshold of [style's] sanctuary.] (*GoA*, p. 23)

The prerequisite for reaching the 'threshold' is the pursuit of the principle of polarity and intensification, with the repeated use of the correlative comparative capturing the sheer dynamism of the process. With Goethe disavowing substance, style (understood as threshold, not ideal) *is* process. To wit, on 2 (8) July 1807, in a conversation with his secretary, Friedrich Wilhelm Riemer, he says: 'Die Kunst stellt eigentlich nicht Begriffe dar, aber die Art, wie sie darstellt, ist ein Begreifen, ein Zusammenfassen des Gemeinsamen und Charakteristischen, d.h. der Stil' [Art does not really represent concepts but the way in which it represents is grasping, bringing together the common and the characteristic, that is, the style].[21] What the qualification 'actually' tells us is that, without style, art would be conceptual; with style, it is dynamic and ambiguous, which Goethe underscores with three verbs — meaning to 'present' or 'represent'; to 'grasp', literally and figuratively; and to 'combine into a coherent whole' — interweaving the 'universal' and the 'particular' into, we infer, a symbol.

While not explicitly placing Lorrain in the antechamber of style, the statement dovetails with the findings of our investigation to such an extent that it can be read as so doing. Corroboration for this can be found in an otherwise baffling assertion in the essay. An imitator, says Goethe, who has been able to access, and make use of, the requisite vivifying and conceptualizing painterly imagination 'hat sich über das

Mögliche hinüber gearbeitet' [has transcended the possible] (*FA*, XVIII, 228; *GoA*, p. 23). One way to make sense of this is to tie it to an 'Italian' landscape painting à la Lorrain. Assuming that the possible is the naturalism of the imitator, the question arises of what comes after the possible. Is it the impossible, the unreachable ideal of style? Leaving the essay's deliberately vague terminology aside, what do we make of the oxymoronic provocation that style makes the impossible possible?

On 14 May 1787, at sea between Capri and the Sorrento Peninsula, Goethe's boat back to Naples was caught in a dead calm for more than a day. While everyone else was 'impatient' and 'out of humor', Goethe and Kniep were able to look at 'the world with painter's eyes', and so 'enjoyed at sunset the most superb view given us on the whole voyage'. Goethe continues:

> In dem glänzendsten Farbenschmuck lag Cap Minerva mit den daranstoßenden Gebirgen vor unseren Augen, indes die Felsen die sich südwärts hinabziehen schon einen blaulichen Ton angenommen hatten. Vom Cap an zog sich die ganze erleuchtete Küste bis Sorrent hin. Der Vesuv war uns sichtbar, eine ungeheure Dampfwolke über ihm aufgetürmt, von der sich ostwärts ein langer Streif weit hinzog [...] Links lag Capri steil in die Höhe strebend; die Formen seiner Felswände konnten wir durch den durchsichtigen, bläulichen Dunst vollkommen unterscheiden. Unter einem ganz reinen, wolkenlosen Himmel glänzte das ruhige, kaum bewegte Meer, das bei einer völligen Windstille endlich wie ein klarer Teich vor uns lag. Wir entzückten uns an dem Anblick, Kniep trauerte daß alle Farbenkunst nicht hinreiche diese Harmonie wiederzugeben [...] ich ermunterte ihn Hand und Auge zum letztenmal anzustrengen; er ließ sich bereden und lieferte eine der genausten Zeichnungen die er nachher kolorierte und ein Beispiel zurückließ, daß bildlicher Darstellung das Unmögliche möglich wird. (*FA*, XV.1, 338–39)

> [Capo Minerva and the mountains adjacent to it lay before our eyes, enhanced by the most glowing colours, while the rocks extending down toward the south had already taken on a bluish tone. The whole illuminated coast stretched from the cape to Sorrento. We could see Vesuvius, over it a towering cloud of smoke, from which a long strip drew eastwards [...] Capri lay to the left, rising up steeply; we could distinguish the outlines of its rocky walls perfectly through the transparent bluish haze. Beneath a completely clear, cloudless sky sparkled the quiet, scarcely stirring sea, which eventually, in total calm, lay before us like a limpid pond. We were enraptured by this sight, Kniep lamented that paints could never be mixed skillfully enough to reproduce this harmony [...] I encouraged him to exert his eye and hand one more time. He let himself be persuaded and produced a very exact drawing, which afterwards he colored, and left an example of how the impossible becomes possible to pictorial representation.] (*CW*, VI, 251)

Goethe's enthusiasm about Kniep's achievement was such that he purchased the watercolour for his Weimar art collection (Fig. 3.1, *Bocca di Capri*).[22] Sicily is, indeed, 'the key to everything'. Goethe 'discovers' not only Lorrain and Homer in Sicily, but also colour.[23] For the first time on his Italian journey, colour is seen as *integral* to the landscape and to landscape painting, reflected, respectively, in the two statements, 'the most superb view' and 'the impossible becomes possible to pictorial

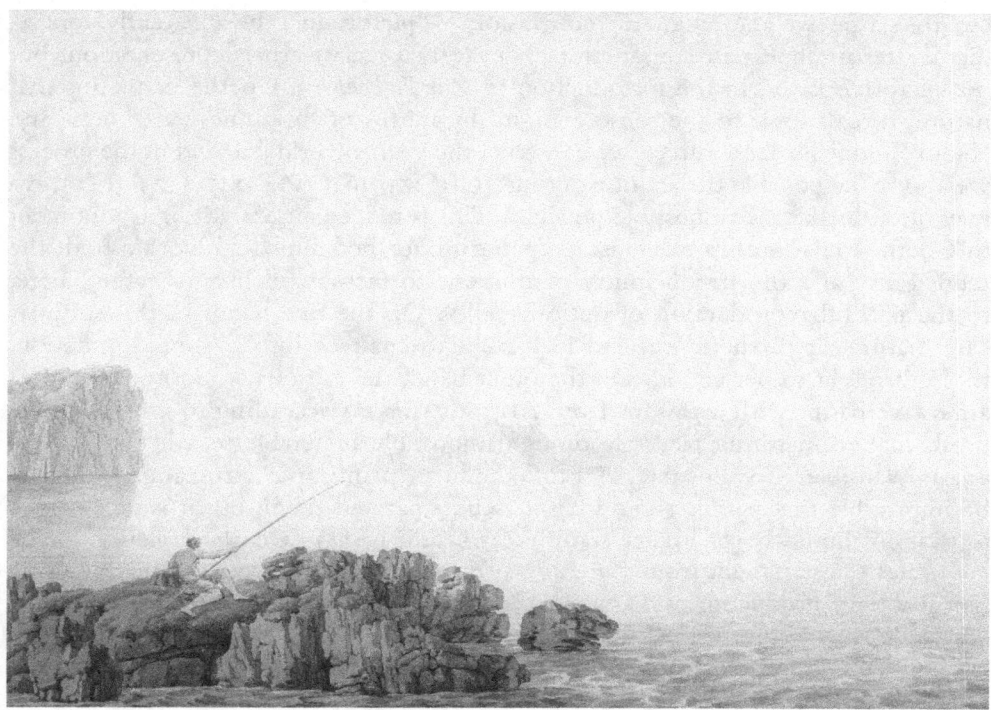

Fig. 3.1. Kniep, *Bocca di Capri*. Klassik Stiftung Weimar, Museen: 27998/ © Angelika Kittel

representation'. Before 'colour' and Goethe's experiential theory thereof start to preoccupy us, though, what we want to try to grasp here is Goethe's paradoxical encapsulation of his perceptual experience and pictorial transposition of Sicily.

What is it in this visual experience that 'enthuses' Goethe — a verb that, according to the *Goethe-Wörterbuch*, denotes, with reference to sight, a feeling so intense that the visual becomes visionary, that natural scenery effects spiritual ecstasy (*GW*, III, 207–09)? Conspicuously placed at the start of the description, it is the sunset and its spectacular colour that enkindles rapture. Beheld as a time of transition, it structures the ensuing description as the interplay of contrasts: day and night, gleaming and faint. In fact, beyond colour and light involving objects, atmosphere, perception, topography, or attributes, the correlation of opposites seems to underlie experience, landscape, and painting: nearby and faraway, water and fire, earth and air, transparent and murky, distinct and nebulous, static and dynamic, domesticated and wild, flat and steep, expansive and soaring. The disjunction in substance correlates with the disjunction in Kniep's painterly approach, sketching, and colouring; his execution correlates with 'darstellen', which, according to the *Goethe-Wörterbuch*, connotes 'to present' and 'to represent' (*GW*, II, 1079–81). Verbally, the disjunctive articulation of Goethe's landscape experience culminates in the oxymoronic 'to make the impossible possible'. However — and this is the key expression in

Goethe's assertive and enigmatic conclusion — 'pictorially', the apparently contradictory terms appear in conjunction. Nature may defy verbal representation, but not pictorial. Later, in the introduction to *Zur Farbenlehre*, Goethe maintains that nature 'reveals itself to the sense of sight' by means of 'brightness, darkness, and colour', and from these three, 'we construct the visible world [...], and in the process we also make possible the art of painting' (*CW*, XII, 164; *FA*, XXIII.1, 24) — or, we may infer, 'make the impossible possible'. This is indeed an extraordinary moment in Goethe's relationship to landscape painting, for he seems to advocate both the reducibility and the irreducibility of mimesis to factual fidelity, or rather, here, to the faithful reproduction of optical reality. On the one hand, in this singular case, nature, art, experience, and idea seem to coalesce into a 'simple imitation' that is brought to perfection. On the other hand, the curious oxymoron resonates almost verbatim with a passage from Aristotle's *Poetics* according to which 'poetic needs make something plausible though impossible preferable to what is possible but implausible'. To illustrate, Aristotle adduces painting as an example: 'It may be impossible that people should be as Zeuxis painted them, but it is ideal, since a paragon should be of higher stature' (25.1461b, p. 135). Goethe concurs, for he continues the statement from *Zur Farbenlehre* quoted above by saying that painting 'is capable of producing on canvas a visible world far more perfect than the real world' (*CW*, XII, 164; *FA*, XXIII.1, 24).

If Kniep entered the antechamber of style with his *Bocca di Capri* aquarelle, did Goethe's decision to give up his painterly pursuits reflect his realization that he could not 'transcend the possible' as stipulated in his programmatic essay? This is not the place to delve into the complexity of Goethe's conundrum, let alone offer an answer. Instead, a glance at Goethe's own praxis as a visual artist might identify, as Peter Hofmann does, *Dampfende Täler bei Ilmenau* [Mist above the Valleys near Ilmenau] (1776) and *Tempel am See bei tiefstehender Sonne* [Temple on a Lake at Sundown] (1806–10) as sketched correlates of simple imitation and style respectively.[24] Alternatively, if we consider colour, we might adduce *Bucht und Kastell bei Neapel* [Bay and Castle near Naples] (1787) as resonating with (Lorrainian) style.

We understand now that when Goethe, in Sicily, couched the landscapist's daunting task of winnowing and essentializing in the language of wishful thinking, he spoke as imitator-cum-stylist. As stated before, the plea to expunge the trivial from mind and drawing is coupled with the anticipation of what the 'queen of islands can do' (*CW*, VI, 188; *FA*, XV.1, 249). Indeed, she hears his appeal for inspiration. Joining Lorrain and Homer, Sicily becomes his muse.

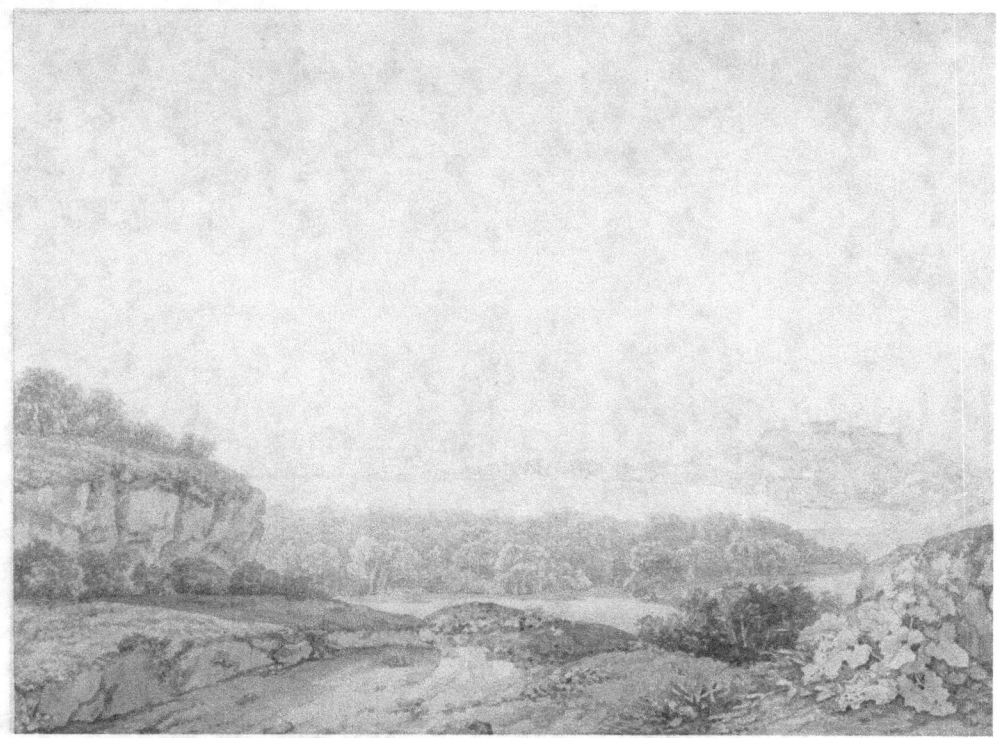

Fig. 3.2. Goethe, *Bucht und Kastell bei Neapel* [Bay and Castle near Naples]. Klassik Stiftung Weimar, Museen: 210521

3.4. Lorrain in Six Lines and One Monologue: *Nausikaa* and Faust's Arcadia

In the spring of 1787, in Taormina, Goethe absorbs 'well-chosen images as contours' and feels compelled

> to create for myself, on and out of this locality, a composition with a spirit and tone unlike anything I had yet produced. The clear sky, the breeze from the sea, the haze which, as it were, dissolves the mountains, sky, and sea into a single element, all of this sustained my project. (*CW*, VI, 238; *FA*, XV.1, 319)

The attempt at sketching a Lorrainian landscape is quickly abandoned for writing a Homeric tragedy on the subject of Nausicaa (*CW*, VI, 238; *FA*, XV.1, 320).[25] Goethe's plan was that the shipwrecked Odysseus would meet, fall for, and desert the Phaeacian Princess Nausicaa, who commits suicide. 'This simple plot was to be made pleasing by a wealth of subordinate themes and particularly by the special sea-and-island tone of the actual finished work' (*CW*, VI, 238; *FA*, XV.1, 320). The aperçu-like 'sea-and-island tone' evokes the hazy clarity enveloping heaven, sky, and earth of Goethe's experience of Sicily cited above. It is also reminiscent of Lorrain's *Seaport with the Embarkation of Ulysses from the Phaeacians* (1646; *LV*, 96).

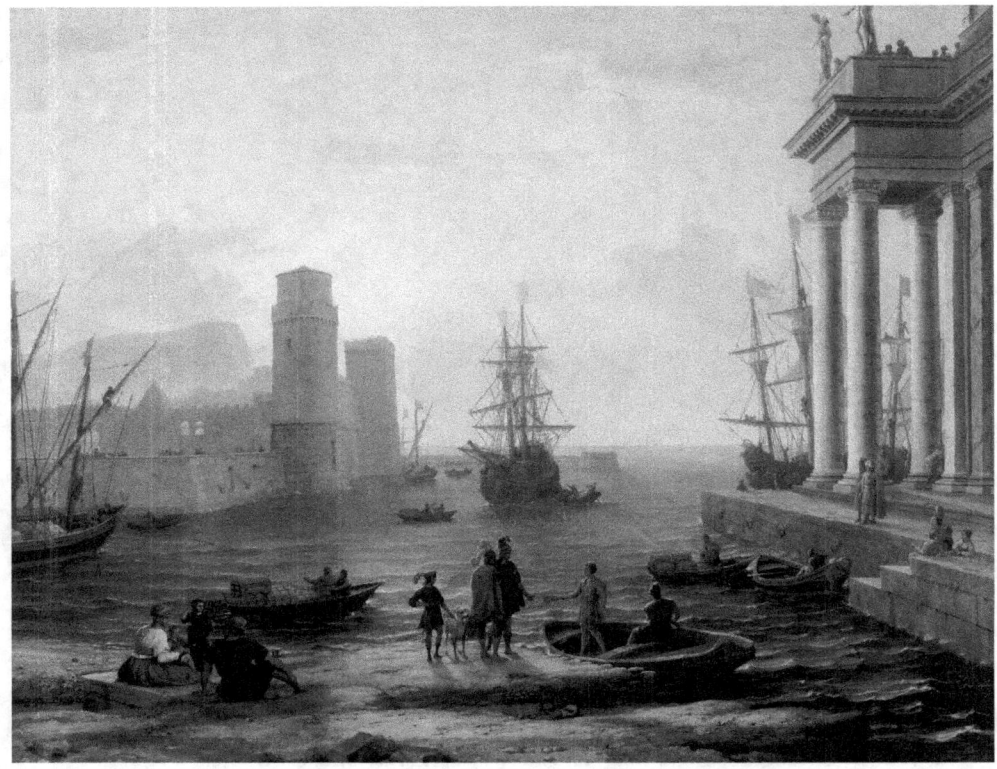

Fig. 3.3. Lorrain, *Seaport with the Embarkation of Ulysses from the Phaeacians*. Musée du Louvre, Paris/© RMN-Grand Palais — Thierry Le Mage — Art Resource, NY

When Ulysses sings the praises of Nausicaa's homeland, a few lines suffice to set the stage with scenery designed by Lorrain, Homer, and Sicily:

> Ein weißer Glanz ruht über Land und Meer,
> Und duftend schwebt der Äther ohne Wolken.
>
> Und nur die höchsten Nymphen des Gebirgs
> Erfreuen sich des leicht gefallnen Schnees
> Auf kurze Zeit.
>
> Und senden ewig frische Quell<en>. (*FA*, v, 1341)
>
> [A white sheen rests upon land and sea
> And the shimmering Aether hovers without a cloud.
>
> And but the highest mountain nymphs
> Amuse themselves in the lightly fallen snow
> For a brief moment.
>
> And launch eternally fresh fountain<s>.]

Read as an ekphrastic rendering of a landscape painting, these six lines of verse evoke an image of nature composed of tensions and harmonies. As striking as the image of snow amidst the radiance and warmth of the Mediterranean climate is, snow was endemic to Sicily. It left such an indelible impression that, in his nostalgic account in the *Italienische Reise*, Goethe couches the experience in the language of the sublime:

> Die Atmosphäre vor uns tief herab mit Wolken bedeckt, wobei sich ein wunderbar Phänomen in der größten Höhe sehen ließ. Es war weiß und grau gestreift und schien etwas Körperliches zu sein; aber wie käme das Körperliche in den Himmel! Unser Führer belehrte uns, diese unsere Verwunderung gelte einer Seite des Ätna, welche durch die zerrissenen Wolken durchsehe: Schnee und Bergrücken abwechselnd bildeten die Streifen, es sei nicht einmal der höchste Gipfel. (*FA*, xv.1, 306)

> [In front of us, the atmosphere was filled with very low-hanging clouds, whereupon a wonderful phenomenon appeared far above us. It was striped white and gray and seemed to be something physical; but how did something physical get into the sky? Our guide informed us that what was causing our astonishment was a side of Mt. Etna, which was showing through rents in the clouds: the stripes were formed by alternating ridges and snow; this was not even the highest peak.] (*CW*, vi, 228)

More striking still are the nymphs frolicking in the snow. Goethe interpolates nature and art by adapting motifs from Books vi and vii of the *Odyssey*, specifically the *locus amoenus* where female voices wake Odysseus as he encounters Nausicaa:

> Listen: shouting, echoing round me — women, girls —
> or the nymphs who haunt the rugged mountaintops
> and the river springs and meadows lush with grass![26] (vi. 134–36)

The anaphoric repetition of 'and' at the start of the second, third, and sixth lines in the *Nausicaa* passage is essential for this landscape that is both disjunctive and conjunctive. There is the obvious additive use of 'and', with the sense that the painting is a composition of various elements, such as mountains, snow, springs, and the nymphs as staffage introducing Antiquity. But there is more than enumeration to this litany; there is invocation, a summoning of the supernatural or, at least, an elicitation of awe in the listener or observer. Rhythmically and melodically, the last two 'and's echo the first two, which themselves evoke an ethereal, indeed otherworldly, vision. Yet, paradoxically, the conjunctions not only unite: they separate, setting up most notably a tectonic and temporal contrast between horizontal, 'sea', and vertical, 'mountain', between permanence, 'to rest', and transience, 'for a brief moment'. The contrast encompasses the atmospheric — luminous warmth and cloudy cold, with 'white' as the subtly implied link — and the metrical — the breaking of the hexametric symmetry by enjambment. Rhetorically, it is the oxymoron that encapsulates the juxtapositional dynamic: the 'eternally fresh' springs of water set in motion by the nymphs. Finally, the emphatic tone of the anaphoric 'and' shows the speaker's attachment to the surrounding nature, which, personified in the nymphs, beckons with erotic allure. As staffage, the petite nymphs blend in with, and enhance, the image of nature as actress.

Crediting a pictorial impulse to Lorrain, yet mindful of pushing the analogic envelope, the following is an attempt at interrelating Goethe's poetry and (an imagined Lorrain) painting. The iambic pentameter measures the seemingly endless diffusion of radiant light, just as the buildings and trees frame Lorrain's beaming sun, while the stanzaic pattern has its analogue in the tectonic pattern of the painting. Similar to Lorrain's vibrant stillness, the tranquillity of Goethe's landscape is both static and dynamic, as implied by the verbs 'to rest' and 'to hover', the latter modified by the present participle 'shimmering', capturing the tremulous essence of the sunlit air. Goethe meets Lorrain in the evocation of unity in diversity as well: 'land', 'sea', and 'Aether', which is synonymous with 'sky' (*GW*, 1, 883). The repetition of (untranslatable) vowel patterns forms a melodious string of assonances, 'ei–ei, a–a, e–e, u–u, o–o', which, together with the sonorous umlauts 'ü' and 'ä', almost dematerializes the material, were it not for the sibilant and plosive consonants, which tether the ethereal vowels to solid ground. If there is an 'airy', quasi-lyrical equivalence in Lorrain, it could be seen in the ways in which light suffuses that which exists in physically concrete form, be it mountain, sea, or tree. Finally, there is the light of the scenery's reflective surfaces — bright, with a steady yet subdued shining — which we recognize by now as the leitmotif interrelating the poetic and the pictorial landscapes, art and nature.

The Hellenic spirit of Sicily and Magna Graecia also suffuses the third act of *Faust II*, in which the eponymous hero, in his guise as imitator-cum-stylist, paints his own Arcadia.[27] Transported to a micro- and macrocosmic Hellenic realm, we witness the romance between Faust and Helena taking place here:

> Und sie [Fausts Ritter] beschützen um die Wette
> Ringsum von Wellen angehüpft,
> Nichtinsel dich, mit leichter Hügelkette
> Europens letztem Bergast angeknüpft.
> Das Land, vor aller Länder Sonnen
> Sei ewig jedem Stamm beglückt
> [...]
> Und duldet auch auf seiner Berge Rücken
> Das Zackenhaupt der Sonne kalten Pfeil,
> Läßt nun der Fels sich angegrünt erblicken,
> Die Ziege nimmt genäschig kargen Teil.
>
> Die Quelle springt, vereinigt stürzen Bäche,
> Und schon sind Schluchten, Hänge, Matten grün,
> Auf hundert Hügeln unterbrochner Fläche
> Siehst Wollenherden ausgebreitet ziehn.
>
> Verteilt, vorsichtig, abgemessen schreitet
> Gehörntes Rind hinan zum gähen Rand,
> Doch Obdach ist den sämtlichen bereitet,
> Zu hundert Höhlen wölbt sich Felsenwand.
>
> Pan schützt sie dort und Lebensnymphen wohnen
> In buschiger Klüfte feucht erfrischtem Raum,
> Und, sehnsuchtsvoll nach höhern Regionen,
> Erhebt sich zweighaft Baum gedrängt an Baum.

Alt-Wälder sind's! die Eiche starret mächtig
Und eigensinnig zackt sich Ast an Ast;
Der Ahorn mild, von süßem Safte trächtig,
Steigt rein empor und spielt mit seiner Last.

Und mütterlich im stillen Schattenkreise
Quillt laue Milch bereit für Kind und Lamm;
Obst ist nicht weit, der Ebnen reife Speise,
Und Honig trieft vom ausgehöhlten Stamm.

Hier ist das Wohlbehagen erblich,
Die Wange heitert wie der Mund,
Ein jeder ist an seinem Platz unsterblich:
Sie sind zufrieden und gesund.

Und so entwickelt sich am reinen Tage
Zu Vaterkraft das holde Kind.
Wir staunen drob; noch immer bleibt die Frage:
Ob's Götter, ob es Menschen sind?

So war Apoll den Hirten zugestaltet
Daß ihm der schönsten einer glich;
Denn wo Natur im reinen Kreise waltet
Ergreifen alle Welten sich.

Neben ihr sitzend

So ist es mir, so ist es dir gelungen,
Vergangenheit sey hinter uns gethan;
O fühle dich vom höchsten Gott entsprungen,
Der ersten Welt gehörst du einzig an.

Nicht feste Burg soll dich umschreiben!
Noch zirkt, in ewiger Jugendkraft
Für uns, zu wonnevollem Bleiben,
Arkadien in Sparta's Nachbarschaft.

Gelockt auf seligem Grund zu wohnen
Du flüchtetest in's heiterste Geschick!
Zur Laube wandeln sich die Thronen,
Arkadisch frei sey unser Glück!

Der Schauplatz verwandelt sich durchaus. An eine Reihe von Felsenhöhlen lehnen sich geschlossene Lauben. Schattiger Hain bis an die rings umgebende Felsensteile hinan. (ll. 9510–73)

[And they [Faust's vassals] will eagerly protect
this almost-island in the dancing waves
that by a slender chain of hills
is linked to Europe's outmost mountain spur!
May every nation share the joys
of this, the sunniest land of all
[...]
Although its jagged heights and ridges
must be content with cold rays from the sun,

one still can glimpse rocks tinged with green
and goats that forage for their scanty fare.

A spring wells forth, the streams unite and plunge,
and soon ravines and slopes and meadows all are green.
Upon the many hills that dot the plain
you see spread out the moving flocks of sheep.

Cattle, careful not to crowd each other,
come singly to the precipice's edge;
still, there is shelter for them all within
the many caves that arch the walls of rock.

Pan guards them there, while nymphs as living creatures dwell
in the moist freshness of shrub-filled ravines
and, in their urgent search for air and light,
the close-set trees raise high their heavy branches.

Primeval woods! The mighty oak stands motionless
with boughs that branch capriciously;
the generous maple with its sugar-sap
rises uncluttered and bears its weight with ease.

And in the shaded stillness the warm flow
of mother's milk provides for lamb and child;
on nearby plains ripe fruit is found,
and honey trickles from the hollow branch.

Contentment is a birthright here,
and cheerful cheek and lips express serenity;
all are immortal where they are,
for they are satisfied, are healthy.

And so, in this untroubled brightness,
each precious child attains maturity.
We see this miracle, and are compelled to ask:
must these be gods, or are they mortal men?

Among the shepherds here, and in their guise,
Apollo was no fairer than the fairest,
for when the sway of nature is unhindered,
all realms of being merge as one.

(*He seats himself beside* HELENA.)

Now that we have achieved this oneness,
let what is past be past forever!
Remember the high god who gave you being,
that only in this primal world do you belong!

No mighty fortress need confine you!
Arcadia, while near to Sparta,
is a domain of ever-youthful vigor
where we can dwell in perfect bliss.

> When we were lured to flee to this fair soil
> fate granted you its greatest favor!
> Our thrones shall now become a bower,
> our happiness Arcadian and free!

The stage set changes completely. Enclosed arbors rest against a series of grottos. A SHADED GROVE *extends to the cliffs that rise on all sides.*]

If the prerequisite for approximating style involves curtailing the subjective for the sake of representing the objective, then most stanzas represent an 'actuality' that seems to exist independent of a lyric 'I'. Even in those instances where an individual perception manifests itself, it is part of a dialogic interaction with an 'objective' interlocutor, as for instance in the verse 'As I succeeded, so did you' — an 'objectivization' enhanced, grammatically speaking, by the use of an impersonal dative construction.[28] Similarly, universal taxonomic units, whether in the singular (e.g. 'father' or 'child') or in the plural ('gods' and 'humans') — with the accumulation in list form of 'ravines', 'slopes', and 'meadows' amplifying the generic quality — predominate over particular 'individualities' identified by nomenclature (e.g. 'Apollo', 'maple', or 'goat').

If style thrives on the tension created by the juxtaposition of contrasting elements, then the dynamic interplay between the subjective and the objective is but one manifestation of this. In fact, Faust makes abundant use of it. Focusing on motifs, examples include: 'hill' and 'cave' contrast with each other (their multiplication by a 'hundred' suggests a numerical link between polar opposites, sonorously corroborated by the echo of alliteration in the German; ll. 9532, 9537); the vertical collocates with the horizontal in 'plunging streams' and 'spreading flocks' (ll. 9530, 9533); the peril implied by 'precipice' is offset by the reassuring prospect of 'shelter' (ll. 9535–36); the static quality conveyed by 'stand motionless' is juxtaposed with the dynamic quality intrinsic to 'rise' or 'play' (ll. 9542, 9545); and, finally, the juxtaposition that is quintessential to Goethe's conception of the symbol is the coincidence of the particular and the universal ('Each is immortal in his sphere'; l. 9552). As this sample proves, and as our study has shown, poetically and pictorially, landscape is a function of the interplay between *natura* and *ars*, or, roughly speaking, between the imitation of optical reality and the self-conscious deployment of artistic means. The first glimpse that Faust offers of his landscape is telling. He describes it as a 'ringsum von Wellen angehüpft[e]' 'Nichtinsel [...] mit leichter Hügelkette' [almost-island in the dancing waves with a slender chain of hills] (ll. 9511–12). The naturalism of the waves 'dancing', or literally 'leaping upon', the shore of the peninsula is juxtaposed with the artifice of, literally, 'not-island', an archaic synonym for 'headland' or 'peninsula', which, however, begins to make poetic sense once we hear the line's consonant pattern echoed in the 'ich' sound three times. The reliance of *ars* on rhetoric comes to the fore in other respects, too: for instance, in 'wool' as a metonym for 'sheep' (l. 9533), or in the 'g–h–r' alliteration and the 'Rind'–'Rand' consonance in the lines 'schreitet | Gehörntes Rind hinan zum gähen Rand' [Horned cattle inch closer to the edge of the steep cliff] (ll. 9534–35). In the line 'In freshly moistened bushy clefts', the physicality of sight and touch, or even (subliminally erotic as the image is) taste and smell, is held in tension by the laboured syntax of the poetic genitive and the conceptual properties of both 'gulf' and 'area' (l. 9539). Even the 'question' of 'whether' Arcadia's inhabitants 'are gods or humans' is a rhetorical one (ll. 9556–57). It is answered in the subsequent stanza's image of Apollo being 'fashioned into the form' of a shepherd, which is literally to be *seen*, as the next couplet reveals, as an instantiation of the notion of the pantheistic interrelatedness of the divine and the human (ll. 9558–61). Hypostatization is also involved in the interplay between the notional and the actual, i.e. in the way that a 'concept' is rendered 'perceptible', as is the case, for instance, in the visualization of 'contentment' in the smile, the 'brightening up', expressed by 'cheek' and 'mouth' (ll. 9550–51). Emotive response to nature and rhetorical transposition feed into each other in the stanza starting with 'Primeval woods!'. Articulating the epiphany as an exclamation, the speaker's excitement is offset by the noticeable use of the alliterative and assonant 'a' (including its umlauted manifestation), as if to produce a sonic encapsulation of (Greek) <u>Arkadía</u> by rhetorical means (ll. 9542–45). Given the intricate and complex fabric of juxtapositions and visual and sonic harmonies, and given that this dynamic interplay culminates in the epithet 'serene',[29] Faust leads us, at it were, into a Lorrainian landscape, much like the one Goethe saw when visiting the Dresden Picture Gallery in 1794. It bears the title *Coast View with Acis and Galatea* (1657; *LV*, 141). Goethe possessed an etched version of it, and considered it 'one of the most beautifully composed' paintings (*FA*, xviii, 306).[30]

Lorrain follows the mythological story, as told by Galatea in Book XIII of Ovid's *Metamorphoses*, quite closely:

> A wedge-shaped promontory with long, sharp point juts out into the sea, both sides washed by the waves. Hither the fierce Cyclops climbed and sat down on the cliff's central point, and his woolly sheep, all unheeded, followed him. Then, laying at his feet the pine-trunk which served him for a staff, fit for a vessel's mast, he took his pipe made of a hundred reeds. All the mountains felt the sound of his rustic pipings; the waves felt it too. I, hiding beneath a rock and resting in my Acis' arm, at a great distance heard the words he sang. (pp. 283–85)

Polyphemus tries to lure Galatea away from Acis by enchanting her with a vivid description of an Arcadian world made up of familiar motifs, culminating in the vision of a paradisal land where, as he puts it, echoing the Bible, 'snow-white milk' flows and fruit grows in abundance (Ovid, pp. 285–87). Faust harks back to this iconic image almost verbatim (ll. 9546–49). Yet, as Polyphemus's siren song falls on deaf ears, his strategy changes from allure to attack. He brutally kills Acis. Galatea, doing 'the only thing that fate allowed' her, 'caused Acis to assume his ancestral powers', for 'suddenly a youth stood forth waist-deep from the water'. It 'was Acis, changed to a river-god' (Ovid, p. 291). Eschewing, as usual, the depiction of violence, Lorrain leaves it to the observer to recognize the thundery storm clouds and the wind-lashed waves as pictorial metaphors for Polyphemus's brutal rage when Galatea spurns him. Ovid's and Lorrain's Arcadias are fraught with premonitions of doom. From its inception, the Arcadian topos had featured death, most notably in Poussin's famous landscape *The Arcadian Shepherds* (1637–38), in which a sarcophagus

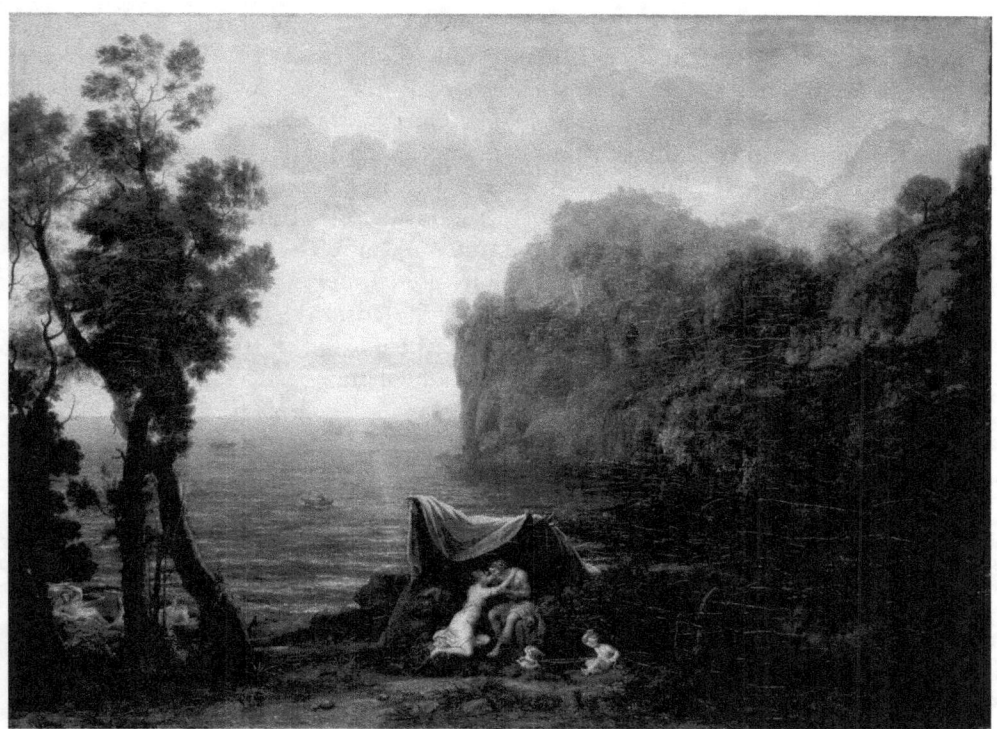

Fig. 3.4. Lorrain, *Coast View with Acis and Galatea*. Gemäldegalerie Alte Meister, Staatliche Kunstsammlungen, Dresden; © bpk Bildagentur — Ursula Maria Hoffmann — Art Resource, NY

bears the inscription 'Et in Arcadia ego' [Even in Arcadia I [death] am present].[31] In Ovid, the tension is played out in the death and resurrection of Acis, while in Lorrain, the dynamic interplay of tranquillity and storm creates an atmosphere of anxiety and excitement. He pits shelter against exposure, light against darkness, heaven against hell, the lyrical against the discordant. This dialectic generates a landscape that is both mythic and real, Arcadian and awe-inspiring.

While resounding with descriptive and verbatim echoes from Ovid, Faust's ekphrasis captures Lorrain's painting with regard to both composition and mood. Like Lorrain, Faust starts his composition at the horizon formed by the 'chain of hills' protruding into the ocean, capped by the 'jagged summit', and then shifts, topographically, layer by layer, from the middle ground to the foreground, where we finally encounter the miniature staffage figures, thus allowing nature to take pride of place. Natural elements are the subjects, and the verbs used drive home the point, almost obtrusively, that it is nature which acts. With an array of action verbs ranging from to 'leap upon' to 'environ', Faust generates the stately dynamism that we identified as an effect of the aesthetics of style. His trees, for instance, are rather like Lorrain's on the left in *Coast View*, reaching for the skies with meticulously delineated leaves, branches, and trunks: 'in their urgent search for air and light, | the close-set trees raise high their heavy branches' (ll. 9540–41). It is not only vegetative nature that acts, but human nature too: the infant in the painting frolics in front of the makeshift shelter; Faust's 'child attains maturity' (ll. 9554–55). The verbal energy is paired with a kind of hyper-realism, which in turn is paired with a kind of hyper-idealism. If the example just quoted is an allusion to procreation, it would be an innocent act, for it would happen 'on a pure day' involving a 'fair' or 'holy' child (ll. 9554–55). Similarly, the maple that is 'pregnant with sweet sap rises aloft in purity', as if the pregnancy were the result of an immaculate conception (ll. 9544–45). The only epithet used three times — 'pure' — acquires the axiomatic significance of a Goethean archetype, for it interconnects all living organisms or spheres, including (in its third manifestation) the cosmos: 'for when the sway of nature is unhindered | all realms of being merge as one' (ll. 9560–61). The three figures forming the centre of Lorrain's foreground can be read as an allusive staging of a nativity scene, which, at the same time, lies on the axis formed by the sun's rays, and thus extends into the celestial sphere. The Chorus in *Faust* describes the 'nativity' of Euphorion, the offspring of Faust and Helena, in metamorphic imagery as the birth of a butterfly soaring into the ether:

> Gleich dem fertigen Schmetterling
> Der aus dem starren Puppenzwang
> Flügel entfaltend behendig schlüpft
> Sonne durchstrahlten Äther kühn
> Und mutwillig durchflatternd. (ll. 9657–61)

> [Like a butterfly ready for life
> and unfolding its wings as it agilely
> slips from pupal confinement
> and ventures, wantonly fluttering,
> into the sunlit air's radiance.]

The wanton body language of Lorrain's child corresponds to Euphorion's wanton flight — expressed in the breathlessness of enjambed, punctuation-free verses — ominously foreboding his Icarus-like death. If the death of Euphorion signals the death of poetry (i.e. Byronic poetry), does it also signal the death of Arcadia?

The dialectic of birth and death also underlies Faust's pictorialization of the sun. While Lorrain's sun may be straining against dark clouds, it still makes its light felt throughout the painting. Faust's ekphrasis is marked by its absence, or rather, by a remarkable reduction of its light and warmth to a menacing 'cold arrow'. Amplifying the flickering light in the upper right-hand corner of Lorrain's painting, the martial image points to the militarism associated with Sparta. Since Faust's landscape poem begins with the 'arrow' and ends with 'Sparta', his Arcadia is framed by the threat of war. Yet, in verses leading up to his Arcadian landscape, Faust likens Helena to the sun:

> Das Land, vor aller Länder Sonnen
> Sei ewig jedem Stamm beglückt,
> Nun meiner Königin gewonnen,
> Das früh an ihr hinauf geblickt.

> Als, mit Eurotas Schilfgeflüster,
> Sie [Helena] leuchtend aus der Schale brach,
> Der hohen Mutter [Leda], dem Geschwister
> Das Licht der Augen überstach. (ll. 9514–21)

> [May every nation share the joys
> of this, the sunniest land of all,
> that now is conquered for my queen,
> to whom it lifted once its eyes

> when as Eurotas' rushes whispered,
> she [Helena] burst resplendent from the shell
> to dazzle her royal mother's [Leda's] eyes
> and those of her two brothers also.]

The likeness is complex. As 'leuchtend' or effulgent as the light radiating from Helena may be, it is also 'stinging' or 'blinding' — the Grimms' *Wörterbuch* defines 'überstechen' (which Goethe uses in the simple past form, 'überstach') as 'to be dazzled by brilliant light' (XXIII, 572). As unexpected as this dichotomous sun imagery may be in the context of the Italian journey, in *Faust* it is not new. In fact, *Faust II* opens with Faust turning away from the 'blinding' light of the sun and toward its reflection in the rainbow, which he perceives as life's 'many-hued reflection' (ll. 4702, 4727).[32] Poetically, in Faust's Arcadia, the sensation of pain is evinced by its rhyming antecedent, 'brach' [broke], which, despite its suggestion of material harm, is part of the imagery of Helena's 'radiant' mythic birth. Moreover, the imagery's inherent dialectic is enhanced by the sonic alternation of feminine and masculine rhymes.

We cannot enter here into a discussion of Helena's symbolism in *Faust*, but Goethe's dialogue with Lorrain opens up a new and intriguing layer of meaning. In the broader context of *Faust*'s 'Hellenic' realm — Goethe called its poetic enactment a 'classical-Romantic phantasmagoria' (*FA*, VII.1, 790)[33] — in which Faust evokes his Arcadia, there is a deeper connection between painting and poetry, the mirroring of Galatea and Faust, and of Homunculus and Helena. Homunculus figures as a test-tube humanoid whose wish it is to 'obtain a body' (l. 8252). Galatea, the drama's amphibian incarnation of natural beauty,[34] brings about Homunculus's metamorphosis into water, while Faust, so to speak, brings about Helena's metamorphosis into earth. Seeking advice on how to embody himself, Homunculus is told by two ancient philosophers: 'Nature! Nature!' (l. 7837), which, on the one hand, echoes to the letter the advice given to the novice painter in Goethe's art theoretical mini-drama written in Rome and entitled *Künstlers Apotheose* [The Artist's Apotheosis] (*FA*, V, 724, l. 61); on the other hand, it echoes in spirit the advice given to Faust, the novice poet. When Faust goes in search of Helena in an imaginary Antiquity, he is told that she is but an idea that must be brought into existence: 'Ganz eigen ist's mit mythologischer Frau; | Der Dichter bringt sie, wie er's braucht zur Schau' [A woman, in mythology, is an exception | whom poets introduce in any way they want] (ll. 7428–29). To this, Faust replies:

> Und sollt ich nicht, sehnsüchtiger Gewalt,
> Ins Leben ziehn die einzigste Gestalt?
> Das ewige Wesen, Göttern ebenbürtig,
> So groß als zart, so hehr als liebenswürdig?
> [...]
> Ich lebe nicht, kann ich sie nicht erlangen. (ll. 7438–45)

> [And shall not I, sustained by poignant longing,
> endow this perfect form with life —
> this timeless being, the true peer of gods,
> tender but grand, august yet gracious too?
> [...]
> and I shall die unless I make her mine.]

'Realizing' Helena is Faust's new project, another ideal in his quest for his own self-realization, and as before — say in his pursuit of the ideal that he made Gretchen represent for him — pursuing it is a matter of life and death, that is to say, he will not rest until he succeeds in 'reaching' it. It is crucial to recognize the ambiguity of the relevant verb: 'erlangen' has intellectual and physical properties insofar as it means 'to achieve' and 'to lay one's hands on'. In his pursuit of Helena, Faust does not differentiate between the two: Arcadia is both abstract and concrete. Just as Pygmalion implores Venus to bring Galatea to life, Faust summons the spirit of Lorrain to 'draw' Helena 'into life', to 'make' her 'perceivable'. And, like Pygmalion, who carved Galatea from a lump of ivory, Faust carves Helena out of a shapeless 'non-island'. Through the transformation of non-island into island, land into landscape, peninsula into Arcadia, Helena becomes embodied as a landscape painting, with a 'form' and 'essence' calling to mind Lorrain. If Helena represents archetypal female beauty, she also comes to represent here archetypal scenic beauty; the common denominator between the two archetypes lies in the epithet 'unique', which is used in reference to her 'form' (l. 9324) and to 'Arcadia' (l. 9565). Significantly, Lynceus, Faust's lookout smitten with Helena's beauty, uses 'unique' on two occasions, one of which involves the phrase 'unique form', which is familiar from the formula Faust uses to 'actualize' Helena: 'to draw into life her unique form' (ll. 9229, 9324, 7439).

The congruence of Helena and landscape begins with the image of her birth, which coincides, in Faust's evocation, with the birth of Arcadia. In a vague allusion to Lorrain's painting, where we see, in the lower left, sea nymphs frolicking after they have brought to shore Galatea in her 'seashell chariot', Helena, as Faust recounts, 'burst from the shell', hatched from the egg laid by Leda on 'Eurotas' whispering rushes' (ll. 8144, 9518–19). The identification is corroborated by the language, specifically the use of the personal pronoun 'du' [you] for Helena. As is typical of Goethe's ekphrastic rendering of landscape, Helena is both subject 'du' and object 'dich', figuratively captured in the as-yet shapeless 'non-island'. But as her manifestation as island is completed, 'du' and 'dich' become sublated into the wholeness of Helena's Arcadian substantiation, marked by the coincidence of 'primal world' and 'uniqueness': 'Remember the high god who gave you being, | that only in this primal world do you belong!' (ll. 9564–65). Arcadia may be singular, as 'uniquely' suggests, but, as we have seen before, in Goethe's ekphrasis the creator inscribes himself in his creation, signalled here by 'we' and its derivatives, 'us' and 'our'. Mephistopheles, disguised as the female hag Phorcyas, seemingly affected by Faust's conjuration of Arcadian oneness, and as if extrapolating from the Lorrain painting, characterizes the Arcadian bivouac as a 'canopy' of safe keeping: 'Here [...] was provided | for our lord and for our lady, just as for idyllic lovers, | shelter and security' (ll. 9586–88). Phorcyas's recalling of the pastoral tradition through the use of simile reminds us once more of the interplay of nature and art that underlies Faust's Arcadia.

The power of his imagination notwithstanding, there is little permanence to Faust's landscape painting, signalled by the paradox of its temporal contingency, existing both 'for the time being' and with 'ever-youthful vigor' (l. 9567). It seems to have the stability of a vision. Both Faust and Helena call it a 'dream' (l. 9883), from which, for Faust, 'time and space have fled', and in which, for Helena, 'beauty and happiness can form no lasting union' (ll. 9414, 9940). As the curtain falls on Arcadia, Goethe leaves his readers guessing as to Arcadia's 'reality'. On the one hand, it could be smoke and mirrors, a 'phantasmagoria' produced by the play's master illusionist, Mephistopheles:

> Der Vorhang fällt.
> PHORKYAS
> *Im Proszenium richtet sich riesenhaft auf, tritt von den Kothurnen herunter, lehnt Maske und Schleier zurück und zeigt sich als Mephistopheles, um, in sofern es nötig wäre, im Epilog das Stück zu kommentieren.* (stage directions after l. 10,038)
>
> [*The curtain falls.* PHORKYAS, *in the proscenium, rises to a gigantic height, then steps down from the cothurni, pushes back mask and veil, and stands revealed as* MEPHISTOPHELES, *prepared to comment on the play, as much as may be necessary, in an epilogue.*]

On the other hand, when Helena joins the dead Euphorion in Hades, she leaves behind her garment and her veil — the metaphorical embodiment of the idea of Arcadia as a 'serene' landscape.

As a landscapist, is Faust a latter-day Kniep who makes the impossible possible? In the landscape's sublation of the primeval and the transcendent, natural verisimilitude and artistic truth do not blend but are interlocked in a dynamics of irreducible polar opposites. Blending them would be too facile a solution to the nature–art dilemma. It would be but a 'beautiful semblance', shiny yet hollow. With Euphorion as enlivening staffage, the landscape evokes a related sublation. Goethe associated Euphorion with Lord Byron, whom he saw as 'the representative of the modern poetical era' because he sublated the 'antique' and the 'Romantic', elaborating that 'his pictures have an air of reality, as lightly thrown off as if they were improvised', citing as examples his 'sea scenes, with a sail peeping out here and there [making] us feel the sea-breeze blowing'.[35] If this is an instance of the suspension of disbelief or, similarly, making the impossible possible — if Byron is, while rarely 'serene', always 'poetic' (*CV*, p. 210; *FA*, xxxix, 250) — the Lorrainian echoes resound unmistakably. With them comes the realization that Lorrain is now part of the much larger aesthetic debate on classicism and romanticism. One can argue that Lorrain, just like Byron, in Goethe's curious 'sublative' wording, 'is not antique and is not Romantic' — with the 'and' reminding us of the sublative 'and' in *natura et ars*. Goethe's well-known, indeed notorious, differentiation between classical and Romantic art is, it turns out, also a statement about landscape painting:

> Das Antike ist nüchtern, modest, gemäßigt, das Moderne ganz zügellos, betrunken. Das Antike erscheint nur ein idealisiertes Reales, ein mit Großheit (Stil) und Geschmack behandeltes Reales; das Romantische ein Unwirkliches, Unmögliches, dem durch die Phantasie nur ein Schein des Wirklichen gegeben wird. Das Antike ist plastisch, wahr und reell; das Romantische täuschend wie die Bilder einer Zauberlaterne.[36]
>
> [Classical art is sober, modest, measured; modern art is completely unbridled, intoxicated. Classical art has only the appearance of being an idealized real, a reality transmuted by a highly developed sense of style and taste; Romantic art seems unreal, impossible, the imagination gives it only the appearance of being real. Classical art is plastic, true, and realistic; Romantic art is illusionary like the images of a magic lantern.]

The nature–art duality and the question of balancing the two is of foundational importance for the English Garden, which engaged Goethe both as a horticulturalist and as a writer. Since eighteenth-century garden art regarded Lorrain as the father of the *jardin anglais*, the dialogue between Lorrain and Goethe had a new topic of focus. The other major topic concerned colour and its proper handling in painting. It is striking that Faust's Arcadia is, were it not for 'green', colourless, while the Arcadias of Ovid and Lorrain pulsate with the full palette of Goethe's famous colour circle — as does the last poetic fruit of the Italian journey, which we analyse in the next and final section of this chapter.

3.5. *Natura et Ars* as Comedy: 'Amor ein Landschaftsmaler'

> Amor ein Landschaftsmaler (1788)
>
> Saß ich früh auf einer Felsenspitze,
> Sah mit starren Augen in den Nebel,
> Wie ein grau grundiertes Tuch gespannet,
> Deckt' er alles in die Breit' und Höhe.
>
> Stellt' ein Knabe sich mir an die Seite,
> Sagte: Lieber Freund, wie magst du starrend
> Auf das leere Tuch gelassen schauen?
> Hast du denn zum Malen und zum Bilden
> Alle Lust auf ewig wohl verloren?
>
> Sah ich an das Kind, und dachte heimlich:
> Will das Bübchen doch den Meister machen!
>
> Willst du immer trüb' und müssig bleiben,
> Sprach der Knabe, kann nichts kluges werden:
> Sieh, ich will dir gleich ein Bildchen malen,
> Dich ein hübsches Bildchen malen lehren.

Und er richtete den Zeigefinger,
Der so rötlich war wie eine Rose,
Nach dem weiten ausgespannten Teppich,
Fing mit seinem Finger an zu zeichnen:

Oben malt' er eine schöne Sonne,
Die mir in die Augen mächtig glänzte,
Und den Saum der Wolken macht' er golden,
Ließ die Strahlen durch die Wolken dringen;
Malte dann die zarten leichten Wipfel
Frisch erquickter Bäume, zog die Hügel,
Einen nach dem andern frei dahinter;
Unten ließ er's nicht an Wasser fehlen,
Zeichnete den Fluß so ganz natürlich,
Daß er schien im Sonnenstrahl zu glitzern,
Daß er schien am hohen Rand zu rauschen.

Ach da standen Blumen an dem Flusse,
Und da waren Farben auf der Wiese,
Gold und Schmelz und Purpur und ein Grünes,
Alles wie Smaragd und wie Karfunkel!
Hell und rein lasiert er drauf den Himmel
Und die blauen Berge fern und ferner:
Daß ich ganz entzückt und neu geboren
Bald den Maler, bald das Bild beschaute.

Hab' ich doch, so sagt' er, dir bewiesen,
Daß ich dieses Handwerk gut verstehe;
Doch es ist das schwerste noch zurücke.

Zeichnete danach mit spitzem Finger
Und mit großer Sorgfalt an dem Wäldchen,
G'rad an's Ende, wo die Sonne kräftig
Von dem hellen Boden wiederglänzte,
Zeichnete das allerliebste Mädchen,
Wohlgebildet, zierlich angekleidet,
Frische Wangen unter braunen Haaren,
Und die Wangen waren von der Farbe,
Wie das Fingerchen, das sie gebildet.

O du Knabe, rief ich, welch ein Meister
Hat in seine Schule dich genommen,
Daß du so geschwind und so natürlich
Alles klug beginnst und gut vollendest?

Da ich noch so rede, sieh, da rühret
Sich ein Windchen, und bewegt die Gipfel,
Kräuselt alle Wellen auf dem Flusse,
Füllt den Schleier des vollkommnen Mädchens,
Und, was mich Erstaunten mehr erstaunte,
Fängt das Mädchen an, den Fuß zu rühren,
Geht zu kommen, nähert sich dem Orte.
Wo ich mit dem losen Lehrer sitze.

Da nun alles, alles sich bewegte,
Bäume, Fluß und Blumen und der Schleier
Und der zarte Fuß der Allerschönsten;
Glaubt ihr wohl, ich sei auf meinem Felsen,
Wie ein Felsen, still und fest geblieben? (*FA*, 1, 351–53)

[Amor as Landscape Painter

Sat upon a rocky peak at daybreak,
Staring fix-eyed through the mist before me;
Stretched like canvas primed with gray it mantled
Everything on either side and upward.

A little boy now came and stood beside me;
Friend, he said, I wonder what you're up to,
Peering, supine, at that empty canvas.
Might you have lost for now, if not for ever,
Pleasure in painting, shaping out an image?

Glancing at the child, I thought in secret:
Perhaps the boy thinks he can act the master.

If you sit there, sullen, doing nothing,
Said the boy, no good will be the outcome.
Watch, I'll paint a smidgeon of a picture
Now, for you, a pretty one to learn from.

Then he lifted up his index finger,
Which was quite as rosy as a rose is;
Pointing to the fabric stretched before him,
Now the boy began to trace a picture.

At the top a beauteous sun he painted,
I was almost blinded by the dazzle;
Borders of the clouds, he made them golden,
Rays of sun to perforate the cloud mass;
Painted then the delicate and tender
Tops of freshly quickened trees, with hillocks
Touched into place and freely grouped behind them;
Lower down — water he put, and plenty,
Drew the river, as it is in nature,
So much so, it seemed to glint with sunlight
And murmur as it rose against its edges.

Ah, beside the river flowers sprouted,
And the meadow was a blaze of colour,
Gold, enamel sheen, a green, and crimson,
All aglow like emerald and carbuncle.
Bright and clear, above, he glazed the sky in,
Mountains, blue, receding in the distance,
So that born anew I looked, ecstatic,
Now upon the painter, now the picture.

You'll admit, says he, I've demonstrated
This is handiwork I have some skill in;

The hardest part is still to come, however.

Then, with pointing fingertip and very
Solicitously, by the little forest,
Right on the brink of it, where sunlight gathered
To be reflected off the shining humus,
He traced the loveliest girl you could set eyes on,
Pretty figure, and a graceful garment,
Cheeks a fresh complexion, all around them
Tawny hair, and more, the cheeks were tinted
Like the tiny finger that had shaped them.

Little boy, I now exclaimed, what master
Can it be who took you as his pupil,
That your designs should be so swift, so clever,
And finished, as by nature, to perfection?

Even as I'm speaking, look, a zephyr
Gently stirs, it agitates the treetops,
Ruffles all the river into wavelets,
Fills the filmy robe that she is wearing,
The perfect girl, amazed I am, and more so
When she starts to set her feet in motion,
And she moves, she walks, she's coming this way
To where I sit beside my wicked teacher.

Now everything, but everything was moving,
Trees, the flowers, filmy robe, the river,
Delicate feet of the girl in all her beauty —
Do you think I sat so calm and steadfast
Rocklike on my rock a moment longer?] (*CW*, 1, 99–101)

The master of the school that the poem's painter attended, is, we intend to argue, Claude Lorrain. In fact, it has been claimed that one of the latter's most accomplished paintings that Goethe may have seen while in Rome — the 1648 *Landscape with Dancing Figures* (*LV*, 113), widely known as *The Mill*, in the Galleria Doria Pamphilj (Fig. 3.5) — may have served as an inspiration for 'Amor ein Landschaftsmaler'.[37]

There are, however, other 'riverscapes' by Lorrain, not to mention the differences both small and large (e.g. the flowers, architecture, position of the sun). It is probably more useful to regard the landscape in 'Amor ein Landschaftsmaler' as generically Lorrainian, especially in terms of compositional elements and techniques, which Goethe seems to emphasize. The risk involved in deploying the notion of the generic is that it might suggest a kind of construction kit from which pieces are plucked in order to assemble the landscape. The poem's casual style and bantering tone may be read as fitting the generic substance. Yet, as we shall see, the poem is about deception and duplicity, and that applies to its language, too.

The poem creates, or allows us to witness the creation of, a landscape painting and its effect on the observer, while at the same time embedding Lorrain's art in a broad aesthetic discussion and making it its cornerstone, its testing ground. The discussion centres on the conundrum of whether, in landscape painting, nature and

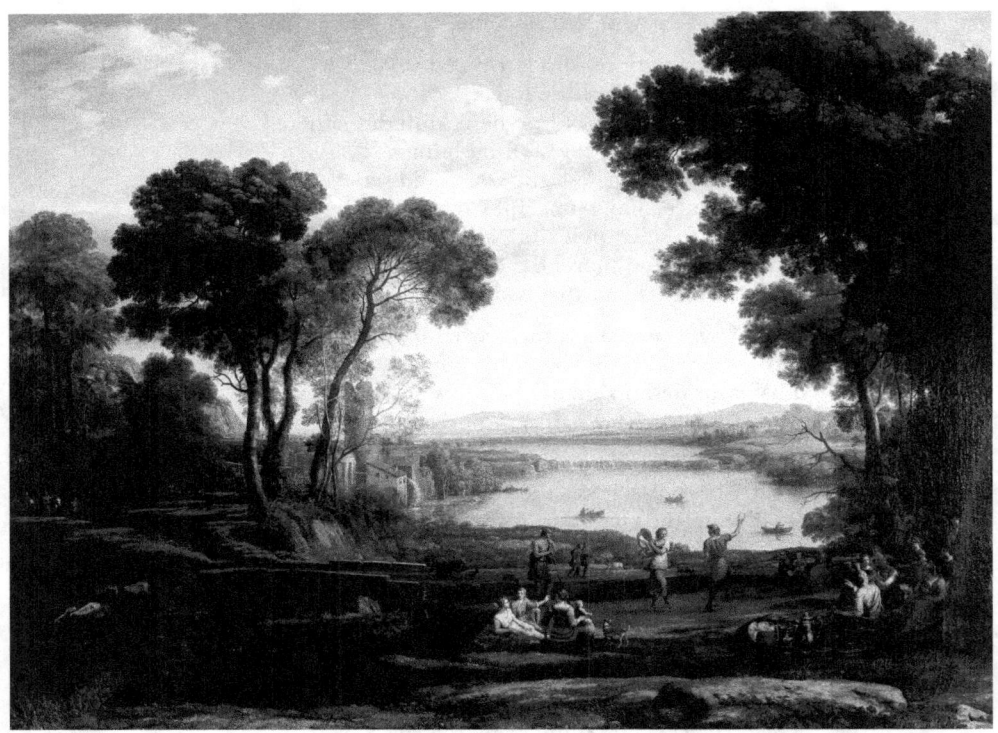

Fig. 3.5. Lorrain, *Landscape with Dancing Figures* [*The Mill*]. Galleria Doria Pamphilj, Rome/© Luisa Ricciarini — Bridgeman Images

art can be perceived as distinct. The poem can be read as enacting, in and through language, an example of 'lively conception', in the sense that the poetic practice renders the invisible aporetic concept 'anschaulich' [visible], enabling the observer to experience its vivification as an epiphanic moment. It summarizes the aesthetic questions that have preoccupied us in this chapter. Since it does so in a seemingly light-hearted, playfully ironic fashion, we start to suspect that the poem might be both the culmination of, and a distancing from, Goethe's thinking about the conundrum and his artistic practice. Our analysis will show that, on the level of both substance and style, the poem enacts the juxtaposition as a riddle that remains unresolved.

Composed in unrhymed trochaic pentameters, what catches most readers' attention right away is the inverted syntax in which the subject–verb order common in German is reversed, literally 'sat I' instead of 'I sat'. Goethe seems to employ this rhetorical device for dramatic effect because the inversion emphasizes the verbs and therefore action. It gives the poem a balladesque, narrative, even epic quality: we are told a story, with actors and interlocutors engaging in spirited dialogue. Another startling effect of the inversion is a foregrounding of the actors' physical presence. They enact the scene, literally turning the process of painting into a *tableau vivant* in which we as observers and readers become participants (note the plural 'you' in the penultimate line). As we become aware of their presence, we begin to realize that the rhetorical device relates language to space. The verbs have a visual impact in that they act like the outlines of a drawing. Thus, the inversion emphasizes structure and 'constructedness', or artifice, which is indeed a leitmotif of the poem. Finally, the unconventional placement of the verb gives the language an unconventional, even flippant tone, which calls attention to Goethe's ironic attitude vis-à-vis the poem's subject matter.

The poem's longest section (twenty-nine lines) is devoted to Amor's 'construction' of the painting — a landscape à la Lorrain. As the inverted syntax tells us, the composition begins 'at the top', with the 'sun', then proceeds downward through spaces layered vertically, 'trees', and horizontally, 'clouds', 'hillocks', 'river', until we reach the 'meadow' at the bottom in the foreground. To be precise, the bottom is where river and meadow meet. The point of view, as the first line establishes, is from up on 'a rocky peak'. If *The Mill* was indeed the model, the elevated position helps condense the painting's depth, because by the time the observer's eye reaches the horizon, which appears to be directly across from the rocky peak (i.e. at the same height), it has travelled down the sloped foreground and up the rapidly receding, tectonically segmented middle ground until it reaches the expansive background.[38] The lyric 'I' is 'enraptured' by the magic of this dynamic simultaneity of nearness and farness. Equally dynamic is the segments' interplay of light and shadow: the rays of the sun permeate the clouds, the treetops, and the small forest, and reflect off the water and the ground. Although the 'horizontal' and 'vertical' structure stabilizes the picture and gives it a sense of repose, the 'stabilizers' are imbued with an energy of their own: the trees appear 'fresh' and 'quickened', and the vocabulary used to sketch the hills and mountains bespeaks momentum: 'freely', 'one by one', and 'far and farther'.

After filling in the foreground with a vivid array of colourful flowers, Amor leads us back up to the sky, giving it a lustrous and transparent sheen by applying a coat of varnish, and finally to the hills and mountains, which, as they recede in the distance, turn fainter and bluer, as the technique of aerial perspective requires. 'Height', 'width', and 'depth', or 'lower down', 'at the top', and 'in the distance', are brought together to form a consistent whole. The energy that brings everything together is the light emanating from the sun whose rays 'perforate the cloud mass', and as they reach the river, the water 'glints with sunlight'.

While the range of Amor's characterizations — from 'child' to 'master' — is initially puzzling, the alliterative oxymoron of 'Lust' [desire], 'lose' [frivolous], and 'Lehrer' [teacher] reveals the complexity and ambiguity of this incarnation of inspiration. While 'desire' reverberates with the inspiration brought on by Venus, this Amor no longer instils the poetic fury that brings about an unconscious burst of creativity. That *Sturm und Drang* demon and his frenzy have been replaced by a friendly imp who teases and tickles with, for instance, an offer — brazenly stated using an untranslatable diminutive — of 'painting without further ado a small picture'. When he restates the offer, with a significant modification, of 'teaching how to paint a small picture', we realize that this Amor, at one point called 'Bübchen' [little fellow] — a sonic echo of his diminutive creation — is a tamed *furor poeticus*, who, in his naughty playfulness, may be mischievous but not malicious, insisting that creativity is not, or at least not solely, a frenzied involuntary process but one that requires schooling to change the 'divinely' inspired vision into something 'wise'. Espousing 'to paint' *and* 'to form', he proceeds to compose his painting according to rules that are so strict that, after its completion, he, teasingly, calls his work of art an expression of 'handiwork'. To remedy the Pygmalion-like situation, he has yet to accomplish the 'hardest' step in the creative process: to inspire, that is, to breathe life into his artful landscape by inserting a human figure, a 'loveliest maiden'. Her 'fresh' and 'ruddy' cheeks, her luxuriant 'brown' locks, and her fit with elemental features of the landscape — on the forest's edge brightly reflecting the sun — make her out to be a creature of nature. Yet other features make her out to be a creature of art, or rather, a product of her creator's skills: he draws her with 'pointed finger' and places her 'with anxious care' into the scenery; most significantly, the red of her cheeks matches that of his finger-cum-pencil, which 'forms' her 'well-formed' figure. To underscore the importance of the staffage, Amor casts the maiden as the personified imagination that vivifies, aphrodisiac-like, the landscape painting. She is phenomenon and noumenon in one.

The speaker who, as interlocutor and observer is 'outside' the painting, yet, as participant in the *tableau vivant*, also belongs to the staffage 'in' the painting, brings the poem's fundamental duality, or even duplicity, to the fore. The duality infiltrates the speaker's perception of, assessment of, and reaction to Amor and his art. Tellingly, with minor linguistic modifications and an infusion of exclamatory rhetoric, his reaction changes from condescension, 'Would the boy pretend to be a master?', to enthusiasm, 'Oh you boy! [...] what master'. He is enthusiastic about Amor's imitative and compositional skills and cleverness, 'so true to nature' and 'Wisely to begin, and well to finish', and especially his command of execution — note the double use of 'to let',[39] with the sense of 'to effect', 'cause', or 'induce'. Yet the speaker's language betrays the fact that the verisimilitude may only be apparent, the 'reality' only 'semblance'. Making use of anticlimax and antithesis, rhetoric helps him to tease out the tension between nature and art more dynamically. As part of the figure 'so much so ... that', the climax expressed in 'so completely true to nature' ought to result in 'that it [the river] glittered in the sun's beams'. Yet, unable to persuade himself that nature and art are indistinguishable, the speaker relativizes the hyperbolic proposition by inserting the verb 'to seem'[40] into his conclusion, not once but twice. With Amor's masterful imitation of the — quintessentially Lorrainian — translucent sky and bluish mountains, the speaker adheres to the logic of the 'so ... that' conjunction and declares himself to be 'truly enraptured and reborn'. The resolution of the conundrum in favour of nature is called into question immediately. The following line restates the juxtaposition of imitation and execution in brilliantly worded ambivalence: 'gazed on now the painter, now the picture'. While the 'now'–'now' parallelism suggests irresolution, the preponderance of the 'b' alliteration in the stanza's last line tips the scale toward art. While the final alliterated 'b', in 'beschauen', increases the musical quality, it also causes irritation, for the prefix 'be-' deviates from 'an-', the obligatory prefix for Goethe's aesthetic-epistemological principle of 'anschauen' [perceive].

With the insistence on movement, 'Now everything, but everything was moving', the *tableau* seems to have indeed become *vivant*; even the onlooker seems swept up in the activity stirred by the breeze and eventually seizes 'trees' and 'flowers', 'river' and 'foot', thus integrating landscape and staffage. A new motif, the maiden's 'veil', is introduced and given unusual (syntactic) prominence, suggesting that illusion and deception are inherent to the nature–art riddle, just as concealment and revelation are inherent to a veil. It blurs the boundary between fact and fiction, making it indecipherable or imperceptible. In a startling oxymoron, the maiden appears simultaneously 'to come and go', and the last couplet leaves the riddle unanswered. The poem ends with a question and a simile: the 'rock' partakes in nature and in art.

Nature is transposed into art by means of similes starting in the first stanza with the 'fog' that is 'like a canvas primed with grey', and continuing with colours that are rendered in terms of what they resemble, 'like a rose', 'like emerald', 'like carbuncle'. The rhetoric of transposition culminates in the simile of the final verse, 'like a rock', implying that the rock frames the landscape, painting, and poem. The spring meadow ablaze with the colours of fresh flowers rings conventional; the 'gold', reflecting the 'golden' glow of the clouds, suggests a microcosmic totality of heaven and earth. Sticking out from the list of colours is 'green', not due to its nominal form (that applies to the other colours, too) but its singularity: 'a' or 'one green'. 'Green', the *Goethe-Wörterbuch* (IV, 507–08) informs us, is the main colour for vegetative nature *in toto* but also for nature reawakening in spring. Its symbolism is both physical — fertility — and spiritual, for Goethe associates 'green' with his vision of paradise, as he does in these verses from a poem resonating with similar language and motifs:

> Once the sheep leave the meadow
> It lies there stretched out, a pure green,
> Yet soon in paradise
> It will flower in colourful bloom. (*FA*, II, 695)

In the context of the poem as a whole, 'green' symbolizes 'creation', be it vegetative, erotic, or divine — the latter tied to the analogy between nature and art insofar as artistic creativity and divine creativity mirror each other.

Such kaleidoscopic colour anticipates Goethe's colour wheel, in which colours are perceived as evolving out of polar opposites that are complementary, contrastive, and dynamic, such as yellow and blue amalgamating into green, red and blue into purple. Returning to 'Amor ein Landschaftsmaler', with the metonymical 'colours' for 'flowers', the colours seem to gain an expressionistic quality; they seem to acquire a life of their own. Yet, if we bear in mind the growth of Goethe's mineralogical expertise in Italy (including volcanic rock, thanks to his ascent of Mount Vesuvius), with 'enamel sheen', the precious metal 'gold', and especially with the precious stones 'emerald' and 'carbuncle', the colours appear pellucid (or, to use a technical term, desaturated), their glassy or crystalline substance allowing light to pass through. Since we will discuss *Zur Farbenlehre* and its relation to Lorrain in the last chapter, it suffices for now to say that Goethe discovered colour in Italy and began, despite his obsession with the dynamic interplay of light and darkness, to appreciate, via the discovery of landscape, its artistic possibilities, indeed importance. The lyric 'I' also uses the motif of the coloured flower for the painter's instrument, his rose-coloured finger with which he both 'draws' and 'paints'. And he uses it for the staffage, the figure of the maiden whose cheeks have a rosy-red glow. It is a colour that serves as the intermediary between the creator and the created. In fact, it is also the intermediary between nature and art, because when the maiden comes alive and steps out of nature into the canvas, she breaks down the barriers between nature and art.

Amor's boyish charm and mischievous nature have prevented critics from discovering his serious side. Read against the backdrop of the argument in the late Renaissance between the two major schools of painting — the 'ideational' Florentine approach of *disegno*, advocating invention, clear form, and flowing line, and the 'observational' Venetian approach of *colore*, espousing imitation, rich colour, and naturalistic light — the poem reflects the reverberations of that debate in the classicism–romanticism discussion around 1800, including the execution, perception, and epistemology of landscape painting.[41] Given that Amor assumes the dual role of designer and colourist, he may be read as a go-between in the debate's antiphonal exchange on the spirituality of the 'design' and the sensuality of the 'colour'. The gendering of the juxtaposition aligns design with reason as the domain of the male, and colour with soul as the domain of the female. Rather than seeing the maiden as a reflection of a mysterious love relationship of Goethe — identified in the *Italienische Reise* as 'a Milanese girl' (*CW*, VI, 333; *FA*, XV.1, 445)[42] — she can be read as a metaphorical embodiment of the vivifying power of colour, providing the skeletal draft with a unifying and therefore beautiful body. True to his ancient ancestor, Goethe's Amor acts as a catalyst for the interplay of drawing and colouring, which in its duality and complementarity transcends Renaissance art theory by harking back to the differing epistemologies of Plato and Aristotle. In terms of perception, the Pygmalion-like animation suggests that colour replaces rhetoric in bringing the landscape 'as if before our eyes', which in turn implicates colour as playing a role in the artwork's power to seduce and deceive.

Ultimately, there is no answer to the question of where nature ends and art begins. Even after the maiden steps out of the canvas and into the surrounding landscape, the boundaries between nature and art remain, or rather, keep shifting. A marker of the ambivalence that permeates the poem is the irony that lends the nature–art dilemma a comedic air. Contemplating his fascination with the Roman comedy in which men played the role of women to perfection, the speaker sees its cause in the fact that, in such performances, nature and art engage so cleverly in a lively play that they produce a kind of '*self-conscious illusion*' (*FA*, XV.2, 858) — yet another oxymoron encapsulating the theatricality, albeit not comedy, of Lorrainian landscape painting.

Finally, the poem might be read as a comedic reckoning with Lessing, for what arises out of the mist is an image (like Achilles' shield): we *hear* Amor narrating it, in consecutive mode, and we *see* Amor painting it, in coexistent mode — which raises an interesting question: is Amor flirting with white or black magic to conjure up (as if) before our eyes and ears a landscape that exists as painting, poem, and — nature? As we begin the next chapter, nature undergoes a metamorphosis. As Tivoli transforms into Twickenham, Amor's *concordia discors* suggests that *ut pictura poesis* becomes *ut pictura poesis et hortus*. The English Garden and its relationship to Lorrain and Goethe is the subject to which we now turn.

Notes to Chapter 3

1. See Robson-Scott, pp. 110–49, and Beyer, 'Italienische Reise', for succinct overviews of the journey's significance for Goethe the artist; cf. *FA*, xv.2, 1603–10, for salient scholarship. Particularly useful for the purposes of this study were Gerstenberg, 'Goethe und die italienische Landschaft'; Formanek; Busch; Beyer, '"Poussinsche Vorderteile"'; Miller, 'Der Dichter ein Landschaftsmaler', *Insel der Nausikaa*.
2. See Femmel, II. On Goethe's Italian drawings (and aquarelles), see Mildenberger, 'Goethe als Zeichner', pp. 35–39; Bergmann and Berndt, pp. 71–162; Maisak, *Goethe: Zeichnungen*, pp. 22–24, 115–76, 'Der Zeichner Goethe', pp. 110–12, 128–35, 439; Münz, pp. 53–73; Nohl; Hecht, pp. 97–133.
3. Letter to Carl August, 18 March 1788 (*FA*, xv.2, 1256). On Lorrain's art of etching, cf. Mannocci; Rümelin, 'Claude Lorrain', 'Search'; Sonnabend.
4. To the extent that von Ramdohr's 1787 guide is reliable, there were twenty-nine Lorrain paintings on display in Rome in the mid-1780s: eleven at Palazzo Colonna (II, 61, 74–75, 77, 78, 79, 107, 109), four at Palazzo Doria Pamphilj (II, 127, 129, 131), four at Palazzo Barberini (II, 314), two at Palazzo Pallavicini-Rospigliosi (III, 60, 64), one at Palazzo Costaguti (III, 69), two at Palazzo Altieri (III, 104), and five at Palazzo Chigi (III, 106, 107). Cf. Moses; Weidner, *Jakob Philipp Hackert*, pp. 96–98.
5. According to Kurbjuhn's comprehensive study, pp. 4, 542–51, Goethe does not strictly differentiate between the 'graphic' outline ('Umriß') and the 'plastic' contour ('Kontur', 'Contour[e]'), but in the *Italienische Reise*, he increasingly uses 'contour' to articulate his experience of, *and* reflection on, nature.
6. Nohl, p. 98. For details on the *disegno–colore* debate, see our reading of 'Amor ein Landschaftsmaler' below.
7. Robertson, p. 52. On Moritz's aesthetics, see also Boyle, I: *The Poetry of Desire*, pp. 495–500; Pfotenhauer, 'Weimar Classicism', pp. 267–72; Schreiber.
8. See Lange.
9. For the biblical echoes, cf. e.g. Psalms 63. 35, 96. 11; on Homer, see E. G. Schmidt.
10. See e.g. Lehmann; Striehl, pp. 72–73.
11. These are the paintings identified by Femmel, ed., p. 88. For difficulties identifying the eleven Colonna Lorrains listed by von Ramdohr, cf. Roethlisberger (MRP, II, 197, 375); Weidner, *Jakob Philipp Hackert*, pp. 228–29.
12. Putting more emphasis on Hackert's criticism of Lorrain, Miller, '"Über die Kunst ist es ein ander Ding"', pp. 63–69, offers a slightly differing reading of the evidence analysed in the following pages.
13. Here and in the following paragraphs, quotations are again from Maul's edition of Hackert's original letters.
14. Robertson, p. 31.
15. Even though scholars do not read the essay as a theory of landscape painting, my attempt at doing so evolves from Grätz; Wolf; Frank. Although I am sceptical about her assertion that Goethe understood 'style' as a synthesis of 'imitation' and 'manner', Grätz rightly draws attention to tensions within the types and the typology as a whole.
16. I have in mind here 'wahr', 'gewissenhaft', 'fehlen', and 'unglaublich' in the German.
17. According to Ritter, pp. 156–57, there is, in man's relation to nature, a similar split between

an objective and subjective language in Kant and Carus, with Kant using the same term ('spelling' [buchstabieren]) for the experiential rendering of nature. Cf. Kant, IV, 312: 'Sie [die reinen Verstandesbegriffe] dienen gleichsam nur, Erscheinungen zu buchstabieren, um sie als Erfahrung lesen zu können' (*Prolegomena*, §30).

18. The more literal translations here correspond in the first group to the German verbs 'aufopfern', 'fehlen', and 'erreichen', and in the second group to 'enthalten', 'sich aufhalten', and 'festhalten'.
19. Ditner, pp. 158–59.
20. See Grätz, p. 137; Frank, p. 571.
21. Herwig, II: *1803–1817*, p. 235.
22. Striehl, p. 367 (cf. pp. 87–88, 135, 293). For other Sicilian landscapes by Kniep in Goethe's possession, see Striehl, pp. 95–97; for Lorrain as Kniep's model in general, see Striehl, pp. 38, 75–77, 161–76, 243, 283, 286. Cf. Formanek.
23. See Pfotenhauer, 'Farbe'.
24. Hofmann, pp. 269, 270–71. For reproductions, see Schulze, ed., pp. 119, 140.
25. Cf. the section 'Nausikaa' in Gerstenberg, 'Goethe und die italienische Landschaft', pp. 659–64. Cf. also Atkins, p. 43, who points to Lorrain and, above all, to Pellegrino Tibaldi (1527–96) and his Bolognese Ulysses frescos, among them *Ulysses Introduced to Alcinous by Nausicaa*, as Goethe's 'first strong — pictorial — impulse' for *Nausikaa*. A Lorrainian stimulus not mentioned in the Goethe literature might be *Coast View of Naxos with Ariadne and Bacchus*, now exhibited as *Ulysses Discovering Himself to Nausicaa* (1656; *LV*, 139); cf. Russell, pp. 175–76, on the arguments for and against each title. Cf. furthermore Miller, *Insel der Nausikaa*, pp. 39–55, who, in his reading of the tragedy fragment, highlights Sicily and Homer as inspiration but not Lorrain. For a survey of research on *Nausikaa*, see Sauder.
26. Cf. Homer, VI. 85, 122–25, VII. 113–34. On the relationship of nymphs and snow, see the *Theoi Project* at <http://www.theoi.com> [accessed 26 March 2018]. Kione (Chione), a nymph on Mount Haimos in the north of Greece, was considered a goddess of snow. Among the snow similes in Homer is that of melting snow for a flood of tears, such as those of Odysseus at the Phaeacian court (VIII. 522). On the significance of nymphs in the *Odyssey*, cf. Malkin.
27. For a useful introduction to the 'Helena act', and the nature and function of the Arcadia episode in it, see J. Schmidt, pp. 234–64. The episode has not hitherto been read through the lens of landscape painting.
28. Required by the German 'gelingen' for 'succeed'.
29. Implied by the verb 'heitern' [to brighten up] (l. 9551).
30. See the Appendix. Cf. Femmel, ed., pp. 217, 219; Schuchardt, p. 204 (no. 98).
31. Cf. Panofsky, p. 296; Lagerlöf, pp. 7–11.
32. Contemplation as an antidote to being dazzled is anticipated in the *Italienische Reise* in a letter to Charlotte von Stein from 25 December 1787: 'Der Glanz der größten Kunstwerke blendet mich nicht mehr, ich wandle nun im Anschauen, in der wahren unterscheidenden Erkenntnis' [The splendor of the greatest artworks no longer dazzles me. I now go around in contemplation, with true, discerning perception] (*FA*, XV.1, 478; *CW*, VI, 358).
33. Cf. *FA*, VII.2, 582 (commentary).
34. Here, Goethe drew inspiration from another painting he saw and studied in Rome, Raphael's 1514 fresco *The Triumph of Galatea* (*FA*, VII.2, 574, commentary).
35. To Eckermann, 5 July 1827 (*CV*, pp. 210–11; *FA*, XXIX, 249–50). Goethe reviewed Byron's works, such as *Cain* (1821), *Don Juan* (1819–24), and *Manfred* (1817), pointing out the latter's link to *Faust* (cf. *FA*, XXII, 973–75). See Butler for a detailed account of their 'fascination' with each other, including Goethe's contention that Byron had 'completely absorbed [his] *Faust*' for *Manfred* (letter of 13 October 1817 to Karl Ludwig von Knebel; Butler, p. 33; *FA*, XXXV, 145).
36. Conversation with Riemer, 28 August 1808 (*FA*, XXXIII, 362).
37. See Ziolkowski, 'Die Natur'. Drawing attention to the poem's ekphrastically executed composition, Renner, pp. 8–10, imagines Amor's painting to be a cross between Hackert and Lorrain, but identifies only 'vibrant expression' and the 'handling of light' as characteristics. Miller, 'Der Dichter als Landschaftsmaler', p. 382, sees Amor as a tribute to Hackert, while Pape,

in '"Die Sinne triegen nicht"', p. 109, more concerned with reading the poem as an example of Goethe's increasing objectivization of perception, sees 'its ideality [as] a homage to Claude Lorrain'. While acknowledging the *Mill* link, Eilert, pp. 130, 133–36, suggests another persona of the master painter could be Watteau, whose *L'Amour paisible* (c. 1718) and *Le Reve de l'artiste* (c. 1710) accentuate the erotic-lascivious aspect of artistic inspiration and thus transcend the Lorrainian landscape model.
38. See Gerstenberg, *Landschaftsmalerei*, p. 102.
39. The German verb is 'lassen', here used in its simple past tense form, 'ließ'.
40. The German verb is 'scheinen', here used in its simple past tense form, 'schien'.
41. See V. Krieger's cogent account of the debate and its resurgence in the controversy between the 'classicist' Poussinists and the 'Romantic' Rubenists in the eighteenth and early nineteenth centuries. Cf. also Freedberg.
42. Cf. *FA*, xv.2, 1398 (commentary).

CHAPTER 4

Painting into Poetry into Park: Lorrain and Goethe as English Gardeners

> No work of art can be great, but as it deceives; to be otherwise is
> the prerogative of nature only. (Burke, pp. 58–59)

'The human being', writes Rudolf Borchardt in his book *The Passionate Gardener*, 'embodies a tension between a nature which has since been lost and an unreachable Divine Creator' (originally published in German in 1938). He continues:

> The garden stands at precisely the center of this tension and displaces itself, in accord with its fluctuations in the epoch and the individual, toward one or the other: toward nature or creativity. This is the deepest reason for which the human being dreams that our origins lie in a garden, and that the garden is the place in which we achieve enlightenment; this is why we hope to find redemption in a garden, and why we look for solace there.[1]

Borchardt maps out a compelling conceptual and experiential framework for our expansion of the sister arts to include gardening. What he articulates so well is that a garden is not just an enactment of a tension between nature and cultivation but also an experience with potential to deliver us from this tension. Moreover, the idea of the gardener as a secularized creator fits squarely into the Age of Enlightenment because it underscores that the garden is a man-made art form. This is important insofar as our argument continues to be aesthetic, for it is in art (i.e. in garden art) that a resolution to the nature–art divide is sought.

The resolution, a state of repose, is found in Lorrain:

> The peculiar beauty of the most beautiful of all landscape painters is characterized by *il riposo di Claudio*, and when the mind of man is in the delightful state of repose, of which Claude's pictures are the image — when he feels that mild and equal sunshine of the soul which warms and cheers but neither inflames nor irritates — his heart seems to dilate with happiness, he is disposed to every kind of kindness and benevolence, to love and cherish all around him.

This is an excerpt from one of the influential treatises on eighteenth-century British garden art, the 1794 *Essay on the Picturesque, as Compared with the Sublime and the Beautiful; and on the Use of Studying Pictures, for the Purpose of Improving Real Landscapes* by Uvedale Price.[2] In the following, we will delve into the meaning of Price's terminology; suffice it to say for now that by 1794 Lorrain and the English

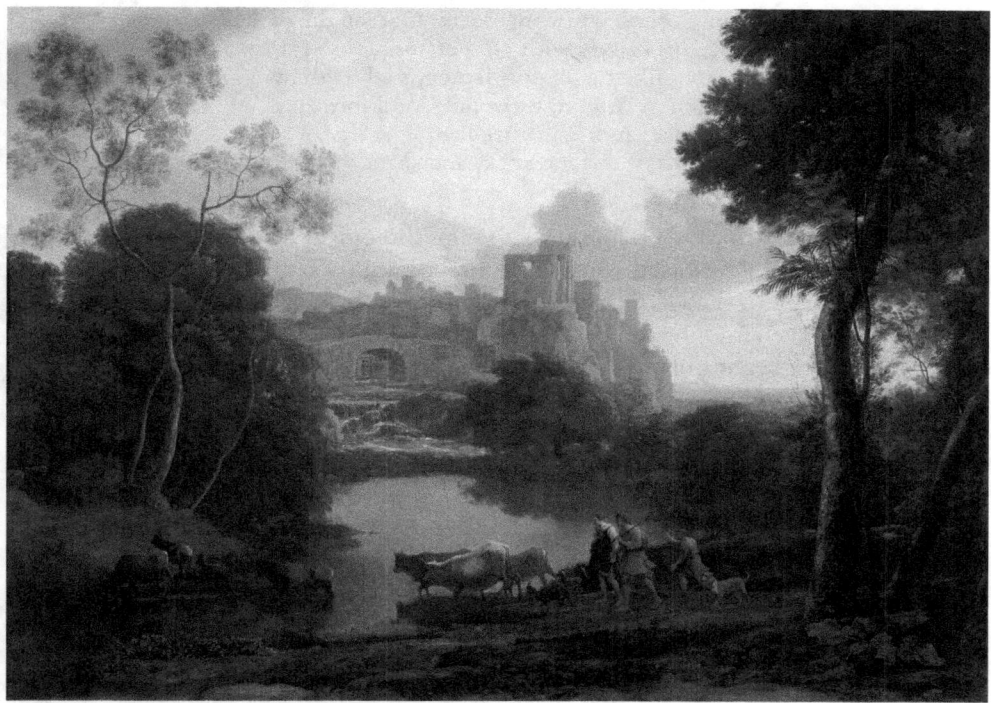

FIG. 4.1. Lorrain, *View of Tivoli at Sunset*. The Fine Arts Museums of San Francisco; gift of the Samuel H. Kress Foundation, 61.44.31

landscape garden seem to have become synonymous.³ We begin, therefore, by tracing the history of this marriage of painting and park.

When Faust lands on Grecian soil in search of Helena, Mephistopheles conjectures about the figures they encounter:

> Sind Briten hier? Sie reisen sonst so viel,
> Schlachtfeldern nachzuspüren, Wasserfällen,
> Gestürzten Mauern, klassisch dumpfen Stellen;
> Das wäre hier für sie ein würdig Ziel. (ll. 7118–21)
>
> [Are any British here? They're usually great travelers,
> looking for battlefields and waterfalls,
> dilapidated walls and dreary ancient sites;
> this is an ideal place for them to visit.]

Before the British made Greece their travel destination in the nineteenth century, they went seeking Arcadia in Italy en masse — here invoked by the picture of the iconic *View of Tivoli at Sunset* (1644; *LV*, 81), with the ruined temple of the Sibyl atop the cascade.

To counter Mephistopheles' anachronism with a genuinely British perspective, in William Mason's poem *The English Garden* (1772–81),⁴ Lorrain figures as the missing link between Antiquity, the 'Italian', and the 'English' Arcadias:

> Meanwhile, of old and classic aid
> [...] your eyes entranc'd.

> Shall catch those glowing scenes, that taught a Claude
> To grace his canvas with Hesperian hues:
> And scenes like these, on Memory's tablet drawn,
> Bring back to Britain; there give local form
> To each Idea; and, if Nature lend
> Materials fit of torrent, rock, and shade,
> Produce new TIVOLIS.[5]

With the allusion to the Hesperides, the mythological 'Daughters of Evening' glowing in the golden sunset, Mason intones a by now familiar motif of Lorrain's classical landscape. What has changed is that Lorrain is brought 'back to Britain' by scores of travellers who embarked on their own Italian journeys long before Goethe. They brought Lorrain back not just figuratively but also literally. The first pair of paintings arrives in 1644, and by the end of the eighteenth century, more than eighty works by Lorrain are in English hands, including the *Liber Veritatis* from which Richard Earlom etches a complete set of prints published in 1777.[6] For historians, theoreticians, and practitioners of the arts — poetry, painting, horticulture — Lorrain was everyone's darling. And this infatuation was not short-lived. It ranges from the first printed source, Richard Graham's 1695 biographical entry on Lorrain in a supplement to John Dryden's English translation of Du Fresnoy's *Art of Painting*, to J. M. W. Turner's paintings *Thomson's Aeolian Harp*

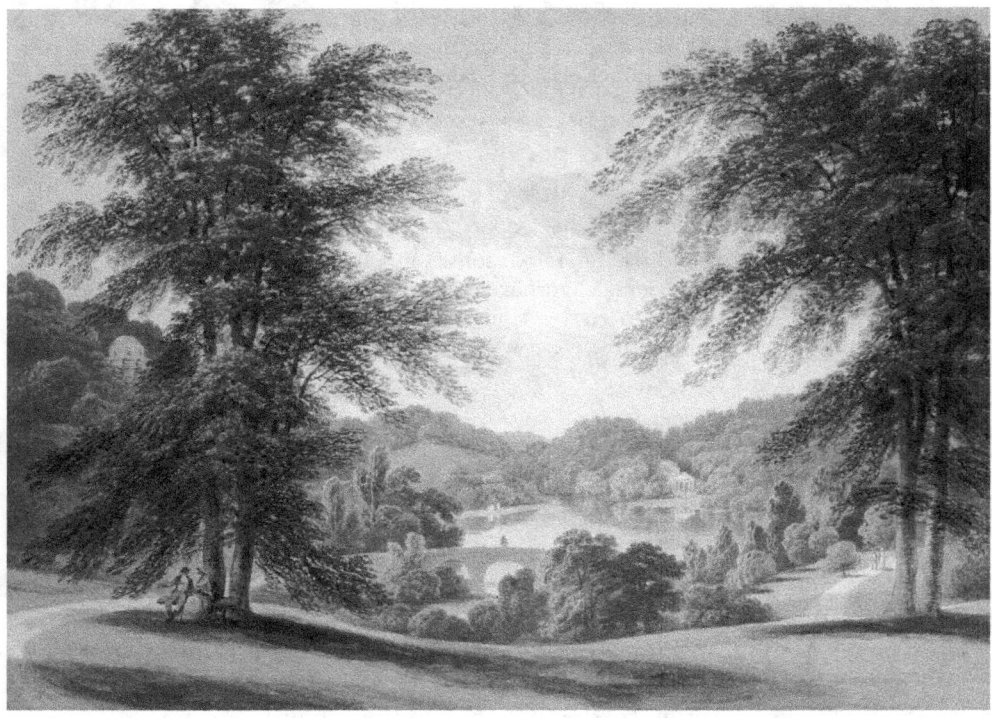

FIG. 4.2. Nicholson, *Rural Scenery at Stourhead*. British Museum, London/ © Trustees of the British Museum

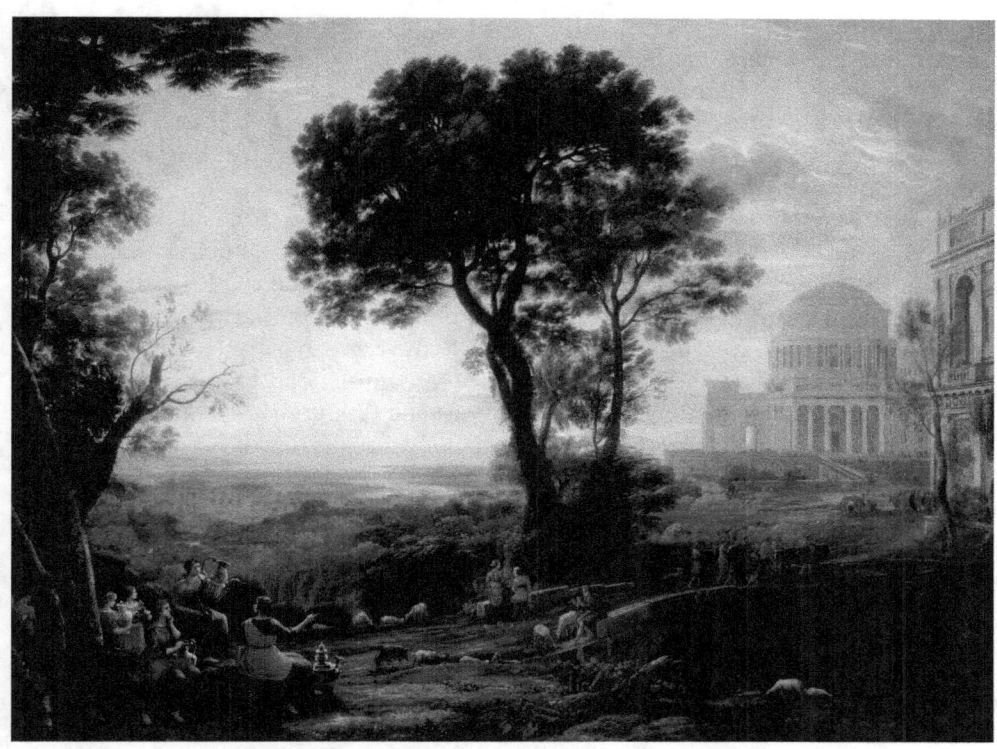

Fig. 4.3. Lorrain, *Coast View of Delphi with a Procession.* Trust Doria Pamphilj; Archivio Doria Pamphilj/© 2018 ADP s.r.l.

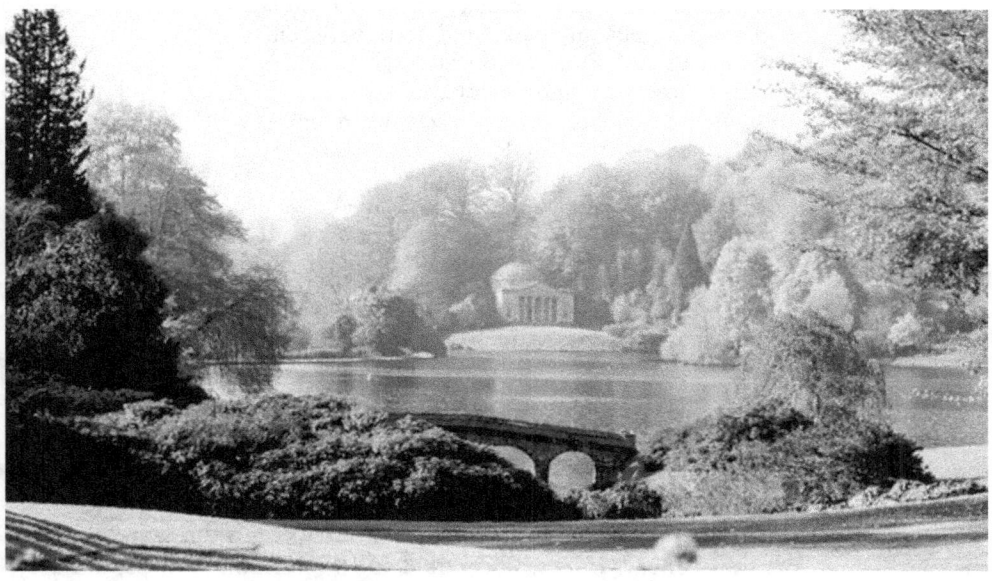

Fig. 4.4. Contemporary view of Stourhead.
<http://geographic.org.uk/p/484205>/© Chris Downer

(1805) and *Crossing the Brook* (1815). In between, an array of *jardins à l'anglaise* are laid out looking like *jardins à la Lorraine*, among them the Stourhead landscape garden, here represented by Francis Nicholson's watercolour *Rural Scenery at Stourhead* (*c.* 1810), which is in part based on Lorrain's *Coast View of Delphi with a Procession* (*c.* 1648; *LV*, 119), as well as by a contemporary view of the bridge, the lake, and the Pantheon in the background (Figs 4.2–4.4).

In order to explore the interrelation between painting, poetry, and park, we will focus here on James Thomson (1700–48) and Alexander Pope (1688–1744).[7] In and through their poetry, they can be seen as linking Lorrain and the English Garden.[8] An exceptional number of translations attests to their popularity in eighteenth-century Germany.[9] Goethe's familiarity with the two spans virtually his whole life. Before he reached the age of twenty, he recommended to his sister — with quotations in English — Pope's *The Happy Life of a Country Parson* and *Phryne* (*FA*, XXVIII, 31–32, 589), and shortly before he died aged eighty-two, his admiration for Thomson had not waned.

4.1. James Thomson's Lorrainian Landscapes

Another example of an English Arcadia is Hagley Park, admired for its undulating contours and vast vistas, and a frequent retreat for James Thomson. After Thomson travelled to Italy, where he was exposed to the 'reality' of Lorrain's landscapes, the experience prompted him to rework *The Seasons*, adding, for instance, this view from Hagley Park to the poem 'Spring' in 1744:

> Meantime you gain the height, from whose fair brow
> A bursting prospect spreads immense around;
> And, snatched o'er hill and dale, and wood and lawn,
> And verdant field, and darkening heath between,
> And villages embosomed soft in trees,
> And spiry towns by surging columns marked
> Of household smoke, your eye excursive roams —
> Wide-stretching from the Hall in whose kind haunt
> The hospitable Genius lingers still,
> To where the broken landscape, by degrees
> Ascending, roughens into rigid hills
> O'er which the Cambrian mountains, like far clouds
> That skirt the blue horizon, dusky rise.[10]

As with Goethe's poetic landscapes, the link between Thomson and Lorrain is ekphrastic.[11] The main Lorrainian motifs are rather obvious; aspects of composition and effect deserve closer scrutiny. With regard to sight, the experience of park, poetry, and painting mirror each other. The ekphrasis relies on the eye — specifically, its movement — to convey this experience. The conveyance, in turn, relies on the syntax, on the extreme separation between verb, 'snatched', and subject, 'eye', across five lines. From the moment the 'immense' 'prospect' bursts onto the field of vision, the eye flies across the scenery, irresistibly pulled to the horizon and, presumably, the vanishing point. Descending from there, in a semi-orderly paratactic staccato of 'and's, the eye piles sight upon sight, plane upon plane, until it finally comes to rest, as is literally and figuratively marked by the dash. Relaxed, and immersed in the present — reflected in the tense of the verbs — the eye now surveys the landscape, able to notice discrete features evolving 'by degrees'. The calm is such that the 'inner eye' joins the perceptional process by contributing a simile ('like far clouds') to enhance the picture — and bring the cross-fertilization of park, painting, and poetry to completion. In another poem, *Liberty* (1736), Thomson invokes the 'bright *muse*' (my emphasis) of painting to create an aura of tranquillity by shaping a stretch of countryside into bucolic scenery:

> [...] to rural life,
> The softer canvas oft reposed the soul.
> There gaily broke the sun-illumined cloud;
> The lessening prospect, and the mountain blue,
> Vanished in air [...]
> In closing shades, and where the current strays,
> With peace, and love, and innocence around,
> Piped the lone shepherd to his feeding flock. (p. 334, ll. 350–62)

Thomson figures prominently in Lorrain's reception in England, especially when we broaden our perspective and look at the aesthetic concepts used to characterize his art, and how these concepts are 'translated' into the theory and practice of the English Garden. In his poem *The Castle of Indolence* (1748), we read:

> The rooms with costly tapestry were hung,
> Where was inwoven many a gentle tale;
> Such as of old the rural poets sung,
> Or of Arcadian or Sicilian vale:
> [...]
> While flocks, woods, streams around, repose and peace impart.
>   (p. 265, l. 36)

> Sometimes the pencil, in cool airy halls,
> Bade the gay bloom of vernal landskips rise,
> Or Autumn's varied shades imbrown the walls:
> Now the black tempest strikes the astonished eyes;
> Now down the steep the flashing torrent flies;
> The trembling sun now plays o'er ocean blue,
> And now rude mountains from amid the skies;
> Whate'er *Lorrain* light-touched with softening hue,
> Or savage *Rosa* dashed, or learned *Poussin* drew.
>   (p. 265, l. 38; my emphasis)

Reminding us of Goethe's Tasso and his indulgence in nostalgia for a bygone Golden Age, and longing for the tranquillity offered by a Roman country house and garden, Thomson brings together the English landscape and Lorrain in a single poem. The final couplet cites, on the one hand, the familiar motif of Lorrain's handling and purposing of light; on the other hand, it encapsulates the prevalent reception of seventeenth-century Italian landscape painting in eighteenth-century England. Grouping together Lorrain, Salvator Rosa (1615–73), and Gaspard Poussin, it anticipates the aesthetic-philosophical assessment that would soon take hold of deliberations regarding man's novel relationship to, and perception of, nature and its effects, as well as their enactment in landscape painting — Lorrain as 'beautiful', Rosa as 'sublime', and Gaspard Poussin as 'picturesque' — and, by extension, in landscape gardening.[12]

4.2. Lorrain, the Beautiful, the Sublime, and the Picturesque: Edmund Burke and Uvedale Price

According to Edmund Burke's treatise *A Philosophical Enquiry into the Origin of our Ideas of the Sublime and Beautiful* (1757),[13] the 'beautiful' and the 'sublime' emanate from 'real objects' (p. 175), excite the 'passion of love' or 'terror' (pp. 91, 134), and have a soothing or a frightening effect. He sums up the contrasts as follows:

> For sublime objects are vast in their dimensions, beautiful ones comparatively small; beauty should be smooth, and polished; the great, rugged and negligent; beauty should shun the right line, yet deviate from it insensibly; the great in many cases loves the right line, and when it deviates, it often makes a strong deviation; beauty should not be obscure; the great ought to be dark and gloomy; beauty should be light and delicate; the great ought to be solid, and even massive. They are indeed ideas of a very different nature, one being founded on pain, the other on pleasure. (p. 124)

There is little doubt that he would subsume Lorrain under the rubric of beauty. To wit: without naming any painter or gardener, two of his examples for beauty — 'smooth slopes' and 'smooth streams' in 'gardens' and 'landscapes' respectively (p. 114) — could certainly be derived from Lorrain or the then-current theory and practice of garden design. The idea of the 'whole', the *'hidden soul of harmony'* as he calls it at one point, quoting Milton, pertains to beauty, too (p. 122). 'The softness, the winding surface, the unbroken continuance, the easy gradation', writes Burke, are properties of beauty, as long as the objects that appeal to our senses and affect us 'throw lights from one another to finish one clear, consistent idea of the whole [and] not obscure it by their intricacy and variety' (p. 122). Yet Burke's distinction is more complex than the clear-cut categorization suggests. The presumed borders are porous. While Lorrain hardly strikes any 'pain' or 'terror' in us, Burke, in presenting 'awe' as a subcategory of the sublime, allows for a mixture of pain and terror. 'Poetry [and] painting [are] capable of grafting delight on wretchedness, misery, and death' (p. 44), he maintains, resulting in the 'delightful terror' of 'awe' (p. 136). With its tension between 'consummated passion' and 'suicidal despair' — a tension mirrored in the storm clouds gathering in the bright morning sky — one of the many Lorrain paintings with a mythological subject that resonate with this definition would be the *View of Carthage with Dido, Aeneas, and their Suite Leaving for the Hunt* (1676; LV, 186).[14] In addition to affecting 'tranquility shadowed by horror', i.e. 'awe' (p. 34), this painting could also be cited as a source for Burke's notion of *'infinity'*. It 'has a tendency', writes Burke, 'to fill the mind with that sort of delightful horror which is the most genuine effect, and truest test of the sublime' (p. 73). As a cause, Burke identifies 'the eye not being able to perceive [...] bounds'

(p. 73), which is applicable to Lorrain's painting insofar as he pushes his horizon line, that is, the point where sky and land or water meet, to a barely discernible vanishing point. The painting's architecture, perceived as endlessly extendable, illustrates another manifestation of the 'infinite'. Here, the 'sublime' arises from 'an uniform succession of great parts', such as columns in 'a colonnade or a rotunda', which 'impresses the imagination with the idea of their progress beyond their actual limits' (pp. 74–75). While, extrapolating from Burke, the seemingly boundless prospects and columned architecture can be seen as a 'sublime' link between painting and park, this does not correlate with the 'picturesque', for his emphasis on the uniformity of the architecture anticipates Wine's suggestion that its 'severity [...] reinforces the painting's tragic import'.[15] Inadvertently aligning himself with Goethe, it is noteworthy that, for Burke, both painting and poetry have the capacity to evoke the beautiful and the sublime (thus uniting what Lessing split) through the sensuousness or effect of the depicted object:

> In reality, poetry and rhetoric do not succeed in exact description so well as painting does; their business is, to affect rather by sympathy than imitation; to display rather the effect of things on the mind of the speaker, or of others, than to present a clear idea of the things themselves. This is their most extensive province, and that in which they succeed best.[16] (p. 172)

Based on Burke, Uvedale Price developed his own theory of the interrelation between man and nature, between landscape painting and landscape park, in his *Essay on the Picturesque*.[17] According to Price, beauty, sublimity, and picturesqueness arise from diametrically opposed causes such as smoothness and roughness, gradation and abruptness, uniformity and variety, plainness and intricacy, symmetry and irregularity. Equally opposed are their effects: repose on the one hand, curiosity on the other. In opposition to sublime vastness, infinity, and solemnity, the picturesque is more likely to arise from smallness, circumscription, and playfulness. The sublime terrifies, the picturesque captivates.[18] While Price delineates distinctions, he recognizes affinities: 'Picturesqueness when mixed with either of the other characters, corrects the languor of beauty, or the tension of sublimity' (pp. 88–89). Thus, a Grecian temple is beautiful, but when overgrown with vegetation, picturesque; a calm lake is beautiful, a cataract sublime, and a cascade picturesque; a 'fresh and tender ash' is beautiful, and a 'knotty wych elm' is picturesque, as are 'the limbs of huge trees shattered by lightening', but the 'dreaded powers' causing their 'destruction' have 'the tincture of the sublime' (pp. 57–58).

Price's comparison between Rubens and Lorrain makes clear his understanding of these three concepts. Rubens's landscapes show sublime and picturesque elements. Among them are

> striking contrasts in form, colour, and light and shadow: sun-beams bursting through a small opening in a dark wood — a rainbow against a stormy sky — effects of thunder and lightening-torrents rolling down trees torn up by the roots, and the dead bodies of men and animals. (pp. 130–31)

While admiring Rubens for the 'noble' exhibition of these motifs, Price avers that 'these sudden gleams, these cataracts of light, these bold oppositions of clouds and darkness [...] would destroy all the beauty and elegance of Claude' (p. 131). Declaring that Lorrain's beauty is unmatched (p. 156), he singles out the aura created by his deft handling of light. This light, while 'brilliant', is

> so diffused over the whole, so happily balanced, so mellowed and subdued by that almost visible atmosphere, which pervades every part, and unites all together, that nothing in particular catches the eye; the whole is splendor, the whole is repose; every thing is lighted up, every thing is sweetest harmony. (pp. 152–53)

'Repose' echoes Goethe's 'serenity' as *the* effect of Lorrain's aura. And, similarly to Goethe, Price understands 'repose' as the aura's ontological correlative, as peace of mind, or, as he puts it in the passage already quoted, 'that mild and equal sunshine of the soul' (p. 125).

In his preface, Price unequivocally states that painting and gardening are 'distinct, but intimately connected', and that they 'throw a reciprocal light on each other' (p. vi). Price's figurative use of 'light' here is telling: even though the picturesque manifests itself in nature, it is very much a function of sight — that is, unlike the beautiful and the sublime, the picturesque cannot be applied to music (pp. 45–46). Etymologically, Price traces the term back to the Italian '*pittoresco*', which, he maintains, 'marks its relation to the painter', more specifically to the 'painter's eye' (pp. 218, 31, 54). To underscore the painterly way of seeing nature, Price summons an authority from Antiquity. In the preface he writes: 'It is not mere observation of Cicero; it is an exclamation: Quam multa vident pictores! it marks his surprise at the extreme difference which the study of nature by means of the art of painting, seems to make almost in the sight itself' (p. xii). On the title page, the full quotation appears as the epigraph to the entire treatise: 'Quam multa vident pictores in umbris et in eminentia quae nos non videmus!' [How many things painters see in shadows and in the foreground which we do not see!] (*Academica*, II (Lucullus), pp. 492–93). The recourse to Cicero has far-reaching implications. Making the eye sensitive to painting becomes a stimulus for discovering the picturesque in nature and for subsequently translating it into horticulture. But it is not just the physiological eye that sees in the mimetic sense, but also the spiritual eye that sees in the creative sense. In other words, painterly seeing entails imaginative access to, or indeed appropriation of, what was hitherto a *terra incognita*, the world hidden 'in shadows'.

Price cites Charles Hamilton, creator of Painshill Park, as an exemplary garden designer who 'had studied pictures [...] for the express purpose of improving real landscape' (p. 333). Price is especially pleased by the openness of the design: there were 'no edges, no borders, no distinct lines of separation; nothing was done except keeping the ground properly neat, and the communication free from any obstruction. The eye and the footsteps were equally unconfined' (p. 333). Even though Painshill has the typical follies or picturesque eye-catchers (e.g. a temple, a grotto, a fretted, arched bridge, a Gothic ruin), his description leads us to infer that he associates the overall layout with Lorrain.

4.3. Alexander Pope: Gardener and Poet

To explore the nature–art antithesis seemingly inherent in the three sister arts in eighteenth-century England, we turn to the emergence of the English Garden and to Alexander Pope.[19] While first and foremost a poet, Pope dabbled in painting and created his own English Garden at his Twickenham estate, featuring a Palladian-style villa with a portico, as well as a — picturesque — grotto.[20] Invoking *ut pictura poesis et hortus*, Horace greeted the visitor to the grotto with 'A hid recess, where Life's revolving Day, | In sweet Delusion gently steals away', while Pope, shutting the doors, turned the grotto into a camera obscura: 'on the Walls [...] the River, Hills, Woods, and Boats, are forming a moving Picture in their visible Radiations'.[21] This is how the 'garden' looked — transposed into a latter-day Lorrain — in Turner's 1808 painting, *Pope's Villa at Twickenham*.[22]

Pope never made it to Italy, but he was a well-informed armchair traveller, privy to what his friends brought home from their Grand Tours, including, de rigueur, paintings and prints by Lorrain. Apart from the multi-art talent that points ahead to Goethe as a kindred spirit, there is also his predilection for ekphrasis, as proven by the vivid rendering of Achilles' shield in his translation of *The Iliad*. With regard to Lorrain, this passage from *The Temple of Fame: A Vision* (1715) can be read as an ekphrastic description of a Lorrainian landscape:

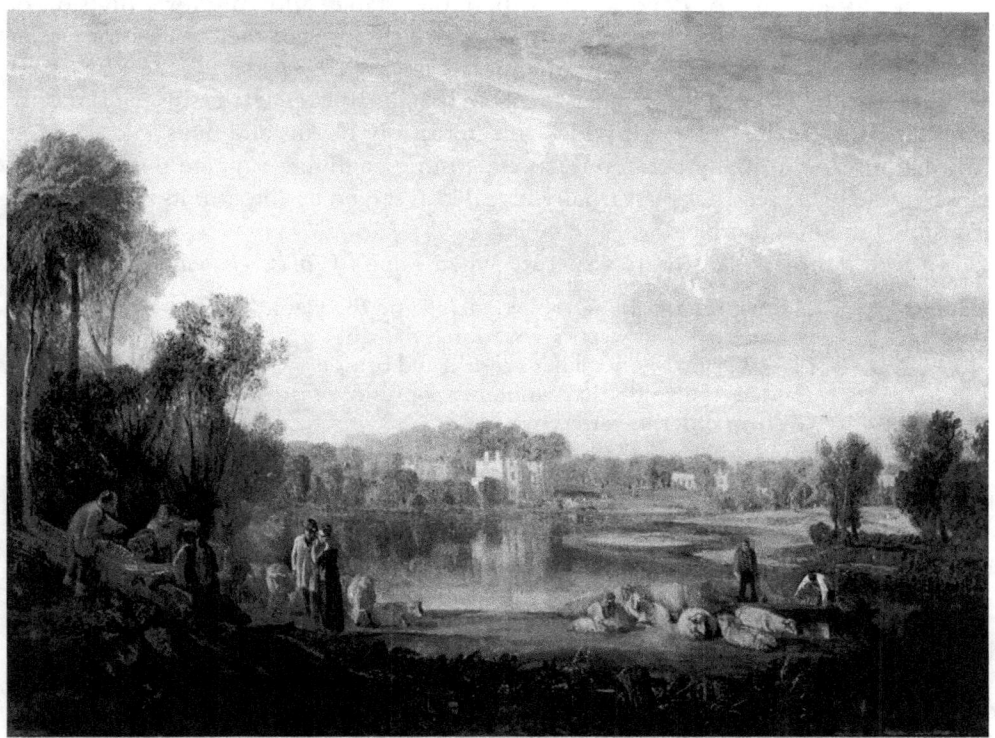

Fig. 4.5. Turner, *Pope's Villa at Twickenham*. Private collection/ © Sotheby's, London; 9 July 2008, lot 91

> (What time the morn mysterious visions brings,
> While purer slumbers spread their golden wings)
> A train of phantoms in wild order rose,
> And join'd, this intellectual scene compose.
> I stood, methought, betwixt earth, seas, and skies;
> The whole creation open to my eyes:
> In air self-balanc'd hung the globe below,
> Where mountains rise, and circling oceans flow;
> Here naked rocks and empty wastes were seen;
> There tow'ry cities, and the forests green:
> Here sailing ships delight the wand'ring eyes:
> There trees and intermingled temples rise;
> Now a clear sun the shining scene displays,
> The transient landscape now in clouds decays.
> O'er the wide prospect as I gaz'd around.[23]

While Pope's 'wand'ring eyes' do follow the movement of the 'sailing ships', and the 'mountains rise' as the 'oceans flow', nature's tempos seem controlled by the observer's gaze ('were seen'). In fact, taking our cue from the last line, 'O'er a wide prospect as I gazed around', the observer, the 'I', has control over the view. To this we can add the fact that the 'phantoms', i.e. the visual impressions, may run 'wild', but they are harnessed to an 'intellect' that 'composes' them into a 'whole'. In terms of point of view, that of Pope seems to be rather stable, allowing for a division of the canvas into 'here' and 'there' sections, which, by dint of their repetition, seem to come into view almost cinematographically (as 'moving pictures'). Maybe this is why the steady gaze catches objects in their non-distinct plural forms — the only singular entity is the sun, with which this 'Creation' begins and ends. Notice how this dreamscape, initially perceived from a cosmic or divine vantage point, then as close-ups (e.g. 'naked rocks'), is finally revealed as staged by the sun: its light renders it visible but also absorbs it.

We find a similar here/there structure when Pope's *Windsor-Forest* (1713) opens:

> Here hills and vales, the woodland and the plain,
> Here earth and water seem to strive again,
> Not Chaos-like together crush'd and bruis'd,
> But, as the world, harmoniously confus'd:
> Where order in variety we see,
> And where, tho' all things differ, all agree.
> Here waving groves a checquer'd scene display,
> And part admit, and part exclude the day;
> As some coy nymph her lover's warm address
> Nor quite indulges, nor can quite repress.
> There, interspers'd in lawns and op'ning glades,
> Thin trees arise that shun each other's shades.
> Here in full light the russet plains extend:
> There wrapt in clouds the blueish hills ascend.
> Ev'n the wild heath displays her purple dyes,
> And 'midst the desert fruitful fields arise,
> That crown'd with tufted trees and springing corn,
> Like verdant isles the sable waste adorn. (pp. 37–38, ll. 11–28)

Famous for their comparison of Windsor Forest to Milton's Garden of Eden, these lines also contain something akin to a theory of landscape, or rather, an aesthetic of landscape painting — a theory and an aesthetic arguably akin to Lorrain's and Goethe's. While in the poem cited above, the subjective 'I' composed a landscape of the mind, here an objective 'we' selects, assembles, and integrates 'natural' elements according to painterly principles — namely, aerial perspective, tectonic segmentation, and receding prospect. When Pope uses 'seeing an order' for his painterly eye, we are reminded of Goethe's notion of 'schauen', or intuiting an essence. Indeed, the 'order in variety' that underlies both land and landscape — namely, a dynamic interplay of contrasts, a coincidence of opposites — seems remarkably in tune with Goethe, e.g. 'agree' *and* 'differ', 'include' *and* 'exclude', 'indulge' *and* 'repress', 'desert' *and* 'orchard'. In this line-by-line assortment of oxymoronically articulated visual perceptions, painterly imagination and poetic inventiveness go hand-in-hand, as in 'harmoniously confused' or the use of the 'chequered scene' technique to verbally paint an alternating pattern of differently coloured spaces, 'verdant' and 'sable', or of 'light' and 'shade'. 'Seeing' the here/there structure of the landscape-cum-painting also reflects 'seeing' the here/there structure of the landscape-cum-park; the walk through the park provides the wandering eye with a succession of ever-changing sights. Or, as Pope's Eckermann, Joseph Spence, remarked after Philip Southcote had laid out the new circuit path at the Woburn Farm garden: the 'rosary that was so close and disagreeable is now a *wilderness of views*, and the new walk by it a *picture-gallery*'.[24] Goethe concurs: the efforts to 'anglicize' the Weimar Ilmpark aimed at producing 'a sequence of aesthetically pleasing pictures' (*FA*, XVII, 392).

Another feature of the landscape park that Pope alludes to is the small groups of trees ('thin trees'), or in horticultural jargon 'clumps', that dot the extensive lawns, breaking their monotony and serving as landmarks. In its allusive reference to order, the clump brings to the fore landscape's ultimate aporia, whereby landscape both realizes the order latent in nature and imposes it at the same time.[25]

With Pope's *Epistle to Burlington* (1731), we move from painting to park. In a passage that can be read as enacting his aperçu that 'all gardening is landscape-painting',[26] we witness the evolution of a garden:

> Consult the Genius of the Place in all;
> That tells the Waters or to rise, or fall,
> Or helps th'ambitious Hill the heav'ns to scale,
> Or scoops in circling theatres the Vale;
> Calls in the Country, catches op'ning glades,
> Joins willing woods, and varies shades from shades;
> Now breaks, or now directs, th' intending Lines,
> Paints as you plant, and as you work, designs.
> Still follow Sense, of ev'ry Art the Soul,
> Parts answ'ring parts shall slide into a whole,
> Spontaneous beauties all around advance,
> Start ev'n from Difficulty, strike from Chance;
> Nature shall join you; Time shall make it grow
> A Work to wonder at — perhaps a Stow. (pp. 316–17, ll. 57–70)

When Pope identifies the garden as, 'perhaps', Stowe, *the* pioneer among the English landscape parks, he is making not only a horticultural-historical statement but a political one as well. Conventional wisdom has it that the eighteenth century witnessed not only a political revolution but also a horticultural revolution, and that the latter mirrored the former — as if the French Garden's transformation into the English Garden reflected a transition from a strictly absolutist to a more enlightened socio-political system. And, while the rectilinear patterns of the French Garden celebrate the omnipotence of reason, the curvilinear shapes of the English Garden celebrate the freedom of nature.

Accordingly, the Pope excerpt cited here is framed by lines charging the architect of the French Garden at Versailles, André Le Nôtre, with lacking British common sense ('good sense') — here represented by the 'Genius of the Place' — which, Pope predicts, will lead to the demise of Versailles: 'proud Versailles! thy glory falls' (p. 316, l. 43, p. 317, l. 71). Unlike Stowe, Versailles feels restrictive, monotonous, overly cultivated, and symmetrical:

> On ev'ry side you look, behold the Wall!
> No pleasing Intricacies intervene,
> No artful wildness to perplex the scene;
> Grove nods at grove, each Alley has a brother,
> And half the platform just reflects the other. (p. 318, ll. 114–18)

While Goethe's ambivalence vis-à-vis the English Garden is fuelled by aesthetic contradiction, the political contradiction should not be disregarded, for Stowe and its continental cousin Wörlitz are 'aristocratic dreamscapes' that are both

> progressive and nostalgic, liberal and conservative; they celebrate natural freedom and natural order. If it is natural for man to be free, it is also natural for princes to rule, not absolutely, as in France, but liberally enough to accommodate ambitious new blood and retain their privileges.[27]

Of classical origin,[28] the 'Genius of the Place' is evoked as a nature spirit inhabiting a Lorrainian landscape in Shaftesbury's *The Moralists, A Philosophical Rhapsody: Being a Recital of Certain Conversations upon Natural and Moral Subjects* (1709):

> To morrow, when the Eastern Sun (as Poets describe) with his first Beams adorns the Front of yonder Hill; there, if you are content to wander with me in the Woods you see, we will pursue those Loves of ours, by favour of the Sylvan Nymphs; and invoking first the Genius of the Place, we'l try to obtain at least some faint and distant View of the Sovereign *Genius* and First Beauty.[29]

Reflecting the rise of secularization, Shaftesbury's sun god evolves into Pope's spirit that gives each garden its locally unique character — as opposed to the French Garden's universality. What is more, Virgil's 'genius loci', the guardian deity Aeneas prays to at his father's tomb after landing in Sicily, is reincarnated as a stone monument in the shape of an altar entwined with — this, too, reminiscent of Virgil's 'genius' — a snake in Weimar's Ilmpark, bearing the inscription 'Genio huius loci'.[30] What is intriguing for our investigation is the striking resemblance of Pope's genius to Goethe's Amor, the landscape painter. The difference is that here the painter has become a gardener — or rather, as the line 'Paints as you plant, and, as you work, designs' suggests, painting and gardening are analogous activities. Similarly to Goethe's Amor, Pope's genius imagines his creation beginning at the horizon where water and earth meet sky, working his way through the 'lines' that separate the various planes ('hills', 'vales', 'woods', 'glades') to the stage-like foreground ('theatre'), where he makes 'spontaneous beauties [...] grow'. Similarly to Goethe's Amor, Pope's genius is a 'dialectician' of sorts in that his creation is a dynamic 'whole' of opposites, including the interplay of light and shadow, of 'design' and 'chance', and — above all — of nature and art. And, in the end, similarly to Goethe, Pope presents us with a riddle ('perhaps'): is the product of his pictorial and horticultural imagination fictitious, 'wonder', or real, 'Stowe'?

Goethe's Amor vivified his landscape painting, and Pope's genius follows suit. Consisting mainly of action verbs, this passage from the *Epistle to Burlington* reads as if Pope's garden were an enactment of Goethe's maxim that it is the dynamic principle of polarity and intensification that makes up nature's pulse:

> To build, to plant, whatever you intend,
> To rear the Column, or the Arch to bend,
> To swell the Terras, or to sink the Grot;
> In all, let Nature never be forgot.
> But treat the Goddess like a modest fair,
> Nor over-dress, nor leave her wholly bare;
> Let not each beauty ev'ry where be spy'd,
> Where half the skill is decently to hide.
> He gains all points, who pleasingly confounds,
> Surprises, varies, and conceals the Bounds. (p. 316, ll. 47–56)

As Pope elaborates on the nature–art dialectic, he gives it an erotic twist that calls to mind Goethe's 'Amor ein Landschaftsmaler', as well as, picking up on Pope's nature goddess being 'spied' on, Hackert's 'surveilling' painterly eye — another example of nature as female other being the product of male fantasy.

4.4. Through the Claude Glass: Lorrain's Protean Art

Against the backdrop of the nature–art dilemma that Pope problematizes here, his mantra of 'consult the Genius of the Place' impacted (directly and indirectly) on Lorrain's reception in Britain in curious ways. Insofar as 'place' meant 'local', it kindled a 'nationalist' awakening which led to the discovery of the British countryside as a 'picturesque' landscape. It turned into a veritable movement led by the first theoretician of the 'picturesque', William Gilpin (1724–1804), and his hugely popular accounts of his explorations of the River Wye and South Wales (1770), the mountains and lakes of Cumberland and Westmoreland (1786), the Scottish Highlands (1789), and the Isle of Wight (1798). Scores of travellers toured the British countryside in search of picturesque beauty, which, for those pictorially challenged, could be discovered anyway with the aid of the Claude glass.[31] Named after Lorrain, the device consisted of a convex oval mirror which presented 'nature' to the onlooker neatly framed and in subdued hues, proving Gilpin's definition of the 'picturesque' as 'a term expressive of that peculiar kind of beauty, which is agreeable in a picture' — a picture à la Lorrain, we hasten to add.[32] Important for the question explored in this chapter is the fact not so much that the picturesque beauty-hunters turned away from nature — with Claude glass in hand, they had to turn their backs to the landscape in sight — but that this is an instance of 'art', in the form of a mechanical device, manipulating nature and making it conform to what boils down to a visual or pictorial artifice. To wit, Gilpin's etchings of his 1769 journey to Norfolk strike one as digitally enhanced by an image-editing application called *Lorrain*, such as this scene with the 'ruins of Castle-acre'.[33]

Despite conjuring up the dreaded image of the traveller turned *homo faber*, in its mirroring function the Claude glass suggests, as Hagstrum notes, 'both faithful realism and stylized idealism',[34] and thus reflects the aesthetic conundrum under scrutiny here. In its unique way, the Claude glass corroborates the notion that landscape means shaping land, here in the form of a frame, which harks back to the theatricality of landscape painting by turning nature into spectacle — thus establishing a lineage, via Gilpin, from Lorrain to René Magritte,[35] with Goethe's *Die Wahlverwandtschaften* somewhere in between, for the novel's male protagonist sits down in a moss hut 'so that he could take in at a glance the various scenes that showed the landscape as if framed by door and window' (*CW*, XI, 94; *FA*, VIII, 272). As the taste for the picturesque increased, Lorrain became a pawn in a protracted and acerbic dispute between the followers and detractors of 'Capability' Brown, England's most prominent garden architect.[36]

The main bone of contention was the naturalness of the new garden. To give an impression of the dispute, we turn to Richard Payne Knight (1751–1824), who saw Lorrain, in his *Analytical Inquiry into the Principles of Taste* (1805), as the paragon of picturesqueness: 'The mouldering ruins of ancient temples, theatres, and aqueducts, enriched by such a variety of tints, all mellowed into each other, as they appear in the landscapes of Claude, are, in the highest degree, picturesque'.[37] To illustrate Brown's neoclassical style, and to contrast it with the picturesque, he added two etchings (Figs 4.7–4.8) to his didactic poem *The Landscape* (1794).

Knight's comments on the two plates allow the reader to compare the same scene 'dressed up in the modern style' (plate 1) and 'undressed' (plate 2), specifying that the brook in the middle distance has 'its banks dressed up by an improver' in plate 1, while in plate 2 it 'flows in its natural banks'.[38] According to the *OED Online*, the verb 'to dress' denotes to 'cultivate', 'trim', and 'smooth', implying the use of mechanical and artificial means, while an 'improver' is someone who 'cultivates land'.[39] With his improvements, the devilish Brown sins against the ultimate purpose of the English landscape park — to afford the solitary walker peace of mind:

> Advance triumphant, and alike lay waste
> The forms of nature, and the works of taste!
> To improve, adorn, and polish, they profess;
> But shave the goddess, whom they come to dress;
> Level each broken bank and shaggy mound,
> And fashion all to one unvaried round;
> One even round, that ever gently flows,
> Nor forms abrupt, nor broken colours knows;

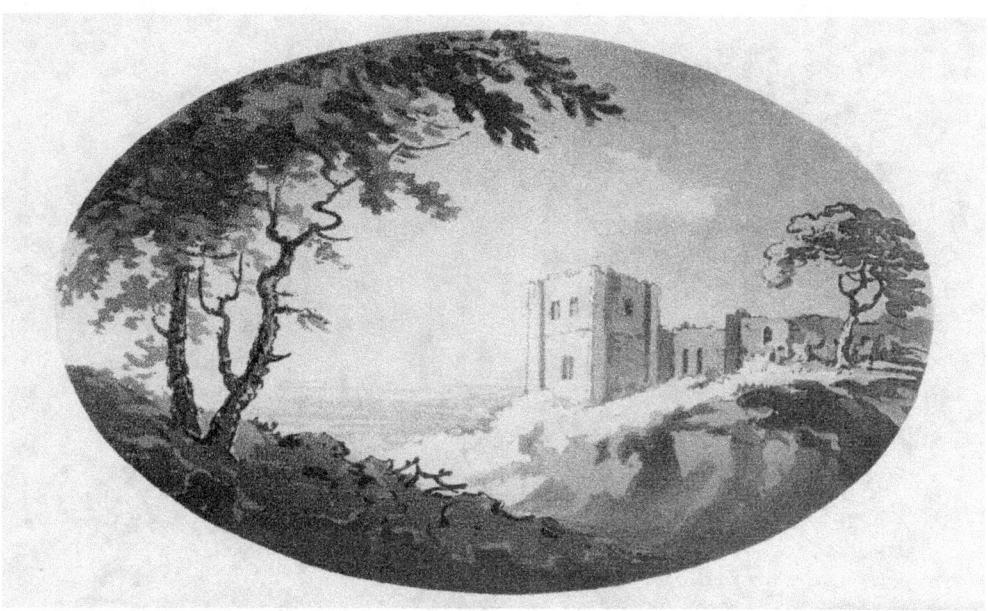

Fig. 4.6. Gilpin, view of Castle Acre. Royal Academy of Arts, London/ © Royal Academy of Arts, London — Prudence Cuming Associates Limited

> But, wrapt all o'er in everlasting green,
> Makes one dull, vapid, smooth, unvaried scene.
> [...]
> Shaved to the brink, our brooks are taught to flow
> Where no obtruding leaves or branches grow;
> While clumps of shrubs bespot each winding vale,
> Open alike to every gleam and gale;
> Each secret haunt, and deep recess display'd,
> And intricacy banish'd with its shade.
> Hence, hence! thou haggard fiend, however call'd,
> Thin, meagre genius of the bare and bald;
> Thy spade and mattock here at length lay down,
> And follow to the tomb thy favourite Brown:
> Thy favourite Brown, whose innovating hand
> First dealt thy curses o'er this fertile land;
> First-taught the walk in formal spires to move,
> [...]
> Banish'd the thickets of high-bowering wood,
> Which hung, reflected, o'er the glassy flood;
> Where screen'd and shelter'd from the heats of day,
> Oft on the moss-grown stone reposed I lay,
> And tranquil view'd the limpid stream below,
> Brown with o'erhanging shade, in circling eddies flow.[40]

As much as the philippic overshadows the horticultural issue, the plates and the poem's litany of juxtapositions would seem to situate Lorrain, contrary to Knight's

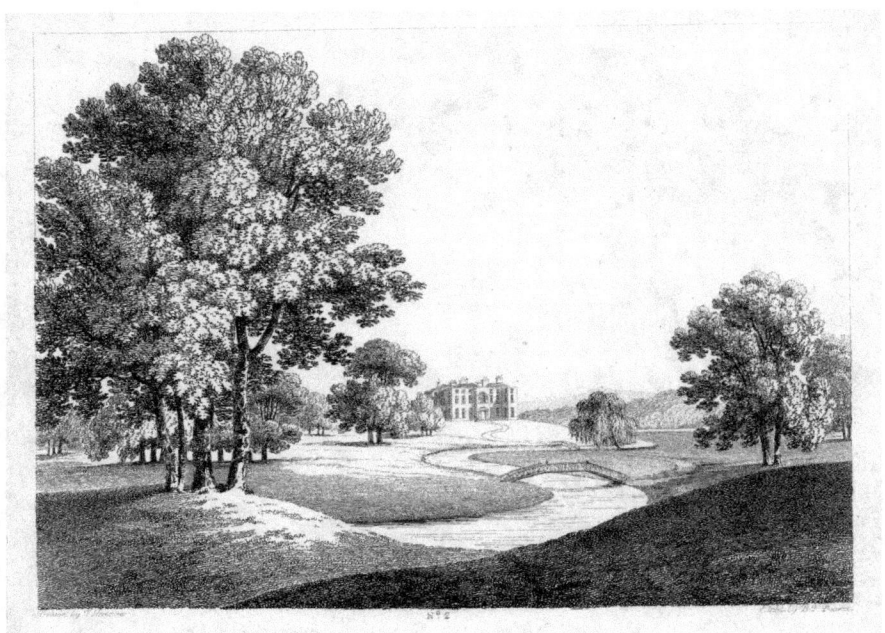

FIG. 4.7. Knight, plate 1. British Museum, London/
© Trustees of the British Museum

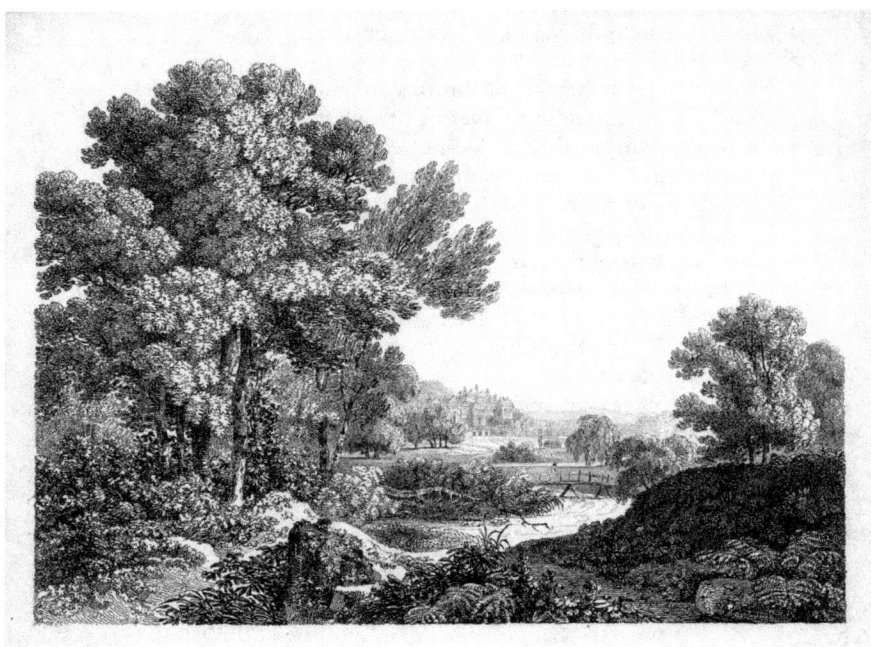

FIG. 4.8. Knight, plate 2. British Museum, London/
© Trustees of the British Museum

claim, somewhere between Brown's neoclassical 'beauty' and Knight's pre-Romantic 'picturesqueness'. Knight collected drawings by Lorrain, and owned two of his paintings — one of which, *View of La Crescenza* (1648–50; *LV*, 118),[41] seems to have served as a model for Knight's estate, Downton Castle in Herefordshire.[42] Knight accompanied Hackert on his 1777 *Expedition into Sicily* — thus the title of Knight's travel diary, which Goethe translated into German and included in his biography of Hackert (*FA*, XIX, 440–90). Just as Goethe would do ten years later, Knight evokes Lorrain to capture the light and the chromatic harmony of the landscape of Magna Graecia: 'The infinite variety of tints were all harmonized together by that pearly hue, which is peculiar to this delicious climate. (This Tint very particularly marks Claude Lorraine's Colouring).'[43] No matter how jarring the disagreements among horticulturalists, Lorrain remained everyone's darling.

The British naturalization of Lorrain overlaps with the Anglomania that had been gaining momentum on the Continent ever since Voltaire dined at Pope's Twickenham estate in 1728 and subsequently wrote *Letters Concerning the English Nation* (1733), his anglophile bible.[44] With Anglomania came the English Garden, and with that came Lorrain, who was repatriated in horticultural praxis and theory. Published between 1779 and 1785 in both German and French, Christian Cay Lorenz Hirschfeld's five-volume *Theorie der Gartenkunst* [Theory of Garden Art], the most erudite and impactful work on this subject in the eighteenth century, references Lorrain twice in the first volume alone.[45] His prolonged and meticulous observation of the atmosphere at dawn and dusk 'in the open field' exemplifies 'the first duty' of both painter and gardener, the in-depth 'study of beautiful nature'. The consequence of obstructing the prospect of the rising or setting sun by 'surrounding buildings, walls, or tall trees' is, Hirschfeld cautions future gardeners, to 'rob' the viewer of 'the most glorious sight in creation'. To shore up his conviction that the 'enlightenment of garden art' originated with the British — namely, that it is 'modestly embellished nature alone that retains the privilege to make a truly agreeable impression and delight the understanding' — he relies on Thomas Whately's *Observations on Modern Gardening* (1770) and — cited above — William Mason's didactic poem *The English Garden*, both of which were translated into German and enlist Lorrain as a model.[46] Right at the start, Hirschfeld introduces his German readers to Hagley Park and the enchanting prospects described by Thomson; he quotes Mason's invocation of nature as the gardener's 'Muse' and likewise references Pope's *Epistle to Burlington*.[47]

Insofar as the horticultural battle can be reduced to 'prospect' vs 'variety', Lorrain finds himself in the midst of a 'nationalist' project that denies the formative influence of Italian Garden design by naturalizing 'prospect' and 'variety' — in tandem with the 'representation of untouched nature' — as 'stock principles' of English Garden design.[48] Aesthetically, the English Garden is an exercise in the liberal arts; politically, it is 'an emblem of English liberty, gained by Whig politics'.[49] This is the poetics and politics of Walpole's seemingly neutral term 'modern' in his history of garden design, to which we now turn.

4.5. Gardening is Painting: Horace Walpole's Essay *On Modern Gardening*

'Perhaps, a Stowe?' Pope's question is answered by the description of Stowe that is part of Horace Walpole's pioneering history of horticulture in eighteenth-century England, *On Modern Gardening* (1771).[50] 'Modern', for Walpole, is not the picturesque style of gardening fashionable at the time of the essay's publication. In fact, he warns against pursuing variety for variety's sake, calling the results 'puerile', 'quaint', even 'barbarous' (pp. 146–47). 'Modern' for him is the gardening style of a William Kent (*c*. 1685–1748) and a Lancelot 'Capability' Brown. Their 'art softens nature's harshness and copies her graceful touch', thus reflecting the 'elegant' and 'noble simplicity of the Augustan age' (p. 146) — an almost verbatim echo of Winckelmann's judgement on Greek sculpture. The 'seed' for the modern school of landscape art was planted in England by Lorrain and Dughet (p. 148), which may be one reason for his assertion that 'the chief beauty of all gardens [is] prospect and fortunate point of view' (p. 145). The 'open country' is, for the gardener, 'but a canvass on which a landscape might be designed' — in the description of Stowe that follows, he repeatedly imagines Kent walking through nature with 'pencil' in hand (p. 149). And his design is such that the walk through the garden is — we already know the simile from Pope and Goethe — like 'a journey [...] made through a succession of pictures' (p. 148). Walpole pays tribute to Pope's role in the emergence of the English landscape park by 'undoubtedly contributing to form [the] taste' of Stowe's first architect — Kent (p. 140).[51]

Walpole pinpoints the emergence of the new garden style as the destruction of the walls enclosing — and the eradication of the symmetries underlying — the Italian and French Gardens, and the introduction of the 'sunk fence', which made for a smooth transition between more and less cultivated grounds (p. 137). According to Walpole, Kent was the first to 'leap the [erect] fence', and in so doing he discovered 'that all nature was a garden' (p. 138). Before he became a landscape gardener, Kent was a landscape painter who went on a Grand Tour to Italy between 1712 and 1719, tasked with acquiring copies of Lorrain for his wealthy patron. Little surprise, then, that one of his most cherished garden 'pictures', the section of Stowe called the Elysian Fields with the Temple of Ancient Virtue situated across the River Styx, invites comparison with Lorrain's *Apollo and the Muses on Mount Helicon* [*Parnassus*] (1680; *LV*, 193). Knowing that Walpole toured Italy too, we read his description of Kent's signature as a garden designer with Lorrain in mind:

> He felt the delicious contrast of hill and valley changing imperceptibly into each other, tasted the beauty of the gentle swell, or concave scoop, and remarked how loose groves crowned an easy eminence with happy ornament, and while they called in the distant view between their graceful stems, removed and extended the perspective by delusive comparison.
>
> Thus the pencil of his imagination bestowed all the arts of landscape on the scenes he handled. The great principles on which he worked were perspective, and light and shade. Groups of trees broke too uniform or too extensive a lawn; evergreens and woods were opposed to the glare of the champain, and where the view was less fortunate, or so much exposed as to be beheld at once, he blotted out some parts by thick shades, to divide it into variety, or to make

the richest scene more enchanting by reserving it to a farther advance of the spectator's step. Thus selecting favourite objects, and veiling deformities by screens of plantation; sometimes allowing the rudest waste to add its foil to the richest theatre, he realized the compositions of the greatest masters in painting. Where objects were wanting to animate his horizon, his taste as an architect could bestow immediate termination. His buildings, his seats, his temples, were more the works of his pencil than of his compasses. We owe the restoration of Greece and the diffusion of architecture to his skill in landscape. (p. 138)

Walpole singles out Kent's 'management of water' as the 'unsurpassed beauty' of his style. With his 'gentle stream' that 'serpentizes seemingly at its pleasure' and 'glitters [...] at a distance where it might be supposed naturally to arrive', he says 'adieu to canals, circular basons, and cascades tumbling down marble steps, that last absurd magnificence of Italian and French villas' (pp. 138–39). The stream's 'borders', Walpole continues,

> were smoothed, but preserved their waving irregularity. A few trees scattered here and there on its edges sprinkled the tame bank that accompanied its meanders; and when it disappeared among the hills, shades descending from the heights leaned towards its progress, and framed the distant point of light under which it was lost, as it turned aside to either hand of the blue horizon. (p. 139)

Evoking a Lorrainian image of trees given 'freedom' to grow, and resembling ancient 'columns' and blending a 'chequered light' with their 'lengthened shadows', Walpole concludes: 'Thus dealing in none but the colours of nature, and catching its most favorable features, men saw a new creation opening before their eyes. The living landscape was chastened or polished, not transformed' (p. 139).

4.6. Goethe: Gardener and Poet

Pondering potential 'imitators', Walpole singles out Germany as 'the most likely' (pp. 149–50). The prospect came to fruition in what was seen at the time as the most famous and elaborate English landscape park in continental Europe, the Dessau–Wörlitzer Gartenreich [Dessau–Wörlitz Garden Realm]. Begun in 1769, and using Stowe and Stourhead as models, it was created by Duke Leopold III of Anhalt-Dessau.[52] Between 1776 and 1797, Goethe visits Wörlitz seven times.[53] On his second visit, from 13 to 14 May 1778, he draws the park's neoclassical palace in chiaroscuro reminiscent of Lorrain,[54] and writes to Charlotte von Stein a letter that may be regarded as his first documented English Garden experience:

> Hier ists iezt unendlich schön. Mich hats gestern Abend wie wir durch die Seen Canäle und Wäldgen schlichen sehr gerührt wie die Götter dem Fürsten erlaubt haben einen Traum um sich herum zu schaffen. Es ist wenn man so durchzieht wie ein Mährgen das einem vorgetragen wird und hat ganz den Charackter der Elisischen Felder in der sachtesten Manigfaltigkeit fliest eins ins andre, keine Höhe zieht das Aug und das Verlangen auf einen einzigen Punckt, man streicht herum ohne zu fragen wo man ausgegangen ist und hinkommt [...] das ganze hat die reinste Lieblichkeit. (14 May 1778; FA, XXIX, 129)

[It is now infinitely beautiful here. I was very moved last night as we strolled through lakes, canals, and woods by how the gods have allowed the Prince to create a dream around himself. As you wander around, it is like a fairy tale being read to you, and it has the ambience of the Elysian Fields, manifold impressions flow most gently into each other, no height draws the eye and one's longing to a single point, you roam about without worrying where you started off and where you were going [...] the whole thing is of the purest loveliness.]

Rather than enumerating the park's comprehensive assembly of English Garden elements, Goethe tries to capture the inner experience that the garden generates. Particularly noteworthy is the parallel between the perceptional and the verbal. The merging of punctuation-less clauses mirrors the flux of impressions and associations with literature and myth. Enchanted, yet acutely aware, Goethe resorts to rhetoric to articulate his emotive response, be it simile ('like a fairy tale') or metonymy ('Elysian Fields'). The interweaving of the emotional with the spiritual is also reflected in that of the real and the unreal, the visible and the invisible: roaming a landscape and sleepwalking in a dreamscape. To 'roam about' implies both mobility and aimlessness; the modification with its riddle about origin and destination adds a sense of losing oneself in the garden's variety, which, oddly, contradicts the precept of English Garden theory that the walk through the park is guided so as to enable the visitor to integrate distinct vistas into a cohesive whole. Instead, Goethe evokes the whole as sheer emotion, as 'purest loveliness' — yet even this affect is tinged with a modicum of reflection, as 'pure' suggests the ideational (wholesomeness, even verity). Is Goethe's English Garden experience, in addition to poetry and Antiquity, also related to landscape painting? His rather striking characterization of his experience — 'no height draws the eye and one's longing to a single point' — lends itself to being read according to painterly principles insofar as Goethe feels uneasy about the lack of a single point up high that would stem the tide of impressions and stabilize the roving eye, and the lack of a vertical point of orientation that would counter the somewhat labyrinthine horizontal meandering of perception. It would seem that what Goethe is seeking is something akin to Lorrain's aerial perspective that clarifies and focuses the varied lines of perception in one vanishing point.

When Goethe moved to Weimar in 1775 to take on his duty as tutor of Duke Carl August, his first main residence, the Garden House, was situated in the 'park' along the river Ilm (*FA*, XXIX, 34, 732). As we enter the Ilmpark with Goethe, we follow in the footsteps of Susanne Müller-Wolff, who has meticulously and comprehensively traced its history and development. Having been neglected for years, the house, its garden, and the park were all in need of restoration. Drawing up a plan for 'an English Garden' (*FA*, XXIX, 38), Goethe began to lay out serpentine paths and patches of lawn, and planted clumps of trees and borders of flowers. Commenting on his efforts, in the summer of 1778, he writes to Johann Heinrich Merck (1741–91) that his 'vale is becoming more and more beautiful [...] and enjoyable' because he, 'at all times, with utmost care, hands over the compositional principles of art to dear nature, and lets her, who always binds together, consolidate and conceal' (5 August 1778; *FA*, XXIX, 138). Strikingly reminiscent of Pope's horticultural aesthetics, gardening, for Goethe, is tied from the start to the question of the relationship between art and nature, in the sense — here — that a garden's beauty and delight are functions of nature's cohesive powers to integrate, and keep from sight, the artist's hand.

With the garden's expansion, 'the wall of the [existing] French Garden is demolished' (*FA*, XXIX, 94). Following the picturesque fashion, Goethe adds a 'flight of stone steps' with a grotto-like structure, an 'abbey' — a cluster of small buildings featuring a steepled chapel, a Gothic ruin, and a moss-covered 'hermitage' — and a stone sculpture dedicated to 'Good Fortune', an allusion to the mythological deities Agathe and Tyche, reminding the visitor of the vagaries of human fate.[55] His fellow writer at the court, Christoph Martin Wieland (1733–1813), feels transported to 'Tempe and Elysium', not without, however, ironically qualifying the sight's 'reality' (Wieland's adjective of choice is 'würk*lich*') with a litany of oxymoronic epithets: 'wunderbar Künstlich Kunstlos anmuthig wild' [marvellous Artificial Artless delightful wild].[56]

From the start, in Goethe's mind, Weimar's English Garden interrelates landscape with illusionistic theatricality and landscape painting. For the courtly society of his sovereign, Duke Carl August, he stages playlets and open-air banquets, followed by nocturnal illuminations. For the mini-drama performed at the Louisenfest, a celebration of the Duchess's name-day (25 August 1777), Goethe asks his first drawing teacher, Friedrich Oeser, for an etching after Poussin to serve as the model for the curtain (*FA*, XVII, 78), while Wieland compares the chiaroscuro effect of the illumination to Rembrandt: 'a sight that resembled more a realized poetic vision than a natural scene. The entire bank of the river Ilm illuminated just as in Rembrandt — a marvellous, magical blend of light and shadow'.[57]

Part mini-drama, part description (of festivity, stage setting, and landscape), Goethe's 'Louisenfest' text is, on the one hand, a history of eighteenth-century horticulture in a nutshell and, on the other, an expression of his ambivalence vis-à-vis the English Garden.[58] The plan to stage it in what remained of the Baroque Garden — 'rectilinear paths and grounds [...] tree-lined avenues [...] large squares for gatherings and entertainment' — was scratched due to heavy downpours flooding the area (*FA*, XVII, 39–93). Taking a leaf from the book of English Garden theory, and using Wörlitz as a model, Goethe resolves to create a picturesque setting on higher ground, or, as he puts it, 'to improve the appearance of the landscape so as to present it as a sequence of aesthetically pleasing images' (*FA*, XVII, 392). As Goethe continues, the line between natural and painted landscape blurs — think of the nature–canvas puzzle in 'Amor ein Landschaftsmaler' or of the subject and composition of Lorrain's *The Mill* — for, once the curtain with the Poussin landscape is lifted, 'the rear door opened [and] there appeared, in stark contrast with the narrow foreground, a splendid and serene view [with] a princely banqueting table in the shadow of the ash trees' (*FA*, XVII, 399). The picturesque *pièce de résistance* is thus:

> ein über Felsen herabstürzender Wasserfall, welcher durch einen kräftigen Zubringer unablässig unterhalten wurde und malerisch genug angelegt war, ertheilte dem Ganzen ein frisches romantisches Wesen, welches besonders

dadurch erhöht wurde, daß man eine Scene der Art, in solcher Nähe, an solch wüster Stelle keineswegs hatte vermuthen können. (*FA*, XVII, 399)

[a waterfall roaring down crags, which was fed continuously by a strong tributary and laid out quite picturesquely, imparted the entire scene with a lively Romantic ambience, which was intensified by the fact that one would not have reckoned at all with such a scene, in such proximity, and in such inhospitable a place.]

Being captivated by an unexpected natural sight is the picturesque effect par excellence, but it is not the only effect. Goethe writes: 'Artistically, everything was seamlessly integrated, anything coarse was completely removed; one felt so close and distant from home, almost like being in a fairy tale' (*FA*, XVII, 399). Mindful of the Louisenfest context, this summary reads like an encapsulation of Lorrain's art, due not just to the comparison with the fairy tale but also, and crucially so, to the tension that this label suggests — real and unreal — as well as the tension inherent in the quasi-oxymoronic 'close'–'distant' formula, implying the simultaneous closeness to and distance from nature *and* art. As sincere as Goethe is about this tension being at the core of Lorrain's art, his ambivalence about English Garden art comes to the fore in his ironic treatment of the play's gardener character, who is seen as not only a 'decorator' but also an illusionist who, in three sleepless nights, 'transforms the valley into a paradise' by 'turning meadows into rocks and rocks into paths, | now straight, now zigzag width and breadth' (*FA*, XVII, 396). In the comedy *Der Triumph der Empfindsamkeit* [The Triumph of Sensibility] (1778), Goethe's satire of picturesque gardening,[59] the 'decorator' has indeed become a magician who regales courtly society with his 'travelling nature', a set of boxes out of which he conjures 'roaring waterfalls', 'singing birds', and a 'shining moon' (*FA*, V, 83, 90; cf. 84). One has to wonder whether this folly of a portable nature is not a veiled attack on another portable folly, the Claude glass. While not the same, both follies provide a mechanized experience of 'nature'. The irony hidden in Goethe's satire is that the garden style meant to lessen man's alienation from nature has ultimately intensified it. The English Garden's aesthetics play a role in this ontological impact. At one point, the court gardener recites a litany of thirty-three picturesque elements, ending with:

> Obelisken, Labyrinthe, Triumphbögen, Arkaden,
> Fischerhüten, Pavillons zum Baden.
> Chinesisch-Gotische Grotten, Kiosken, Tings,
> Maurische Tempel und Monumente,
> Gräber, ob wir gleich niemand begraben,
> Man muß es alles zum Ganzen haben. (*FA*, V, 96)

> [Obelisks, labyrinths, triumphal arches, arcades,
> Fishermen's cottages, pavilions for bathing.
> Chinese-Gothic grottoes, kiosks, Chinese pavilions,
> Moorish temples, and monuments,
> Tombs, even though we bury no one,
> One must have all these to have a whole.]

Just as the rhyme scheme breaks down in the penultimate couplet, so does the purported 'wholeness' of the English Garden, whose aesthetics have been reduced to arithmetic.⁶⁰ As enumeration replaces integration, we are reminded of Faust's opening monologue, in which he laments the lack of a secret thread linking the various subjects he has studied. Goethe's picturesque scepticism also involves the relation between nature and art:

> [...] unsere Elysische Bäume
> Schwinden wie Elysische Träume,
> Wenn man sie verpflanzen will.
> [...]
> Denn in einem Park ist alles Prunk;
> Verdorrt ein Baum und wird ein Strunk,
> Ha! sagen sie, da seht die Spur,
> Wie die Kunst auch hinterdrein der Natur
> Im Dürren ist. (*FA*, v, 96)

> [[...] our Elysian trees
> Vanish like Elysian dreams,
> When you try to transplant them.
> [...]
> For in a park everything is ostentation;
> When a tree withers and turns into a stump,
> Ha! they say, there you have proof,
> How art, following nature,
> Withers, too.]

Goethe's career as picturesque gardener was short-lived. By ignoring the autonomy of both nature and art, the English Garden's facile blending results in a hollow splendour that evaporates the Arcadian dream. But his scepticism ran deeper than the playful criticism articulated here. Even before he began to dabble in gardening, around 1770, he suggested that the new garden was both a *locus amoenus* and a *locus terribilis*. In *Faust*, Gretchen's downfall begins with the seduction in the garden of her licentious friend Martha. Similarly, the site for the only love scene between Faust and Gretchen is a garden cottage where Mephistopheles lurks like a beast of prey (ll. 3073–3210). Likewise, for Werther, the randomness of the new garden art nurtures his capriciousness so as to allow him to project heaven or hell into one and the same spot:

> Erst hast du zwischen Kastanienbäumen die weite Aussicht [...] hohe Buchenwände [schließen] einen endlich ein, und durch ein daran stoßendes Bosket [wird] die Allee immer düsterer, bis zuletzt alles sich in ein geschlossenes Plätzchen endigt, das alle Schauer der Einsamkeit umschweben [...] Ich ahndete ganz leise, was für ein Schauplatz das noch werden sollte von Seligkeit und Schmerz. (*FA*, VIII, 117)

> [From between the chestnuts there is a broad view [...] the tall mass of beech trees at the end, and how the avenue grows darker and darker as it winds its way among them until it ends in an enclosure which has all the mysterious charm of solitude. I can recall the strange feeling of melancholy which came over me the first time I entered that dark retreat, at bright midday. I seemed to

feel even then that it would some day be the scene of so much happiness and misery!] (*CW*, XI, 39)

Such horticultural scruples keep gestating within Goethe until, two decades later, they resurface in programmatic form in the 1799 essay 'Über den Dilettantismus' [On Dilettantism] (see below).

To return to *Der Triumph der Empfindsamkeit*, Goethe's satire on the English landscape park includes its 'source', that is, landscape painting. To bring his catalogue of disjointed picturesque eye-catchers to a close, the court gardener declares that for the 'perfect park' to be 'complete', one element is needed — a 'wooden bridge' featuring an 'arch' decorated with 'fretwork'. He justifies his request by arguing that 'no park can exist | Without it, as we can see in every copper engraving' (*FA*, V, 96–97). Does this mean that landscape painting is part of the pretence that the 'regulated wild' is still natural, or does it mean that landscape painting is still the model to be emulated? There may be yet another possibility here — namely, that Goethe mistrusts the seemingly unquestioned premise that a landscape painting can be translated into landscape garden. Our discussion of Goethe's ambivalence about the English Garden will shed light on this question. From the late 1770s on, he disengages from the Weimar Park project, but his critical stance on landscape gardening gives way to his reinvolvement ten years later.

While still in Italy, Goethe began to discuss with Duke Carl August plans for the construction of the Roman House, a retreat for the Duke styled in the tradition of the Renaissance country estate,[61] as depicted in his poem 'Mignon' (1795) and in his pen-and-ink drawing *Roman House*.

> Kennst du das Land? wo die Citronen blühn,
> Im dunkeln Laub die Gold-Orangen glühn,
> Ein sanfter Wind vom blauen Himmel weht,
> [...]
> Kennst du das Haus? Auf Säulen ruht sein Dach,
> Es glänzt der Saal, es schimmert das Gemach. (*FA*, II, 103)
>
> [Knowst thou the land of flowering lemon trees?
> In leafage dark the golden orange glows,
> From azure sky there wafts a gentle breeze,
> [...]
> Knowst thou the house? Its column-bedded roof,
> The shining hall, the inner room aglow.] (*CW*, I, 133)

In both setting and atmosphere, the poem and the drawing resonate with lines from 'Summer' in Thomson's *Seasons*:

> Bear me, Pomona! to thy citron groves;
> To where the lemon and the piercing lime,
> With the deep orange glowing through the green,
> Their lighter glories blend. Lay me reclined
> Beneath the spreading tamarind, that shakes,
> Fanned by the breeze, its fever-cooling fruit. (p. 78, ll. 663–68)

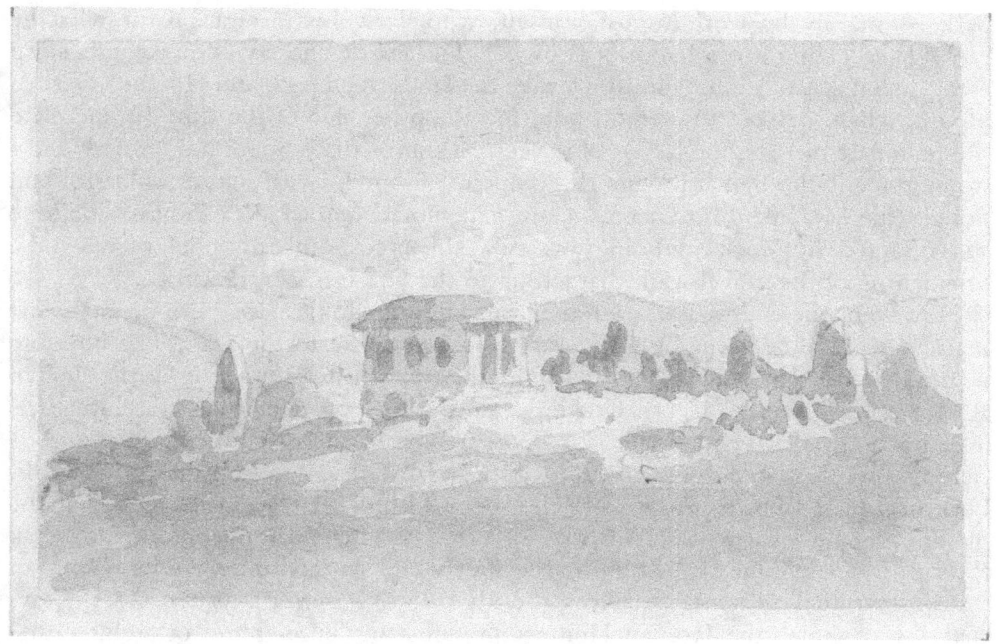

Fig. 4.9. Goethe, *Roman House*. Klassik Stiftung Weimar, Museen: 212535/ © Angelika Kittel

The remarkable verbal echoes[62] are evidence of how thoroughly Goethe had read Thomson, whom, days before he (Goethe) died in March 1832, he remembered as a poet who did not suffer from 'want of poetry' when he penned the 'very good poem on the Seasons' (*CV*, p. 425; *FA*, xxxix, 493).

In the drawing, Goethe integrates architecture and nature through the drama of chiaroscuro, producing a rich pattern of contrasts: vertical vs horizontal lines, foreground vs middle ground. The columns and trees in their darkness mirror each other, as do windows and shrubbery. The brightness of the portico connects the groomed area in front of the building to the clouds, which are contoured so as to mirror each other. The foreground is submerged in darkness, giving the illuminated building a sense of grandeur. The scenic setting invites comparison with the elevated locale and prospect of the ancient Greek temple of Segesta described in the *Italienische Reise*:[63] 'Die Lage des Tempels ist sonderbar: am höchsten Ende eines weiten Tales, auf einem isolierten Hügel, aber doch noch von Klippen umgeben, sieht er über viel Land in eine weite Ferne, aber nur ein Eckchen Meer' [The temple has an exceptional location: at the highest end of a long, wide valley, on an isolated hill, but nevertheless surrounded by cliffs, it looks into the far distance, across much land but just a small corner of the sea] (20 April 1787; *FA*, xv.1, 290; *CW*, vi, 216–17).

After his return to Weimar, between 1793 and 1798, Goethe was put in charge of realizing the plan, not just in terms of constructing the actual building but also of choosing its location in the greatly expanded and much 'improved' landscape park — mainly by Carl August himself, who drew his inspiration for what he called 'anglicizing' from Lancelot Brown.[64] The site he chose was on top of a steep escarpment, with a commanding view of the landscaped park and Goethe's Garden House, which marked the far-off point on the other side of the Ilm. To complete the Italianate picture, the layout of the retreat's immediate surroundings included a stone semicircular bench unique to Pompeii, a fountain with statues of Castor and Pollux (the San Ildefonso Group), a stone memorial named after Euphrosyne, one of the Graces in Greek mythology, as well as planted Lombardy poplar trees and a broadening of the gravel walk that led up to the building's entrance.

However, these antique, or rather picturesque, follies are peripheral. What matters for Goethe is the building and its integration into the park. The building is modelled after Andrea Palladio, Goethe's favourite architect of the Italian Renaissance — indeed, for Goethe, the Lorrain of neoclassical architecture. The feature meant to integrate it into nature lies in the bottom half of the two-tiered structure, which consists of roughly hewn Doric columns and brick walls, both of which seem to grow from the rocky hillside. They also suggest that the plastered upper level with its portico supported by graceful Ionic columns rests on the ruins of a bygone age, imbuing the stately and static structure with a kind of transformational dynamic (recalling the idyll 'Der Wandrer'). When Goethe says that, 'as a whole', the Roman House represents the 'purer sense of architecture' (*FA*, XVIII, 390), he likely sees it as an architectural example of 'formative imitation of the beautiful', Moritz's aesthetic credo according to which a work of art evolves out of a dialectic between a natural inner coherence and inventive composition.[65] In short, the Palladian Roman House is 'poetic'. While Goethe's documented input into the design and construction of the building, as well as the minutiae of its decoration and ornamentation, both inside and outside, is extensive, we look in vain for his horticultural ideas.[66] Given his apprehension about the English Garden, this is no surprise. If, in its Weimar incarnations, Palladio's neoclassical architecture is 'poetic', Brown's neoclassical garden is decidedly not. The closest Goethe comes to applying this ultimate accolade in a horticultural context is the expression 'ästhetische Landschaftsbildung' [aesthetic landscape design], which he applies to the Botanical Garden in Jena — a project in which he was, for scientific and seemingly aesthetic reasons, heavily involved (*FA*, XXIV, 537).[67] The Roman House as *drawing* reveals something significant — that a natural landscape can be 'translated' into a painted one. Viewing the Roman House as edifice reveals that a painted landscape cannot be translated into a horticultural landscape. From here, it is useful to look back to the British reception of Lorrain.

4.7. The English Garden: A Testing Ground for the Nature–Art Dilemma

Goethe's blending of Lorrain with his discovery of the British landscape, and his integration of it into the English Garden, both clarifies and complicates the Goethe–Lorrain dialogue. When Pope opines that 'all gardening is landscape painting [...] just like a landscape hung up',[68] he advocates, through the use of gerunds and a metaphor, not only for an equivalency of creative processes but also for a resolution of the nature–art antithesis. Similarly, Walpole maintains that, on the one hand, 'an open country is but a canvass on which a landscape might be designed' (p. 149); on the other hand, however:

> The very extensive lawns at [Stansted Park], particularly when you stand in the portico of the temple and survey the landscape that wastes itself in rivers of broken sea, recall such exact pictures of Claud [sic] Lorrain, that it is difficult to conceive that he did not paint them from this very spot. (p. 143)

If Pope and Walpole argue for an equivalency of method, Price argues for an equivalency in effect, recounting 'how [soothingly] *broad* the lights and shadows are on a fine evening in nature, or (what is almost the same thing) in a picture of Claude' (p. 148). Were it not for the parenthetical afterthought, 'nature', 'painting', and 'garden' would be indistinguishable in terms of experiencing landscape as nature and as art. Yet, as we shall see, the parenthetical 'almost' is precisely at the heart of the matter, for within its hidden oxymoron — similarly dissimilar — lies the paradox that *is* the English Garden.

Behind the shopworn cliché of Lorrain being the father of the English Garden, fundamental questions of aesthetics and intellectual history begin to emerge. For instance, does nature imitate art, or does art imitate nature? Or, as the Turner paintings and Thomson's and Pope's ekphrastic poetry suggest, is art imitating art? Consequently, does the English Garden only act the part of nature, and thus, given the frequently acknowledged theatricality of a park's sights, enact an illusion, pretence, or deception?[69] After all, it can be argued that there would be no English Garden without the invention of the sunk fence or 'ha-ha', which is a *trompe-l'œil*, an optical illusion that deceives the eye into believing that different pieces of parkland are one. In other words, is resolution of the nature–art antithesis even possible or feasible — a resolution that does not tamper with the integrity of either, thus avoiding the charge of being a sham?

Joseph Addison (1672–1719), already using the term 'English Garden' in 1712, in his essay on gardening in the *Spectator* (no. 414, 25 June), conjoins contradictory propositions when he states that 'there are [...] wild Scenes, that are more delightful than any artificial Shows; yet we find the Works of Nature still more pleasant, the more they resemble those of Art', such as a 'prospect which is well laid out, diversified with Fields and Meadows, Woods and Rivers'. For him, the dilemma is actually a source of pleasure, because we can 'represent' objects like these 'to our Minds, either as Copies or Originals'. Addison's argument that, in the final analysis, it is the 'mind' that resolves the nature–art ('original'–'copy') dilemma is symptomatic of the English Garden discussion throughout the century. As we shall see, Goethe, relying on Lorrain, will criticize this resolution as a deceitfully fabricated semblance and insist that the dilemma *is* the solution.

The dilemma harks back to the rhetorical tradition of the 'dissimulation of art' (*dissimulatio artis*) or the 'art of concealing art' (*ars celare artem*); that is, in our context, disguising the gardener's hand in creating the garden and thus giving the appearance of authenticity. To put it differently, is the beautiful semblance of the English Garden artificial or artful, false or genuine? In maintaining that the writer, painter, and gardener alike should avoid being 'plainly and avowedly artificial' and 'conceal' their presence behind seemingly untouched nature — note the remarkable contrast to the *Sturm und Drang* conviction of the artist *as* nature — Price (pp. 334–36) evokes Renaissance rhetoric to promote this 'precept'. He excerpts a couplet from Tasso's description of the garden of Armida in *The Liberation of Jerusalem*: 'and (what perfects the pleasure in each part) | the art that makes it never seems like art' (XVI. 9, p. 287). At stake here is judiciousness in applying art to nature — recall Bellori's directive for the soul-searching selection of natural beauties — and, insofar as the English Garden at Painshill is a transplanted Arcadia, the allusion to *The Liberation of Jerusalem* is apposite, for Tasso, in presenting nature as Edenic, brings to the fore the issue of authentic and artificial nature, and the attendant suspicion of deception.[70]

The evocation of Arcadia and its imagined wholeness and wholesomeness interrelates the English Garden's antithetical method and effect. In Thomson's 'Autumn', Stowe's coincidence of oppositions lulls the visitor into a carefree Arcadian daydream: in this 'fair majestic paradise'

> [...] the enchanted round I walk,
> The regulated wild, gay fancy then
> Will tread in thought the groves of Attic Land.
> (p. 170, ll. 1042, 1054–56)

In the *Epistle to Burlington*, Pope's coupling of his plea 'let Nature never be forgot' with his insistence on 'hiding' and 'concealing' art's role makes for an English Garden experience that 'pleasingly confounds' (p. 316, ll. 50, 55). This is a curious oxymoron. Is Pope's argument here mainly aesthetic? That is, is choosing 'confounds' over 'confuses' a mere matter of rhyming (with 'bounds' in the next line), or is it that the indistinguishable 'con-fusion' of nature and art is so harmonious that it is enjoyable? Yet, given the adverse connotations of 'confound', his argument might be more philosophical-ontological. According to the *OED Online*, 'confound' expresses a sense of disorientation, even alienation: 'To throw into confusion of mind or feelings; so as to surprise and confuse (a person) that he loses for the moment his presence of mind, and discernment what to do.'[71] In combination with the verb 'please', which the *OED Online* glosses as to 'satisfy', 'appease', 'pacify', or 'relieve',[72] Pope seems to suggest, then, that the English Garden, as a secularized 'paradise regained', restores the peace of mind lost during the Age of Reason. When the cultivated self mirrors itself in unspoiled nature, a feeling of alienation infiltrates the experience, which the English Garden promises to overcome with the ideal of balanced synthesis evoked by its cultivated naturalness. The pervasive oxymoron, e.g. in terms of method, 'regulated wild', and in terms of effect, 'pleasingly confound', encapsulates the paradox of the horticultural resolution. Broadly speaking, enmeshed in the process of secularization, the English Garden seeks a non-theological redemption that is paradoxical because, by healing us from (the excesses of French Garden) art through (the English Garden's concealed) art, it disavows the Fall without renouncing the fruit from the tree of knowledge.[73] This explains the persistence in horticultural theory of Renaissance aesthetics, manifested in the concept of the dissimulation of art. To wit, in an anonymous 1804 review of *Observations on the Theory and Practice of Landscape Gardening* (1803) by Humphry Repton (1752–1818), in the major German horticultural journal, the *Allgemeines Teutsches Garten-Magazin* [General German Garden Magazine],[74] the writer declares that the 'main principle is to avoid any appearance of regularity'. To avoid the manifestation of 'systematic beautification', garden art — 'nourished and edified' by nature through a process of 'observation', 'experience', and 'exercise' — is enabled to produce 'works of art in reality as Salvator Rosa, Caspar Dughet, and Claude Lorrain accomplished in painting'. To lend credence to his appeal for horticultural dissimulation, the reviewer quotes Tasso's *Liberation of Jerusalem*:

> a garden opens in a blithe expanse.
> Still ponds and crystal fountains, mossy cells,
> bright varied blooms and sundry trees, green plants
> of all kinds, sunlit hillocks, shady dells,
> forests and caves it offers at one glance;
> and (what perfects the pleasure in each part)
> the art that makes it never seems like art.[75] (XVI. 9, p. 287)

Before we articulate our enquiry into Goethe's criticism of this resolution and his insistence that the dilemma *is* the solution — all the while relying *also* on Lorrain — we need to glance at the emergence of the English Garden on the Continent in order to see how entrenched the dilemma, in its literary manifestations, is. Rousseau's most celebrated 'return to nature', the retreat to the peasants' rustic domesticity, is exemplified, in his novel *Julie; ou, La Nouvelle Héloïse* (1761), by Clarens, the town at the foot of the Swiss Alps. Of specific concern for our purposes is the inner sanctum of this rustic idyll, Julie's garden, 'Elysium'. To the eyes of her lover and tutor, St Preux, 'everything' in this garden 'is verdant, fresh, vigorous', and 'nowhere' does one see 'the slightest trace of cultivation'.[76] In fact, however, rather than untouched nature, the Elysium is an abandoned orchard turned wilderness, a French Garden metamorphosed into an English Garden. Julie therefore corrects St Preux: 'nature did it all, but under my direction, and there is nothing here that I have not designed' (VI, 388).

Since unspoiled nature can only be found in faraway locations, Julie had to settle for a compromise, that is, an artificial wilderness. Yet, in her effort to re-naturalize nature, she admits, she has done 'violence' to nature, 'forcing her in a way to come and live with' her. 'And', she continues significantly, 'all this cannot be done without a modicum of illusion' (VI, 394). If, as David Gauthier points out, 'Julie is able to create only the illusion of natural wilderness', then Rousseau's 'solutions' can create only the illusion of inner wholeness, and thus 'only the illusion of human freedom'.[77] The peasants of Clarens appear to be free. Yet this is a liberation achieved through the control of artificers: Julie or, much more pronouncedly, her husband Wolmar. What is more, Rousseau is an artificer himself. In one of his *Reveries of a Solitary Walker* on the island of St Pierre in the Swiss lake of Bienne, he experiences, while lying on a boat adrift, a 'perfect and full happiness which leaves in the soul no emptiness it might feel a need to fill' (VIII, 46). Ominously foreboding Faust's final words, he laments the moment's transitoriness: '*I would like this instant to last forever*' (VIII, 46). More lasting than this recovery of inner wholeness reminiscent of the original *bête* (that is, the inhabitant of Rousseau's ideal natural state not ravaged by the excesses of modern 'culture'), is the artificial recreation of inner wholeness. While on the island of St Pierre, the *bête* turns into the botanizer:

> The more sensitive a soul a contemplator has, the more he gives himself up to the ecstasies this harmony arouses in him. A sweet and deep reverie takes possession of his senses then, and through a delicious intoxication he loses himself in the immensity of this beautiful system with which he feels himself one. Then, all particular objects elude him; he sees and feels nothing except in the whole. (VIII, 59)

The botanizer's oneness with nature is far from the animalistic oneness of yore. It is a oneness brought about by aesthetic sensibility and a scientifically trained eye, for when Rousseau returns to nature and experiences a moment of supreme happiness, he does so, ironically, equipped with the tools of excessive 'art': a magnifying glass and Linnaeus's *Systema naturae* (VIII, 43). As we shall see, artificers are also at work in the extensive garden projects in *Die Wahlverwandtschaften*, and in *Faust*, where the quintessential artificer, Mephistopheles, helps Faust create a counterfeit Eden. Replicating Rousseau's English Garden experience, and thus healed from artifice through artifice, are those jaunting through the British countryside in search of picturesque oneness with nature with Claude glass in hand.

4.8. Counterfeit Eden: Goethe's Critique of the English Garden in *Die Wahlverwandtschaften* and in *Faust*

If *Julie; ou, La Nouvelle Héloïse* (1761) marks the start of the continental literary English Garden cult, then Goethe's *Die Wahlverwandtschaften* (1809) marks its culmination and demise.[78] Reading like a history and theory of garden art, the novel is his laboratory. In it, the English Garden figures as Utopia and dystopia — and landscape painting serves, so to speak, as the fermenting agent.

Goethe's erstwhile horticultural ambivalence turns into abnegation, for, as Helmut J. Schneider — focusing on *Die Wahlverwandtschaften* — argues, he mistrusts the English Garden's merging of nature and art for the sake of creating a beautiful semblance.[79] We first get a sense of the English Garden's utopian potential in the schoolmaster's ruminations on the old manor's French Garden:

> Er [der Gehülfe] war durch den großen alten Schloßgarten gegangen und hatte die hohen Lindenalleen, die regelmäßigen Anlagen, die sich von Edwards Vater herschrieben, bewundert. Sie waren vortrefflich gediehen, in dem Sinne desjenigen der sie pflanzte, und nun, da sie erst anerkannt und genossen werden sollten, sprach Niemand mehr von ihnen; man besuchte sie kaum und hatte Liebhaberei und Aufwand gegen eine andere Seite hin ins Freie und Weite gerichtet. (*FA*, VIII, 453)
>
> [He [the schoolmaster] was out walking through the expansive old manor garden, admiring the avenues of tall linden trees and the formal beds that Edward's father had created. They had flourished wonderfully well, just as

their creator would have wished, but now that they were ready to be seen and enjoyed, nobody spoke of them anymore; hardly anyone went there, and everyone's attention and energy had turned in another direction, towards the free, open spaces.] (*CW*, XI, 213)

In his ensuing conversation with Charlotte, she expands on his allusion to the 'freedom' of the English Garden, tying it to a longing for the wholesomeness of the Golden Age:

> Niemand glaubt sich in einem Garten behaglich, der nicht einem freien Lande ähnlich sieht; an Kunst, an Zwang soll nichts erinnern, wir wollen völlig frei und unbedingt Atem schöpfen [als ob] das goldne Zeitalter vor der Türe [stünde]. (*FA*, VIII, 454)

> [No one feels comfortable now in a garden that does not resemble the open countryside; nothing may create the impression of artifice or constraint; we wish to breathe quite freely and unrestrictedly [as if we were] on the brink of the golden age.] (*CW*, XI, 214)

Freedom is felt *and* practised, for castle and village, nobility and commoner, come together to celebrate the 'utility' of the English Garden. For the student of Rousseau's Clarens idyll, it comes as no surprise that this concept is expressly identified with 'Swiss order and cleanliness' (*CW*, XI, 123, 135–36; *FA*, VIII, 315–16, 335). As we will see, it is during this celebration that the fateful decision is made to combine three ponds into one lake, which brings about the dystopian turn.

Once the novel's main horticultural project is completed, a travelling Englishman serves as judge and advisor. Unlike the sarcasm with which Goethe censured the new garden cult in *Der Triumph der Empfindsamkeit*, his ridicule is now slightly subtler. He has the Englishman speak in a 'strangely accented French', as if he had not quite given up on French Garden art, and calls him a 'Liebhaber', or connoisseur, thus making him a representative of dilettantism and its flights of picturesque fancy:

> Durch seine Bemerkungen wuchs und bereicherte sich der Park [...] keine Stelle blieb ihm unbemerkt, wo noch irgend eine Schönheit hervorzuheben oder anzubringen war. Hier deutete er auf eine Quelle, welche gereinigt, die Zierde einer ganzen Buschpartie zu werden versprach; hier auf eine Höhle, die ausgeräumt und erweitert, einen erwünschten Ruheplatz geben konnte, indessen man nur wenige Bäume zu fällen brauchte, um von ihr aus herrliche Felsenmassen aufgetürmt zu erblicken. (*FA*, VIII, 465–67)

> [His observations expanded and enriched the gardens [...] he overlooked no spot where a beautiful effect might be brought out or added. Here he pointed out a spring which, if cleaned up, promised to add a decorative touch to a whole group of bushes, here a cavern which, if cleared and enlarged, would provide a welcome resting place, while they would only have to fell a few trees to have a view of the splendid cliffs rising behind them.] (*CW*, XI, 221–22)

As noted before, here is the motif again — that the English Garden's main feature, the serpentine path, is designed to offer fresh and surprising views with every turn, as if wandering through a gallery of landscape paintings. The pictures for the gallery are no longer provided by the outdated Claude glass but by the latest technological invention, 'a portable camera obscura', with which the Englishman 'captures the picturesque views of the garden' (*CW*, XI, 222; *FA*, VIII, 466). In choosing art over nature, the Englishman mirrors the method of the garden's principal architect, the Captain. He is obsessed with 'drawing and cross-hatching' and 'colouring with water paints' a map of the estate's topography so vividly that it seemed to 'hervorwachsen aus dem Papier wie eine neue Schöpfung' [grow out of the paper like a new creation] (*FA*, VIII, 290; *CW*, XI, 106, trans. modified). To help his fellow horticulturalists imagine his design even more vividly, he suggests consulting 'English Garden descriptions with copper engravings'. In the books, one found

> den Grundriß der Gegend und ihre landschaftliche Ansicht in ihrem ersten rohen Naturzustande gezeichnet, sodann auf andern Blättern die Veränderung vorgestellt, welche die Kunst daran vorgenommen, um alles das bestehende Gute zu nutzen und zu steigern. Hiervon war der Übergang zur eigenen Besitzung, zur eignen Umgebung, und zu dem was man daran ausbilden könnte, sehr leicht. (*FA*, VIII, 318)

> [a map of the area and a view of the landscape in its natural state, then on separate flaps the change artfully made to utilize and enhance its original good properties. From this the transition to their own estate, their own surroundings, and what could be made of them, was an easy one.] (*CW*, XI, 124–25, trans. modified)

The overlays of 'before' and 'after' views recall the pictorial 'rhetoric' invented by Humphry Repton, the most prolific of the English landscape gardeners.[80] In the introduction to his *Sketches and Hints on Landscape Gardening* (1794) — widely discussed in Weimar around 1800 (and reviewed and translated in excerpts in relevant journals)[81] — he writes that the 'art' of landscape gardening 'can only be advanced and perfected by the united powers of the *landscape painter* and the *practical gardener*. The former must conceive a plan, which the latter may be able to execute'.[82] Finding 'a mere *map* insufficient' for visualizing the transformative potential of his designs, he 'invented the peculiar kind of slides to [his] sketches', that is, aquatint plates slipping over one another. Among the slides which he collected and published in the famous *Red Books* is a before-and-after view of an estate in North Wales, illustrating his principle that 'the love of unity acting on the mind in landscape gardening' prompts the designer to 'form [...] separate pieces of water [...] into one'.

The Lorrainian character of his illustrations is undeniable, but not surprising, since Repton 'adopted enthusiastically' Gilpin's 'vocabulary and imagery for the Red Books'.[83]

Beyond garden design, Charlotte's allusion to the Golden Age establishes another link to landscape painting and to Lorrain, specifically his *Landscape with Narcissus and Echo* (1644; *LV*, 77) (Fig. 4.11).[84]

Painting into Poetry into Park 169

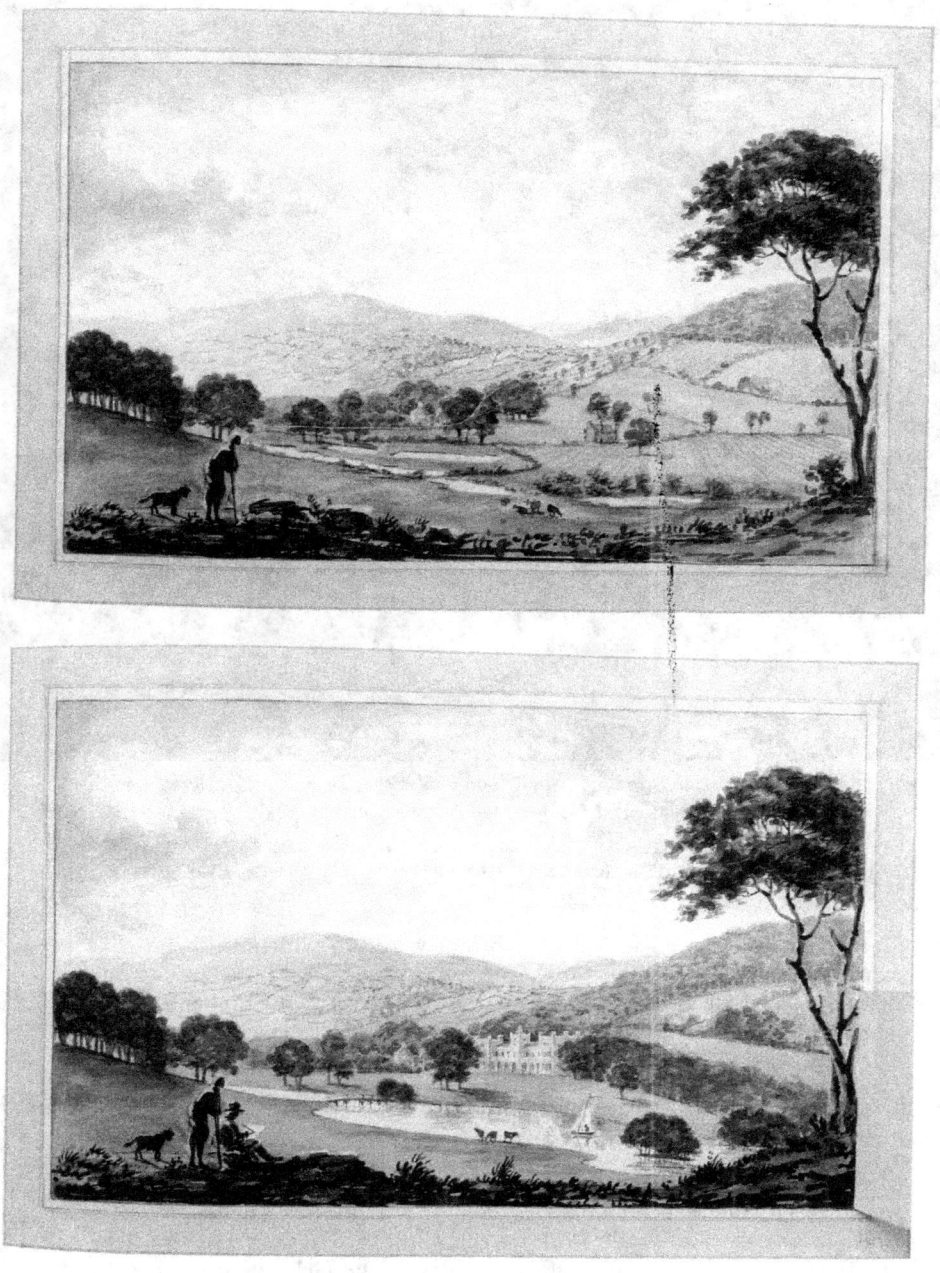

Fig. 4.10. Repton, sketches from *Red Book 65*. *Red Book 65*; private collection, Wales/ © André Rogger

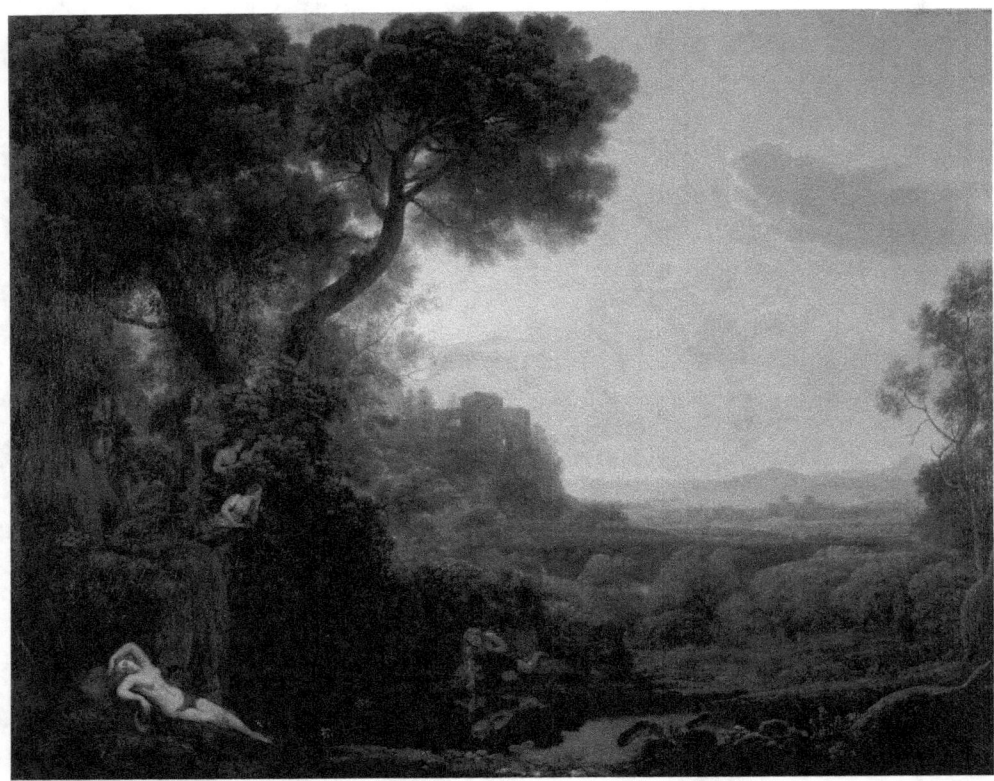

Fig. 4.11. Lorrain, *Landscape with Narcissus and Echo*. National Gallery, London/© National Gallery — Art Resource, NY

The place where Echo observes Narcissus smitten with his own reflection is introduced, in Ovid's story, as follows:

> There was a clear pool with silvery bright water, to which no shepherds ever came, or she-goats feeding on the mountain-side [...] whose smooth surface neither bird nor beast nor falling bough ever ruffled. Grass grew all around its edge, fed by the water near, and a coppice that would never suffer the sun to warm the spot. (Ovid, p. 153)

Ottilie evokes Ovid in describing her favourite spot for the planned summerhouse opposite, and thus echoing, the existing mansion:

> Man sähe zwar das Schloß nicht: denn es wird von dem Wäldchen bedeckt; aber man befände sich auch dafür wie in einer andern und neuen Welt, indem zugleich das Dorf und alle Wohnungen verborgen wären. Die Aussicht auf die Teiche, nach der Mühle, auf die Höhen, in die Gebirge, nach dem Lande zu, ist außerordentlich schön; ich habe es im Vorbeigehen bemerkt. (*FA*, VIII, 325–26)

> [You would not see the manor from there, of course, since it would be hidden by the clump of trees; instead, you would be in a new and different world, with the village and all the houses hidden from sight. The view of the lakes, towards

the mill, the hills, mountains and countryside, is extraordinarily beautiful; I noticed it as we went past.] (*CW*, XI, 129)

Even though the Narcissus myth is regarded as constitutive for *Die Wahlverwandtschaften*,[85] one of its manifestations has escaped the critics. Ottilie-Echo's landscape reverberates with Edward-Narcissus's earlier landscape so loudly that if verbally the echo reflects their (much-noted) taciturn and talkative dispositions, then pictorially her echo is like a condensed, i.e. engraved, version of his painting — which, in turn, resonates with Lorrain's. To wit: when they rove the country estate in search of areas suitable for picturesque landscaping, Edward takes them to what Ottilie will eventually choose as the site of the rustic building, enticing his friends with the assurance that 'on the very top of the rise [...] the view is freer':

> Dorf und Schloß hinterwärts waren nicht mehr zu sehen. In der Tiefe erblickte man ausgebreitete Teiche; drüben bewachsene Hügel, an denen sie sich hinzogen; endlich steile Felsen, welche senkrecht den letzten Wasserspiegel entschieden begrenzten und ihre bedeutenden Formen auf der Oberfläche derselben abbildeten. Dort in der Schlucht, wo ein starker Bach den Teichen zufiel, lag eine Mühle halb versteckt, die mit ihren Umgebungen als ein freundliches Ruheplätzchen erschien. Mannigfaltig wechselten im ganzen Halbkreise den man übersah, Tiefen und Höhen, Büsche und Wälder, deren erstes Grün für die Folge den füllereichsten Anblick versprach. Auch einzelne Baumgruppen hielten an mancher Stelle das Auge fest. Besonders zeichnete zu den Füßen der schauenden Freunde sich eine Masse Pappeln und Platanen zunächst an dem Rande des mittleren Teichs vorteilhaft aus. Sie stand in ihrem besten Wachstum, frisch, gesund, empor und in die Breite strebend. (*FA*, VIII, 289)

> [The village and manor house could no longer be seen. Down below they saw an expanse of ponds; beyond them green hills, whose contours they followed; and final steep cliffs forming a clearly defined vertical boundary to the furthest watery expanses, in whose surface their majestic outlines were mirrored. Down in the valley, where a rapidly flowing brook ran into the ponds, was a half-hidden mill, forming together with its surroundings an inviting resting-place. Heights and depths, bushes and woodland alternated throughout the whole semicircular view, and the leaves on the trees promised greater fullness later in the season. Separate groups of trees caught the eye at various spots. In particular a clump of poplars and plane trees stood out most attractively near the edge of the middle pond, at their feet. The trees were in their prime: fresh, healthy, reaching upward and outward.] (*CW*, XI, 105)

Faint as the echoes of Lorrain may be, they resound unmistakably once the view opens up from the top of the scaffolding, including the compositionally crucial aerial perspective, the *repoussoir* (i.e. the trees guiding the viewer's eye), and the 'whole': 'Further out in the countryside several new villages came into view; the silver streak of the river could be seen distinctly [...] Behind the wooded hills rose the blue summits of a far-off mountain range, and the nearby countryside could be seen in its entirety' (*CW*, XI, 135; *FA*, VIII, 334–35). The topographical analogy between the verbal and the pictorial landscapes extends to the existential analogies involving the motif of death. When the gardeners decide to 'combine the three ponds to make one lake' for the sake of magnifying 'the grandeur of the view', they turn a blind eye to unspoiled nature just as Narcissus overlooks natural beauties around him (*CW*, XI, 135, trans. modified; *FA*, VIII, 335). The result of 'single-mindedly forcing [nature] into shape' (*CW*, XI, 152; *FA*, VIII, 360) is the death of Otto (the child of Charlotte and Edward), who slips into the lake, while Narcissus vanishes by the water's edge.

The principle underlying the 'chemistry' of the elective affinities is that 'opposites [...] seek each other out, combine, modify each other and form through their interaction a new compound' (*CW*, XI, 114; *FA*, VIII, 302–03). In the novel, this seemingly transformative and harmonizing principle is a recipe for disaster. The new compound, the expanded lake, forces Ottilie to forgo the once safe pathway between the ponds and take the shortcut across the lake in a boat that rocks so hard she topples overboard, drowning the boy as its 'pure and wholesome' surface turns out to be a 'faithless and unfathomable' depression (*CW*, XI, 238–40; *FA*, VIII, 491, 494). 'Elective affinity' is the oxymoronic metaphor with which Goethe problematizes 'marriage', in human and in horticultural terms. 'Free' and 'wholesome' become associated with libidinal abandon and renunciation, with picturesque caprice and forceful improvement.[86] The marriages that give birth to Otto and the park are adulterous: Otto's parents dream of their respective lovers during his conception, the park's parents engage in fancy and whim. The result is a veneer that disguises the truth. The boy's facial beauty is easily mistaken for that of the lovers (*CW*, XI, 238; *FA*, VIII, 492). The park's colourful beauty disguises the demonic, even unleashes it. Just as the baby boy is neither Edward nor Charlotte, the English Garden is neither nature nor art. The azure sky of Italy transmutes into the moribund kitsch of the 'azure heaven' bedecking the vault of Ottilie's funerary chapel (*CW*, XI, 182; *FA*, VIII, 406). While the marriage of Faust and Helena gives birth to Arcadia, Helena's death signals the death of Arcadia. The death of Otto signals the death of the park.

To finish our exploration of Goethe's problematization of the English Garden, we turn to his *Faust* once more. The nature–art dilemma is bookended by Faust's first and last monologues. In the first, art, in the form of erudition, is purely accumulative. Fragmented knowledge leads to a fragmented self. In his existential desperation, Faust yearns to escape by invoking the moon beaming down into his dungeon-esque study:

> Ach! könnt' ich doch auf Berges-Höh'n
> in deinem lieben Lichte gehn,
> Um Bergeshöhle mit Geistern schweben,
> Auf Wiesen in deinem Dämmer weben,
> Von allem Wissensqualm entladen
> In deinem Tau gesund mich baden! (ll. 392–97)

> [If only I, in your kind radiance,
> could wander in the highest hills
> and with spirits haunt some mountain cave,
> could rove the meadows in your muted light
> and, rid of all learned obfuscation,
> regain my health by bathing in your dew!]

Although nature and art are seen as incompatible in the opening monologue, they come together in the closing one. With echoes ranging from Pope's 'nature methodiz'd' and Thomson's 'regulated wild' to Kent's and Brown's bold 'improvements' of water and land, from Rousseau's *jardin anglais* to Lorrain's *Acis and Galatea*, it is, in bold terms, an English Garden. In it, the cross-fertilization of nature and culture produces an earthly paradise in which happiness signals the overcoming of self-alienation and the achievement of human self-realization:

> Ein Sumpf zieht am Gebirge hin,
> Verpestet alles schon Errungene;
> Den faulen Pfuhl auch abzuziehn
> Das Letzte wär das Höchsterrungene.
> [...]
> Grün das Gefilde, fruchtbar; Mensch und Herde
> Sogleich behaglich auf der neusten Erde,
> Gleich angesiedelt an des Hügels Kraft,
> Den aufgewälzt kühn-emsige Völkerschaft.
> Im Innern hier ein paradiesisch Land,
> Da rase draußen Flut bis auf zum Rand,
> [...]
> Und so verbringt, umrungen von Gefahr,
> Hier Kindheit, Mann und Greis sein tüchtig Jahr.
> Solch ein Gewimmel möcht ich sehn,
> Auf freiem Grund mit freiem Volke stehn. (ll. 11,559–80)
>
> [A marsh stretching along those mountains
> contaminates what's been reclaimed so far;
> to drain that stagnant pool as well
> would be a crowning last achievement.
> [...]
> in green and fertile fields, with man and beast
> soon happy on the new-made soil
> and settled in beside the mighty hill
> a dauntless people's effort has erected,
> creating here inside a land of Eden —
> then there, without, the tide may bluster to its brim,
> [...]
> And so, beset by danger, here childhood's years,
> maturity, and age will all be vigorous.
> If only I might see that people's teeming life,
> share their autonomy on unencumbered soil.]

Thus, for Faust, ten thousand lines after stating under what conditions he would surrender his soul to the 'Devil' (with 'If I should ever say to any moment: | Tarry, remain! — you are so fair!'), it is an English Garden that brings about his fulfilment ('Envisioning those heights of happiness, | I now enjoy my highest moment'; ll. 1699–1700, 11,585–86).

Faust the English Gardener? Faust has not fared well with his critics, and justifiably so, for, after all, in a court of law, he would be indicted for involuntary manslaughter in at least three cases.[87] Unsurprisingly, he hires, as it were, a PR agent who euphemizes as 'progress' his ruthless exploitation of nature, people, trade, and colonies.[88] The catalyst for Faust's reinventing himself as a gardener is 'Sorge' [Care], a spectral figure and, quintessentially, a force greater than him, that he encounters in the scene preceding his English Garden vision. 'Care' derives from the Latin *Cura*, which Goethe found in his favourite mythological encyclopedia, where Cura is identified as the 'goddess of care, anxiety, and bad conscience'.[89] While *Faust* critics have exhausted possible readings of the Care figure, ranging from the ontological to the ethical, the following creation myth (from Hyginus's *Fabulae*), which is part of the Cura entry, has gone unnoted in *Faust* scholarship.[90] It presents Care not as a debilitating tormentor but as a creator, a cultivator, an ur-gardener:

> Once when Care was crossing a river, she saw some clay; she thoughtfully took up a piece and began to shape it. While she was meditating on what she had made, Jupiter came by. Care asked him to give it spirit, and this he gladly granted. But when she wanted her name to be bestowed upon it, he forbade this, and demanded that it be given his name instead. While Care and Jupiter were disputing, Earth arose and desired that her own name be conferred on the creature, since she had furnished it with part of her body. They asked Saturn to be the arbiter, and he made the following decision, which seemed a just one: 'Since you, Jupiter, have given its spirit, you shall receive that spirit at its death; and since you, Earth, have given its body, you shall receive its body. But since Care first shaped this creature, she shall possess it as long as it lives. And because there is now a dispute among you as to its name, let it be called *homo*, for it is made out of *humus* (earth).'[91]

When Faust rejects Care, she blinds him, forcing him to rely on, as he puts it, the 'radiant light [...] in my inner being' (l. 11,500). Attempting to proceed without Care has, up to his final hours, been typical of Faust, for 'sorglos' means as much as 'reckless'. It also implies 'having nothing to care for', as is the case with Odysseus on Calypso's enchanted island, or Adam and Eve in Eden.[92] For Faust, however, this meaning is equal to stagnation and is thus anathema to his quintessential disposition, 'striving'. The blinding then suggests that Faust is afflicted by Care, not in the enfeebling sense but in the edifying sense of 'concern', or even 'cure'; that is, he becomes a gardener — an English Gardener, to be precise. The blindness shows him that chasing after the sun (or, his less hubristic ambition at the start of the second part, rainbows) was narcissistic, while a life of care requires the extension of the self into the world, born of a love of something other than himself.[93]

'Human happiness', Robert Pogue Harrison reminds us, seems to have been, since the time of the *Gilgamesh* epos, 'conceived of as a garden existence'[94] — not in a Garden of Eden but, abiding by Candide's plea, 'Il faut cultiver notre jardin', in a garden of one's own making, of one's own cultivation, requiring daily toil and, above all, care. It should come as no surprise, then, in an epoch as obsessed with both happiness and horticulture as the eighteenth century, that Faust should enjoy his supreme moment of happiness as a gardener.

On closer scrutiny, however, Faust's synthesis of nature and art unravels. Philemon decries Faust's 'park' as 'a counterfeit of Eden', while Mephistopheles sneers: 'That things might just as well have never been' (ll. 11,085–86, 11,601). Faust's great triumph is just an illusion, both because it is spoken 'im Vorgefühl' [in anticipation] and couched in the hypothetical subjunctive ('möcht" [would like], 'dürft" [might]; ll. 11,579, 11,581, 11,585), and also because it is the product of magic, which always denotes the beautiful semblance created by the triumph of art over nature, and which ranges, in the play, from alchemy to counterfeit to technology. Magic is identified with Mephistopheles, the proverbial liar and purveyor of illusions.[95] Cold and calculating, he is reminiscent of Rousseau's artificers.

Goethe's rejection of the English Garden is a matter of aesthetics and his self-understanding as an artist. His objections are twofold. First, the English Garden, as art, foregoes 'objectivity' for the sake of 'subjectivity'. Following up on his satire of extravagant sentimental gardening in *Der Triumph der Empfindsamkeit* in 1778, he, together with Schiller, clarifies his position in 'Über den Dilettantismus' (1799):

> Die Gartenliebhaberei verewigt die herrschende Unart der Zeit, im ästhetischen unbedingt und gesetzlos sein zu wollen und willkürlich zu phantasieren, indem sie sich nicht, wie wohl andere Künste korrigieren und in der Zucht halten läßt. (*FA*, XVIII, 760–62)

> [The art of gardening perpetuates the current bad habit of wanting to be unrestrained and lawless, and of fantasizing capriciously in aesthetic matters, for it can, unlike the other arts, neither be corrected nor disciplined.][96]

Second, the English Garden destroys both art and nature. Under the rubric 'Adverse Effect', Goethe does not mince his words when he characterizes the new garden art as 'Vermischung von Kunst und Natur. Vorliebnehmen mit dem Schein. Reales wird als ein Phantasiewerk behandelt. Sie verkleinert das erhabene der Natur, und hebt es auf, indem sie es nachahmt' [Mishmash of art and nature. Makes do with semblance. Turns reality into fantasia. It diminishes the sublime of nature and nullifies it by simulating it] (*FA*, XVIII, 760).

In order to avoid 'artificiality' and preserve the 'sublime', nature must be authentic, yet 'artistically' (or 'bildend' [formatively], to use Moritz's term) — not artificially or artfully — formed so as to 'Platonize' it. Goethe's model is Lorrain. Echoing the poietics of *Die Wahlverwandtschaften* — 'kein Strich, der nicht erlebt, aber kein Strich so, *wie* er erlebt worden' [not a touch that he had not experienced, and at the same time not a touch just as he had experienced it][97] — he maintains that Lorrain's landscape

> uns sehr natürlich erscheinet, die wir aber in der Wirklichkeit vergebens suchen. [Lorrain spricht] zur Welt durch ein Ganzes; dieses Ganze aber findet er nicht in der Natur, sondern es ist die Frucht seines eigenen Geistes, [...] des Anwehens eines befruchtenden göttlichen Odems. (to Eckermann, 18 April 1827; *FA*, XXXIX, 603–04)

> [appears very natural to us, but that we vainly seek it in the actual world. [Lorrain speaks] to the world through an entirety; he does not find this entirety in Nature — it is the fruit of his own mind; [...] of the aspiration of a fructifying divine breath.] (*CV*, pp. 196–97)

Mindful of the credo that the 'whole' is more elevated than — indeed, supersedes — reality, Goethe's already-cited bon mot that in Lorrain 'nature proclaims herself to be eternal' gains new meaning (*FA*, XXII, 534).

Goethe questions the utopian potential of the English Garden. For him, it is neither nature nor culture; it meddles with nature's authenticity, thus voiding its grandeur and masking its barbarity. It is susceptible to the whims of subjectivity and unrestraint. Its beautiful semblance is a shiny surface, a *laterna magica*-type illusion, a delusion without essence. It fails to make visible the whole, the idea, which can only emerge from the dynamics of dichotomy and heightening. For Goethe, the English Garden is dystopian, and fails to redeem because it fails as art.

In 1825, while on a coach ride to the baroque-style Belvedere Castle on the outskirts of Weimar, in a conversation with Chancellor von Müller, Goethe praises the French Garden for its 'spacious canopies of leaves, vaulted trellis, [and] quincunxes, which allow a sizeable party to disperse and assemble graciously', while faulting the English Garden for causing people 'everywhere to bump or hamper each other or go their separate ways' (*FA*, XXXVII, 280; cf. 889). As interesting as it is to see how Goethe ties horticulture to sociability, even conviviality, the wit of his verbal imagination is truly striking when he characterizes the English Garden as 'Naturspäßig' [quirkily natural] (*FA*, XXXVII, 280) — an aperçu-like neologism that encapsulates the English Garden's untruth, for, as Goethe explains to Eckermann at about the same time (using 'Spaß' [jest] again): '*Nature* understands no jesting; she is always true, always serious, always severe; she is always right, and the errors and faults are always those of man.'[98] If the English Garden's return to nature smacks of mischief, the French Garden's underlying geometry elicits Goethe's return to rhetoric. The source for the quincuncial pattern of planting trees is Quintilian's *Orator's Education*. In his chapter on 'Ornament', he writes, 'I shall plant my trees in order and at fixed distances apart. What can be more handsome than the quincunx, which presents straight lines whichever way you look?' (Quintilian, VIII. 3. 9). For Goethe, at the age of seventy-six, a landscape's visual appeal is still, or again, tied to the perception of order, and thus not unlike the aesthetic experience rhetorically articulated when he first discovered Lorrain half a century earlier.

If Faust's horticultural moment of happiness is predicated upon a perception — indeed experience — of balance, then it is also a chromatic moment of happiness — at least if we rely on the 'sensory-moral effect' that Goethe grants green, the only colour used in his English Garden vision, in *Zur Farbenlehre*: 'The eye finds a physical satisfaction in green. When the mixture of the two colours [yellow, blue] which yield green is [...] evenly balanced [...] the eye and the soul come to rest' (*CW*, XII, 279, 283; *FA*, XXIII.1, 247, 256). The interplay of colour and mood — Lorrainian 'serenity' in the case of green — is a perfect segue to a discussion of Goethe's colour theory, with which the next chapter commences.

Notes to Chapter 4

1. Borchardt, p. 33.
2. U. Price, pp. 125–26. Henceforth cited with page numbers in parentheses in the text. For an intellectual biography of 'Mr Price the Picturesque' and the horticultural feats at his Foxley estate, see Watkins and Cowell.
3. For brevity's sake, and in contradistinction to 'French Garden', we will mostly use 'English Garden' to refer to the new movement in garden design originating in the British Isles. As

boundaries are permeable, Turner, in his comprehensive *European Gardens: History, Philosophy and Design*, pp. 261–311, subsumes the English Garden under the heading 'Neoclassical and Romantic Gardens, 1770–1810'.
4. The poem was popularized in Germany by a partial translation in Christian Cay Lorenz Hirschfeld's acclaimed *Theorie der Gartenkunst* (see e.g. I, 128).
5. Mason, pp. 3–4.
6. See Brink, pp. 3–4; Manwaring, pp. 57–94; Kitson, pp. 29–30. As mentioned in the Introduction to this study, the Weimar court library owned a copy of this 'portable' Lorrain, and it must have been consulted so often, mainly by Goethe, that it began to fall apart.
7. While neither their connection to the landscape park nor, in Pope's case, landscape poetry are the focus of Hagstrum's *Sister Arts*, the individual chapters on Pope's and Thomson's 'pictorialism' are still instructive (pp. 210–42, 243–67).
8. Brownell, pp. 39–117; Manwaring, pp. 91–92, 97, 101–08, 127–28. Hagstrum, pp. 165, 263, 266, maintains that Lorrain's 'influence' on Pope and Thomson is overestimated, and that their neoclassical pictorialism (even Thomson's sun imagery) has more in common with Annibale Carracci, Guido Reni, and Nicolas Poussin.
9. See Guthrie; Jung; Fabian and Spieckermann. Cf. Fabian; L. M. Price, pp. 61–72, 73–84.
10. Thomson, *Complete Poetical Works*, pp. 38–39, ll. 950–62. Further references to this edition are given in parentheses in the text.
11. I am adopting in this section Barrell's approach to reading Thomson; my indebtedness to him extends to reading a landscape poem like a landscape painting, and vice versa. Stated later, but coincident with Barrell, is the view of McCormick, '*Poema Pictura Loquens*', pp. 201–02, that a landscape poet like Thomson 'imitates the *process* of composition and the pictorial organization of painting', and 'words, in their syntax, grammar, and word order come to equal the schemata of painting'. While the painter 'registers objects in the landscape and arranges them into a composition [...], so does the poet select, arrange, and ultimately compose'.
12. For a succinct summary of the three concepts (to be discussed in the next section) in relation to 'landscape', see Lobsien. To get a compact sense of the impact of this painterly trinity on British painters, see Bicknell. For Richard Wilson (1713–86), Alexander Cozens (1717–86), Jonathan Skelton (1735–59), and J. M. W. Turner (1775–1851), see Howard; Ditner.
13. On the essay, see Boulton, pp. xv–cxxvii. All quotations, accompanied by page number in parentheses in the text, are from Boulton's text, which follows the second (1759) edition of the original. For Burke and the place of his notion of the sublime in aesthetic theory going back to Longinus, see Bullard. For Burke's sublime and its reverberations in landscape painting into the nineteenth century, see Andrews, *Landscape and Western Art*, pp. 129–49.
14. See Wine, pp. 51–52, 100.
15. Wine, p. 100.
16. On the relation between Burke and Lessing, especially their shared view of poetry as a non-imitative art, see Boulton, pp. cxxi–cxxv; McCormick, '*Poema Pictura Loquens*', p. 199.
17. On Price's understanding of the picturesque and on his familiarity with Lorrain, see Watkins and Cowell, pp. 61–78, 127–28, 152, 188. For Britain in the second half of the eighteenth century, the authoritative study on the picturesque in poetry, painting, and 'tourism' (but not in garden art) is Andrews, *Search for the Picturesque*. It should be noted that he is sceptical both of drawing too close an equivalency between Lorrain's paintings and Pope's and Thomson's poetry, and of granting Lorrain a 'monopoly of influence' in light of the popularity of Dutch and Flemish landscape painters in the early eighteenth century (p. 22). For a succinct discussion of the picturesque in and as garden art, as well as the controversy between its two main proponents, Uvedale Price and Richard Payne Knight, see Ross, pp. 121–54; for a painterly 'morphology of the picturesque' and on the 'fate of the picturesque' in Humphry Repton's garden designs around 1800, see Rogger, pp. 149–74.
18. U. Price, p. 86. Quotations will subsequently be accompanied by page numbers in parentheses in the text.
19. This section draws on the detailed investigation of Pope's horticultural poetics and politics in Brownell, pp. 39–241. Shorter, but no less pertinent, are the essays from the *Cambridge*

20. *Companion to Pope* by Erskine-Hall; Kelsall; Rogers. Also helpful, but much broader in scope, is the study by Buttlar.
21. On Twickenham as the site where Pope the gardener and Pope the poet meet, see Brownell, pp. 118–45; Batey, pp. 42–73; Ross, pp. 55–59.
22. Quoted in Ross, pp. 56–57.
23. On Pope and Turner, see Batey, pp. 127–31.
24. Pope, *Poetical Works*, pp. 132–33, ll. 7–21. Further references to this edition are given in parentheses in the text.
25. Spence, I, 426.
26. Cf. Barrell, p. 49.
27. Spence, I, 252.
28. Buruma, p. 86.
29. See Virgil, v. 32–119.
30. Shaftesbury, II. 1, p. 62.
31. Schneider, p. 97; Müller-Wolff, pp. 158–59.
32. On Gilpin's understanding of the picturesque, his use of the Claude glass, and his Wye Valley tour, see Andrews, *Search for the Picturesque*, pp. 56–58, 61–70, 85–94. See also the section 'The Smoking Mirror' (with a sample of Gilpin's pictorial excursion practice; pp. 112–17) and the chapter 'The Idealizing Mirror' (pp. 137–46) in Maillet's comprehensive account of this optical device. For Gilpin's 'Lorrainian' aquatints, see Figure 4.6 here, as well as Rogger, pp. 115–17.
33. The definition is from Gilpin, *Essay on Prints*, p. xii (1768).
34. Gilpin, *Observations on Several Parts of the Counties of Cambridge, [...]*, pp. 32–33.
35. Hagstrum, p. 142.
36. See Andrews, *Landscape and Western Art*, pp. 115–29.
37. See Brown and Williamson; Rutherford.
38. Knight, *Inquiry*, p. 156.
39. Knight, *The Landscape*, pp. 15, 25, pp. 105–06 (plates).
40. *OED Online* <http://www.oed.com/view/Entry/57672> [accessed 14 September 2019].
41. Knight, *The Landscape*, pp. 22–25, ll. 277–96.
42. The painting resurfaced after Roethlisberger's catalogue raisonné had appeared, and is now in the Metropolitan Museum of Art in New York.
43. See Kitson, pp. 126–27.
44. Knight, *Expedition into Sicily*, p. 26.
45. See Buruma, pp. 26, 31.
46. For a brief but comprehensive account of Hirschfeld's role in the theory of, and debate on, garden art in late eighteenth-century Germany, see Parshall. I quote from Hirschfeld's German original with my own translations (here: I, 146, 168, 37).
47. Hirschfeld, I, 128; Whately, p. 53; Mason, pp. 4, 10, 73, 135.
48. See Hirschfeld, I, 64–65, 67–68 (for the Thomson reference), I, 116 (for the reference to Mason, *English Garden*, pp. 5–6, ll. 93–111), I, 125 (for the Pope reference).
49. Bending, 'Walpole', p. 218.
50. Bending, 'Walpole', p. 222; cf. Buttlar, pp. 98–120, 129–66.
51. Henceforth quoted with page numbers in parentheses in the text. It should be noted that the writing of the essay dates back to 1770. It was translated into German by Hirschfeld in 1789.
52. On Pope, Kent, and Stowe, see Batey, pp. 64–65, 89–95.
53. See Pochat; Küster; Trauzettel. Cf. Buruma, pp. 83–86.
54. See Jena.
55. See Maisak, *Goethe: Zeichnungen*, p. 92.
56. See *FA*, XXIX, 85, 782 (commentary), 123, 128, 814 (commentary), 137, 142; cf. Müller-Wolff, pp. 41–42, 49, 60. For drawings by Goethe of his picturesque gardening, see Maisak, *Goethe: Zeichnungen*, pp. 96, 98; Hecht, pp. 51–61 ('Goethes Gartenhaus und der Weimarer Park'). For photographic evidence of some of these 'follies', see Huschke and Vulpius, plates 33, 34b, 38, 39, 42, 43.
57. Wieland, VII.1, 74, 113, 126.
58. Wieland, VII.1, 114.

58. The author of the mini-drama itself was not Goethe but Sigmund von Seckendorff.
59. See Gerndt, pp. 85–88.
60. Goethe is not the first, nor the last, to satirize the faddish gallimaufry of the English Garden. See e.g. Anglomania Domen [Justus Möser]; Bertuch.
61. Not just in terms of its (Palladian) architecture and bucolic setting but also its use for leisure, cultivation, and negotiation (see Pace, 'Free from Business').
62. See Williams, pp. 11–13.
63. Cf. Müller-Wolff, p. 309.
64. Letter to Goethe, 29 August 1795 (*Briefwechsel des Herzogs-Großherzogs Carl August mit Goethe*, I: 1775–1806, p. 202).
65. See Müller-Wolff, pp. 290–91.
66. See Müller-Wolff, p. 311.
67. See Müller-Wolff, p. 282.
68. Spence, I, 252.
69. Cf. Schneider, pp. 100–01.
70. See Zatti, pp. 132–33. Walpole, p. 147, deems 'deceptions' artful enhancements of nature and therefore necessary: 'Those deceptions, as a feigned steeple of a distant church, or an unreal bridge to disguise the termination of water, were [...] intended to improve the landscape' just as 'they would be if employed by a painter in the composition of a picture.'
71. *OED Online* <http://www.oed.com/view/Entry/38962> [accessed 14 September 2019].
72. *OED Online* <http://www.oed.com/view/Entry/145560> [accessed 14 September 2019].
73. See Kempf, pp. 423–25.
74. *Allgemeines Teutsches Garten-Magazin*, 1.8 (1796), 319–27. The following quotations are from pp. 319, 323; the Tasso quotation is on p. 327.
75. We substitute here Wickert's English translation of the Tasso passage for the German used in the review. Note that Wickert, p. 424, explains the last line as a version of the Ovidian maxim about 'the art which consists in concealing art', which gained new currency in the Italian Renaissance.
76. Rousseau, VI, 393. Further references to this edition are given by volume and page number in parentheses in the text.
77. Gauthier, p. 98; see also Neumeyer.
78. For a concise overview of Goethe and the contemporary debate on garden art, as well as the place of *Die Wahlverwandtschaften* in it, see Hennebo. For a more strictly horticultural-ontological comparison between Rousseau and Goethe, see Neumeyer, pp. 197–209. Klotz shows how, in *Die Wahlverwandtschaften*, horticultural and societal transitions mirror each other around 1800. The argument for Goethe's synthetic nature–art ideal notwithstanding, the chapter on Goethe in Finney, pp. 58–74, is instructive. For the integration of Lorrain into the mythic dynamic (life and death in Arcadia) of the novel, see Buschendorf, pp. 66–122.
79. In addition to Schneider, see also Gerndt, pp. 129–44 (on Goethe and garden design in general), 145–66 (on *Die Wahlverwandtschaften* in particular).
80. See Rogger. Cf. Lauterbach; Wegner.
81. Repton's *Sketches* and aforementioned *Observations* are in the Anna Amalia Library in Weimar (see Schwartz, p. 283). For the review of the original English version of the *Observations*, see n. 74 above; a review in instalments of the German translation of the *Observations* appeared in *Allgemeines Teutsches Garten-Magazin*, 1.11 (1804), 451–60, 1.12 (1804), 491–98, 2.1 (1805), 8–21, 2.2 (1805), 45–54. A review of the *Sketches* appeared in *Journal des Luxus und der Moden*, 11 (1796), 454–64. See Müller-Wolff, pp. 274–76.
82. Repton, p. xiii. The next two quotations are from pp. xv, 31.
83. Rogger, p. 106.
84. Of the three nymphs depicted, Echo is generally identified as the one in the middle, while the one in the front (clothed in the original painting) may be Liriope, Narcissus's mother, or his twin sister (MRP, I, 222; Wine, pp. 14–15, 106). Similar in composition, Domenichino's *Dying Narcissus* (c. 1603), a fresco in the Palazzo Farnese, may have been a source for both Lorrain and Goethe.
85. See *FA*, VIII, 1023–24 (commentary).

86. See Klotz, p. 129; Schwartz, pp. 152–53; Constantine, pp. 182–83; Finney, p. 66.
87. For a précis of the quarrel in Faust criticism between the perfectibilists and the imperfectibilists, see Laan, pp. 67–69. Given the compelling argument in Kaiser, *Ist der Mensch zu retten?*, that Faust is both a vision and a critique of modernity, one-sided exculpatory, incriminatory, or even nihilist readings (Laan, p. 161) seem equally problematic, especially in light of the play's ironies, ambiguities, and open-endedness.
88. Lynceus delivers his media-savvy panegyric on Faust 'through a speaking-trumpet' [durchs Sprachrohr] (ll. 11,143–50).
89. Hederich, p. 814.
90. See, for instance, Reich. The sole attempt to relate the Cura fable to Faust is not via horticulture but via Heidegger, who 'names Sorge as the constitutive being of time-bound Dasein' (see Hamilton; quotation: p. 268). According to Hamilton, Heidegger happened to come upon the Cura fable in Burdach, pp. 41–42. See also Dye.
91. Hederich, p. 814 (here cited as trans. by Harrison, pp. 5–6). My discussion of Care as a gardener draws on Harrison.
92. Harrison, pp. 4–9.
93. I am adopting here Harrison's dictum on Adam, p. 9.
94. Harrison, p. 1. On the Gilgamesh garden, see also Turner, pp. 42–43.
95. On magic, Mephistopheles, and technology, see J. Schmidt, pp. 229–34; Laan, pp. 98–109, 121. See also Barnouw.
96. For the broader implications of the 'trauma of dilettantism' from which Goethe suffered as a (visual) artist, see Vaget.
97. Conversation with Eckermann, 17 February 1830 (*FA*, xxxix, 385; *CV*, p. 351).
98. 13 February 1829 (*CV*, p. 293; *FA*, xxxix, 308).

CHAPTER 5

❖

Light – Eye – Colour: The Metamorphosis of Landscape Painting

> One remarkable point: among the painters who have most loved and best managed to dispense with colour, it is the great 'colourists' — Rembrandt, Claude, Goya, Corot — who are supreme. But then all these painters were essentially *poets*. (Valéry, p. 145, trans. modified)

In a conversation with Ludwig Tieck (1773–1854) in early September 1801, on a visit to the Old Masters Gallery in Dresden, Friedrich Schiller bemoaned:

> It is all quite beautiful. If only they weren't painted over! [I] cannot help but think that these colours appear untrue to me, since they, depending on my point of view or on how the light is cast on them, appear variously coloured; the mere contour would provide me with a truer picture.[1]

At first blush, Schiller's comment seems to esteem black-and-white sketching more highly than colourized painting when it comes to producing a verisimilar image of, say, a landscape.[2] On a closer look, though, he is describing his experience of viewing paintings in a gallery and the pivotal role that lighting plays in the display and perception of a painting's colours.

If we adopt the argument that Wolfgang Schöne makes in his study on the nature and function of light in painting, *Über das Licht in der Malerei* (1954), Schiller's seemingly casual comment gains in significance. Schöne argues, in brief, that one of the features that distinguishes sixteenth- and seventeenth-century painting from that of previous periods is the practice of locating the light source, increasingly, within the painting itself — as is, needless to say, typical of Lorrain. Illumination of a painting's subject from within puts a premium on the compositional distribution of light and shadow, and thus on tone rather than hue, or, more technically, on the lightness and darkness of colours rather than their saturation.[3] If a painting is exhibited — and this brings us back to Schiller's objection — in essentially too much light from without, the light from within is overshadowed by the spectacle,[4] or, to use Schiller's term, the 'Unwahre' [untruth], of colour. Another reason for Schiller's apprehensiveness vis-à-vis colour may be related to the 'black-and-white' viewing culture of his time, which, feeding off the 'mass' reproduction and distribution of etchings and engravings, was amazingly adept at colourless seeing, at imagining and appreciating beauty — the 'poetic' in Goethe's (*and* Valéry's) sense — without colour.[5] Indeed, Valéry's aperçu alludes to the Goethean paradox of colour: Goethe was so obsessed with colour as to write a 1500-page 'gospel' of colour, considering it his most important work,[6] yet when it comes to landscape depiction (including his own visual work), colour played a seemingly minor role, most notably in his verbal landscapes.[7]

In *Zur Farbenlehre*, Goethe sets out to discuss colour's 'esthetic effect' by beginning with 'the general requirements for pictorial representation, i.e. light and shadow' and only then proceeding to 'the appearance of colour' (*CW*, XII, 288; *FA*, XXIII.1, 267). The first 'effect' Goethe discusses is 'chiaroscuro', for the 'artist will more easily resolve the riddle of depiction by thinking of chiaroscuro as independent of colour' (*CW*, XII, 288; *FA*, XXIII.1, 268). If we heed Goethe's advice for the time being, Lorrain's light may be soft or effulgent, in plain sight or out of sight, but it is always 'within', allowing him, compositionally, to dispense with colour (to use Valéry's term) and hence resolve the riddle of depiction poetically. It is this inner light that first and foremost, even literally, elucidates Goethe's reverence for Lorrain's art. In *Zur Farbenlehre*, colour is introduced as the second effect, and then only half-heartedly, as the 'striving of colour' mainly 'to please the eye', given the 'forced abstraction [of] copperplate engravings and mezzotints' (*CW*, XII, 289, trans. modified; *FA*, XXIII.1, 270). Typical is an instance in *Wilhelm Meisters Wanderjahre*. When Wilhelm goes in search of Mignon in Italy, he and his painter friend accomplish their mission when 'all scenes and localities referring to Mignon had been not only sketched but partly brought into light, shade, and colour' (*WMT*, p. 197; *FA*, X, 133).[8] The sequencing is telling: landscape comes into existence by drafting its contours, distributing light and shadow, and, lastly, applying colour. This concatenation is of biblical proportion, divinely enacted in the poem 'Wiederfinden' [Reunion] in the *West–Östlicher Divan* [West–Eastern Divan] (1819):

> Als die Welt im tiefsten Grunde
> Lag an Gottes ew'ger Brust,
> Ordnet' er die erste Stunde
> Mit erhabner Schöpfungslust,
> Und er sprach das Wort: Es werde!
> [...]
> Auf that sich das Licht! sich trennte
> Scheu die Finsterniß von ihm,
> Ein erklingend Farbenspiel,
> Und nun konnte wieder lieben,
> Was erst auseinander fiel. (*FA*, III.1, 96–97)
>
> [When buried deep the whole world lay
> In God's eternal breast, elate
> He summoned forth the primal day
> Urged by the rapture to create.
> He spake the fiat 'Let there be!'
> [...]
> Light broadened in the firmament,

> The darkness shrank with timorous start,
> Colours, a soft harmonious play,
> And things had power to love anew
> Which each from each had fallen away.] (*WED*, p. 134)

Finally, as mentioned before, Goethe's favourite source of Lorrain's work was, in addition to the black-and-white prints of original etchings, Richard Earlom's engravings — using mezzotint for the ink washes — of the *Liber Veritatis*. In a curious way, the preface to this collection anticipates Goethe's dilemma between, to put it bluntly, the pointlessness of colour and the science of colour. On the one hand, the 'excellence' of Lorrain's pictures can be 'considered independently of their colouring', namely 'the warmth and clearness of his Skies, the brilliant effects of his rising and setting Suns, the luxuriant richness of his Trees, the delicacy of his distant Tints, and his exact knowledge altogether of the *aerial* Perspective'.[9] On the other hand, 'the tone and complexion' of Lorrain's pictures are so 'astonishing' that he must have

> attained [...] the proper knowledge of a Philosopher, rather than a Painter, and could discourse with much exactness as if he had been well versed in physics, on the causes of the differences of the same view [...] at different times; on the morning dews and evening vapors, and on the several various reflections and refractions of light.

Light, and, crucially, its transposition into the *painting*'s source of illumination, *is* nature and art *in actu nascendi*.

5.1. Mediterranean Colours

'But what about colour?' This seems to have been the question on the minds of those left behind in Weimar by the late autumn of Goethe's second sojourn in Rome, for on 24 November 1787, he writes to Charlotte von Stein:

> Du fragst in deinem letzten Briefe wegen der Farbe der Landschaft dieser Gegenden. Darauf kann ich dir sagen: daß sie bei heitern Tagen, besonders des Herbstes so *farbig* ist, daß sie in jeder Nachbildung *bunt* scheinen muß. Ich hoffe dir in einiger Zeit einige Zeichnungen zu schicken, die ein Deutscher macht, der jetzt in Neapel ist; die Wasserfarben bleiben so weit unter dem Glanz der Natur, und doch werdet ihr glauben, es sei unmöglich. Das Schönste dabei ist, daß die lebhaften Farben, in geringer Entfernung schon, durch den Luftton gemildert werden, und daß die Gegensätze von kalten und warmen Tönen (wie man sie nennt) so sichtbar dastehn. Die blauen klaren Schatten stechen so reizend von allem erleuchteten Grünen, Gelblichen, Rötlichen, Bräunlichen ab, und verbinden sich mit der bläulich duftigen Ferne. Es ist ein Glanz, und zugleich eine Harmonie, eine Abstufung im Ganzen, wovon man nordwärts gar keinen Begriff hat. Bei euch ist alles entweder hart oder trüb, bunt oder eintönig. (*FA*, xv.1, 464–65)

> [In your last letter you inquire about the colour of the landscape in this area. I can answer that on sunny days, especially in the autumn, it is so *colourful* that in any picture it would look *mottled*. I am hoping to send you fairly soon some

drawings made by a German who is now in Naples; the watercolours by no means match the brilliance of nature, and yet none of you will believe it. The most beautiful feature is that, even at a slight distance, the vivid colours are muted by the tint of the air, and that the contrasts between cool and warm tones (as they are called) emerge so visibly. The clear blue shadows stand out very attractively from all the brightly lit green, yellowish, reddish, brownish parts, and combine with the bluish haze in the distance. There is a brilliance, and at the same time a harmony, a gradation, in the whole that cannot be imagined at all in the north. Where you are, everything is either hard or dull, mottled or monotonous.] (*CW*, VI, 348)

From this impressionistic account, we can already glean some of the principles of Goethe's nascent thinking about colour. Although he appreciates the variety of colours, he cautions that the translation into painting might be obtrusively 'mottled'. This first chromatic term is fraught with tension: what is perceived as colourful in nature might come across as garish in art. What is crucial for Goethe's aesthetic sense is that the atmospheric turbidity softens the brightness of the colours and that hues are tempered with complementary or adjacent colours. Equally important are the interplay of 'light' and 'shadow' and the rendering of the aerial perspective in a bluish cast. Finally, contrary to the North's dullness and starkness, the South has a harmonizing effect that softens the colours' brilliance and smoothens their transitions. While Goethe sees complementarity in both hue and effect, the emphasis is on modulation, notably in green, which can modulate toward yellow or blue and thus be either warm or cold — a differentiation he considers uniquely 'Southern', as evidenced by his characterization of green in the public garden of Palermo: 'ein Grün, das wir nicht gewohnt sind, bald gelblicher, bald blaulicher als bei uns' [a green colour we are not accustomed to, sometimes more yellowish, sometimes more bluish than at home] (*FA*, XV.1, 258; *CW*, VI, 194). The modulation's linguistic marker, the suffix '-lich' [-ish], marks the range from, say, Naples yellow to orpiment and on to lead-tin yellow, while variations of ochre and umber make up the brown palette. But there is more to the ubiquitous suffix '-lich', which is too close to '*Lich*t' [light] to be overlooked. That is to say, as much as the range and variety of tints is a matter of pigment, it is also, maybe even more so, a matter of light: for Goethe, colour is light, and light is colour. Recall the 'Gold-Orangen' in the 'Mignon' poem (*FA*, II, 103): perceived as suffused with light, yellow-red or red-yellow becomes golden.[10] The chromatic aura of the Mediterranean landscape is generated by, it would seem, an iridescent magnetic field of repulsion and attraction, effulgence and softness, discord and concord.

As apprehensive as Goethe may be about colour, for landscape painting it is a *sine qua non*. The 'blue shadows' and the 'bluishly hazy distance' evidence two principles of his chromatic thinking — coloured shadows, which he is credited for having discovered, and colourization of the aerial perspective (more on these below). Landscape painting's dependence on colour is not just 'natural', it is also 'epistemological'. In the introduction to *Zur Farbenlehre*, he maintains that nature 'reveals itself to the sense of sight' by means of 'brightness, darkness, and colour'. From these three, 'we construct the visible world [...], and in the process we also make possible the art of painting'. He continues by saying that painting 'is capable of producing on canvas a visible world far more perfect than the real world' (*CW*, XII, 164; *FA*, XXIII.1, 24). As often as Goethe may waver between apprehensiveness about and advocation of colour — Jacques Le Rider contextualizes the conundrum as one between Goethe the 'colourophile' Romantic *avant la lettre* and Goethe the classicist draughtsman[11] — it seems that colour is a prerequisite for landscape painting if it is to make the world visible and, thus, comprehensible. As Faust puts it when, at the opening of Part 2, he awakens in an idyllic landscape and perceives a rainbow arching through the vaporous sky:

> of human striving it's a perfect symbol —
> ponder this well to understand more clearly
> that what we have as life is many-hued reflection.[12] (ll. 4725–28)

As a mist veils the sun, colours emerge and reveal it as a symbol. It is as if colours were enacting Goethe's favourite aesthetic-epistemological paradox, the 'holy open secret' (*FA*, XXIV, 440). To the extent that 'many-hued reflection' interweaves light and colour, it encapsulates what Christian Klemm calls Lorrain's 'most important contribution to landscape painting' — the 'integration of the local colours', the unadulterated hues of natural objects, 'into an encompassing pearly tone' — adding that the 'riddle' and 'paradox' of Lorrain's unique achievement lies in evoking 'this translucent atmosphere, yet making it appear as completely transparent'. Klemm further maintains that both brush and pigment as such serve a purely representational function, that of enacting a chromatic achromatism that effects a 'dematerialization', a 'transcending of the material to pure phenomena of light'.[13] This brings us back to Valéry, for, thanks to Klemm's keen observation, his provocative claim that Lorrain dispenses with colour in order to produce the poetic begins to make sense.

5.2. Goethe's *Zur Farbenlehre* and Lorrain's *Landscape with Tobias and the Angel* (1663)

Goethe's first publication on colour theory, his 1791 *Beiträge zur Optik* [Contributions to Optics], opens with Lorrain — or at least with his memory of Italian nature evoking in him the vision of a Lorrainian painting (note 'Gemälde' [picture] at the end of the following quotation). This memory is so insistent that he resolves to suppress it in order to embark on a systematic examination of colour:

> Ebenso wird es uns, wenn wir eine Zeitlang in dem schönen Italien gelebt, ein Märchen, wenn wir uns erinnern, wie harmonisch dort der Himmel sich mit der Erde verbindet und seinen lebhaften Glanz über sie verbreitet. Er zeigt uns meist ein reines, tiefes Blau; die auf- und untergehende Sonne gibt uns einen Begriff vom höchsten Rot bis zum lichtesten Gelb; leichte hin und wider ziehende Wolken färben sich mannigfaltig, und die Farben des himmlischen Gewölbes teilen sich auf die angenehmste Art dem Boden mit, auf dem wir stehen. Eine blaue Ferne zeigt uns den lieblichsten Übergang des Himmels zur Erde, und durch einen verbreiteten reinen Duft schwebt ein lebhafter Glanz in tausendfachen Spiegelungen über der Gegend. Ein angenehmes Blau färbt selbst die nächsten Schatten; der Abglanz der Sonne entzückt uns von Blättern

> und Zweigen, indes der reine Himmel sich im Wasser zu unsern Füßen spiegelt. Alles, was unser Auge übersieht, ist so harmonisch gefärbt, so klar, so deutlich, und wir vergessen fast, daß auch Licht und Schatten in diesem Bilde sei. Nur selten werden wir in unsern Gegenden an jene paradiesischen Augenblicke erinnert, und ich lasse einen Vorhang über dieses Gemälde fallen, damit es uns nicht an ruhiger Betrachtung störe, die wir nunmehr anzustellen gedenken. (*FA*, XXIII.2, 16)

> [Remembrance of some sojourn in Italy, may also live in our thoughts like a fairytale. We recall how the southern sky blends harmoniously with the earth, and sheds its vivid light upon the land. We remember its pure deep blue; the rising and setting sun ranges in colour from brightest red to palest yellow; the graceful forms of passing clouds take on so many different hues, and all the colours of the sky are mirrored on earth. The horizon lies folded in the blue of the distance, and a vivid brilliance seems to float like a radiant veil over the landscape. Blue tinges even the nearest shadows; the reflection of the sunlight sparkles from leaves and branches, while the clear sky is imaged in the waters of the foreground. All that we see is so harmoniously coloured and is so clear, that we almost forget there is both light and shadow there. It is seldom in our own country that such heavenly moments repeat themselves; so now let us put these pictures aside, and not let them distract our attention from the serious study of our subject.] (*CtO*, p. 6)

Zur Farbenlehre is based primarily on perception and experience rather than on 'mathematics' as the system of Goethe's opponent, Newton, and — as Schopenhauer shrewdly hinted — the exhaustive compilation of 'data *for* a theory'.[14] As empirical as *Zur Farbenlehre* is, it is fraught with rhetoric, part of which is the tripartite compositional strategy: the 'Didactic' section concerns the perception, formation, and effect of colours; the 'Polemical' section covers the feud with Newton; and the 'Historical' provides a chronological survey of chromatism.[15] The latter includes an essay by Goethe's lifelong adviser on matters of the visual arts, Johann Heinrich Meyer (1760–1832),[16] entitled 'Geschichte des Kolorits seit der Wiederherstellung der Kunst' [History of Colourizing since the Restoration of Art]. Considered, according to Pamela Currie, whose *Goethe's Visual World* (2013) has been invaluable for this section, the first historical outline of colour in painting,[17] it assesses Lorrain's achievement as a colourist:

> Das Fach der Landschaft verehrt zwar in Claude Lorrain seinen größten Meister, und vorzüglich ist das Kolorit desselben im höchsten Grade heiter, zart und wahrhaft; allein die Landschaftsmalerei läßt dem Koloristen, vermöge ihrer Natur, weniger Freiheit und Spielraum als im historischen Fache der Fall ist. (*FA*, XXIII.1, 772)

> [To be sure, adepts in landscape painting revere Claude Lorrain as its greatest master, and most notably his art of colourizing is supremely cheerful, gentle, and truthful; however, due to its very nature, landscape painting leaves the colourist less freedom and license than history painting.]

Goethe himself applies 'cheerful' or 'serene' to Lorrain's use of colour, and this is clearly the epithet for the most impressive aesthetic effect a painter can achieve. In addition to Lorrain, Meyer, in tacit agreement with Goethe, uses the term for

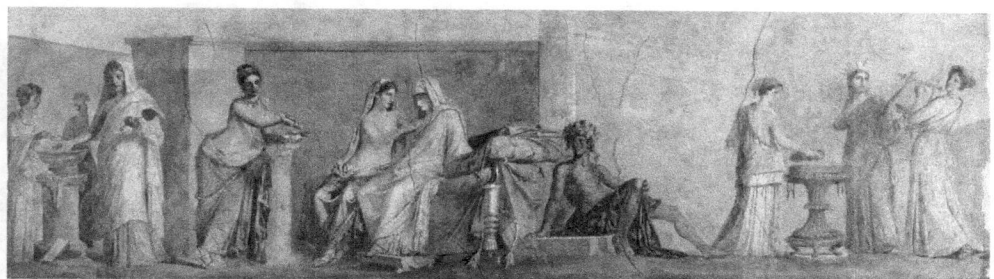

FIG. 5.1. *The Aldobrandini Wedding*. Biblioteca Apostolica Vaticana, Vatican City/ © Vatican Museums

Paolo Veronese's *Family of Darius before Alexander* (1565–70) and Pietro da Cortona's *Triumph of Divine Providence* (1639), a large ceiling fresco in the Palazzo Barberini in Rome.

'Serene' is also Meyer's epithet of choice for the ancient Roman fresco *The Aldobrandini Wedding* (27 BCE–14 CE) by an unknown artist, discovered around 1600. Meyer copied it for Goethe, who placed it on display in his Weimar residence in the room named after the Roman goddess Juno, drawing back the curtains to expose its delicate watercolours for cognoscenti only. In an 1810 essay devoted to the fresco's art, Meyer uses 'serene' for the distribution of light and shade, and for the exemplary handling of colours.[18] He speaks of 'the serene cheerful interplay of colours', which 'contrast with each other pleasantly, not glaringly, and which respond to each other through reflected light; another chromatic means is the tone that suffuses the whole resulting in even more correlations'.[19] Not only does this expert commentary encapsulate essential aspects of Goethe's chromatic ideal; the significance of the *Aldobrandini Wedding* is also underscored by the fact that it is the only antique painting mentioned in *Zur Farbenlehre* — once in the context of chiaroscuro in the 'Didactic' section, and once in that of ancient Roman painting in the 'Historical' section (*CW*, XII, 289; *FA*, XXIII.1, 269, 589–95). The latter elaborates on the commentary just quoted, detailing the use of 'bright purple hue', 'varnish', or '*cangianti* mode' to 'warm shadows' and thus 'contribute' to the 'overall harmony of the whole' (*FA*, XXIII.1, 592); furthermore, after identifying familiar 'Italian' colours such as 'golden yellow ochre' or 'Neapolitan red earth', Goethe describes the fresco's ultimate quality as a kind of chromatic trinity, a tonality that is 'cheerful, serene, and truthful' (*FA*, XXIII.1, 593). To this we can add Meyer's statement from the *Aldobrandini* essay according to which the anonymous painter makes use of his 'poetic freedom' to transcend mere naturalism for the sake of 'symbolic representation'.[20] Taken together, if 'serene' is the golden thread running through the various statements on *The Aldobrandini Wedding*, it pertains to both nature ('truthful') and art ('symbolic'), making colour intrinsic to painting; insofar as colour is intrinsic to landscape painting, it is intrinsic to man's 'poetic' bond with nature.

While Lorrain, Veronese, and Cortona are united by their achievement of 'serene' colouring, their use of colour differs insofar as Lorrain reaches the goal with restricted means for 'landscape painting'; 'coloration' and 'nature' imply colouring in imitation of optical reality, while 'history painting', 'freedom', and 'space for play' (literally: 'Spielraum') lay claim to artful licence. Reflected in this differentiation between the 'colourist' and the 'harmonist' is, once again, the dialectic of nature and art — with, schematically speaking, Rubens and Titian as exponents of a verisimilar or naturalistic style of colouring, and Veronese and Cortona as examples of a decorative, fresco method of colouring.[21] Using 'clear local colours without garishness' and 'harmonizing them through tricks of lighting that blur boundaries and contrive gentle transitions', Federico Barocci's *Madonna del Popolo* (1575–79) sublates the two opposites.[22] Since Lorrain's name occurs nowhere else in *Zur Farbenlehre*, the inference is that, with his dexterity in handling local colours, Lorrain fulfils Goethe's ideal of a harmony of hues; with his dexterity in handling lightness and darkness, Lorrain also fulfils Goethe's expectation of a harmony of tone — which derives, as we now know, in large measure, from placing the source of light inside the painting and generating the landscape from it. Another inference is that Lorrain strives for 'the effect of fresco in oils' insofar as his 'serenity' has the richness and vibrancy of true-to-life paints and the lightness and translucence of decorative fresco paints. The bon mot 'the effect of fresco in oils' is, according to Currie, from Gottlieb Schick, whom both Goethe and Meyer saw as neoclassicism's answer to (excessive) Romantic chromatism.[23] It seems fitting that only an oxymoron can capture the Goethean colour conundrum: chromophilic classicist. Currie writes: 'Goethe's campaign for chromatic harmony, though unique among classical aestheticians in his time, remained within the bounds of classical thought, rather than making common cause with classicism's opponents.'[24]

When Goethe visited Landgrave William VIII's collection of paintings in Kassel in 1779 and 1783, he viewed what has come to be known as the tetraptych 'Four Times of the Day',[25] consisting of *Landscape with Jacob, Rachel, and Leah at the Well [Morning]* (1666; *LV*, 169), *Landscape with the Rest on the Flight into Egypt [Noon]* (1661; *LV*, 154), *Landscape with Tobias and the Angel [Evening]* (1663; *LV*, 160), and *Landscape with Jacob Wrestling with the Angel [Night]* (1672; *LV*, 181). On the basis of later comments (in the fragments for a history of landscape painting) that are directly or indirectly related to the Kassel tetraptych, we can surmise that Goethe is thinking of *Landscape with Tobias and the Angel*[26] when he writes that Lorrain 'surpasses everyone by far in regard to the richness and loftiness of thought, the delightful effect of light and shade, the inimitable grace, serenity, and harmony of colours' (*FA*, XIX, 33). Goethe then highlights how 'the rays of the sinking sun dance and glimmer on the sea's softly rippled surface, leaves quiver, water wells up from springs, small, colourful clouds float in pure air' (*FA*, XIX, 33). Finally, he adds that Lorrain 'ins Freye, Ferne, Heitere, Ländliche, Feenhaft-architectonische sich ergeht' [indulges himself in the open, distant, serene, pastoral, the fairy-like architectural] (*FA*, XXII, 534).

Using and elaborating on key terms and phrases from Goethe's characterization of Lorrain — misty transparency; the harmonious interplay of light, shade, and colours; fairy-land architecture; wholeness; prospect; serenity — and relying on *Zur Farbenlehre* as a guide, we turn now to the evening scene in *Landscape with Tobias and the Angel* (Fig. 5.2).[27]

Late in the 'Didactic' section, Goethe starts to address the 'aesthetic effect' of colours that the artist is now in a position 'to deduce' (*CW*, XII, 288; *FA*, XXIII.1, 267). After reiterating that the linear and the aerial perspectives, as well as their respective gradations in the size and distinctness of objects, are the *sine qua non* of pictorial depiction (*CW*, XII, 290; *FA*, XXIII.1, 271), Goethe states that 'colouration first appears' together with the gradations of the aerial perspective: 'We see the sky, distant objects, and even nearby shadows as blue. At the same time, sources of illumination and illuminated objects appear in gradations from yellow to purple' (*CW*, XII, 291; *FA*, XXIII.1, 272). Admittedly, Goethe describes colour phenomena in nature, but they seem to correspond to Lorrain's handling of colour in *Tobias and the Angel*. Not only that: in regard to aerial perspective, colour has a spatial function; that is to say, the tectonic layering is achieved not so much by compositional lines as by gradations of hue, which in turn are functions of light.[28]

To elaborate on 'perspective' as enacted here, recall Goethe's Sicilian discovery of 'turbid clarity' as the catalyst for colour formation. Oxymoronic only at first glance, it has to do with Goethe's chromatic concept of 'Trübe', 'Dunst', or 'Duft', the 'colourless medium' or 'atmospheric vapour'. It has various degrees of transparency, which are all more or less light-transmitting or 'translucent' (*CW*, XII, 190; *FA*, XXIII.1, 73). As Goethe explains in *Zur Farbenlehre*, the light of the sun is 'blinding and colourless' (*CW*, XII, 191; *FA*, XXIII.1, 73), but the sun 'viewed through a certain degree of haze [...] appears as a yellowish disk'; seen through 'a layer of fine dust', it 'appears ruby red' — an appearance intensified by 'the sirocco in southern regions', where the clouds surrounding the sun take on the same colour, 'radiating the colour by reflection' (*CW*, XII, 191; *FA*, XXIII.1, 74–75). In one of the 'Zahme Xenien' [Tame Xenia], Goethe identifies the sirocco-enhanced turbidity as *the* catalyst for the generation of colour:

> Wenn der Blick an heitern Tagen
> Sich zur Himmelsbläue lenkt
> Beim Siroc der Sonnenwagen
> Purpurrot sich niedersenkt,
> Da gebt der Natur die Ehre
> Froh, an Aug' und Herz gesund,
> Und erkennt der Farbenlehre
> Allgemeinen ewigen Grund.[29] (*FA*, II, 678)
>
> [When, on bright days, you direct your gaze
> Toward the azure sky, and,
> While the sirocco blows,
> The sun's chariot, shining ruby-red, descends,
> Then pay tribute to Nature, and,
> With radiant eye and healthy heart
> Recognize the doctrine of colour's
> Everlasting fundamental premise.]

The poem's interweaving of the phenomenal with the noumenal reminds us why Schiller famously remarked that Goethe's archetypal phenomenon — here suggested by the functional exemplariness of 'turbidity' — is not derived from an 'experience' but is rather an 'idea' (*CW*, XII, 20; *FA*, XXIV, 437).

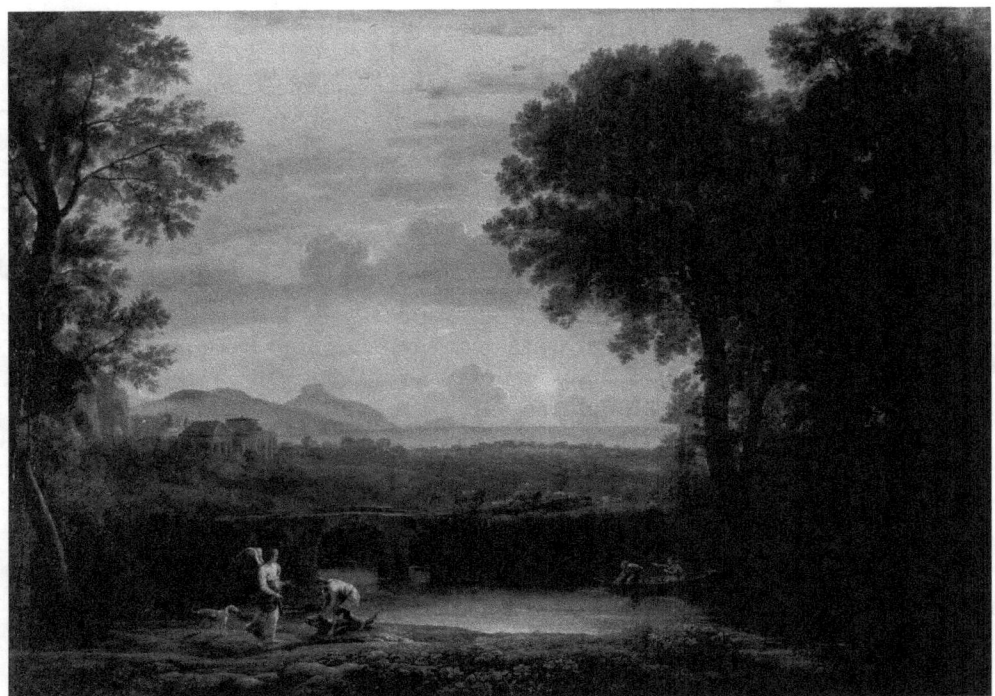

Fig. 5.2. Lorrain, *Landscape with Tobias and the Angel* [*Evening*]. The State Hermitage Museum, St Petersburg/© The State Hermitage Museum — Svetlana Suetova

Goethe's reasoning behind the blue appearance of the mountains on the left-hand side of the painting is linked to turbidity and can be found in *Zur Farbenlehre*: 'when so distant that the colours of their features are no longer visible and the light reflected from their surfaces no longer affects our eye, they will act as completely dark objects and look blue through the intervening haze' (*CW*, XII, 192; *FA*, XXIII.1, 75). Lorrain transposes the atmospheric haze of the Italian landscape to his canvas by exquisitely bathing his painting in light, thus adapting and perfecting Leonardo's *sfumato*. Goethe's characterization of Lorrain as 'otherworldly architectural' begins to make sense when we try to capture the effect of *sfumato*: it draws a veil over hues and objects, gradually merges colours, warms and softens objects, creates harmonies between natural forms and human artefacts; it blends all parts into one whole and produces an effect of ethereal repose. With the disappearance of sharply contrasting colours and with soft transitions, Lorrain achieves the ideal of the 'Harmoniespiel der Farben' [harmonious interplay of colours] (*FA*, XXIII.1, 774), as Goethe calls it, referencing 'play' in Schiller's sense of free aesthetic play.[30] An important aspect of the complementarity and totality of harmonizing colour is the 'iridescent reflection of light' on the water in the foreground of *Tobias and the Angel*. Tremulously, it shimmers with varying shades of blue which mirror and harmonize heaven, sea, and earth, and whose softly changing hues — reddish-brown to green or, where tinged with yellow, to sea-green — are identified by Goethe, in the 'Coloured

Shadows' section of *Zur Farbenlehre*, as 'pleasing' or 'magic' in their effect:

> Waren Tag über, bei dem gelblichen Ton des Schnees, schon leise violette Schatten bemerklich gewesen, so mußte man sie nun für hochblau ansprechen, als ein gesteigertes Gelb von den beleuchteten Teilen widerschien.
> Als aber die Sonne sich endlich ihrem Niedergang näherte, und ihr durch die stärkeren Dünste höchst gemäßigter Strahl die ganze mich umgebende Welt mit der schönsten Purpurfarbe überzog, da verwandelte sich die Schattenfarbe in ein Grün, das nach seiner Klarheit einem Meergrün, nach seiner Schönheit einem Smaragdgrün verglichen werden konnte. Die Erscheinung ward immer lebhafter, man glaubte sich in einer Feenwelt zu befinden, denn alles hatte sich in die zwei lebhaften und so schön übereinstimmenden Farben gekleidet. (*FA*, XXIII.1, 55)

> [Because of the snow's yellowish cast, pale violet shadows had accompanied us all day, but now, as an intensified yellow reflected from the areas in the light, we were obliged to describe the shadows as deep blue.
> At last the sun began to disappear and its rays, subdued by the strong haze, spread the most beautiful purple hue over my surroundings. At that point the colour of the shadows was transformed into a green comparable in clarity to a sea green and in beauty to an emerald green. The effect grew ever more vivid; it was as if we found ourselves in a fairy world for everything had clothed itself in these two lively colours so beautifully harmonious with one another.] (*CW*, XII, 181)

To the extent that one can read into this passage a correlation between painting and (chromatic) poetry, it could be characterized as 'narrative', for, in striking fashion, both Lorrain and Goethe tell the creation myth of colour as ensuing from, and governed by, light.[31] The observer, or rather the observer's eye, accompanies light on its pilgrimage from 'sun' to 'fairy world', from natural to symbolic luminosity. Readers follow as the narrator weaves, like *Faust*'s Earth Spirit, light's garment of nuanced hues, values, and saturations. In accord with this story, in the art-historical vocabulary of Goethe and his contemporaries, the epithet 'schillernd' [iridescent] harks back to the *cangianti* colouring technique, whose gentle transitions and soft blending (and avoidance of black for shadows) Goethe came to admire in the frescoes he studied in Rome.[32] Also at work in the creation of a visual harmony is what Goethe subsumes under the terms 'das Freye' [the wide-open] and 'die Ferne' [prospect, panorama, or vista], by which he means not just the painting's depth — that is, the immense distance from nearest to farthest point — but also the way the sun acts as the focal point from which the light rays emanate and on which they converge. The sun is both a siren that enchants and a magnet that captivates. Suffusing even the darkest hues with light and harmonizing the colours, it effects a sense not only of wholeness but of wholesomeness too.

Metonymically speaking, Lorrain relaxes and expands the mind and engenders 'serenity' — an expansion of the visual into the psychological and the 'ultimate goal' of the colours' aesthetics of effects (*CW*, XII, 294; *FA*, XXIII.1, 279). Framed and anchored by the trees, the scenery exudes an air of tranquillity. Yet the trees represent not just permanence but also change. The intricate effects of light and shade on the trees call forth the dynamics of the entire chromatic scale: darkness weakened by light leads to the darker colours of green, blue, and violet, whereas light dimmed by darkness creates the lighter colours of yellow, orange, and red. On closer inspection, it is through colour that the scenery's complementary movements are enlivened, indeed energized: reminiscent of the mythological Yggdrasil, the trees grow, as it were, from the underworld into the sky, an upward movement reinforced by the transition from a rich soily brown to an airy translucent green with yellow or reddish edges; the movement is counterbalanced by the sinking sun following a trajectory from yellow to orange to red; lacing the trees is a zigzag motion with its own polarity and heightening from right to left and back to right — the iridescent shimmer of the brook fades into the murky water only to resurface in the streaks of reflected light on the path that seems to carry it through glimmering meadows as it snakes toward the shore where it turns pale blue before the soaring larks intensify and raise it into the golden evening sky. There is the contrast between the hectic movement of the glossy fishermen and the languid movement of the muted shepherds. The background is animated by a feathery-white boat that seems to sail faster than the wind and clouds that float overhead in reddish-yellow tufted streaks and globs. Finally, while the vanishing sun marks the end of day, or even life, the brightly lit, lush vegetation in the foreground suggests growth and rebirth.

As noted before, in *Wilhelm Meisters Wanderjahre*, Wilhelm meets and travels for a while with a young landscape painter. While not per se a description of *Landscape with Tobias and the Angel*, the following 'judgment of a critic' on the art of this latter-day Lorrain abounds with ekphrastic resonances that evoke the original painting and serve to summarize the above discussion:

> Der Farbenton ist heiter, fröhlichklar; die Fernen mit milderndem Duft wie übergossen [...].
> Trefflich weiß er, in mächtig schattenden Bäumen des Vordergrundes, den unterscheidenden Charakter verschiedener Arten, so in Gestalt des Ganzen, wie in dem Gang der Zweige, den einzelnen Partien der Blätter befriedigend anzudeuten; nicht weniger in dem auf mancherlei Weise nüancierten frischen Grün, worin sanfte Lüfte mit gelindem Hauch zu fächeln und die Lichter daher gleichsam bewegt erscheinen.
> Im Mittelgrund ermattet almählig der lebhafte grüne Ton und vermählt sich, auf entferntern Berghöhen, schwach violet mit dem Blau des Himmels [...]. [Die Staffagen] zeichnet er all gleich gut und geistreich; immer am schicklichen Ort, und in nicht zu großer Fülle angebracht zieren und beleben sie dieses Bild, ohne seine ruhige Einsamkeit zu stören oder auch nur zu mindern. Die Ausführung zeugt von der kühnsten Meisterhand, leicht mit wenigen sichern Strichen und doch vollendet. (*FA*, x, 138–40)

> [The tone of colouring is serene, mirthfully clear; the distances, as if overflowed with softening vapour [...].
> With exquisite skill, in the deep shady trees of the foreground, he gives the distinctive character of the several species; satisfying us in the form of the whole, as in the structure of the branches, and the details of the leaves: no less so, in the fresh green with its manifold shadings, where soft airs appear as if fanning us with benignant breath, and the lights as if thereby put in motion.
> In the middle ground, his lively green tone grows fainter by degrees; and at last, on the more distant mountain-tops, passing into weak violet, it weds itself

with the blue sky [...]. [The staffage] he paints with equal truth and richness; still introduced in the proper place, and not in too great copiousness, they decorate and enliven the scene, without interrupting, without lessening their peaceful solitude. The execution testifies to a master's hand; easy, with a few strokes, and yet complete.] (*WMT*, pp. 204–06, trans. modified)

What we can gather from this generic colour scheme for our landscape painting is the transitional quality articulated by the virtually exclusive use in the German of verbs indicating flux, meaning to 'soften', 'pour over', 'shadow', 'soothe', 'nuance', 'diminish', 'shift', 'weaken', 'wed', 'enliven'. The deliberate choice seems to serve a dual purpose. On the one hand, the verbs capture the vibration between light and darkness (for instance, depending on whether green inclines toward light or darkness, it takes on a yellow or bluish sheen respectively), enhancing and enriching the palette by contrast. On the other hand, the verbs capture the successive stages of turbidity: the denser the air between us and the receding landscape, the more its manifold colours vanish; the heavier the mists at sundown, the more the yellow passes into orange and red. The verbs carry our eye from the transparency of the fresh and distinguishable local colours of the foreground to the increasingly opaque middle ground, which is dominated by an olive tint that absorbs (or vibrates with) the hues of the colour wheel, and then to the background where the intensification of turbidity turns the topography into 'weak violet' and then muted blue masses, until a yellow shimmer weds them to the vaporous sky.[33] Interestingly, Goethe, in *Zur Farbenlehre*, counts the (painting's main) blend of yellow and green among the 'combinations without character', precisely due to its almost imperceptible oscillation, calling its effect 'mundane but serene' (*CW*, XII, 286; *FA*, XXIII.1, 263).

5.3. The Eye: Perception and Production

Lorrain's idealized landscape is a product of both imitation and intimation. The organ that enables Lorrain to deconstruct and reconstruct nature is the eye. In a letter to Schiller on 10 February 1796, Goethe wrote that *Zur Farbenlehre* (on which he was working at the time) is really about '*the world of the eye*' (*FA*, XXXI, 260). 'The eye', Goethe claims in the introduction to *Zur Farbenlehre*, 'owes its existence to light', is 'called forth by light' (*CW*, XII, 164, trans. modified; *FA*, XXIII.1, 24). At work in the affinity between 'inner [and] outer light' is a reciprocity of perception and production that is of mystical proportion, for, as Goethe avers:

> Wär' nicht das Auge sonnenhaft
> Wie könnten wir das Licht erblicken?
> Lebt' nicht in uns des Gottes eigne Kraft,
> Wie könnt' uns Göttliches entzücken? (*FA*, XXIII.1, 24)

> [Were the eye not of the sun,
> How could we behold the light?
> If God's might and ours were not as one,
> How could His work enchant our sight?] (*CW*, XII, 164)

In the act of seeing,

the retina is simultaneously in different — indeed, in opposite — states. Strong but not blinding illumination works side by side with absolute darkness. At one and the same time, we perceive all the intermediate degrees of light and shadow, and all the distinct qualities of colour. (*CW*, XII, 169; *FA*, XXIII.1, 14)

The *Landscape with Tobias and the Angel* seems to impact the observer's retina as described here by enacting a veritable drama of chiaroscuro and colourization that enriches the scene and gives it grandeur.

At work in the formation of colours are the dynamic principles of polarity (yellow calls forth purple) and of heightening (yellow intensifies to orange). Moreover, since 'the eye exhibits an exacting need for wholeness', it strives to encompass the entire colour circle (*CW*, XII, 178; *FA*, XXIII.1, 50). The sight of a single colour subjects us to pathological constraints, while the demand for completeness releases us, arousing a moment of serenity: 'But the eye's inborn need for totality allows us to escape this limitation; it finds its freedom by creating the opposite of the colour forced on it, thus producing a satisfying whole' (*CW*, XII, 284; *FA*, XXIII.1, 259). To underscore the eye's perceptive and creative powers, Goethe compares 'the retina's great vitality' to 'the eternal rule of life', that is, 'inhaling presupposes exhaling and vice versa; each systole presupposes its diastole' (*CW*, XII, 173; *FA*, XXIII.1, 41). And he adds that, through the polar dynamics of brightness and darkness, the eye 'demonstrates its living quality, its right to take hold of an object, by bringing forth out of itself an element which is the opposite of the object' (*CW*, XII, 173; *FA*, XXIII.1, 41).

'To bring forth' — as Tantillo[34] and Förster point out in their enquiries into Goethe's specular epistemology — suggests that the processes of perception and production require the contribution of another 'organ', a 'stimulus' from 'within' that enables us to 'evoke dazzling inner images in the dark through the power of our imagination' or to 'see, in dreaming, objects as though in clear light' (*CW*, XII, 164; *FA*, XXIII.1, 24–25). Therefore, natural phenomena such as colours can only be seen and studied by having them 'present before our physical eyes, and those of the mind' (*CW*, XII, 205; *FA*, XXIII.1, 100).[35]

Only when sight and intuition — the physical eye and the spiritual eye — 'continuously work in a living union' (*FA*, XXIV, 432) can Goethe's demands for proper observation of nature be met: 'Wenn wir einen Gegenstand in allen seinen Teilen übersehen, recht fassen und ihn im Geiste wieder hervorbringen können, so dürfen wir sagen, dass wir ihn im eigentlichen und im höhern Sinne anschauen' [When we are able to survey an object in every detail, grasp it correctly and produce it again in our mind, we can say that we intuit it in a real and higher sense] (*FA*, XXV, 142; trans. by Förster, p. 93).

While Lorrain's practice overlaps with Goethe's workings of the eye, a question arises: if Lorrain's physical eye receives only light, shade, and colour, then what exactly does his 'higher nature', his spiritual eye, contribute to the act of seeing? Does it reassemble the phenomena and give them shape and contour? Or does it imbue the visual experience with conceptual understanding? Is to 'intuit' a phenomenon in a 'higher sense' related to Goethe's epistemology of 'Anschauung' [intuiting an essence]? If so, what would the 'form', the 'concept', the 'essence' be? Elaborating on the findings that our investigation has yielded so far, it seems tenable that Goethe's epistemology advances a reciprocity of subject and object, with the eye as intermediary. Speaking of the eye, *Zur Farbenlehre* explains that in the eye 'is mirrored from without the world, from within, the person' (*FA*, XXIII.2, 269), and Schopenhauer reports a conversation in which Goethe had occasion to retort: 'What? [...] Light exists only insofar as you see it? No, *you* would not exist, if the light did not see *you!*'.[36] It seems equally tenable that Goethe's 'idea' is less constitutive and more regulative. The creation of yellow or blue by light passing through turbid media, or the dynamic complementarity inherent in the creation of coloured shadows, is a regulative principle that the spiritual eye allows us to perceive. As exemplified by Faust, who relates his quest for understanding 'what, deep within it, | binds the universe together' to 'perceiving all seminal forces' (ll. 382–85), Goethe's 'idea' should be viewed not as a static, abstract entity but rather as a process, a formative energy. Goethe's insistence that Lorrain knew nature implies that, through intuitive perception rather than discursive judgement, the latter grasped its archetypal formative law and enacted it anew in his pictorial imagination.[37] In Goethe's cognitive practice, the eye of the mind presupposes an agile mind, for 'if we wish to arrive at some living perception of nature, we ourselves must remain as quick and flexible as nature herself and follow the example she gives' (*CW*, XII, 64; *FA*, XXIV, 392). The living union of the physical eye and the spiritual eye enables us to 'see a whole' comprised of parts which grow 'simultaneously and sequentially', that is, 'in spacio-temporal variations'[38] — think of Lorrain's tree as the ever-changing realization of the *idea* of the protean 'Urpflanze'. It is through such seeing that 'we may become worthy of participating spiritually in nature's eternal creativity' (*CW*, XII, 31, trans. modified; *FA*, XXIV, 448).

Further comments by Goethe on Lorrain not only resonate with these epistemological musings but also reveal the striking convergence of Goethe's eye and Lorrain's eye at the intersection of nature and art. In his reflections on the Kassel paintings, Goethe maintains that Lorrain 'succeeded in, as it were, eliciting from nature its secrets' and was uniquely able 'to transpose its quiet stirrings and its vitality onto the canvas' (*FA*, XIX, 33). Read through the lens of Goethe's intuitive perception, Lorrain's mind is so astute, perceptive, and agile that, on the canvas, he can weave nature into a 'rich', 'full', and 'pleasing' tapestry while at the same time enacting its 'secret', that is, the dynamics of its formative forces. Recall that Goethe used the epithet 'eternal' to characterize nature's ceaseless creativity, which may explain why he categorically states that 'in Lorrain, nature declares herself eternal'.

If the eye is the alpha and omega of Goethe's 'scientific' method, epistemology, colour theory, and poiesis, then Lorrain is its artistic epitome. Mediating between nature and art, between experience and idea, Lorrain's eye sees light and produces colour; and it is his eye that intuits nature's 'holy open secret' and engages it in creating his paintings.

The staffage, as is typical of Lorrain, serves as the narrative element embedded in the landscape. The apocryphal Book of Tobit tells of Tobias's father losing his eyesight during sleep: in a Job-like trial, 'warm droppings out of a swallow's nest fell upon his eyes, and he was made blind' (2. 11).[39] With the (initially disguised) archangel Raphael as his guide, Tobias sets out on a journey and, followed by his dog, he

> lodged the first night by the river of Tigris. And he went out to wash his feet, and behold a monstrous fish came up to devour him. And Tobias being afraid of him, cried out with a loud voice, saying: Sir, he cometh upon me. And the angel said to him: Take him by the gill, and draw him to thee. And when he had done so, he drew him out upon the land, and he began to pant before his feet. Then the angel said to him: Take out the entrails of the fish, and lay up his heart, and his gall, and his liver for thee: for these are necessary for useful medicines. (6. 1–5)

After returning home,

> Raphael said to Tobias: As soon as thou shalt come into thy house [...] immediately anoint his [the father's] eyes with this gall of the fish, which thou carriest with thee. For be assured that his eyes shall be presently opened, and thy father shall see the light of heaven, and shall rejoice in the sight of thee [...] And his father that was blind, rising up, began to run stumbling with his feet: and giving a servant his hand, went to meet his son [...] Then Tobias taking of the gall of the fish, anointed his father's eyes. And he stayed about half an hour: and a white skin began to come out of his eyes, like the skin of an egg. And Tobias took hold of it, and drew it from his eyes, and immediately he recovered his sight. (11. 7–15)

As we have seen, Goethe's attraction to this painting springs from its enactment of an Arcadian landscape, a landscape about whose nature, beyond the Tigris River setting, the biblical story offers no clues. There are, however, other reasons for his engagement with the story. Raphael, after all, is the patron saint of travellers, and Tobias, in his quest for salvation, faintly echoes the wanderer in Goethe's eponymous idyll (see Chapter 2). To this we should add the tension between the polar opposites of sight and blindness, the divine and the human, or, manifested in the image of the fish, healing and destruction. It comes as little surprise, then, to learn that Goethe reacted, if not ekphrastically, then poetically, to the story and the painting. The poem in question bears the title 'Antikritik' [Anti-Criticism] and appertains to *Zur Farbenlehre*:

> Antikritik
>
> Armer Tobis, tappst am Stabe
> Siebenfarbiger Dröseleien,
> Kannst dich jener Himmelsgabe
> Reinen Lichtes nicht erfreuen.
>
> Nicht erlustigen dich im Schatten,
> Wo mit urgebotner Liebe
> Licht und Finsternis sich gatten,
> Zu verherrlichen die Trübe.
>
> Werd' ihm doch die kräft'ge Salbe,
> Diesem Armen, bald gesendet,

Dem die theoretische Schwalbe
Augenkraft und -Lust geblendet. (*FA*, II, 758–59)

[Anti-Criticism

Poor Tobis, stumbling on your probing cane
Of seven strands of colour twisted together,
Unable to rejoice in that
Heavenly gift of pure light.

Nor to take pleasure in the shadow
Where light and darkness mate
For a love proffered eons ago
To glorify the mist in the air

May the strong ointment be sent
To the poor sap before long
Blinded to the power and pleasure of sight
By the swallow of theory.]

Starting with the curious title, Goethe's intention is to retaliate a perceived attack on him by a Danish follower of Newton called Ludolph Hermann Tobiesen (*FA*, II, 1219–20). The details of the Newton–Goethe controversy need not concern us here.[40] What is crucial is that the biblical story functions as the missing link between Goethe, Lorrain, and *Zur Farbenlehre*. The poem not only deploys its main motifs but even quotes it. To wit, Raphael's prediction that the blind man's 'eyes shall be opened, and [he] shall see the light of heaven, and shall rejoice in [its] sight' reoccurs almost verbatim. Yet, with the insinuated juxtaposition of 'Dröseleien' [snarls] and 'gatten' [to couple], Goethe adds another layer of meaning to the symbolism of this biblical story. He invokes it (and, indirectly, the Bible) in what amounts to a veritable crusade against Newton, the infidel who, in Goethe's eyes, had the audacity to proclaim that a prism 'aufdröselt' [decomposes] white light into the seven colours of the rainbow. Goethe, by contrast, was unshaken in his faith that colours were the result of a generative process likened to procreation: the offspring of the copulation of light and shadow, of light penetrating 'atmospheric vapour', which is why the latter should be 'glorified' as the chromatic divinity — a veneration reminiscent of the subliminally erotic veneration of the Virgin Mary, as 'Liebe' and the ambiguous and twice-repeated 'Lust' [joy or lust] (in 'erlustigen' and 'Lust') reveal. As other *Zur Farbenlehre* poems reveal, 'to couple' is foundational to Goethe's concept of colour formation.[41] But, significantly, he also uses 'to couple' to characterize the experience of a landscape that combines polar opposites to effect a pleasurable sensate union. In the 1829 edition of *Wilhelm Meisters Wanderjahre*, we read: 'Gradually, as the charming coupled with the wild, all of the wanderers were affected by the delightful view' (*FA*, X, 625).

In its logical consequence, the poem's tension between 'blind' and 'seeing', 'decrepit' and 'virile', 'soiled' and 'pure' strikes a discordant note in the conversation between Goethe and Lorrain. For, if the biblical story is about fidelity to God, 'Antikritik' is about fidelity to the gospel according to Goethe, with Lorrain as his disciple. What is troubling is that Lorrain, beyond the chromatic-theory fracas,

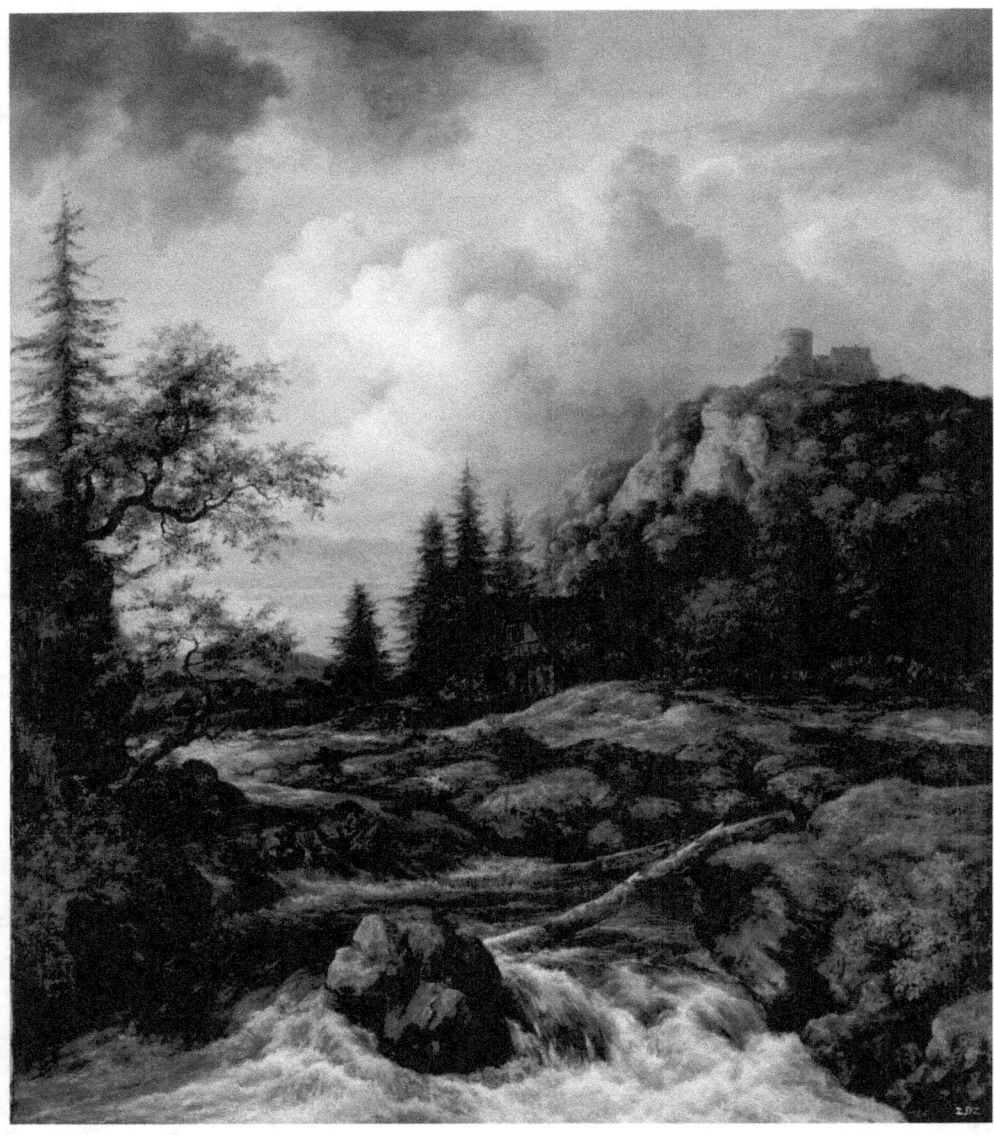

FIG. 5.3. Ruisdael, *Waterfall with Castle on a Mountain*.
Gemäldegalerie Alte Meister, Staatliche Kunstsammlungen, Dresden/
© bpk Bildagentur — Elke Estel — Art Resource, NY

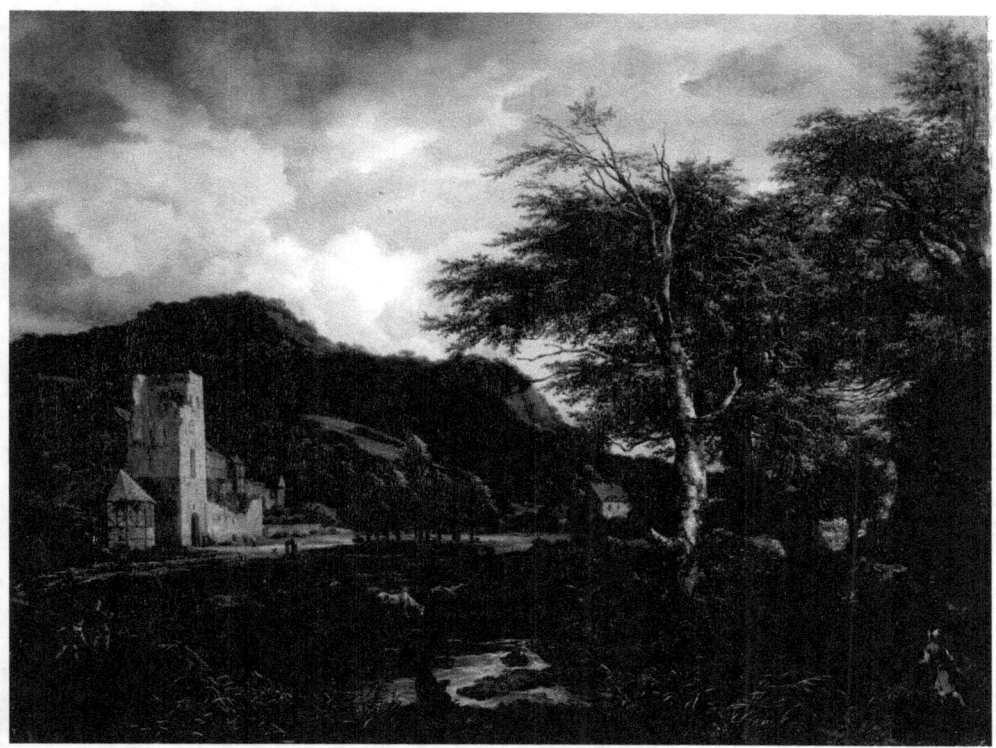

Fig. 5.4. Ruisdael, *The Monastery*.
Gemäldegalerie Alte Meister, Staatliche Kunstsammlungen, Dresden/
© bpk Bildagentur — Hans-Peter Klut — Art Resource, NY

becomes, in the broadest sense, a pawn in the dilemma of progress, the debate pitting the theoretical against the procreative, modernity against the 'ur'.

5.4. Jacob van Ruisdael and Peter Paul Rubens: Lorrains of the North

Goethe's discovery of the beauty of the Mediterranean landscape fills him with a yearning for a comparable Northern beauty. As we have already seen, on his way to Sicily, he couples his epiphanic understanding of Lorrain with 'the hope that [he] shall be able, even some day in the north, to summon up mental images of this happy domain', while back in Rome he is rather sanguine about finding 'more beauty in the North' now that his 'eye is better trained' (*CW*, vi, 188, 348; *FA*, xv.1, 249, 465). Goethe finds 'beauty in the North' in Jacob van Ruisdael. In his 1816 essay 'Ruysdael als Dichter', he discusses three paintings he encountered on visits to the Old Masters Gallery in Dresden, the first time in 1768, then twice more in 1813: *Waterfall with Castle on a Mountain* (1665/1670), *The Monastery* (1655/1660), and *The Jewish Cemetery* (c. 1655) (Figs 5.3–5.5).

Goethe frames the discussion of the three paintings with a general claim relating to what makes Ruisdael a 'poet'.[42] Foregrounding his artistry as such, he describes it, in terms of means, process, and effect, as distinctly dialectic, an interplay of 'outer sense' and 'inner sense', of imitation and intimation, of the visible grasped through the bodily eye and the invisible evoked through the mental eye. Executed in this manner and 'überliefert' [handed down] to the observer, such a work of art 'spricht einen Begriff aus, ohne sich darin [im Kunstwerk] aufzulösen oder zu verkühlen' [expresses a concept without fully exhausting or restricting its [the work's] meaning] (*GoA*, p. 210, trans. modified; *FA*, xix, 632). Associative significance abounds in the solemn, if not sacred, language of this statement: 'überliefern', as 'deliver to posterity', imbues the work of art with semi-religious eternity; 'aussprechen' reverberates with the gravity of a 'pronouncement' or 'revelation'. With the phrase 'to express a, or one, concept' (the German 'einen' allows for both), Goethe references — verbatim — his definition of 'allegory' in his *Maximen und Reflexionen*: 'Die Allegorie verwandelt die Erscheinung in einen Begriff, den Begriff in ein Bild, doch so, daß der Begriff im Bilde immer begrenzt und unvollständig zu halten und zu haben und an demselben auszusprechen sei' [The allegory transforms the phenomenon into a concept, the concept into an image; but in such a way that the image expresses the concept only in finite and incomplete fashion] (*FA*, xiii, 207). While a landscape painting may be read as allegory, the 'concept' or 'idea' intuitively graspable through the 'image' pushes the allegorical envelope. That is, before truth becomes doctrine, Goethe opens the door to polyvalence; the signification of the artwork neither 'auflöst' [dissipates] nor 'verkühlt' [congeals, i.e. solidifies by cooling].[43] Adding a layer of complexity to the dialectic's sublation in the polyvalence of truth, Goethe comes full circle as he concludes the frame of his essay: 'Der reinfühlende und klardenkende Künstler, sich als Dichter erweisend, erreicht eine vollkommene Symbolik und ergetzt, belehrt, erquickt und belebt uns zugleich durch die Gesundheit seines äußern und innern Sinnes' [The artist, in the purity of his feeling and the clarity of his thought, shows himself to be a poet, achieves a perfect symbolism, and at once delights, teaches, refreshes and revitalizes us by the wholesomeness of his outer sense and his inner sense] (*FA*, xix, 636; *GoA*, p. 215).

Goethe sublates the polarity between 'purely feeling' and 'clearly thinking', and between 'outer sense' and 'inner sense', into a double synthesis: 'wholesomeness' and 'symbolism'. In the former, a landscape painting's metaphysical solace is to be understood as an effect engendered by the interplay of perceiving nature objectively and reflectively *as well as* subjectively and experientially. In the latter, a landscape painting's signification is engendered by the interplay between representing nature imitatively and naturally *and* imaginatively and artfully. In the 196th 'Aphorismus', Goethe defines 'perfect symbolism' as that 'wo das Besondere das Allgemeinere repräsentirt, nicht als Traum und Schatten, sondern als lebendig augenblickliche Offenbarung des Unerforschlichen' [in which the particular represents the more general principle, not as a dream or shadow but as the evanescent, living revelation of that which is impenetrable] (*FA*, xiii, 33). It is crucial to heed Goethe's peculiar wording here, because the use of the comparative 'the *more* general' transforms the closed correspondence between 'the particular' and 'the general' into an open-ended association.

With 'lebendig augenblickliche Offenbarung', literally 'lively eye-blinking revelation', Goethe interrelates the trinity of landscape painting: eye, experience, and perception. Once again, he resorts to rhetoric to reinforce the importance of the visual. The 'Augenblick', or blink of the eye, is pleonastic in that it suggests 'seeing with one's eyes' or 'the eyes of the gaze'. Yet the link to revelation also suggests cognition, intuitive understanding. Landscape painting is the medium in and through which nature and self take turns between being 'in sight' and having 'insight'. Finally, the crucial moment suggests beauty. One of Goethe's excerpts from Moritz's *Über die bildende Nachahmung des Schönen* for the *Italienische Reise* reads: 'For us, the connectedness of the whole of nature would be the ultimate beauty, if we were able to grasp it [the connectedness] for one moment' (*FA*, xv.2, 907).[44] And from Faust we already know that 'painting' an English Garden brings about the moment of supreme beauty for which he has long been searching (ll. 11,581–82).

Although Goethe advocates the eighteenth-century faith in the *prodesse et delectare* maxim derived from Horace's *Art of Poetry*, his terminology goes beyond 'moralistic' instrumentalization of art. Goethe uses 'to delight' and 'to invigorate' also in the much broader sense of to 'delight soul, mind, and eye', to 'provide aesthetic pleasure and satisfaction', and to 'stimulate intellectually' (*GW*, III, 299, 380). A couplet by Goethe links 'reinvigorate' to the aesthetic of landscape painting: 'If you want the whole to reinvigorate you, | You must perceive the whole in the smallest thing' (*FA*, II, 380).

What are we to make of the self-contradictory proposition of sighting the invisible, of perceiving the imperceptible? What does the visually vivid epiphany reveal about the 'unfathomable, inscrutable, incomprehensible, enigmatic', i.e. 'das Unerforschliche', that which is incapable of being fully explored or understood?

As Goethe delves into the particulars of Ruisdael's art, which is — given the essay's broad frame of reference — landscape painting as such, we quickly realize that the complex dialectic delineated in the frame is at the core of Ruisdael's style and substance. Rather lapidarily, Goethe summarizes the paintings' subject matter as 'verschiedene Zustände der Erdoberfläche' [different aspects of the inhabited world], which are visualized by the familiar motifs of landscape painting, be they rock or river, building or bridge, village or valley, meadow or moss, tree or tomb, light or shade (*FA*, XIX, 632; *GoA*, p. 210). Executed with 'utmost freedom' yet achieving the 'most precise perfection', their composition into a whole follows the familiar painterly principles of aerial perspective, tripartite topography, and contrast (*GoA*, p. 210, trans. modified; *FA*, XIX, 632). Indeed, juxtaposition in the motifs' relation to time is, in Goethe's mind, the crux of Ruisdael's compositions. To cite but a few examples, in *The Monastery*, Goethe sees 'well-kept buildings' next to the 'ruined, indeed desolated, convent'; a 'decrepit, leafless and branchless beech with pitted bark' is surrounded by 'thriving, luxuriantly growing trees'; and, as 'destroyed' as the 'bridge' may look, it 'cannot stop the lively traffic'. In *The Jewish Cemetery*, the 'once fruitful surroundings of the convent' are now a 'wilderness, overgrown with shrubs and bushes'; a 'shaft of light' struggles through a 'passing rain shower'; and the 'tombs in their ruinous condition' contend with

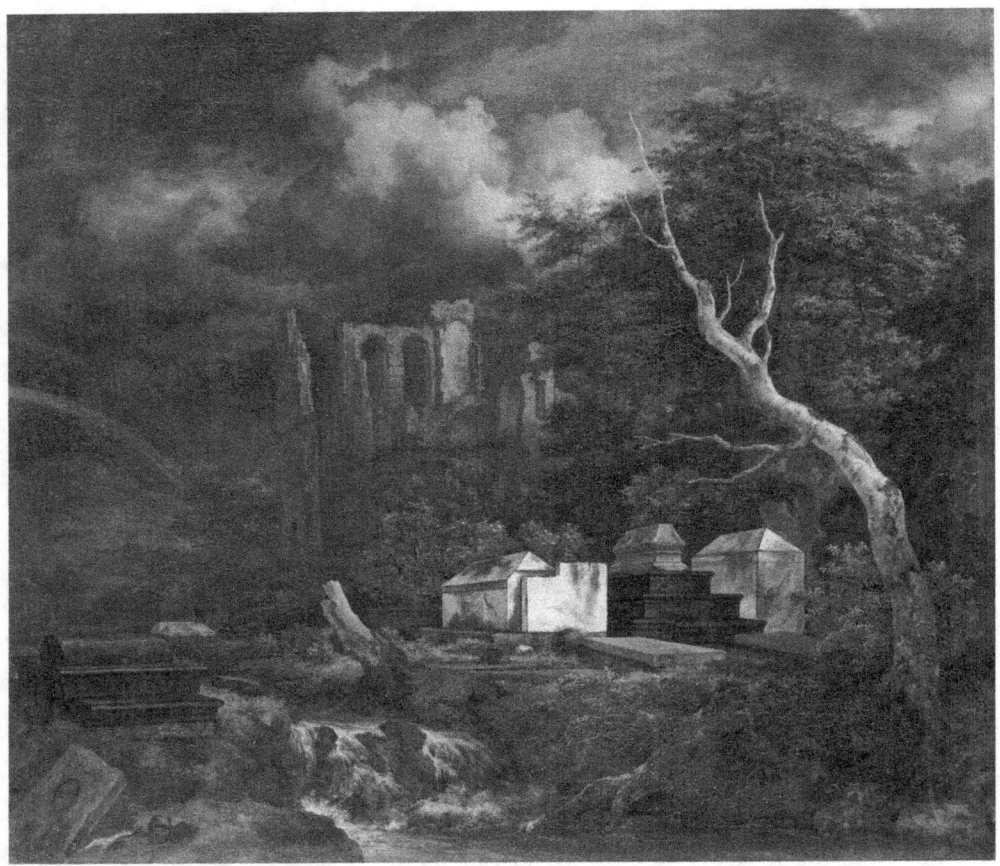

Fig. 5.5. Ruisdael, *The Jewish Cemetery*. Gemäldegalerie Alte Meister, Staatliche Kunstsammlungen, Dresden/© bpk Bildagentur — Elke Estel, Hans-Peter Klut — Art Resource, NY

the 'advancing stream of water with its flashing falls and foam' (*GoA*, pp. 212–15; *FA*, XIX, 633–35). Of critical importance is not that the imagery is comprised of polar opposites but that such opposites are integral to a dynamic, kinetic energy that permeates each painting: nature is 'forever growing', human life a 'continual ebb and flow'. Not surprisingly, Goethe makes out a 'wanderer' as the archetypal peripatetic amidst the lively comings and goings on the dilapidated bridge: is he still seeking an Arcadia that he can call his own, this time in the North (*GoA*, p. 212, trans. modified; *FA*, XIX, 633–34)? Goethe sums up Ruisdael's dialectic of composition, which, while part of *The Monastery* discussion, he sees as applicable to the other paintings too — namely, to 'represent the past in the present' and 'bring into vivid union that which has died with that which is alive' (*GoA*, p. 212, trans. modified; *FA*, XIX, 633). If this dialectic is an aspect of the 'impenetrable', it is light that makes the scene acessible to sight:

Indem nun ein sanftes Licht von dem Kloster zu den Linden und weiter hin sich zieht, an dem weißen Stamm der Buche wie im Widerscheine glänzt, sodann über den sanften Fluß und die rauschenden Fälle, über Herden und Fischer zurückgleitet und das ganze Bild belebt, sitzt nah am Wasser im Vordergrund, uns den Rücken zukehrend, der zeichnende Künstler selbst, und diese so oft mißbrauchte Staffage erblicken wir mit Rührung hier am Platze, so bedeutend als wirksam. Er sitzt hier als Betrachter, als Repräsentant von allen, welche das Bild häufig beschauen werden, welche sich mit ihm in die Betrachtung der Vergangenheit und Gegenwart, die sich so lieblich durch einander webt, gern vertiefen mögen. Glücklich aus der Natur gegriffen ist dies Bild, glücklich durch den Gedanken erhöht, und da man es noch überdies nach allen Erfordernissen der Kunst angelegt und ausgeführt findet, so wird es uns immer anziehen. (*FA*, XIX, 634–35)

[While a soft light passes from the convent to the limes and beyond, and seems to be echoed in the pale trunk of the beech, and as it returns over the gentle stream and the rushing falls, over herds and fishermen, bringing the whole picture to life, the artist himself sits drawing in the foreground, with his back to us, and we are touched to find this figure, which is so often abused, used so aptly and effectively here. He sits here as the observer, the representative of all who look at the picture in the future, and who will willingly immerse themselves in this spectacle of the past and the present so lovingly interfused. This picture has been most happily conceived from nature, and elevated by thought, and since it aspires to and fulfills every expectation of art as well, it will always fascinate us.] (*GoA*, p. 213)

Goethe's eye is truly a painter's, for it is captivated by light, by the zigzag path travelled by the light as it moves from background to foreground, coming to rest on the figure of the artist integrated into the painting. This staffage figure may be an allusion to Lorrain in terms of both his habit of plein-air sketching and his inclusion of the artist among his staffage. However, the fact that Goethe's poetic prose builds up to the artist being caught in the spotlight — note that the tension created by the series of dependent clauses is not released until the main clause introduces the artist — deserves closer scrutiny. For a start, Goethe uses Ruisdael's name just twice, once in the title and once in the essay's first sentence. After that, he substitutes 'artist' for Ruisdael. Specifying here that it is the artist as draughtsman, and not as painter, highlights Goethe's predilection not only for drawing but also for etchings and engravings, for the interplay of line, contour, lighting, and shading (the primary source for his essay is prints after Ruisdael, as he points out, not the original paintings). The self-conscious choice of 'artist' harks back to the equally deliberate designation for the creator of Goethe's exemplary form of art, 'style', which, as we have seen, is a sublation of 'simple imitation of nature' and 'manner'. By presenting Ruisdael as a particular Dutch landscape painter *and* as a more general 'stylist' within his theory of art, Goethe's understanding of symbolism is reflected throughout his essay. Infused with ekphrastic quality, the essay's poetic prose reminds us of his first essay on Lorrain in the *Frankfurt Literary Advertiser* in 1772. Finally, drawing attention to the artist figure, throws — yet again — the nature–art dialectic into sharp relief. It is personified in the painting's two agents who create analogously: the light that traces its winding course over natural objects, illuminating, connecting, and blending them, and the artist who selects natural objects, stringing them together, reflectively, imaginatively, and skilfully, into the story of an unending metamorphosis, that is, a landscape. Both light and the artist are mediators: light presents nature and makes it accessible to the artist, while the artist represents nature and makes it accessible to the spectator — aesthetically, experientially.

Curiously, Goethe uses the adverb 'durcheinander' [muddlingly] to modify 'weave', thereby suggesting, unlike the standard prefixed verb 'ineinanderweben', not 'interlacing' or 'combining into a whole' but the continual back-and-forth, not the synthesis of the finished product but the tension of the open-ended process. In other words, in contemplating the landscape painting, Goethe intuits an analogy between the natural particular — the sinuous trail of light and river — and the abstract universal — the mind weaving in and out of past and present. The synonymous modifiers (all meaning 'gentle') for light, river, and the process of interweaving validate the analogy.

The motif of the artist as 'observer' and 'contemplator' of phenomena and noumena calls to mind a poem from the same era as the Ruisdael essay, 'Epirrhema'. It encapsulates the convictions that guide Goethe's work as a morphologist. Yet, strikingly, it can also be read as encapsulating the ideals that guide the landscape painter:

> Müsset im Naturbetrachten
> Immer eins wie alles achten;
> Nichts ist drinnen, nichts ist draußen
> Denn was innen das ist außen.
> So ergreifet ohne Säumnis
> Heilig öffentlich Geheimnis.
>
> Freuet euch des wahren Scheins,
> Euch des ernsten Spieles:
> Kein Lebendiges ist Eins,
> Immer ist's ein Vieles. (*FA*, II, 498)
>
> [You must, when contemplating nature,
> Attend to this, in each and every feature:
> There's nought outside and nought within,
> For she is inside out and outside in.
> Thus will you grasp, without delay,
> The holy secret, clear as day.
>
> Joy in true semblance take, in any
> Earnest play:
> No living thing is One, I say,
> But always Many.] (*CW*, I, 159)

Extending upon the weaving trope from the Ruisdael essay, Goethe's style of landscape painting features a warp-and-weft aesthetic: just as the shuttle interlaces warp and weft into a fabric, so the painter, in a process of observation and contemplation, using outer eye and inner eye, interlaces distinct elements into a varied whole to create a re-presentation both real and unreal, that both reveals and conceals. The verbal analogue of this criss-crossing dynamic is the conjunction of contradictory concepts, e.g. one and all, internal and external, homogeneous and multifarious, or the straight oxymoron ('open secret', 'earnest play', 'true semblance' (as opposed to the 'false' semblance of the English Garden)). The woven fabric is a 'living thing' inhabited by spirituality, or a kind of numen — if 'holy' allows for this inference. Finally, the warp-and-weft aesthetic engenders 'joy'. Among the uses and meanings that the *Goethe-Wörterbuch* lists for the verb 'sich freuen' [to rejoice], the following seem apposite: 'delightful, open-minded, rapt experience, assimilation of, especially, phenomena in nature and of works of art, their soothing, invigorating effect; spontaneous awareness of, and deliberately sought aesthetic-intellectual relish' (*GW*, III, 920). A verbatim reminiscence of Ruisdael occurs in the title of a contemporaneous poem, namely 'Im Gegenwärtigen Vergangenes' [The Past in the Present]. As the title suggests, the poem weaves together past and present, and by so doing brings together self and other for the sake of 'merrymaking' (*FA*, III.1, 21). If this is a case of intuiting nature's 'open secret', the verbal equivalent that makes it visible is encapsulated in the nature image 'Nun die Wälder ewig sprossen' [Now [that] the forests have sprouted forever] (*FA*, III.1, 21). In just four words in the German — the definite article is irrelevant here — Goethe weaves a dynamic fabric of the present ('now') the past ('sprouted'), nature ('forests'), and eternity ('forever'). Oxymoronically poetic, the image is symbolic in Goethe's sense: the particular and the more general correlate.

The broader implication of the Ruisdael essay is that, for landscape painting to 'aspire to and fulfill every expectation of art', and to reveal 'how far art can and should go' (*GoA*, pp. 213, 215; *FA*, XIX, 635, 636), it is not predicated on Italy and a bygone Antiquity as subject matter. The artist as painter-poet transcends his respective realm, be it 'Northern' as in Ruisdael or 'Southern' as in Lorrain. Goethe's seemingly peculiar phrase describing the substance of this realm is not so peculiar after all. 'Verschiedene Zustände der Erdoberfläche', literally 'varying strata of the earth's surface' — this is Goethe the geologist speaking, and he purposely uses this 'physical' language to insist on the authenticity, even the rawness, of the painter-poet's 'material'. The ever-present epithet 'true' needs to be understood not just in its figurative sense but also in its literal sense of accurately conforming to (optical) reality. As such, it is indispensable to Goethe's understanding of 'poetic', for poetic signifies the relationship between self and (optically real) nature. And since this relationship is aesthetic, it signifies — fundamentally — the poietic process that shapes land into landscape. 'Poetic' denotes creativity in action, nourished by the interplay of nature and art — a dynamic that, of course, appertains to art in general. We need only recall Moritz, who, with Goethe's approval, defines this bringing-into-being as 'formative imitation of the beautiful'. An excerpt from Moritz's essay in the *Italienische Reise* is strikingly fitting as it interrelates, twice in the same paragraph, poiesis and beauty, saying that 'beauty has already attained its highest goal in its emergence, in its becoming', and 'beauty's inner essence lies in its emergence and becoming' (*CW*, VI, 432–33; *FA*, XV.1, 575). That is, to adapt

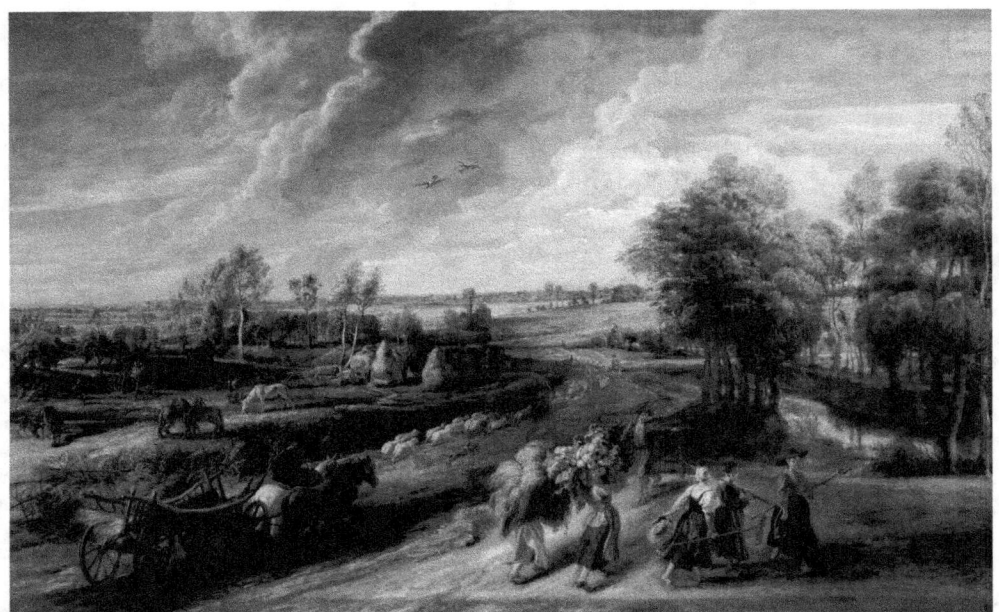

FIG. 5.6. Rubens, *The Peasants' Return from the Fields*. Gallerie degli Uffizi, Florence/© Gabinetto Fotografico

Goethe's epiphany in contemplating the common crab in Venice in October of 1786, beauty is 'lebendig' [lively] yet 'abgemessen' [measured], 'seiend' [authentic] yet 'wahr' [revelatory] (*CW*, VI, 78; *FA*, XV.1, 99). Faintly echoing Pope's 'nature methodiz'd', Goethe's 'crab formativ'd' transmutes into a metaphor for painting and poetry, conjoining science and art.

If, in his Ruisdael essay, Goethe holds the nature–art dynamic in tension, Friedrich Schlegel (1772–1829) disagrees. For Schlegel, Ruisdael's use of raw nature requires more artistry to transform it into beauty than Lorrain's use of refined nature. Ruisdael, he writes, 'affords us a genuine artistic vision', whereas Lorrain 'aspires to compete with nature herself in the reproduction of her most exalted spectacles', and, he concludes, 'the admiration of nature sweeps away all other feelings and drowns the voice of pure artistic sensibility'.[45] Goethe, it would seem, remains conflicted, as evidenced by another conversation with Eckermann (18 April 1827), this one involving Rubens and Lorrain. While it focuses on Rubens's handling of light in his *Peasants' Return from the Fields* (c. 1640),[46] it harks back to the start of our study and the relevance of Tasso's theory of poetry for Goethe's aesthetics of landscape painting and aesthetics in general.

Rubens's use of two light sources, resulting in shadows that point in opposite directions, provides Goethe with an opportunity to elaborate on the dialectic of fact and fiction:

> Der Künstler [...] muß freilich die Natur im Einzelnen treu und fromm nachbilden, er darf in dem Knochenbau und der Lage von Sehnen und Muskeln eines Tieres nichts willkürlich ändern, so daß dadurch der eigentümliche

Charakter verletzt würde. Denn das hieße die Natur vernichten. Allein in den höheren Regionen des künstlerischen Verfahrens, wodurch ein Bild zum eigentlichen Bilde wird, hat er ein freieres Spiel, und er darf hier sogar zu *Fiktionen* schreiten, wie Rubens in dieser Landschaft mit dem doppelten Lichte getan. (*FA*, XXXIX, 603)

[The artist [...] must, indeed, in his details faithfully and reverently copy Nature; he must not arbitrarily change the structure of the bones, or the position of the muscles and sinews of an animal, so that the peculiar character is destroyed. This would be annihilating Nature. But in the higher regions of artistical production, by which a picture really becomes a picture, he has freer play; and here he may have recourse to *fictions*, as Rubens has done with the double light in this landscape.] (*CV*, p. 196)

Shifting from practice to theory, Goethe writes:

Der Künstler hat zur Natur ein zwiefaches Verhältnis: er ist ihr Herr und ihr Sklave zugleich. Er ist ihr Sklave, insofern er mit irdischen Mitteln wirken muß, um verstanden zu werden; ihr Herr aber, insofern er diese irdischen Mittel seinen höheren Intentionen unterwirft und ihnen dienstbar macht.
Der Künstler will zur Welt durch ein Ganzes sprechen; dieses Ganze aber findet er nicht in der Natur, sondern es ist die Frucht seines eigenen Geistes, oder, wenn Sie wollen, des Anwehens eines befruchtenden göttlichen Odems. (*FA*, XXXIX, 603)

[The artist has a twofold relation to Nature; he is at once her master and her slave. He is her slave inasmuch as he must work with earthly things, in order to be understood; but he is her master inasmuch as he subjects these earthly means to his higher intentions, and renders them subservient.
The artist would speak to the world through an entirety; he does not find this entirety in Nature — it is the fruit of his own mind; or, if you like it, of the aspiration of a fructifying divine breath.] (*CV*, p. 196)

This applies to Lorrain too, for Goethe concludes:

Betrachten wir diese Landschaft von Rubens nur so obenhin, so kommt uns Alles so natürlich vor, als sei es nur geradezu von der Natur abgeschrieben. Es ist aber nicht so. Ein so schönes Bild ist nie in der Natur gesehen worden, ebensowenig als eine Landschaft von Poussin oder Claude Lorrain, die uns auch sehr natürlich erscheinet, die wir aber gleichfalls in der Wirklichkeit vergebens suchen. (*FA*, XXXIX, 604)

[If we observe the landscape by Rubens cursorily, everything appears as natural to us as if it had been copied exactly from Nature. But this is not so. So beautiful a picture has never been seen in Nature — any more than a landscape by Poussin or Claude Lorrain, which appears very natural to us, but which we vainly seek in the actual world.] (*CV*, pp. 196–97)

The act that transmutes 'land' into 'landscape', literal into symbolic, is the crux of Goethe's last real note on Lorrain, as recorded by Eckermann on 10 April 1829:

Da sehen Sie einmal einen vollkommenen Menschen [...] der schön gedacht und empfunden hat und in dessen Gemüt eine Welt lag, wie man sie nicht leicht irgendwo draußen antrifft. — Die Bilder haben die höchste Wahrheit, aber keine Spur von Wirklichkeit. Claude Lorrain kannte die reale Welt bis ins

> kleinste Detail auswendig, und er gebrauchte sie als Mittel, um die Welt seiner schönen Seele auszudrücken. Und das ist eben die wahre Idealität, die sich realer Mittel so zu bedienen weiß, dass das erscheinende Wahre eine Täuschung hervorbringt, als sei es *wirklich*. (*FA*, XXXIX, 346)
>
> [Here you see, for once, a complete man [...] who thought and felt beautifully, and in whose mind lay a world such as you will not easily find out of doors. The pictures have the highest truth, but no trace of actuality. Claude Lorrain knew the real world by heart, down to the minutest details, and used it only as a means to express the world of his beautiful soul. That is the true ideality which can so use real means that the truth evolved produces an illusion of actuality.] (*CV*, p. 321)

Noteworthy is the dual connotation of 'auswendig', which — as used here, in the expression 'to know by heart' — signifies the acquisition of complete knowledge, or, in the specifically Goethean sense, having a replica of land in one's mind that serves as a template for a landscape (*GW*, I, 285). The other connotation of 'auswendig' is 'nach außen wenden' [to turn inside out]; that is, as reality is filtered through Lorrain's soul and mind, he sublates what he sees and what he perceives, natural verisimilitude and artistic truth. The result is a beautiful, elevated symbol. As self-consciously crafted as the symbol may be, it is also an outpouring of the thoughts and feelings of Lorrain's soul. With 'inside out', Goethe finds a new way of articulating the inside–outside dialectic at work in the creative process: 'to know something inside out' and 'to turn something inside out'. The first idiom recalls the previously cited conversation with Eckermann (18 January 1827), in which Goethe says that, through the 'drawing of landscapes, I learned Nature by heart to the minutest details so that, when I needed anything as a poet, it is at my command' (*CV*, p. 156; *FA*, XXXIX, 211). The second idiom echoes the 'formative imitation of the beautiful' insofar as the creative process filters reality through the beautiful soul and draws it outside where it manifests itself as a 'true semblance'. Unlike the English Garden's 'simulation' of naturalness, Lorrain's 'deception' takes us back to the rhetoric of Longinus's sublime — 'as if a landscape manifested itself before our eyes'. While announcing an edition of etchings of his own selected drawings with accompanying poems (1821), Goethe expresses the hope that the cross-fertilization of drawing and poetry will 'awaken the inner sense and laudably deceive the observer into believing that he saw before his eyes what he feels and thinks, that is, an approximation of the sketcher's disposition when he committed a handful of strokes to paper' (*FA*, XXI, 278).

Given that Goethe repeatedly applies the distinction 'poetic' to Lorrain's art, one wonders why he never wrote an essay entitled 'Lorrain the Poet'. One reason is that 'poetic' becomes bound up with Goethe's quarrel with the Romantics. Presenting Ruisdael as a model for Northern landscape painting, he uses 'poetic' polemically against Romantic painters such as Caspar David Friedrich (1774–1840). Despite an initial enthusiasm for Friedrich, and despite overlaps in style and substance, Goethe denigrates his landscapes as 'mystical-allegorical' (*FA*, XX, 120). They suggest to Goethe transcendence instead of immanence, fragmentation instead of wholeness. In short, they are not symbolic because they are 'wanting in poetry' and thus not 'poetic'.⁴⁷ Polemics aside, Goethe clearly saw Lorrain as being right up there on Mount Parnassus with him, for when Eckermann, in the conversation just quoted, draws the conclusion 'This, I think, is good doctrine and would apply to poetry as to the plastic arts', Goethe laconically replies: 'Indeed it would' (*CV*, p. 321, trans. modified; *FA*, xxxix, 347).

5.5. Faust: Poet and Painter of Landscapes

In the landscapes from *Faust* to be discussed here, Goethe invokes poetry and painting one last time as sister arts. The question that arises is: how does the true artist relate nature and art so that 'semblance' becomes 'symbol', and so that 'authentic' is analogous to 'truth'?⁴⁸ Faust's pivotal monologues *are* landscape poetry, and they show that regarding Ruisdael and Lorrain as pendants is more a matter of complementation than of provocation.

As Faust's opening monologue revealed (see Chapter 4), the dynamic between nature and art is antithetical rather than synthetic, leaving the dichotomy intact. With the exception of Faust's improbable English Garden concoction, all of his other monologues significantly take place in pristine nature. Goethe returns to Rousseau's original nature, which, according to Julie in *La Nouvelle Héloïse*, can only be found 'on the tops of mountains or 'deep in the forest'.⁴⁹ In the 'Forest and Cave' monologue, Faust invokes the Earth Spirit, who, as an earlier scene reveals, personifies nature's primordial, inborn energy that weaves her 'lively garment' (l. 509). Given the focus and findings of our study, this raises the question of whether the 'sublime spirit' to whom Faust's 'prayer of thanks' is addressed might also be the spirit, if not of Lorrain, then of landscape painting:

> Erhabener Geist, du gabst mir, gabst mir Alles,
> [...]
> Gabst mir die herrliche Natur zum Königreich,
> Kraft, sie zu fühlen, zu genießen. Nicht
> Kalt staunenden Besuch erlaubst du nur,
> Vergönnest mir in ihre tiefe Brust
> Wie in den Busen eines Freund's zu schauen.
> [...]
> Und wenn der Sturm im Walde braus't und knarrt,
> Die Riesenfichte stürzend Nachbaräste
> Und Nachbarstämme quetschend nieder streift,
> [...]
> Dann führst du mich zur sichern Höhle, zeigst
> Mich dann mir selbst, und meiner eignen Brust
> Geheime tiefe Wunder öffnen sich.
> Und steigt vor meinem Blick der reine Mond
> Besänftigend herüber: schweben mir
> Von Felsenwänden, aus dem feuchten Busch,
> Der Vorwelt silberne Gestalten auf,
> Und lindern der Betrachtung strenge Lust. (ll. 3217–39)

> [Spirit sublime, all that for which I prayed,
> [...]
> You gave me for my realm all Nature's splendour,
> with power to feel and enjoy it. You grant
> not only awed, aloof acquaintanceship,
> you let me look deep down into her heart
> as if it were the bosom of a friend.
> [...]
> And when the storm-swept forest creaks and groans,
> When, as it falls, the giant fir strips down,
> and crushes neighboring boughs and trunks, and when
> [...]
> you guide me to the safety of a cave,
> reveal my self to me, and then my heart's
> profound and secret wonders are unveiled.
> And when I see the calming moon ascend
> and pass unblemished, into view there float
> from walls of rock and out of dripping glade
> the argent shapes of ancient times that serve
> to temper contemplation's stern delight.]

Recognizing nature as an objective presence outside of his self, Faust paints a landscape with a 'storm' that 'creaks and groans' through the forest as 'giant firs' keep 'crashing' into neighbouring trees. Both visually and auditorily, the scene arouses awe in Faust, the amalgam of fear and reverence that Burke identified as the sublime. In its rawness, it is an effect enkindled not by a Lorrainian landscape (with the exception of *Acis and Galatea*) but by the alpine scenery of a Salvator Rosa or the storm-swept landscapes of a Ruisdael. Yet Faust also paints a moonscape that is purely visual, and that, with an ethereality reminiscent of Lorrainian landscapes at twilight or night, engenders the soothing effect that Burke called beautiful. While Goethe wrote and drew and painted moonlit landscapes all his life,[50] moonlight plays an important role in his Italian experience. A passage from the *Italienische Reise* anticipates Faust's quasi-somnambulistic hallucination. The moonlight's 'magic', he writes in April 1788, is not just 'felt' but 'most vividly palpable' so as to transport us to 'a different [...] grander world' (*CW*, VI, 447; *FA*, XV.1, 595). However, Goethe appreciates the moon for its effect not just on mood and ambience but, more importantly, on form. In September 1787, Goethe reports on an outing with fellow artists to Frascati: 'Especially indescribable is the richness of the moonlight scenes, where the individual [...] details recede, and there are only the great masses of light and shadow, which fill the eye with hugely graceful, symmetrically harmonious, colossal shapes' (*CW*, VI, 326; *FA*, XV.1, 437). The moon here seems indispensable as a draughting tool because its light, through an intricate interplay with darkness, contours an amorphous mass into a visually pleasing composition. Another compositional reflection of the moon is its function in the scenery's symbolism, in the sense that it highlights the correlation of the particular, the 'individual detail', with the more general, the 'large mass'. Similarly, in terms of staffage, the figures emerging from the mists of a 'bygone world' and 'floating' in the foreground bring the intimacy of selfhood and the grandeur of myth into a reciprocally symbolic relation.

Although it is not meant to illustrate Faust's verbal moonscape, one of Goethe's wash drawings may serve as a pictorial enactment of his lunar aesthetics as discussed here. It is entitled *Aesculap-Tempel in der Villa Borghese im Mondschein* [The Temple of Aesculapius at the Villa Borghese in Moonlight] (1787).

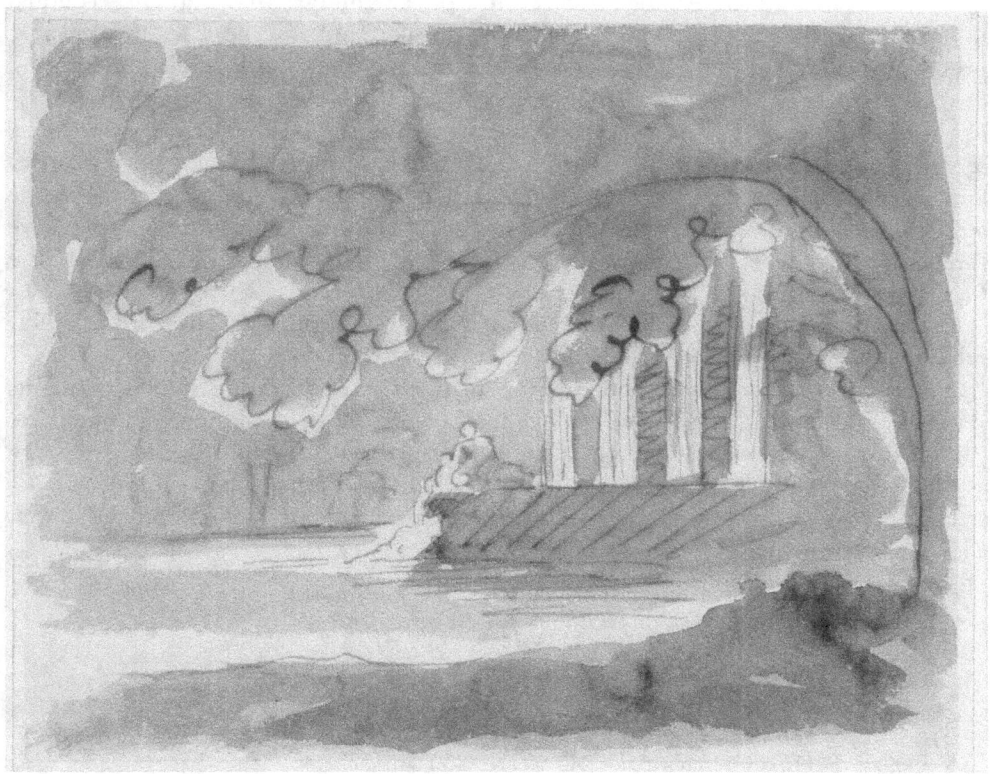

FIG. 5.7. Goethe, *Aesculap-Tempel in der Villa Borghese im Mondschein* [The Temple of Aesculapius at the Villa Borghese in Moonlight]. Klassik Stiftung Weimar, Museen: 210564/© Olaf Mokansky

The moon engenders a landscape in which the dynamic contrast between bright and dark creates structure and atmosphere. For Goethe, the moonlight sharpens and softens contours — note the gorgeous lines and washes, especially the highlight on the outermost reaches of the tree — and, while it solidifies myth into actual form, it also evokes the Aesclepeian reciprocity of death and resurrection.

The structure of Faust's monologue-cum-landscape poem bears striking resemblance to the composition of a (Lorrainian?) landscape: the eye moves from the panoramic background down to the forest in the middle ground, and then narrows in on the cave up front. Taking note of the 'thickets' there, it wanders up the 'high cliffs' and comes to rest on the lucent moon. The pronouncedly poetic analogue to this well-proportioned design is the monologue's iambic pentameter, which contours Faust's multifarious thoughts and feelings into an audibly pleasing rhythm. While in Rome, in the realm of Lorrain's 'classical' landscape, Goethe recast his most famous 'classical' drama, *Iphigenie auf Tauris*, in blank verse, and this is the only time he uses blank verse in *Faust* — significantly, to articulate a landscape experience. What is crucial about this experience is that 'landscape' *is* the medium in and through which subject and object interact in a dialogue as equal interlocutors: the 'I' that thinks, feels, and speaks, and the 'you' as an objective presence outside the self. It is precisely this tension between the self praying and the storm raging, between the self reflecting and the moon soothing, the cross-fertilization of 'experience of nature' and 'knowledge of self', that 'reveals' the 'deep, secret wonders'. Landscape poetry, like landscape painting, *is* fraught with polarity and intensification; thus, it is only fitting that their fundamentally oxymoronic aesthetics generates an oxymoronic effect: 'stern delight' — with the polarity here intensified by the erotic twist inherent in the 'delight'/'desire' ambiguity of the German word 'Lust'.

Even the idyllic landscape in which Faust and Helena consummate their relationship is partly comprised of features that remind us of Salvator Rosa — 'jagged heights' and 'ridges', 'ravines', or 'primeval woods'. Yet, since Faust paints with an alpine and an Arcadian — indeed, a Lorrainian — brush (see Chapter 4), he can claim that 'when the sway of nature is unhindered | all realms of being merge as one' (ll. 9526, 9531, 9542, 9560–61). According to Goethe, the monologue at the start of Part 2 was inspired by his visit to the Rhine Falls in Switzerland (*FA*, VII.2, 410–411, commentary).

> Des Lebens Pulse schlagen frisch lebendig
> Ätherische Dämmerung milde zu begrüßen;
> [...]
> Im Dämmerschein liegt schon die Welt erschlossen,
> [...]
> Ein Paradies wird um mich her die Runde.
> Hinaufgeschaut! — Der Berge Gipfelriesen
> Verkünden schon die feierlichste Stunde,
> Sie dürfen früh des ewigen Lichts genießen. (ll. 4679–97)

> [Life's pulses beat with fresh vitality
> And gently greet the sky's first glimmering;
> [...]
> But now the light of dawn unveils the world;
> [...]
> All that surrounds me forms a paradise!
> Look now, above! The mountains' mighty peaks
> Herald the hour of full solemnity,
> By right partaking of the everlasting light.]

As the monologue opens, the landscape is suffused by the exquisite light of the dawning day, redolent of the celestial airiness of the Mediterranean sky ('Aether') in *Nausikaa*. Given the literal and figurative sense of 'erschlossen', Faust experiences the 'world' as both 'unfolding' and 'revealing' itself in its totality; he perceives himself as 'immersed' in a supernal yet sensate world, a 'paradise'. However, as the sun rises and, fully alight, 'blinds' Faust, he 'turns away, his eyesight wounded, pierced':

> So bleibe denn die Sonne mir im Rücken!
> Der Wassersturz, das Felsenriff durchbrausend,
> Ihn schau' ich an mit wachsendem Entzücken.
> Von Sturz zu Sturzen wälzt er jetzt in tausend
> Dann abertausend Strömen sich ergießend,
> Hoch in die Lüfte Schaum an Schäume sausend.
> Allein wie herrlich diesem Sturm entsprießend
> Wölbt sich des bunten Bogens Wechsel-Dauer
> Bald rein gezeichnet, bald zerfließend,
> Umher verbreitend duftig kühle Schauer.
> Der spiegelt ab das menschliche Bestreben.
> Ihm sinne nach und du begreifst genauer:
> Am farbigen Abglanz haben wir das Leben. (ll. 4715–27)
>
> [I am content to have the sun behind me.
> The cataract there storming through the cliff —
> the more I watch it, the more is my delight.
> From fall to fall it swirls, gushing forth
> in streams that soon are many, many more,
> into the air all loudly tossing spray and foam.
> But see how, rising from the turbulence,
> the rainbow forms its changing-unchanged arch,
> now clearly drawn, now evanescent,
> and casts cool, fragrant showers all about it.
> Of human striving it's a perfect symbol —
> ponder this well to understand more clearly
> that what we have as life is many-hued reflection.]

Faust the landscape painter turns from Lorrain to Ruisdael, substituting the Southern landscape, an Edenic realm drenched with light, for a Northern one, an aquatic realm drenched in foamy spray, the sun for a rainbow. In terms of time, Lorrain's landscape encompasses past, present, and future — suggested by the verbs used: 'revealed', 'greet', and 'begins to be', 'turns into'. Ruisdael's landscape is one of sheer presence, ongoing action and perception — expressed by the virtually exclusive use of the verbs' present participle forms, such as 'roaring', 'pouring', or 'flowing'. Audibly, the action's kinetic energy is enhanced by the sharp sibilance of the 'sh' or 'sht' alliteration (e.g. 'Schaum', 'Sturz'), linking motion and image. The sun's reversal from radiating light to attracting the eye is analogous to the rainbow's alternation between permanence and change. Finally, and this is crucial for landscape's significance in the play's symbolism, the sun as an emblem for superhuman striving is replaced by the rainbow as an emblem of human striving. Is Goethe abandoning the sun-worshipper Lorrain? In 'Versuch einer Witterungslehre' [Toward a Theory of the Weather] (1825), Goethe writes:

> Das Wahre, mit dem Göttlichen identisch, läßt sich niemals von uns direkt erkennen, wir schauen es nur im Abglanz, im Beispiel, Symbol, in einzelnen und verwandten Erscheinungen; wir werden es gewahr als unbegreifliches

Leben und können dem Wunsch nicht entsagen, es dennoch zu begreifen. (*FA*, XXV, 274)

[We can never directly see what is true, i.e. identical with what is divine; we look at it only in reflection, in example, in the symbol, in individual and related phenomena. We perceive it as a life beyond our grasp, yet we cannot deny our need to grasp it.] (*CW*, XII, 145)

Faust sees a rainbow rising from the crashing water's turbulence:

> Of human striving it's a perfect symbol —
> ponder this well to understand more clearly
> that what we have as life is many-hued reflection. (ll. 4725–27)

With its culmination in the rainbow, nature — or, perhaps we should say, this painting of nature — has become 'eternal' à la Lorrain, or, in the words of a couplet which reads almost like a commentary on this scene: 'When Nature, from herself, created nature, | she made this globe complete and perfect' (ll. 10,097–98).

Furthermore, there is the monologue after the 'Helena act' where Faust in the 'High Mountains' steps 'with care' onto 'rugged, serrated peaks', watching 'a cloud float in and touch a peak, then settle on a projecting ledge'.[51] Just as the rainbow was 'eternal', so are the clouds: one evokes Helena, the other Gretchen, that is, Faust's aesthetic and ethical essences respectively. Finally, there are the 'forest' and 'rock' of the 'Mountain Gorges', the final landscape of the entire play:

> Wie tausend Bäche strahlend fließen
> Zum grausen Sturz des Schaums der Flut,
> Wie strack, mit eignem kräftigen Triebe,
> Der Stamm sich in die Lüfte trägt,
> [...]
> Ist um mich her ein wildes Brausen,
> Als wogte Wald und Felsengrund,
> Und doch stürzt, liebevoll im Sausen,
> Die Wasserfülle sich zum Schlund,
> Berufen gleich das Tal zu wässern;
> [...]
> Das sind Bäume, das sind Felsen,
> Wasserstrom, der abestürzt
> Und mit ungeheuerm Wälzen
> Sich den steilen Weg verkürzt. (ll. 11,868–913)

> [when jetting streams in thousands plunge
> into the seething cataract,
> when with its strong innate compulsion,
> a tree will rise straight to the sky,
> [...]
> When all about me there is tumult —
> woods and ravines a surging sea —
> the roar is pleasant as the streams,
> bringing water to the valley,
> gush and plunge into the gorge
> [...]

> Those are trees, and those are rocks,
> that's a stream — its falling waters
> tumble down in giant loops
> to make short the steep descent.]

The pictorial quality of Goethe's poetry is deceptive. At first it all seems, to quote from his programmatic 'Einleitung in die Propyläen' [Introduction to the *Propylaea*] (1798), 'raw material'. But the lines: 'Those are trees, and those are rocks, | that's a stream — its falling waters', preceded by 'gaze upon the landscape here!' (ll. 11,909–11), reveal the hand of the artist who selects for the sake of 'artistic truth' (*GoA*, pp. 6, 11; *FA*, XVIII, 461, 469). It is no coincidence that Goethe uses the verb 'schauen', which for him means not just 'to gaze' but 'to intuit an essence'. Goethe invites us, as he puts it in 'Über Wahrheit und Wahrscheinlichkeit der Kunstwerke: Ein Gespräch' (1798), into an imaginary landscape to perceive with him 'the excellence of the selection and the ingenuity of the composition, the otherworldly beauty of the small artistic world' (*GoA*, p. 30, trans. modified; *FA*, XVIII, 506).

If we try to interrelate painting and poetry one last time, Ruisdael's craggy streams and waterfalls come to mind. And there is, of course, the inspiration that Goethe drew from other pictorial sources, be it a fresco depicting hermits in rocky dwellings in Pisa or an etching illustrating Luke Howard's nomenclature of cloud formation.[52] Yet at least two paintings by Lorrain from around 1635 would seem to open up fresh considerations for *Faust* scholarship. Both feature a setting and a staffage that correspond, physically and metaphysically, to the 'Mountain Gorges' scene. One depicts an anchoress, *Landscape with St Mary of Cervello* (*c.* 1636), the other an anchorite, *Landscape with St Onuphrius* (*c.* 1636) (Figs 5.8–5.9).

Admittedly, the originals were not accessible for Goethe (in the Buen Retiro Palace of Philip IV), and, since they pre-date the *Liber Veritatis*, Goethe could not have found them in Earlom's engraved versions.[53] Yet if we pursue the likelihood that Goethe saw copies or printed versions — it was the widespread piracy of Lorrain's works that motivated the *Liber Veritatis* — we quickly realize that there is enough circumstantial evidence to tie Lorrain convincingly to *Faust*'s last scene.

As the curtain opens, with a few strokes of the verbal brush, Goethe sets a scene strikingly similar to the paintings: 'mountain gorges', 'forest', 'rocks', 'solitude', 'mountain range', and 'crevices'.[54] In the vivid description that follows, we are reminded of Longinus's sublime, for it feels as if we are stepping into the picture:

> Waldung, sie schwankt heran,
> Felsen, sie lasten dran,
> Wurzeln, sie klammern an,
> Stamm dicht am Stamm hinan. (ll. 11,844–47)

> [Woods seek to come near
> as rocks press them down,
> roots try to take hold
> as trees crowd together.]

The dynamic interaction between nature and art is palpable. 'Waldung' rings primeval and poetic. Even though the word does not derive from a verb (as is

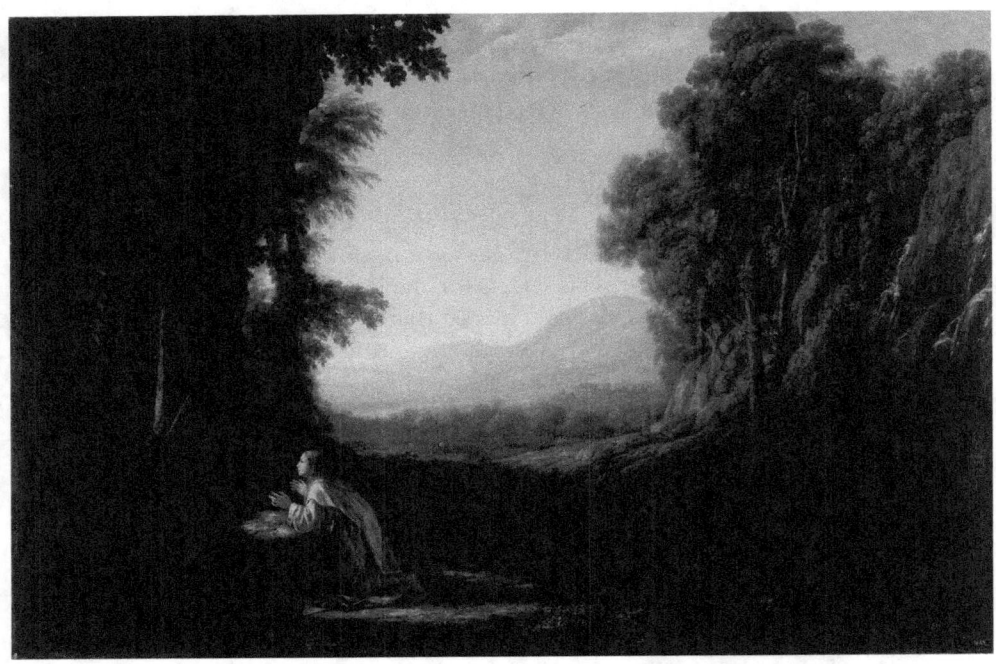

Fig. 5.8. Lorrain, *Landscape with St Mary of Cervello*. Museo del Prado, Madrid/ © Photographic Archive Museo Nacional del Prado

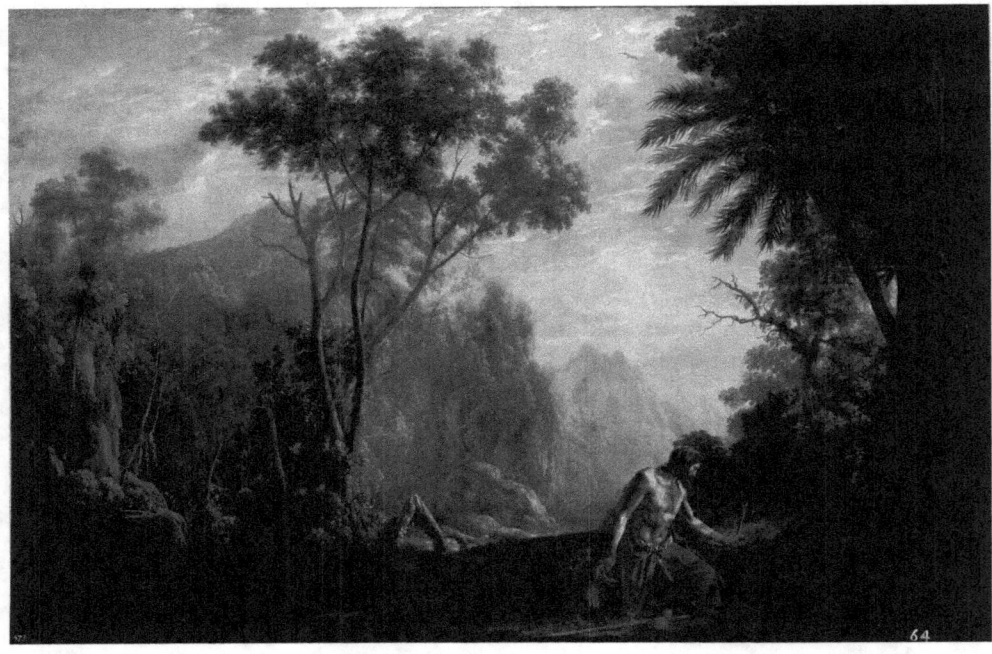

Fig. 5.9. Lorrain, *Landscape with St Onuphrius*. Museo del Prado, Madrid/ © Photographic Archive Museo Nacional del Prado

typical for the use of the suffix '-ung') it seems to conjoin the concrete and the abstract and suggest both action and result. Nature is the subject, both visually and grammatically: the peculiar syntax tells us that nature first strikes the eye with full force. Art, then, incorporates it into a composition that structures the scene in layers from the horizon, 'woods', down to the foreground, 'roots', and back up, 'upward'. Split as it is into 'CHORUS *and* ECHO',[55] the voice articulating these lines is dynamic, too, as is the staccato rhythm enhanced by the alliteration of 'a' in words and rhymes in the German. Finally, in its magnet-like effect, Lorrain's handling of the sun's light is a kind of visual analogue to the audible antiphony between the Chorus and its Echo. The scene ends with the same word, 'upward', only now it is not the physical — the trees — pushing from below, but the metaphysical — the 'eternal feminine' — pulling from above (ll. 12,110–11). Reciprocity completes the dynamic *and* the landscape as 'a whole'.

Engaged in rituals of expiation and seeking spiritual redemption in solitary wilderness, the figures fit squarely into the the play's last scene. Like one of the 'penitent women' in Goethe's scene, the floodlit woman in Lorrain partakes of the mythic light that emanates from the heavens and extends to the waters around her:

> Bei dem Bronn, zu dem schon weiland
> Abram ließ die Herde führen,
> [...]
> Bei der reinen reichen Quelle
> Die nun dorther sich ergießet,
> Überflüssig, ewig helle,
> Rings durch alle Welten fließet. (ll. 12,045–52)
>
> [By the well to which of old,
> the flocks of Abraham were driven
> [...]
> By the pure, abundant waters
> that since then spring up from it
> and in everlasting brightness
> overflow and flood the universe.]

Known for his retreat to the Theban desert in Upper Egypt, St Onuphrius is likely one of the hermits in the Campo Santo fresco. But Goethe 'encountered' him also in one of his favourite haunts in Rome, the monastery and church of Sant'Onofrio on Janiculinum Hill. After participating in a stifling service at the Sistine Chapel, Goethe writes in *Italienische Reise* that he 'sought the open air and at the end of a long walk reached San Onofrio, in a corner of which Tasso lies buried' (*CW*, VI, 140; *FA*, XV.1, 183). Offering a commanding view of Rome and the Vatican City, this most likely is the site Goethe used for his 1788 drawing 'Peterskirche in Rom' [St Peter's Basilica in Rome].[56] The Onuphrius thread that interweaves painting, poetry, and drawing extends even to colour theory, for, in the cloister, the fresco afficionado must have been dazzled by the lunette frescoes from around 1600 depicting episodes from the life of St Onuphrius.[57] One shows him being buried with the help of lions, which, curiously enough, appear in the landscape conjured by Goethe's Chorus and Echo: 'Lions roaming about, | silent and friendly' (ll. 11,850–51). Another shows the apogee of the saint's pilgrimage, his soul ascending to the heavens, just as Faust's 'immortal part' is carried aloft by angels.[58] In other frescoes, we see the saint eking out an ascetic existence in an alpine setting, similar to the self-flagellating figure in Lorrain's painting — note the scourge and the girdle of thorns — and in Goethe, where Pater Ecstaticus entreats the agents of punishments:

> Pfeile durchdringet mich,
> Lanzen bezwinget mich,
> Keulen zerschmettert mich,
> Blitze durchwettert mich. (ll. 11,858–61)

> [Arrows, transpierce me,
> lances, subdue me,
> batter me, cudgels,
> lightning, crash through me.]

It is only in this scene's nature — so pristine that Goethe employs a dialect form, the Swiss German 'abe' for 'down' (*FA*, VII.2, 799) — that redemption seems possible. 'Art' begins with Anchorites in 'crevices of the mountain-side',[59] and expands into a hierarchy of ever-more sublimated representations of 'love', not of *agape* (as the nomenclature might suggest) but of Platonic Eros, from 'Penitent Women' to the 'Mater Gloriosa' and on to the 'Eternal Feminine'.[60] But nature and art, the primeval and the transcendent, never blend. They are interlocked in a dynamic upward movement of irreducible polar opposites.[61]

Not even the Chorus Mysticus, with which the play concludes, is enough to resolve the tensions:

> Alles Vergängliche
> Ist nur ein Gleichnis;
> Das Unzulängliche
> Hier wird's Ereignis;
> Das Unbeschreibliche
> Hier ist es getan;
> Das Ewig-Weibliche
> Zieht uns hinan. (ll. 12,104–11)

> [All that is transitory
> is only a symbol;
> what seems unachievable
> here is seen done;
> what's indescribable
> here becomes fact;
> Woman, eternally,
> shows us the way.]

If we read the Chorus as intoning a commentary on the final scene's landscape, we cannot help but recall the oxymoronic formula for the tension in Kniep's 'most exquisite' Sicilian landscape, *Bocca di Capri* (Chapter 4): 'in pictorial representation the impossible becomes possible'. Similarly, in the last eight lines of *Faust*, Goethe falls back on rhetoric to conjoin contradictions: transitory permanence, manifest intangibility, effable indescribabilty, and eternal womanhood. The oxymoron used to describe Faust's dialectic essence as 'geeinte Zwienatur' [united duality] just a few lines before is, analogously, applicable to Lorrain too. The *et* in *natura et ars* is additive, contrastive, sublative.

Musically, the lyrical quality of the poetry might evoke a pastorale by Beethoven. The mystical chant suggests a dissolution into ethereal music, but at its most symphonic ('Hier ist es getan' [Here it is accomplished]), the metrical irregularity generates cacophony — Goethe breaks the rhythm with his 'ist es' [it is] instead of 'ist's' [it's].[62] Thus, the play is open-ended, as alluded to by Goethe in his comment to Eckermann: *Faust* is 'quite incommensurable'.[63] Significantly, the very last word is 'hinan' [upward, onward].

Visually, the landscape's serenity calls to mind a Lorrain painting, for, after all, it is the dawn of a 'new day' (l. 12,093). Enacted as if before our eyes — note the Chorus's insistent use of 'here' (ll. 12,107, 12,109) — it is a landscape suffused with the dynamic of polarity and intensification. The sublation of 'nebulous rocks' and 'clear cloudlets', the 'earth's burden' and the 'higher spheres', engenders a 'fresh spring' of 'rising perfection' (ll. 11,966–79).

Just as Faust *is* in a state of transformation between the physical and the spiritual — 'Puppenstand' [chrysalis] and 'sich umarten' [to form oneself into] (ll. 11,982, 12,099) are the ciphers of transition — so too *is* the landscape: between the physicality of tangible natural phenomena and the immateriality of intangible natural phenomena. To verbalize the latter, Goethe falls back on the 'Sicilian' vocabulary of the *Nausikaa* fragment: 'sheen' and its variant 'to shine', as well as its substantiation in the figure of the Mater Gloriosa, 'float', and 'Aether'. It is a landscape that relies on contrasts of light and shade, rather than colour, for its compositional structure, except for the aerial perspective which ends in a luminescent 'azure', the proverbial blue of the Italian sky. Beyond the 'wide prospect', the sun, the 'heaven's High Queen', rises in all her 'glory', shining 'splendidly' and 'exalting the spirit'. It is a sight that 'enraptures', holding out the promise of 'perceiving [her] mystery' in the 'azure of heaven's canopy'.[64] Faust's 'redemption' may begin in the darkness of the Northern 'mountain gorges', but it ends in a Mediterranean landscape where all is light upon light, or 'eternal', as is nature in Lorrain.

Notes to Chapter 5

1. Schiller, XLII, 328.
2. On the history of apprehensiveness vis-à-vis colour, and its ubiquity among Goethe's contemporaries, see Pape, '"Richtige Zeichnung und Charakter"'.
3. See W. Schöne, pp. 111, 115, 117, 149–50.
4. See W. Schöne, p. 109.
5. Cf. Traeger, pp. 130–31, who argues for Goethe's ability to 'see' an equivalency of black-and-white copy and coloured original, as well as for the duality, or even duplicity, that inheres in the notion of 'reproducing' the already 'produced'. Typical for Goethe's participation in the 'copper-engravings culture' is his advertisement, in the *Propyläen* (1799; *FA*, XVIII, 635–37), of the work of the Chalkographische Gesellschaft zu Dessau, which was an institution founded in 1795 for the sole purpose of commercially distributing reproductions of well-known paintings, among them numerous Lorrains; see Heine, pp. 58–59 (Goethe's announcement reprinted), 44, 53–54 (engravings after Lorrain).

6. Appearing in two volumes in 1810, the first edition had a total of 1487 pages.
7. Cf. P. Schmidt, pp. 247–48.
8. Cf. Beitl, p. 76.
9. This and the next quotation are from the preface to the *Liber Veritatis* (Earlom, I, 10).
10. See Beitl, p. 81.
11. Le Rider, p. 42.
12. It should be noted that one of the ironies of *Faust* is that, *chromatically*, the rainbow is a less than 'perfect symbol' because it lacks what Goethe considered the purest manifestation of the process of colour formation, 'purple'. See Evans, pp. 57–58.
13. Klemm, pp. 71, 74.
14. Schopenhauer, p. 43. Charles Lock Eastlake, whose 1840 translation of the 'Didactic' portion has remained authoritative, renders the title *Farbenlehre* as *Theory of Colours*, but elsewhere in the text he uses 'Doctrine of Colours' for 'Farbenlehre' (p. 164), which is given preference here in light of the religious fervour with which Goethe pursued and defended his chromatic beliefs. Cf. A. Schöne. For a succinct and competent introduction to the theory, see Wenzel. Cf. also A. Schöne; Allert, 'Goethe's *Farbenlehre* (*Treatise on Color*)'; Basfeld. For an elaborately annotated English edition of the 'Didactic' segment and other relevant texts, such as excerpts from Goethe's 'Confessions of the Author', see Matthaei, ed.
15. On this tripartite structure as a self-conscious literary strategy for producing a dynamic whole of differing voices and perspectives, see Moore, pp. 205–39.
16. See Wyder. Cf. Schillemeit; Gombrich, 'Goethe'.
17. Currie, p. 73.
18. Cf. Wyder, pp. 67–71.
19. Meyer, pp. 189, 183.
20. Meyer, p. 177. The details of the fresco's significance for Goethe's *Zur Farbenlehre* have been worked out, most recently, by Currie, pp. 67–69, 122, and Rössler.
21. Currie, pp. 72–73.
22. Currie, p. 72.
23. Currie, p. 83.
24. Currie, p. 83.
25. See Friedlaender, pp. 90–96.
26. Cf. Petz, 'Lorrain'.
27. Most recently, the painting has been linked to Goethe's 1780 poem 'Ein Gleiches' [Another Night Song] (*CW*, I, 59; *FA*, II, 65), mainly due to its compositional layering and the self's objectifying stance vis-à-vis the surrounding space; cf. Ziolkowski, 'Ich und die Vögel', pp. 33–36, 44.
28. Cf. Gerstenberg, 'Goethe und die italienische Landschaft', p. 657.
29. For a critically edited collection of more than sixty poems constituting a 'short versified doctrine of colours', see A. Schöne, pp. 165–228. Cf. also Fischer.
30. Currie, p. 117.
31. See Rueger, pp. 219–20, who points out the storytelling approach underlying Goethe's 'phenomenological' data collection in *Zur Farbenlehre*.
32. Cf. Rössler, pp. 156–57; Currie, pp. 67–69, 122–26, 142–43.
33. P. Schmidt, pp. 109–10.
34. See Tantillo, *Will to Create*, pp. 37–47.
35. Cf. Förster, 87–88; Tantillo, *Will to Create*, p. 43.
36. Herwig, II: *1803–1817*, p. 937.
37. I adapt here the epistemological reading of Goethe's essay 'Anschauende Urteilskraft' [Judgement through Intuitive Perception] (*CW*, XII, 31–32; *FA*, XXIV, 447–48) in Förster, p. 95.
38. Förster, pp. 94, 98.
39. Quotations are from <http://biblescripture.net/Tobias.html> [accessed 17 September 2019].
40. See Mandelartz; Burwick, pp. 9–53; Rueger, pp. 215–21.
41. For instance, *Zahme Xenien*, 6 (published in 1827): 'Einheit ewigen Lichts zu spalten, | Müssen wir für törig halten, | Wenn euch Irrtum schon genügt. | Hell und Dunkel, Licht und Schatten |

Weiß man klüglich sie zu gatten, | Ist das Farbenreich besiegt' [To split eternal light's unity | We must consider foolish, | Unless fallacy is all you need. | Brightness and darkness, light and shadow | If you know how to couple them wisely, | The problem of colour formation is solved] (*FA*, II, 677).
42. Cf. Osterkamp's reading of the Ruisdael essay (*Im Buchstabenbilde*, pp. 318–56). For an analysis of *The Monastery*, cf. also Petz, 'Ruisdael'.
43. Goethe may have borrowed the idiosyncratic term 'verkühlen' to suggest hermeneutic 'tempering' from processes involving heating and cooling, such as enamelling or encaustic painting.
44. Cf. *CW*, VI, 432; *FA*, XV.1, 574.
45. Translated in Bätschmann, p. 17. For the original, see Schlegel, pp. 473–74 ('Nachtrag italiänischer Gemälde', 1803).
46. See Lüders, pp. 15–18, who comments on Goethe and Rubens in the broader context of Goethe's subject–object aporia.
47. Conversation with Eckermann, 11 April 1827 (*CV*, p. 189; *FA*, XXXIX, 240). See Osterkamp, *Im Buchstabenbilde*, pp. 328–39; Allert, 'Goethe, Runge, Friedrich', pp. 73–78, 86–90. Cf. Grave, 'Illusion'. For Friedrich's 'Romantic' appropriation of Goethe-cum-Lorrain's 'Amor ein Landschaftsmaler', cf. Grave, 'Amor als romantischer Landschaftsmaler?'. Cf. Carus's fifth letter, pp. 105–12, on landscape painting for a contemporary comparison of Lorrain and Ruisdael from a 'Romantic' point of view.
48. For a succinct discussion of the interrelation of nature, art, and symbol in Goethe, see Noé-Rumberg, pp. 214–22.
49. Rousseau, VI, 394.
50. Cf. Mayer, ed.
51. Stage directions before ll. 10,039, 10,040.
52. *CW*, XII, 332–33; *FA*, VII.2, 793–94 (commentary), xiv, xvi (illustrations).
53. Roethlisberger catalogues the paintings as no. 218 (MRP, I, 481–82, II, 86) and no. 219 (MRP, I, 483, II, 87), with the alternative titles *Landscape with St Mary Magdalen in Penitence* and *Landscape with Anchorite*. The Museo del Prado, where they are now on display, uses the titles given here, as does Roethlisberger, ed., pp. 70–72. For the identification of the Anchorite with St Onuphrius, see Barghahn, I, 201–02.
54. Stage directions before l. 11,844.
55. Personae before l. 11,844.
56. Cf. Bergmann and Berndt, p. 137.
57. Witte, pp. 136–41; Abromson, pp. 200–07, 357, illustrations 146, 175–79.
58. Stage direction after l. 11,824.
59. Stage direction before l. 11,844.
60. J. Schmidt, p. 285.
61. On the inherent dialectics of *Faust* (and references to relevant scholarship), see Tantillo, *Goethe's Modernisms*, pp. 23–37.
62. As noted by Wolfgang Schöne in his commentary on the Frankfurt *Faust* edition (*FA*, VII.2, 815–16).
63. 3 January 1830 (*CV*, p. 341; *FA*, XXXIX, 373).
64. For the vocabulary and imagery of 'light' cited here, see ll. 11,864, 11,890, 11,923, 11,989–96, 11,998–99, 12,018, 12,090, 12,093; stage directions after ll. 11,933, 11,996, 12,031.

APPENDIX

Goethe's Lorrain Collection

The main sources for the list of original works are the catalogues raisonnés by Mannocci (etchings) and Roethlisberger (paintings and drawings). Also included are reproductions by other artists, who are listed in alphabetical order. '*M*', followed by plate number, title, and date, refers to original etchings by Lorrain following Mannocci's catalogue. The drawings and, where possible, the paintings related to the listed reproductions are identified with reference to Roethlisberger's catalogues ('*LV*' for paintings in the *Liber Veritatis*, 'no.' for paintings not in the *Liber Veritatis*, and '#' for drawings). Other sources: Femmel, ed., pp. 71–89, plates K 25, 1–40; Friedlaender, pp. 113–54. The entries have been checked against the extant holdings at the Klassik Stiftung Weimar, Abteilung Graphische Sammlungen, with the gratefully acknowledged help of Margarete Oppel and Dorothee Proft. The Goethe Nationalmuseum database number is given in square brackets. The Goethe Nationalmuseum's catalogue entries may need to be reviewed. The Barrière etching [23349] and its doublet [23352] are of *Coast View with Mercury and Aglauros* (*LV*, 70), not of *Seaport with Ulysses Restituting Chryseis to her Father Chryses* (*LV*, 80); the Barrière etching [23353] seems to be after *Seaport with the Embarkation of Ulysses from the Phaeacians* (*LV*, 96); the entry for the Lorrain etching *Landschaft* [20198] should include the addendum '*Der Rinderhirt*' ['The Cowherd' — the designation by which it is known as Lorrain's most accomplished etching (the related painting is *LV*, 85)]; and Schlicht and Schlotterbeck title their aquatint [23360] of *Landscape with Jacob, Rachel, and Leah at the Well* (*LV*, 169) *Evening*, instead of *Morning*, and their aquatint [23359] of *Landscape with Tobias and the Angel* (*LV*, 160) *Morning*, instead of *Evening*.

1. Drawings by Lorrain

1. *Reconciliation of Cephalus and Procris* (*c.* 1645; #586) [27832]
  Related paintings: *Landscape with Diana, Cephalus, and Pocris Reunited by Diana* (1645; *LV*, 91); *Landscape with Cephalus and Procris Reunited by Diana* (*c.* 1646; no. 233)
2. *Pastoral Landscape* (*with Shepherd Playing the Flute*) (no date; #1166; attribution doubtful) [28935]

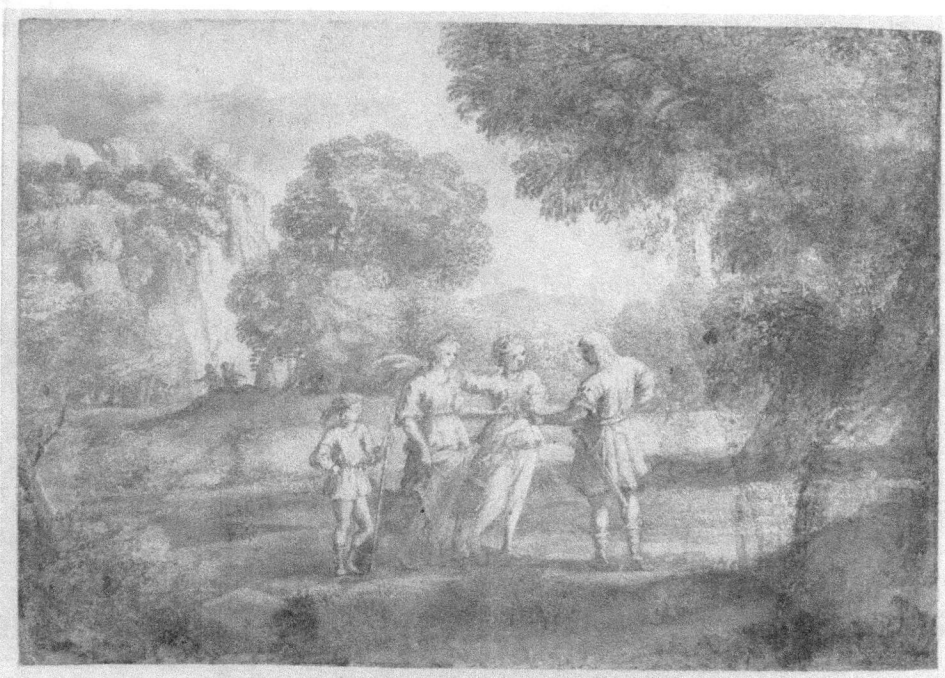

Fig. A.1. Lorrain, *Reconciliation of Cephalus and Procris* (c. 1645). Klassik Stiftung Weimar, Museen: 27832/© Olaf Mokansky

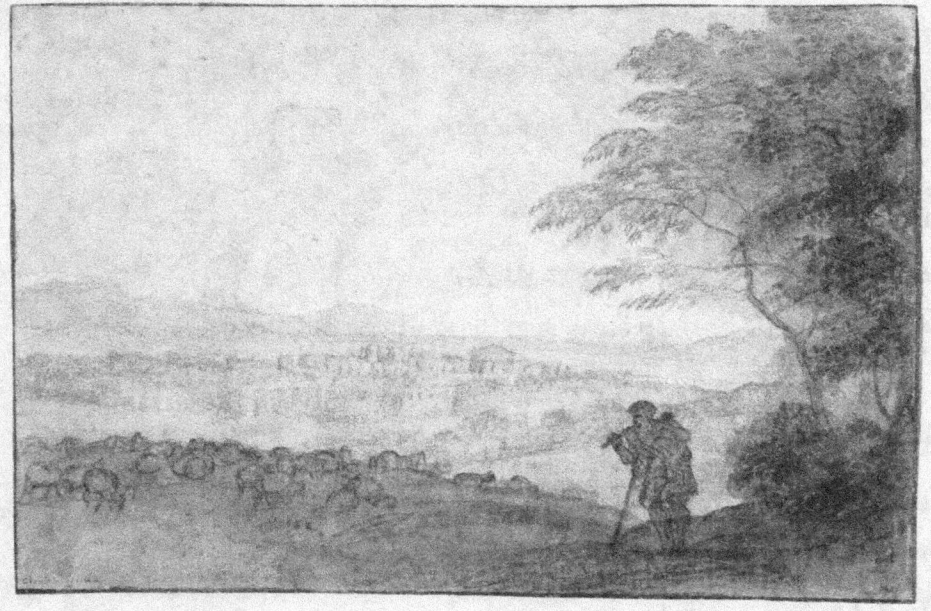

Fig. A.2. Lorrain, *Pastoral Landscape [with Shepherd Playing the Flute]* (no date). Klassik Stiftung Weimar, Museen: 28935/© Renno

2. Etchings by Lorrain

Total: 28 (including multiple prints)

1. M, 6: *The Tempest* (1630) [23328]
2. M, 9: *The Flight into Egypt* (c. 1630–33) [20195]
   Pastoral Landscape with the Flight into Egypt (1642; *LV*, 60)
3. M, 11: *Landscape with Brigands* (1633) [23336]
   Landscape with Brigands (c. 1633–34; *LV*, 3)
4. M, 12: *The Ford* (1634) [20196]
5. M, 13: *The Dance on the River Bank* (c. 1634); two prints [23329, 20197]
   Pastoral Landscape (c. 1638; no. 210)
6. M, 14: *The Rape of Europa* (1634); two prints [23344, 23345]
   Coast View with the Rape of Europe (1647; *LV*, 111)
7. M, 15: *Harbour Scene with Rising Sun* (1634) [20200]
   Coast Scene (1634; *LV*, 5)
8. M, 17: *The Roman Forum* (1636) [23346]
   View of the Campo Vaccino (1636; *LV*, 9)
9. M, 18: *The Cowherd* (1636) [20198]
   Pastoral Landscape (c. 1644–45; *LV*, 85)
10. M, 19: *The Country Dance* (c. 1637; small plate, third version); four prints [20199, 23333, 23334, 24144]
    Landscape with Rural Dance (1637; *LV*, 13)
    Landscape with Rural Dance (1639; *LV*, 36)
11. M, 20: *The Country Dance* (c. 1637, large plate) [23347]
    Landscape with Rural Dance (c. 1637; no. 208)
12. M, 34: *Departure for the Fields* (c. 1638–41) [20201]
    Pastoral Landscape (1637; *LV*, 20)
13. M, 35: *The Shipwreck* (c. 1638–41); two prints [23330, 23331]
    Sea Storm (c. 1638–39; *LV*, 33)
14. M, 36: *Coast Scene with an Artist* (c. 1638–41) [23332]
    Coast View (1639; *LV*, 44)
15. M, 37: *Harbour Scene with a Lighthouse* (c. 1638–41) [23335]
    Coast Scene (c. 1633–34; *LV*, 4)
16. M, 38: *The Wooden Bridge* (c. 1638–41) [23338]
    Pastoral Landscape (The Voyage of Rebekah?) (c. 1640; *LV*, 52)
17. M, 39: *Seaport with a Large Tower* (c. 1641) [2337]
    Harbour Scene with Large Tower (1637; *LV*, 17)
    Harbour Scene (1637; *LV*, 19)
18. M, 40: *The Herd Returning in Stormy Weather* (c. 1650–51) [23340]
    Pastoral Landscape (1654; *LV*, 133)
19. M, 41: *Shepherd and Shepherdess Conversing in a Landscape* (c. 1651) [23343]
    Pastoral Landscape (c. 1644–45; *LV*, 87)
    Pastoral Landscape (c. 1637–38; *LV*, 23)
20. M, 42: *Mercury and Argus* (1662) [23339]
    Landscape with Mercury and Argus (1661; *LV*, 150)
21. M, 43: *Time, Apollo, and the Seasons* (1662) [23342]
    Pastoral Landscape (1637; *LV*, 15)
22. M, 44: *The Goatherd* (1663) [23341]
    Pastoral Landscape (1661; *LV*, 155)

3. Etchings by Dominique Barrière

1. *Coast View with Mercury and Aglauros* (1662; *LV*, 70); two prints, 1668 [23349, 23352]
2. *Landscape with St George* (1643; *LV*, 73); one print, 1668 [23351]
3. *Seaport with the Embarkation of St Ursula* (1641; *LV*, 54); two prints, 1665 [23350, 210853]
4. *Seaport with the Embarkation of Ulysses from the Phaeacians* (1646; *LV*, 96); one print, 1660 [23353]
5. *Seaport with Ulysses Restituting Chryseis to her Father Chryses* (1644; *LV*, 80); one print, 1664 [23348]

4. Engravings by Friedrich Wilhelm Gmelin

1. *Coast with Acis and Galatea* (1657; *LV*, 141); one print, 1816 [23358]
2. *Landscape with Bacchus at the Palace of the Dead Staphylus* (1672; *LV*, 178); one print, 1804 [23356]
3. *Landscape with Dancing Figures [The Mill]* (1648; *LV*, 113); one print, 1804 [23355]
4. *Pastoral Landscape with the Flight into Egypt* (1647; *LV*, 110); one print, 1802 [23357]

5. Engraving by James Mason

1. no. 279: *River Scene* (c. 1629–31; attribution doubtful)
Engraving's title: *A View of the River Po in Italy*; one print, 1769 [23363]

6. Aquatint by Benedikt Piringer

1. no. 226: *Pastoral Landscape* (c. 1633); one print, 1820 [23364]

7. Aquatints by Abel Schlicht and Wilhelm Friedrich Schlotterbeck

1. *Landscape with Jacob, Rachel, and Leah at the Well [The Morning]* (1666; *LV*, 169); one print, 1800 [23360]
2. *Landscape with Jacob Wrestling with the Angel [The Night]* (1672; *LV*, 181); one print, 1800 [23361]
3. *Landscape with Tobias and the Angel [The Evening]* (1663; *LV*, 160); one print, 1798 [23359]

8. Engraving by William Woollett

1. *Landscape with Jacob, Laban, and his Daughters* (1654; *LV*, 134); one print, 1783 [23354]

9. Painting after Lorrain (unknown artist)

1. *Landscape with the Three Heliads Searching for the Dead Phaeton* (c. 1657; *LV*, 143) [111]

REFERENCES

ABROMSON, MORTON COLP, *Painting in Rome during the Papacy of Clement VIII (1592–1605): A Documented Study* (New York: Garland, 1981)
ADDISON, JOSEPH, '[Essay on Landscape Gardening]', *The Spectator*, 25 June 1712 (no. 414)
ALLERT, BEATE, 'Goethe's Farbenlehre (*Treatise on Colour*)', in *The Literary Encyclopedia*, ed. by Robert Clark (2006) <http://www.litencyc.com/php/sworks.php?rec=true&UID=5189> [accessed 23 June 2015]
—— 'Goethe, Runge, Friedrich: On Painting', in *The Enlightened Eye: Goethe and Visual Culture*, ed. by Evelyn K. Moore and Patricia Anne Simpson (Amsterdam: Rodopi, 2007), pp. 73–92
ANDREWS, MALCOLM, *The Search for the Picturesque: Landscape Aesthetics and Tourism in Britain, 1760–1800* (Stanford: Stanford University Press, 1989)
—— *Landscape and Western Art* (Oxford: Oxford University Press, 1999)
ANGLOMANIA DOMEN [JUSTUS MÖSER], 'Das englische Gärtgen', in Justus Möser, *Patriotische Phantasien*, 4 vols (Berlin: Nicolai, 1776), II, 465–67
APEL, FRIEDMAR, 'Der lebendige Blick: Goethes Kunstanschauung', in *Goethe und die Kunst*, ed. by Sabine Schulze (Ostfildern: Hatje, 1994), pp. 571–78
ARISTOTLE, 'Poetics', trans. by Stephen Halliwell, in *Aristotle: 'Poetics', Longinus: 'On the Sublime', Demetrius: 'On Style'*, Loeb Classical Library, 199 (Cambridge: Harvard University Press, 1995), pp. 1–141
ATKINS, STUART, 'Goethe's Nausicaa: A Figure in Fresco', in *Form und Innerlichkeit: Beiträge zur Geschichte und Wirkung der deutschen Klassik und Romantik*, ed. by Werner Kohlschmidt (Munich: Lehmen, 1955), pp. 33–49
BALDINUCCI, FILIPPO, 'Claudio Gellee Lorenese: Pittore di Paesi', in Filippo Baldinucci, *Notizie de' Professori del Disegno*, 6 vols (Florence: Per Santi Franci, 1728), III (1728), 353–59
BARBAULT, JEAN, *Les plus beaux Monuments de Rome ancienne; ou, Recueil des plus beaux Morceaux de l'Antiquité Romaine qui existent encore: Dessinées par Monsieur Barbault Peintre, ancien Pensionnaire du Roy a Rome, et gravés en 128 planches avec leur explication* (Rome: Bouchard & Gravier, 1761)
BARGHAHN, BARBARA VON, *Philip IV and the 'Golden House' of the Buen Retiro: In the Tradition of Caesar*, 2 vols (New York: Garland, 1986)
BARNER, WILFRIED, and OTHERS, eds, *Lessing: Epoche — Werk — Wirkung* (Munich: Beck, 1987)
BARNOUW, JEFFREY, 'Faust and the Ethos of Technology', in *Interpreting Goethe's 'Faust' Today*, ed. by Jane K. Brown (Columbia, SC: Camden House, 1994), pp. 29–42
BARRELL, JOHN, 'The Idea of Landscape in the Eighteenth Century', in John Barrell, *The Idea of Landscape and the Sense of Place, 1730–1840: An Approach to the Poetry of John Clare* (Cambridge: Cambridge University Press, 1972), 1–63
BASFELD, MARTIN, 'Zur Farbenlehre', in *Goethe-Handbuch*, ed. by Bernd Witte and others, 4 vols (Stuttgart: Metzler, 2004), III, 719–43
BATEY, MAVIS, *Alexander Pope: The Poet and the Landscape* (London: Barn Elms, 1999)

BÄTSCHMANN, OSKAR, 'Carl Gustav Carus (1789–1869): Physician, Naturalist, Painter, and Theoretician of Landscape Painting', in Carl Gustav Carus, *Nine Letters on Landscape Painting, Written in the Years 1815–1824; with a Letter from Goethe by Way of Introduction*, trans. by David Britt (Los Angeles: Getty Research Institute, 2002), pp. 1–73

BEAVEN, LISA, 'Claude Lorrain's Harbour Scenes: Sun, Science and the Theatre in the Barberini Years', *Melbourne Art Journal*, 9/10 (2007), 147–61

BEITL, RICHARD, *Goethes Bild der Landschaft: Untersuchungen zur Landschaftsdarstellung in Goethes Kunstprosa* (Berlin: de Gruyter, 1929)

BELLORI, GIOVAN PIETRO, *The Lives of the Modern Painters, Sculptors and Architects*, trans. by Alice Sedgwick Wohl (Cambridge: Cambridge University Press, 2005)

BENDING, STEPHEN, 'Horace Walpole and Eighteenth-Century Garden History', *Journal of the Warburg and Courtauld Institutes*, 57 (1994), 209–26

—— 'Literature and Landscape in the Eighteenth Century', in *Oxford Handbooks Online* <https://www.oxfordhandbooks.com/view/10.1093/oxfordhb/9780199935338.001.0001/oxfordhb-9780199935338-e-133> [accessed 5 April 2018]

BENES, MIRKA, 'Pastoralism in the Roman Villa and in Claude Lorrain', in Mirka Benes, *Villas and Gardens in Early Modern Italy and France* (Cambridge: Cambridge University Press, 2001), pp. 88–113

BERGMANN, GÜNTHER, *Claude Lorrain: Das Leuchten der Landschaft* (Munich: Prestel, 1999)

BERGMANN, GÜNTHER, and JESSICA BERNDT, *Goethe — Der Zeichner und Maler: Ein Porträt* (Munich: Callway, 1999)

BERNHART, TONI, 'Die neuere Forschung zu Goethes Ästhetik und Kunsttheorie', in *Johann Wolfgang Goethe: Romane und theoretische Schriften*, ed. by Bernd Hamacher and Rüdiger Nutt-Kofoth (Darmstadt: Wissenschaftliche Buchgesellschaft, 2007), pp. 164–89

BERTRAM, ERNST, *Nietzsche: Attempt at Mythology*, trans. by Robert E. Norton (Urbana: University of Illinois Press, 2009)

BERTUCH, FRIEDRICH JUSTIN, 'Ueber Englische Garten-Anlagen auf beschränkten Plätzen', *Journal des Luxus und der Moden*, 5 (June 1790), 300–22

BEYER, ANDREAS, '"Poussinsche Vorderteile"; oder, Von den Versuchen, die italienische Landschaft in Worten zu malen', in *Kennst du das Land: Italienbilder der Goethezeit*, ed. by Frank Büttner and Herbert W. Rott (Munich: DuMont, 2005), pp. 45–53

—— 'Italienische Reise', in *Goethe-Handbuch: Supplemente*, 3 vols (Stuttgart: Metzler, 2008–12), III: *Kunst*, ed. by Andreas Beyer and Ernst Osterkamp (2011), pp. 404–13

BEYER, ANDREAS, and ERNST OSTERKAMP, eds, *Goethe-Handbuch: Supplemente*, 3 vols (Stuttgart: Metzler, 2008–12), III: *Kunst* (2011)

BICKNELL, PETER, *Beauty, Horror and Immensity: Picturesque Landscape in Britain, 1750–1850* (Cambridge: Cambridge University Press, 1981)

BIRCHER, MARTIN, and BRUNO WEBER, *Salomon Gessner* (Zurich: Orell Füssli, 1982)

BISANZ, RUDOLF M., 'The Birth of a Myth: Tischbein's "Goethe in the Roman Campagna"', *Monatshefte*, 80.2 (1988), 187–99

BOEHM, GOTTFRIED, 'Bildbeschreibung: Über die Grenzen von Bild und Sprache', in *Beschreibungskunst — Kunstbeschreibung: Ekphrasis von der Antike bis zur Gegenwart*, ed. by Gottfried Boehm and Helmut Pfotenhauer (Munich: Fink, 1995), pp. 23–40

BORCHARDT, RUDOLF, *The Passionate Gardener*, trans. by Henry Martin (Kingston: McPherson, 2006)

BOULTON, JAMES T., 'Editor's Introduction', in Edmund Burke, *A Philosophical Enquiry into the Origin of our Ideas of the Sublime and Beautiful*, ed. by James T. Boulton (Notre Dame: University of Notre Dame Press, 1968), pp. xv–cxxvii

BOWRING, EDGAR ALFRED, TRANS., *Poems of Goethe: Translated in the Original Metres* [1853] (New York: Hurst, 1921)

BOYLE, NICHOLAS, *Goethe: The Poet and the Age*, 2 vols (Oxford: Oxford University Press, 1992–2000)
Briefwechsel des Herzogs-Großherzogs Carl August mit Goethe, ed. by Hans Wahl, 3 vols (Berlin: Mittler, 1915–18)
BRINK, ANDREW, *Ink and Light: The Influence of Claude Lorrain's Etchings on England* (Montreal: McGill–Queen's University Press, 2013)
BROWN, DAVID, and TOM WILLIAMSON, *Lancelot Brown and the Capability Men: Landscape Revolution in Eighteenth-Century England* (London: Reaktion, 2016)
BROWN, JANE K., 'Claude's Allegories and Literary Neoclassicism', in Jane K. Brown, *The Persistence of Allegory: Drama and Neoclassicism from Shakespeare to Wagner* (Philadelphia: University of Pennsylvania Press, 2007), pp. 15–45
BROWNELL, MORRIS R., *Alexander Pope & the Arts of Georgian England* (Oxford: Clarendon Press, 1978)
BULLARD, PADDY, 'Burke's Aesthetic Psychology', in *The Cambridge Companion to Edmund Burke*, ed. by David Dwan and Christopher J. Insole (Cambridge: Cambridge University Press, 2012), pp. 53–66
BURDACH, KONRAD, 'Faust und die Sorge', *Deutsche Vierteljahrsschrift für Literaturwissenschaft und Geistesgeschichte*, 1 (1923), 1–60
BURKE, EDMUND, *A Philosophical Enquiry into the Origin of our Ideas of the Sublime and Beautiful*, ed. by James T. Boulton (Notre Dame: University of Notre Dame Press, 1968)
BURUMA, IAN, *Anglomania: A European Love Affair* (New York: Random House, 1998)
BURWICK, FREDERICK, *The Damnation of Newton: Goethe's Color Theory and Romantic Perception* (Berlin: de Gruyter, 1986)
BUSCH, WERNER, 'Die "große, simple Linie" und die "allgemeine Harmonie" der Farben: Zum Konflikt zwischen Goethes Kunstbegriff, seiner Naturerfahrung und seiner künstlerischen Praxis auf der italienischen Reise', *Goethe-Jahrbuch*, 105 (1988), 144–64
——— ed., *Geschichte der klassischen Bildgattungen in Quellentexten und Kommentaren*, 5 vols (Darmstadt: Wissenschaftliche Buchgesellschaft, 1996), III: *Landschaftsmalerei*
BUSCHENDORF, BERNHARD, *Goethes mythische Denkform: Zur Ikonographie der 'Wahlverwandtschaften'* (Frankfurt a.M.: Suhrkamp, 1986)
BUTLER, E. M., *Byron and Goethe: Analysis of a Passion* (London: Bowles & Bowles, 1956)
BUTTLAR, ADRIAN VON, *Der englische Landsitz 1715–1760: Symbol eines liberalen Weltentwurfs* (Mittenwald: Mäander, 1982)
BÜTTNER, FRANK, 'Schinkel, Goethe und die "Gefährlichkeit der Landschaftsmalerei"', in *Geschichte und Ästhetik: Festschrift für Werner Busch zum 60. Geburtstag*, ed. by Margit Kern and others (Munich: Deutscher Kunstverlag, 2004), pp. 331–48
CANTOR, SARAH, 'The Pastoral Landscape: Politics, Poetry, and Piety in the 17th Century', in *Art and Social Change: Essays on the Collection of La Salle University Art Museum*, ed. by Klare Scarborough and Susan M. Dixon (Philadelphia: La Salle University Art Museum, 2016), pp. 17–33
CARRDUS, ANNA, '"Und mir's vom Aug' durchs Herz hindurch in'n Griffel schmachtete": Rhetoric in Goethe's "Erlebnislyrik"', *Publications of the English Goethe Society*, n.s., 62 (1993), 35–58
CARUS, CARL GUSTAV, *Nine Letters on Landscape Painting, Written in the Years 1815–1824; with a Letter from Goethe by Way of Introduction*, trans. by David Britt (Los Angeles: Getty Research Institute, 2002)
CICERO, MARCUS TULLIUS, '*De natura deorum*', '*Academica*', trans. by H. Rackham, Loeb Classcial Library, 268 (Cambridge: Harvard University Press, 1933)
——— *De Oratore*, trans. by E. W. Sutton, 2 vols, Loeb Classical Library, 348–49 (Cambridge: Harvard University Press, 1942)

CLARK, KENNETH, *Landscape into Art* (Edinburgh: Penguin, 1956)
CLARKE, MICHAEL, 'Ideal Landscape', in Michael Clarke, *The Concise Oxford Dictionary of Art Terms* (Oxford: Oxford University Press, 2010), p. 126
COLERIDGE, SAMUEL TAYLOR, *Biographia Literaria; or, Biographical Sketches of My Literary Life and Opinions*, 2 vols (London: Fenner, 1817)
COLLATZ, CHRISTIAN-FRIEDRICH, 'Pindar', in *Goethe-Handbuch*, ed. by Bernd Witte and others, 4 vols (Stuttgart: Metzler, 2004), IV.2, 853
CONSTANTINE, DAVID, 'Rights and Wrongs in Goethe's *Die Wahlverwandtschaften*', in *Johann Wolfgang Goethe*, ed. by Harold Bloom (Broomall, PA: Chelsea House Publishers, 2003), pp. 173–88
CURRIE, PAMELA, *Goethe's Visual World* (London: Legenda, 2013)
DANIEL, SERGEI, *Claude Lorrain (1600–1682)* (New York: Packstone Press, 2012)
DELP, WILHELMINA E., 'Goethe and Geßner', *Modern Language Review*, 20 (1925), 333–37
DITNER, DAVID, 'Claude and the Ideal Landscape Tradition in Great Britain', *Bulletin of the Cleveland Museum of Art*, 70.4 (1983), 147–63
DU FRESNOY, C. A. *De Arte Graphica: The Art of Painting, Translated into English by Mr. Dryden* (London: J. Heptinstall, 1695)
DYE, ELLIS, 'Sorge in Heidegger and in Goethe's *Faust*', *Goethe Yearbook*, 16 (2009), 207–18
EARLOM, RICHARD, *Liber Veritatis; or, A Collection of Prints, after the Original Designs of Claude le Lorrain*, 2 vols (London: Boydell, 1777)
FERNOW, CARL LUDWIG, 'Über die Landschaftsmalerei', in Carl Ludwig Fernow, *Römische Studien*, 3 vols (Zurich: Gessner, 1806–08), II (1808), 11–130
GOETHE, JOHANN WOLFGANG VON, *Theory of Colors*, trans. by Charles Lock Eastlake (Mineola: Dover, 2006)
EGLE, STEFFEN, 'Schriften zur Landschaftsmalerei', in *Goethe-Handbuch: Supplemente*, 3 vols (Stuttgart: Metzler, 2008–12), III: *Kunst*, ed. by Andreas Beyer and Ernst Osterkamp (2011), pp. 278–86
EILERT, HEIDE, '"Amor als Landschaftsmaler": Goethe und die Malerei des 17. und 18. Jahrhunderts', *Bruckmanns Pantheon*, 51 (1993), 129–37
ERSKINE-HILL, HOWARD, 'Pope and the Poetry of Opposition', in *The Cambridge Companion to Alexander Pope*, ed. by Pat Rogers (Cambridge: Cambridge University Press, 2007), pp. 134–49
EVANS, TAMARA S., 'Von der Mangelhaftigkeit des Regenbogens: Chromatische und morphologische Spuren Goethes bei Paul Klee', *Modern Language Studies*, 15.4 (1985), 55–63
FABIAN, BERNHARD, 'Englisch-deutsche Kulturbeziehungen im achtzehnten Jahrhundert', in *Europäischer Kulturtransfer im 18. Jahrhundert: Literaturen in Europa — Europäische Literatur?*, ed. by Barbara Schmidt-Haberkamp and others (Berlin: Berliner Wissenschafts-Verlag, 2003), pp. 13–30
FABIAN, BERNHARD, and MARIE-LUISE SPIECKERMANN, 'Pope in Eighteenth-Century Germany: A Bibliographical Essay (I, II, III)', *Swift Studies*, 15 (2000), 5–32, 16 (2001), 5–32, 17 (2002), 5–35
FEHRENBACH, FRANK, '"Das lebendige Ganze, das zu allen unsern geistigen und sinnlichen Kräften spricht": Goethe und das Zeichnen', in *Goethe und die Verzeitlichung der Natur*, ed. by Peter Matussek (Munich: Beck, 1998), pp. 128–56
FEMMEL, GERHARD, *Corpus der Goethezeichnungen*, 7 vols (Leipzig: Seemann, 1960–73)
—— ed., *Goethes Grafiksammlung: Die Franzosen*, Goethes Sammlungen zur Kunst, Literatur und Wissenschaft (Leipzig: Seemann, 1980)
FICK, MONIKA, *Lessing-Handbuch: Leben — Werk — Wirkung* (Stuttgart: Metzler, 2016)

FINNEY, GAIL, *Counterfeit Idyll: Garden Ideal and Social Reality in Nineteenth-Century Fiction* (Tübingen: Niemeyer, 1984)

FISCHER, F. P., 'Zu Goethes Gedichten zur Farbenlehre', *Gesnerus*, 6.3/4 (1949), 72–110

FLACH, WERNER, 'Landschaft: Die Fundamente der Landschaftsvorstellung', in *Landschaft*, ed. by Manfred Smuda (Frankfurt a.M.: Suhrkamp, 1986), pp. 11–28

FORMANEK, RUTH, '"Die Welt mit malerischen Augen sehen": Goethe und Kniep in Sizilien', in *Les Songes de la raison: Mélanges offerts à Dominique Iehl*, ed. by Université de Toulouse Le Mirail øCERAM et Département d'allemand (Berne: Lang, 1995), pp. 437–56

FÖRSTER, ECKART, 'Goethe and the "Auge des Geistes"', *Deutsche Vierteljahrsschrift für Literaturwissenschaft und Geistesgeschichte*, 75 (2011), 87–101

FRANK, HILMAR, 'Einfache Nachahmung der Natur, Manier, Styl', in *Goethe-Handbuch*, ed. by Bernd Witte and others, 4 vols (Stuttgart: Metzler, 2004), III, 570–77

FREEDBERG, SIDNEY JOSEPH, '*Disegno* versus *Colore* in Florentine and Venetian Painting of the Cinquecento', in *Florence and Venice: Comparisons and Relations (Acts of Two Conferences at Villa I Tatti in 1976–1977)*, 2 vols (Florence: La Nuovo Italia, 1979–80), II: *Cinquecento*, ed. by Sergio Bertelli and others (1980), pp. 309–22

FRIEDLAENDER, WALTER, *Claude Lorrain* (Berlin: Cassirer, 1921)

GAUTHIER, DAVID, *Rousseau: The Sentiment of Existence* (Cambridge: Cambridge University Press, 2006)

GERNDT, SIEGMAR, *Idealisierte Natur: Die literarische Kontroverse um den Landschaftsgarten des 18. und frühen 19. Jahrhunderts* (Stuttgart: Metzler, 1981)

GERSTENBERG, KURT, *Claude Lorrain und die Typen der idealen Landschaftsmalerei* (Berlin: Ebering, 1919)

—— 'Goethe und die italienische Landschaft', *Deutsche Vierteljahrsschrift für Literaturwissenschaft und Geistesgeschichte*, 1 (1923), 636–64

—— *Die ideale Landschaftsmalerei: Ihre Begründung und Vollendung in Rom* (Halle: Niemeyer, 1923)

GESSNER, SALOMON, 'A Letter from M. Gessner to M. Fueslin, Author of the History of the Swiss Painters, on Landscape Painting', in Salomon Gessner, *Idyls; or, Pastoral Poems* (Edinburgh: Mudie & Constable, 1798), pp. 112–40

GILPIN, WILLIAM, *An Essay on Prints: Containing Remarks upon the Principles of Picturesque Beauty, the Different Kinds of Prints, and the Characters of the Most Noted Masters* (London: J. Robson, 1768)

—— *Observations on Several Parts of the Counties of Cambridge, Norfolk, Suffolk, and Essex: Also on Several Parts of North Wales; Relative Chiefly to Picturesque Beauty, in Two Tours, the Former Made in the Year 1769, the Latter in the Year 1773* (London: Strand, 1809)

GOMBRICH, ERNST HANS, 'Renaissance Artistic Theory and the Development of Landscape Painting', *Gazette des Beaux-Arts*, 41 (1953), 335–60; repr. in Ernst Hans Gombrich, *Gombrich on the Renaissance*, 4 vols (London: Phaidon, 1994), I: *Norm and Form*, pp. 107–21

—— *Art and Illusion: A Study in the Psychology of Pictorial Representation* (Princeton: Princeton University Press, 1969)

—— 'Goethe and the History of Art: The Contribution of Johann Heinrich Meyer', *Publications of the English Goethe Society*, 60 (1991), 1–19

GOWING, LAWRENCE, 'Nature and the Ideal in the Art of Claude', *Art Quarterly*, 37 (1974), 91–97

GRÄTZ, KATHARINA, 'Zwischen Empirie und Ideenschau: Goethes System der Kunst in Einfache Nachahmung der Natur, Manier, Styl', in *Wechselleben der Weltgegenstände: Beiträge zu Goethes kunsttheoretischem und literarischem Werk*, ed. by Hee-Ju Kim (Heidelberg: Winter, 2010), pp. 135–51

GRAVE, JOHANNES, 'Amor als romantischer Landschaftsmaler? Nebel und Schleier bei Goethe und Caspar David Friedrich', *Zeitschrift für Kunstgeschichte*, 69.3 (2006), 393–401
—— *Der 'ideale' Kunstkörper: Johann Wolfgang von Goethe als Sammler von Druckgraphiken und Zeichnungen* (Göttingen: Vandenhoeck & Ruprecht, 2006)
—— 'Diesseits und Jenseits der Landschaft: Naturerlebnis und Landschaftsbild bei Goethe', *Euphorion*, 103 (2009), 427–48
—— 'Goethes Kunstsammlungen und die künstlerische Ausstattung des Goethehauses', in *Goethe-Handbuch: Supplemente*, 3 vols (Stuttgart: Metzler, 2008–12), III: *Kunst*, ed. by Andreas Beyer and Ernst Osterkamp (2011), pp. 46–83
—— 'Illusion und Bildbewusstsein: Überraschende Konvergenzen zwischen Goethe und Caspar David Friedrich', *Goethe-Jahrbuch*, 128 (2011), 107–26
GREIF, STEFAN, 'Jenseits von Arkadien: Natur- und Landschaftsästhetik bei Goethe und Schelling', *Zeitschrift für Ästhetik und Allgemeine Kunstwissenschaft*, 44.2 (1999), 5–23
—— 'Das allmähliche Verschwinden des Menschen? Zur anthropologischen Landschaftserfahrung bei Christian Ludwig Hagedorn und Johann Wolfgang Goethe', in *Physis und Norm: Neue Perspektiven der Anthropologie im 18. Jahrhundert*, ed. by Manfred Beetz and others (Göttingen: Wallstein, 2007), pp. 398–414
GRIMM, JACOB, and WILHELM GRIMM, *Deutsches Wörterbuch*, 33 vols (Munich: Deutscher Taschenbuch Verlag, 1971; repr. 1999)
GUTHRIE, JOHN, 'Eighteenth-Century Translations of Alexander Pope's Poetry', *Publications of the English Goethe Society*, 82.2 (2013), 67–84
HACKERT, JAKOB PHILIPP, *Briefe (1761–1806)*, ed. by Claudia Nordhoff (Göttingen: Hainholz, 2012)
HAGEDORN, CHRISTIAN LUDWIG, *Betrachtungen über die Mahlerey* (Leipzig: Wendler, 1762)
HAGSTRUM, JEAN H., *The Sister Arts: The Tradition of Literary Pictorialism and English Poetry from Dryden to Gray* (Chicago: University of Chicago Press, 1987)
HALLER, ALBRECHT VON, *Gedichte*, ed. by Ludwig Hirzel (Frauenfeld: Huber, 1882)
HAMILTON, JOHN T., *Security: Politics, Humanity, and the Philology of Care* (Princeton: Princeton University Press, 2013)
HARRISON, ROBERT POGUE, *Gardens: An Essay on the Human Condition* (Chicago: University of Chicago Press, 2009)
HECHT, WOLFGANG, *Goethe als Zeichner* (Munich: Beck, 1982)
HEDERICH, BENJAMIN, *Gründliches mythologisches Lexicon* (Leipzig: Gleditschens Handlung, 1770)
HEFFERNAN, JAMES A. W., *Museum of Words: The Poetics of Ekphrasis from Homer to Ashbery* (Chicago: University of Chicago Press, 1993)
HEINE, ALBRECHT FRIEDRICH, *Die chalkographische Gesellschaft in Dessau 1795–1803* (Dessau: Schwabe, 1930)
HELBIG, HOLGER, 'Der "Bezug auf sich selbst": Zu den erkenntnistheoretischen Implikationen von Goethes Naturbegriff', *Goethe-Jahrbuch*, 124 (2007), 48–59
HENNEBO, DIETER, 'Goethes Beziehungen zur Gartenkunst seiner Zeit', *Jahrbuch des Freien Deutschen Hochstifts* (1979), 90–119
HENNIGFELD, IRIS, 'Goethe's Phenomenological Way of Thinking and the Urphänomen', *Goethe Yearbook*, 22 (2015), 143–67
HERDER, JOHANN GOTTFRIED, *Selected Writings on Aesthetics*, trans. and ed. by Gregory Moore (Princeton: Princeton University Press, 2006)
HERWIG, WOLFGANG, *Goethes Gespräche*, 5 vols (Zurich: Artemis, 1965–87)
HIBBERD, J. L., 'Salomon Gessner's Idylls as Prose Poems', *Modern Language Review*, 68 (1973), 569–76
HIRSCH, EDWARD, 'Poet's Choice', *The Washington Post*, 26 December 2004, p. BW12

HIRSCHFELD, CHRISTIAN CAY LORENZ, *Theorie der Gartenkunst*, 5 vols (Leipzig: Weidmann, 1779–85)

HOFMANN, PETER, '"Erkenne jedes Dings Gestalt": Goethes Zeichnen als angewandte Erkenntnistheorie', *Deutsche Vierteljahrsschrift für Literaturwissenschaft und Geistesgeschichte*, 77.2 (2003), 242–73

HOMER, *The Odyssey*, trans. by Robert Fagles (New York: Penguin, 1996)

HOWARD, DEBORAH, 'Some Eighteenth-Century Followers of Claude', *The Burlington Magazine*, 111.801 (1969), 726–33

HUSCHKE, WOLFGANG, and WOLFGANG VULPIUS, *Park um Weimar: Ein Buch von Dichtung und Gartenkunst* (Weimar: Böhlau, 1958)

HUTCHINGS, W. B., '"Can Pure Description Hold the Place of Sense?": Thomson's Landscape Poetry', in *James Thomson: Essays for the Tercentenary*, ed. by Richard Terry (Liverpool: Liverpool University Press, 2000), pp. 35–65

JENA, DETLEF, *Wie das Vorüberschweben eines leisen Traumbilds: Goethe, Weimar und das Wörlitzer Gartenparadies* (Weimar: Weimarer Verlagsgesellschaft, 2017)

JØLLE, JONAS, 'Goethe's Translation of Pindar's *Fifth Olympian Ode*', *Goethe Yearbook*, 10 (2001), 50–64

JUNG, SANDRO, 'Print Culture and Visual Interpretation in Eighteenth-Century German Editions of Thomson's *The Seasons*', *Comparative Critical Studies*, 9.1 (2012), 37–59

KAISER, GERHARD, *Wanderer und Idylle: Goethe und die Phänomenologie der Natur in der deutschen Dichtung von Geßner bis Gottfried Keller* (Göttingen: Vandenhoeck & Ruprecht, 1977)

—— *Ist der Mensch zu retten? Vision und Kritik der Moderne in Goethes 'Faust'* (Freiburg: Rombach, 1994)

KANT, IMMANUEL, *Gesammelte Schriften* (Berlin, 1902–)

KEATS, JOHN, *A Critical Edition of the Major Works*, ed. by Elizabeth Cook, The Oxford Authors (Oxford: Oxford University Press, 1990)

KELSALL, MALCOM, 'Landscapes and Estates', in *The Cambridge Companion to Alexander Pope*, ed. by Pat Rogers (Cambridge: Cambridge University Press, 2007), pp. 161–74

KEMPF, FRANZ R., 'Noble Savages and English Gardeners: *Kulturkritik* from Rousseau to Goethe', *Philosophy and Literature*, 39.2 (2015), 422–42

KEUDELL, ELISE, *Goethe als Benutzer der Weimarer Bibliothek: Ein Verzeichnis der von ihm entliehenen Werke* (Weimar: Böhlau, 1931)

KITSON, MICHAEL, *Claude Lorrain: 'Liber Veritatis'* (London: British Museum Press, 1978)

KLEMM, CHRISTIAN, 'Licht, Raum und Atmosphäre: Zu zwei Stimmungslandschaften von Claude Lorrain', in *Von Claude Lorrain bis Giovanni Segantini: Gemäldeoberfläche und Bildwirkung*, ed. by Paul Pfister (Zurich: Kunsthaus Zurich, 1996), pp. 68–76

KLOTZ, PETER, 'Gesellschaftsdiskurs und Gartenkonstruktion: Zur Spiegelung des Ordnungswandels in Goethes Roman *Die Wahlverwandtschaften*', in *Sozialgeschichtliche Aspekte des Gartens: Gardens in Social History*, ed. by Walter Gebhard (Frankfurt a.M.: Lang, 2002), pp. 113–32

KNIGHT, RICHARD PAYNE, *The Landscape, A Didactic Poem*, 2nd edn (London: W. Bulmer, 1795)

—— *An Analytical Inquiry into the Principles of Taste*, 3rd edn (London: L. Hansard, 1806)

—— *Expedition into Sicily*, ed. by Claudia Stumpf (London: British Museum Publications, 1986)

KOETSCHAU, KARL, 'Goethe und Claude Lorrain', *Wallraf–Richartz Jahrbuch*, 6 (1930), 261–68

KRAMER, OLAF, *Goethe und die Rhetorik* (Berlin: de Gruyter, 2010)

KREIKENBOM, DETLEF, 'Über Laokoon', in *Goethe-Handbuch: Supplemente*, 3 vols (Stuttgart: Metzler, 2008–12), III: *Kunst*, ed. by Andreas Beyer and Ernst Osterkamp (2011), pp. 352–56

KRIEGER, MURRAY, *Ekphrasis: The Illusion of the Natural Sign* (Baltimore: Johns Hopkins University Press, 1992)
KRIEGER, VERENA, 'Die Farbe als "Seele" der Malerei: Transformationen eines Topos vom 16. Jahrhundert zur Moderne', *Marburger Jahrbuch für Kunstwissenschaft*, 33 (2006), 91–112
KURBJUHN, CHARLOTTE, *Kontur: Geschichte einer ästhetischen Denkfigur* (Berlin: de Gruyter, 2017)
KÜSTER, HANSJÖRG, 'Das Gartenreich Dessau–Wörlitz: Eine von Natur, Gestaltung und Ideen geprägte Landschaft', in *Landschaft um 1800: Aspekte der Wahrnehmung in Kunst, Literatur, Musik und Naturwissenschaft*, ed. by Thomas Noll and others (Göttingen: Wallstein, 2012), pp. 113–23
LAAN, JAMES M. VAN DER, *Seeking Meaning for Goethe's 'Faust'* (New York: Continuum, 2007)
LAGERLÖF, MARGARETHA ROSSHOLM, *Ideal Landscape: Annibale Carracci, Nicolas Poussin and Claude Lorrain* (New Haven: Yale University Press, 1990)
LANGDON, HELEN, *Claude Lorrain* (London: Guild, 1989)
LANGE, VICTOR, 'Goethe's Journey in Italy: The School of Seeing', in *Goethe in Italy, 1786–1788*, ed. by Gerhart Hoffmeister (Amsterdam: Rodopi, 1988), pp. 147–58
LAUTERBACH, IRIS, 'Werdende Bilder im Übergange: Gartenkunst und Landschaftsmalerei', in *Parkomanie: Die Gartenlandschaften des Fürsten Pückler in Muskau, Babelsberg und Branitz*, ed. by Agnieszka Lulinska (Munich: Prestel, 2016), pp. 41–53
LE RIDER, JACQUES, 'War die Klassik farbenfeindlich und die Romantik farbengläubig? Von Lessings *Laokoon* zu Goethes *Farbenlehre* und deren Nachwirkung', in *Goethe und das Zeitalter der Romantik*, ed. by Walter Hinderer (Würzburg: Königshausen & Neumann, 2002), pp. 31–49
LEHMANN, HERBERT, *Goethe und Gregorovius vor der italienischen Landschaft* (Wiesbaden: Steiner, 1967)
LENZ, CHRISTIAN, 'Claude Lorrain im Urteil Goethes', in *Im Licht von Claude Lorrain: Landschaftsmalerei aus drei Jahrhunderten*, ed. by Marcel Roethlisberger (Munich: Hirmer, 1983), pp. 49–53
LESSING, GOTTHOLD EPHRAIM, *Laocoön: An Essay on the Limits of Painting and Poetry*, trans. by Edward Allen McCormick (Baltimore: Johns Hopkins University Press, 1984)
LEVEY, MICHAEL, 'The "Enchanted Castle" by Claude: Subject, Significance and Interpretation', *Burlington Magazine*, 130 (1988), 812–20
LOBSIEN, ECKHARD, 'Landschaft als Zeichen: Zur Semiotik des Schönen, Erhabenen und Pittoresken', in *Landschaft*, ed. by Manfred Smuda (Frankfurt a.M.: Suhrkamp, 1986), pp. 159–77
LOEHNEYSEN, WOLFGANG FREIHERR VON, 'Goethe und die französische Kunst', *Publications de la Faculté des lettres de l'Université de Strasbourg*, 137 (1958), 237–89
LONGINUS [DIONYSIUS], 'On the Sublime', trans. by Hamilton Fyfe and Donald Russell, in *Aristotle: 'Poetics', Longinus: 'On the Sublime', Demetrius: 'On Style'*, Loeb Classical Library, 199 (Cambridge: Harvard University Press, 1995), pp. 143–307
LÜDERS, DETLEV, *Welterfahrung und Kunstgestalt: Über die Notwendigkeit von Kunst und Dichtung* (Würzburg: Königshausen & Neumann, 2004)
LÜTTEKEN, ANETT, 'Distanz durch Nähe — Goethe (v)erkennt Gessner', in *Idyllen in gesperrter Landschaft: Zeichnungen und Gouachen von Salomon Gessner (1730–1788)*, ed. by Bernhard von Waldkirch (Zurich: Hirmer, 2010), pp. 191–203
MAHON, DENIS, *Studies in Seicento Art and Theory* (Westport, CT: Greenwood Press, 1971)
MAILLET, ARNAUD, *The Claude Glass: Use and Meaning of the Black Mirror in Western Art*, trans. by Jeff Fort (New York: Zone Books, 2009)
MAISAK, PETRA, 'Der Zeichner Goethe; oder, "Die Practische Liebhaberey in den

Künsten"', in *Goethe und die Kunst*, ed. by Sabine Schulze (Ostfildern: Hatje, 1994), pp. 104–48

MAISAK, PETRA, *Johann Wolfgang Goethe: Zeichnungen* (Stuttgart: Reclam, 1996)

MALKIN, IRAD, 'The Odyssey and the Nymphs', *Gaia: Revue interdisciplinaire sur la Grèce Archaïque*, 5 (2001), 11–27

MANDELARTZ, MICHAEL, 'Goethe, Newton und die Wissenschaftstheorie: Zur Wissenschaftskritik und Methodologie der *Farbenlehre*', in Michael Mandelartz, *Goethe, Kleist: Literatur, Politik und Wissenschaft um 1800* (Berlin: Schmidt, 2011), pp. 240–81

MANNOCCI, LINO, *The Etchings of Claude Lorrain* (New Haven: Yale University Press, 1989)

MANWARING, ELIZABETH WHEELER, *Italian Landscape in Eighteenth-Century England: A Study Chiefly of the Influence of Claude Lorrain and Salvator Rosa on English Taste, 1700–1800* (London: Cass, 1925)

MASON, WILLIAM, *The English Garden: A Poem* (York: A. Ward, 1783)

Masters of Arts — Claude Lorrain (Hastings: Delphi Classics, 2017). e-book. <http://www.delphiclassics.com>

MATTHAEI, RUPPRECHT, ed., *Goethe's Color Theory*, trans. by Herb Ach (New York: Van Nostrand Reinhold, 1971)

MAUL, GISELA, 'Johann Wolfgang von Goethe und Jakob Philipp Hackert: Briefwechsel 1796–1806', in Norbert Miller and Claudia Nordhoff, *Lehrreiche Nähe: Goethe und Hackert* (Munich: Hanser, 1997), pp. 86–122

MAYER, MATHIAS, ed., *Goethes Monde: Texte und Zeichnungen* (Berlin: Insel, 2012)

MCCORMICK, EDWARD ALLEN, '*Poema Pictura Loquens*: Literary Pictorialism and the Psychology of Landscape', *Comparative Literature Studies*, 13.3 (1976), 196–213

—— 'Young Goethe in the Landscape', *Modern Language Studies*, 18.4 (1988), 61–67

MEYER, JOHANN HEINRICH, 'Die Aldobrandinische Hochzeit von Seiten der Kunst betrachtet', in Karl August Böttiger, '*Die Aldobrandinische Hochzeit*': *Eine archäologische Ausdeutung* (Dresden: Walthersche Buchhandlung, 1810), pp. 173–206

MILDENBERGER, HERMANN, 'Goethe and French Drawing', in *From Callot to Greuze: French Drawings from Weimar*, ed. by David Mandrella and others (Berlin: G+H Verlag, 2005), pp. 17–37

—— 'Die Baumporträts', in *Jakob Philipp Hackert: Europas Landschaftsmaler der Goethezeit*, ed. by Hubertus Gaßner and Ernst-Gerhard Güse (Ostfildern: Hatje, 2008), pp. 268–83

—— '"Die Hackertsche klare, strenge Manier": Johann Wolfgang von Goethe und Jakob Philipp Hackert', in *Jakob Philipp Hackert: Europas Landschaftsmaler der Goethezeit*, ed. by Hubertus Gaßner and Ernst-Gerhard Güse (Ostfildern: Hatje, 2008), pp. 75–85

—— 'Goethe als Zeichner', in *Goethe-Handbuch: Supplemente*, 3 vols (Stuttgart: Metzler, 2008–12), III: *Kunst*, ed. by Andreas Beyer and Ernst Osterkamp (2011), pp. 28–45

MILLER, NORBERT, 'Der Dichter als Landschaftsmaler: Zu Goethes Umgang mit der Wahrnehmung', in *Goethes Italienische Reise: Auch ich in Arkadien*, ed. by Michael Ruetz (Munich: Hanser, 1985), pp. 9–19

—— 'Der Dichter ein Landschaftsmaler', in *Goethe und die Kunst*, ed. by Sabine Schulze (Ostfildern: Hatje, 1994), pp. 379–407

—— *Die Insel der Nausikaa: Spiegelungen des Sizilianischen Abenteuers* (Stuttgart: Steiner, 1994)

—— '"Die Regeln des großen Stils aus der schönen italiänischen Natur": Jakob Philipp Hackert in Neapel und die Entstehung der Landschaft nach der Natur', in Norbert Miller and Claudia Nordhoff, *Lehrreiche Nähe: Goethe und Hackert* (Munich: Hanser, 1997), pp. 10–46

—— '"Über die Kunst ist es ein ander Ding": Hackerts Fragmente zur Landschaftsmalerei — Ein imaginäres Gespräch', in Norbert Miller and Claudia Nordhoff, *Lehrreiche Nähe: Goethe und Hackert* (Munich: Hanser, 1997), pp. 47–84

—— *Der Wanderer: Goethe in Italien* (Munich: Hanser, 2002)
MILLER, NORBERT, and CLAUDIA NORDHOFF, *Lehrreiche Nähe: Goethe und Hackert* (Munich: Hanser, 1997)
MITCHELL, W. J. T., 'Imperial Landscape', in *Landscape and Power*, ed. by W. J. T. Mitchell (Chicago: University of Chicago Press, 1994), pp. 5–34
MONTANARI, TOMASO, 'Introduction', in Giovan Pietro Bellori, *The Lives of the Modern Painters, Sculptors and Architects*, trans. by Alice Sedgwick Wohl (Cambridge: Cambridge University Press, 2005), pp. 1–39
MOORE, EVELYN K., *The Eye and the Gaze: Goethe and the Autobiographical Subject* (Berne: Lang, 2015)
MORITZ, KARL PHILIPP, 'Über die bildende Nachahmung des Schönen', in Karl Philipp Moritz, *Werke in zwei Bänden*, 2 vols (Berlin: Aufbau Verlag, 1973), I: *Reisen eines Deutschen in Italien, Aufsätze und Abhandlungen*, pp. 253–89
MOSES, STÉPHANE, 'Goethes Entdeckung der französischen Landschaftsmalerei in Rom (1786–1788)', in *Rom — Europa: Treffpunkt der Kulturen 1780–1820*, ed. by Paolo Chiarini and Walter Hinderer (Würzburg: Königshausen & Neumann, 2006), pp. 29–42
MÜLLER-WOLFF, SUSANNE, *Ein Landschaftsgarten im Ilmtal: Die Geschichte des herzoglichen Parks in Weimar* (Cologne: Böhlau, 2007)
MÜNZ, LUDWIG, *Goethes Zeichnungen und Radierungen* (Vienna: Österreichische Staatsdruckerei, 1949)
NEUMEYER, EVA MARIA, 'The Landscape Garden as a Symbol in Rousseau, Goethe and Flaubert', *Journal of the History of Ideas*, 8.2 (1947), 191–209
NOÉ-RUMBERG, DOROTHEA-MICHAELA, *Naturgesetze als Dichtungsprinzipien: Goethes verborgene Poetik im Spiegel seiner Dichtungen* (Freiburg i.Br.: Rombach, 1993)
NOHL, JOHANNES, *Goethe als Maler Möller in Rom* (Weimar: Kiepenheuer, 1962)
NOLL, THOMAS, '"Das fast allen Menschen beywohnende Wohlgefallen an schoenen Aussichten": Zur Theorie der Landschaftsmalerei um 1800', in *Landschaft um 1800: Aspekte der Wahrnehmung in Kunst, Literatur, Musik und Naturwissenschaft*, ed. by Thomas Noll and others (Göttingen: Wallstein, 2012), pp. 27–59
NOLL, THOMAS, and OTHERS, eds, *Landschaft um 1800: Aspekte der Wahrnehmung in Kunst, Literatur, Musik und Naturwissenschaft* (Göttingen: Wallstein, 2012)
NORDHOFF, CLAUDIA, and HANS REIMER, *Jakob Philipp Hackert 1737–1807: Verzeichnis seiner Werke*, 2 vols (Berlin: Akademie Verlag, 1994)
NUTT-KOFOTH, RÜDIGER, 'Erzähltes Leben zwischen Überlieferung und Konstruktion: Goethes "Hackert"-Biographie und das Problem des "congruenten Ganzen"', *Goethe-Jahrbuch*, 128 (2011), 198–216
OSTERKAMP, ERNST, *Im Buchstabenbilde: Studien zum Verfahren Goethescher Bildbeschreibungen* (Stuttgart: Metzler, 1991)
—— 'Lorrain, Claude (eigentl. Claude Gellée, 1600–1682)', in *Goethe-Handbuch: Supplemente*, 3 vols (Stuttgart: Metzler, 2008–12), III: *Kunst*, ed. by Andreas Beyer and Ernst Osterkamp (2011), pp. 513–16
OVID, *'Metamorphoses': Books IX–XV*, trans. by Frank Justus Miller, Loeb Classical Library, 43 (Cambridge: Harvard University Press, 1984; repr. 1999)
PABST, STEPHAN, 'Das Bild der Idylle: Goethes Kritik an Salomon Geßners Idyllen und ihre Spuren im Werther-Roman', *Goethe-Jahrbuch*, 127 (2010), 13–25
PACE, CLAIRE, 'Claude the Enchanted: Interpretations of Claude in England in the Earlier Nineteenth-Century', *Burlington Magazine* 111.801 (1969), 733–40
—— '"The Golden Age ... The First and Last Days of Mankind": Claude Lorrain and Classical Pastoral, with Special Emphasis on Themes from Ovid's "Metamorphoses"', *Artibus et Historiæ*, 23.46 (2002), 127–56

―――― '"Free from Business and Debate": City and Country in Responses to Landscape in 17th-Century Italy and France', *Konsthistorisk Tideskrift*, 73.3 (2004), 158–78
PANOFSKY, ERWIN, '*Et in Arcadia Ego*: Poussin and the Elegiac Tradition', in Erwin Panofsky, *Meaning in the Visual Arts* (Garden City, NY: Double Day Anchor Books, 1955), pp. 295–320
PAPE, WALTER, '"Die Sinne triegen nicht": Perception and Landscape in Classical Goethe', in *Reflecting Senses: Perception and Appearance in Literature, Culture and the Arts*, ed. by Walter Pape and Frederick Burwick (Berlin: de Gruyter, 1995), pp. 96–121
―――― '"Richtige Zeichnung und Charakter" und "reichergiebiger Farbenquast": Umriss und Farbe in Literatur und Malerei um 1800', in *Die Farben der Romantik: Physik und Physiologie, Kunst und Literatur*, ed. by Walter Pape (Berlin: de Gruyter, 2014), pp. 81–100
PARSHALL, LINDA B., 'Introduction', in C. C. L. Hirschfeld, *Theory of Garden Art*, ed. and trans. by Linda B. Parshall (Philadelphia: University of Pennsylvania Press, 2001), pp. 1–54
PETZ, ANJA, 'Claude Gelée, gen. Lorrain: Landschaft mit Tobias und dem Engel (Der Abend)', in *Goethe und die Kunst*, ed. by Sabine Schulze (Ostfildern: Hatje, 1994), pp. 18–20
―――― 'Jacob Isaackz. van Ruisdael: Das Kloster', in *Goethe und die Kunst*, ed. by Sabine Schulze (Ostfildern: Hatje, 1994), pp. 20–22
PFOTENHAUER, HELMUT, 'Farbe: Goethes sizilianische Ästhetik', in *Ein unsäglich schönes Land: Goethes 'Italienische Reise' und der Mythos Siziliens*, ed. by Albert Meier (Palermo: Sellerio, 1987), pp. 180–92
―――― 'Weimar Classicism as Visual Culture', in *The Literature of Weimar Classicism*, ed. by Simon Richter (Rochester: Boydell & Brewer, 2005), pp. 264–93
PINDAR, *Nemean Odes, Isthmian Odes, Fragments*, ed. and trans by Willian H. Race, Loeb Classical Library, 485 (Cambridge: Harvard University Press, 1997)
―――― *Olympian Odes, Pythian Odes*, ed. and trans by Willian H. Race, Loeb Classical Library, 56 (Cambridge: Harvard University Press, 1997)
POCHAT, GÖTZ, 'Gartenkunst und Landschaftsgarten vor Wörlitz', in *Weltbild Wörlitz: Entwurf einer Kulturlandschaft*, ed. by Frank-Andreas Bechtoldt and Thomas Weiss (Ostfildern: Hatje, 1996), pp. 17–49
PONZI, MAURO, '"Eines Schattens Traum": Goethe und Pindar', in *Goethes Rückblick auf die Antike*, ed. by Bernd Witte and Mauro Ponzi (Berlin: Schmidt, 1999), pp. 38–58
POPE, ALEXANDER, *Poetical Works*, ed. by Herbert Davis, Oxford Standard Authors (Oxford and New York: Oxford University Press, 1989)
POWERS, ELIZABETH, 'The Sublime, "Über den Granit", and the Prehistory of Goethe's Science', *Goethe Yearbook*, 15 (2008), 35–56
―――― 'Where are the Mountains? Johann Jacob Bodmer and the "Pre-Kantian Sublime"', *Goethe Yearbook*, 20 (2013), 199–222
PRANGE, PETER, 'Die Entdeckung der Meeresküste', in *Jakob Philipp Hackert: Europas Landschaftsmaler der Goethezeit*, ed. by Hubertus Gaßner and Ernst-Gerhard Güse (Ostfildern: Hatje, 2008), pp. 234–47
PRICE, LAWRENCE MARSDEN, *English Literature in Germany* (Berkeley: University of California Press, 1953)
PRICE, UVEDALE, *An Essay on the Picturesque, as Compared with the Sublime and the Beautiful; and, on the Use of Studying Pictures, for the Purpose of Improving Real Landscape* (London: J. Mawman, 1810)
QUINTILIAN, MARCUS FABIUS, *The Orator's Education*, ed. and trans. by Donald A. Russell, 5 vols, Loeb Classical Library, 124–27, 494 (Cambridge: Harvard University Press, 2002)

RAMDOHR, FRIEDRICH WILHELM BASILIUS VON, *Ueber Mahlerei und Bildhauerarbeit in Rom für Liebhaber des Schönen in der Kunst*, 3 vols (Leipzig: Weidmanns Erben und Reich, 1787)
REED, T. J., ED. and TRANS., *The Flight to Italy: Diary and Selected Letters* (Oxford: Oxford University Press, 1999)
REICH, THOMAS, '"Sorge" in Goethes *Faust*: Goethe als Moralist?', in *Erzählen und Moral: Narrativität im Spannungsfeld von Ethik und Ästhetik*, ed. by Dietmar Mieth (Tübingen: Attempto, 2000), pp. 143–65
REIFF, PAUL, 'Pindar and Goethe', *Modern Language Notes*, 18.6 (1903), 169–73
RENNER, URSULA, 'Eros, Melancholie und Medien: Goethes "Amor als Landschaftsmaler"', *Jahrbuch des Freien Deutschen Hochstifts* (2001), 1–29
REPTON, HUMPHRY, *Sketches and Hints on Landscape Gardening* (London: W. Bulmer, [1794])
RILKE, RAINER MARIA, 'Der Wanderer: Gedankengang und Bedeutung des Goethe'schen Gedichtes', in Rainer Maria Rilke, *Sämtliche Werke*, 6 vols, ed. by Rilke-Archiv in cooperation with Ruth Sieber-Rilke (Frankfurt a.M.: Insel Verlag, 1965), V, 283–87
RITTER, JOACHIM, 'Landschaft: Zur Funktion des Ästhetischen in der modernen Gesellschaft', in Joachim Ritter, *Subjektivität: Sechs Aufsätze* (Frankfurt a.M.: Suhrkamp, 1974), pp. 141–90
ROBERTSON, RITCHIE, *Goethe: A Very Short Introduction* (Oxford: Oxford University Press, 2016)
ROBSON-SCOTT, W. D., *The Younger Goethe and the Visual Arts* (London: Cambridge University Press, 1981)
ROETHLISBERGER, MARCEL, 'Claude Lorrain Revisited', *Artibus et Historiæ*, 32.63 (2011), 101–18
—— ED., *Im Licht von Claude Lorrain: Landschaftsmalerei aus drei Jahrhunderten* (Munich: Hirmer, 1983)
ROGERS, PAT, 'Pope in Arcadia: Pastoral and its Dissolution', in *The Cambridge Companion to Alexander Pope*, ed. by Pat Rogers (Cambridge: Cambridge University Press, 2007), pp. 105–17
ROGGER, ANDRÉ, *Landscapes of Taste: The Art of Humphry Repton's 'Red Books'* (London: Routledge, 2007)
ROSS, STEPHANIE, *What Gardens Mean* (Chicago: University of Chicago Press, 1998)
RÖSSLER, JOHANNES, 'Die *Aldobrandinische Hochzeit* als gemalte Farbentheorie: Kopierpraxis und Notation in Hinblick auf Goethes *Farbenlehre*', in *Farben der Klassik: Wissenschaft — Ästhetik — Literatur*, ed. by Martin Dönike and others (Göttingen: Wallstein, 2016), pp. 147–72
ROUSSEAU, JEAN-JACQUES, *The Collected Writings of Rousseau*, ed. by Roger D. Masters and Christopher Kelly, 13 vols (Hannover: University Press of New England, 1990–2009)
RUEGER, ALEXANDER, 'The Cultural Use of Natural Knowledge: Goethe's Theory of Color in Weimar Classicism', *Eighteenth-Century Studies*, 26.2 (1992–93), 211–32
RÜMELIN, CHRISTIAN, 'The Search for the "True Appearance of Things"', in Martin Sonnabend and Jon Whiteley, *Claude Lorrain: The Enchanted Landscape* (Oxford: Ashomlean Museum, 2011), pp. 151–59
—— 'Claude Lorrain and the Notion of Printed Arcadian Landscapes', *Art in Print*, 4.5 (2015), 12–16
RUSSELL, H. DIANE, *Claude Lorrain 1600–1682* (Washington: National Gallery of Art, 1982)
RUTHERFORD, SARAH, *Capability Brown and his Landscape Gardens* (London: National Trust, 2016)
SANDRART, JOACHIM VON, *Teutsche Academie der Bau-, Bild- und Mahlerey-Künste* [Nuremberg:

Johann-Philipp Miltenberger, 1675–1680], ed. by T. Kirchner and others <http://ta.sandrart.net/en/text/1#tapagehead> [accessed 20 September 2019]

SAPIR, ITAY, 'The Birth of Mediterranean Culture: Claude Lorrain's Port Scenes between the Apollonian and the Dionysian', *Mitteilungen des Kunsthistorischen Institutes in Florenz*, 56.1 (2014), 58–69

SAUDER, GERHARD, 'Nausikaa', in *Goethe-Handbuch*, ed. by Bernd Witte and others, 4 vols (Stuttgart: Metzler, 2004), II, 67–70

SCHADE, WERNER, ed., *Claude Lorrain: Gemälde und Zeichnungen* (Munich: Schirmer, 1996)

SCHILLEMEIT, JOST, 'Goethe und Heinrich Meyer: Zu den römischen Anfängen der klassischen Weimarer Kunstlehre', in Jost Schillemeit, *Studien zur Goethezeit*, ed. by Rosemarie Schillemeit (Göttingen: Wallstein, 2006), pp. 275–88

SCHILLER, FRIEDRICH, *Schillers Werke: Nationalausgabe*, ed. by Julius Petersen and others (Weimar: Böhlau, 1943–)

SCHLEGEL, FRIEDRICH, *Kritische Ausgabe seiner Werke*, ed. by Ernst Behler (Paderborn: Schöningh, 1959)

SCHMIDT, ERNST GÜNTHER, 'Himmel — Erde — Meer im frühgriechischen Epos und im alten Orient', *Philologus*, 125 (1981), 1–24

SCHMIDT, JOCHEN, *Goethes 'Faust': Erster und Zweiter Teil: Grundlagen — Werk — Wirkung*, 2nd edn (Munich: Beck, 2001)

SCHMIDT, PETER, *Goethes Farbensymbolik: Untersuchungen zu Verwendung und Bedeutung der Farben in den Dichtungen und Schriften Goethes* (Berlin: Schmidt, 1966)

SCHNEIDER, HELMUT J., 'Dichter, Herrscher, Natur: Die Entstehung des Ilmparks und das Bild des Parks in Goethes Dichtung', *Goethe Yearbook*, 12 (2004), 93–109

SCHOLL, CHRISTIAN, 'Offenbarung oder Projektionsraum? Theorie und Praxis der Landschaftsmalerei bei Carl Gustav Carus', in *Landschaft um 1800: Aspekte der Wahrnehmung in Kunst, Literatur, Musik und Naturwissenschaft*, ed. by Thomas Noll and others (Göttingen: Wallstein, 2012), pp. 265–97

SCHOLZ, BERNHARD F., '*Ekphrasis* and *Enargeia* in Quintilian's *Institutionis oratoriæ libri xii*', in *Rhetorica Movet: Studies in Historical and Modern Rhetoric in Honour of Heinrich F. Plett*, ed. by Peter L. Oesterreich and Thomas O. Sloane (Leiden: Brill, 1999), pp. 3–24

SCHÖNE, ALBRECHT, *Goethes Farbentheologie* (Munich: Beck, 1987)

SCHÖNE, WOLFGANG, *Über das Licht in der Malerei* (Berlin: Mann, 1954)

SCHOPENHAUER, ARTHUR, 'On Vision and Colors', in Arthur Schopenhauer, *On Vision and Colors*; Philipp Otto Runge, *Color Sphere*, trans. by Georg Stahl (New York: Princeton Architectural Press, 2010), pp. 35–119

SCHREIBER, ELLIOTT, 'Towards an Aesthetics of the Sublime *Augenblick*: Reading Karl Philipp Moritz Reading Goethe's *Die Leiden des jungen Werthers*', in *The Enlightened Eye: Goethe and Visual Culture*, ed. by Evelyn K. Moore and Patricia Anne Simpson (Amsterdam: Rodopi, 2007), pp. 193–217

SCHRIMPF, HANS JOACHIM, 'Gestaltung und Deutung des Wandermotivs bei Goethe', *Wirkendes Wort*, 3.1 (1952/53), 11–23

SCHUCHARDT, CHRISTIAN, *Goethe's Kunstsammlungen, Erster Theil: Kupferstiche, Holzschnitte, Radirungen, Schwarzkunstblätter, Lithographien und Stahlstiche, Handzeichnungen und Gemälde* (Jena: Frommann, 1848)

SCHULZE, SABINE, ed., *Goethe und die Kunst* (Ostfildern: Hatje, 1994)

SCHULZE ALTCAPPENBERG, HEINRICH-THEODOR, 'Zwischen Ideal und Wirklichkeit: Zum Verständnis der Goethe-Zeichnungen', in *'... auf classischem Boden begeistert': Goethe in Italien*, ed. by Jörn Göres (Mainz: von Zabern, 1986), pp. 99–112, 318–30

SCHUSTER, PETER-KLAUS, 'Catel und Goethe: Zur Entstehung der realistischen Bildungslandschaft', in *Literaturwissenschaft und Geistesgeschichte: Festschrift für Richard*

Brinkmann, ed. by Jürgen Brummack and others (Tübingen: Niemeyer, 1981), pp. 164–200

SCHWARTZ, PETER J., *After Jena: Goethe's 'Elective Affinities' and the End of the Old Regime* (Cranbury: Rosemont, 2010)

SHAFTESBURY, ANTHONY ASHLEY COOPER, EARL OF, *The Moralist, a Philosophical Rhapsody: Being a Recital of Certain Conversations upon Natural and Moral Subjects* (London: J. Wyat, 1709)

SMUDA, MANFED, 'Natur als ästhetischer Gegenstand und als Gegenstand der Ästhetik: Zur Konstitution von Landschaft', in *Landschaft*, ed. by Manfred Smuda (Frankfurt a.M.: Suhrkamp, 1986), pp. 44–69

—— ed., *Landschaft* (Frankfurt a.M.: Suhrkamp, 1986)

SONNABEND, MARTIN, 'Claude Lorrain: The Printmaker', in Martin Sonnabend and Jon Whiteley, *Claude Lorrain: The Enchanted Landscape* (Oxford: Ashomlean Museum, 2011), pp. 137–50

SONNABEND, MARTIN, and JON WHITELEY, *Claude Lorrain: The Enchanted Landscape* (Oxford: Ashomlean Museum, 2011)

SPENCE, JOSEPH, *Observations, Anecdotes, and Characters of Books and Men*, ed. by James M. Osborn, 2 vols (Oxford: Oxford University Press, 1966)

STEPHENSON, ROGER H., 'Mind and Nature: Making Sense of Sense', in Roger H. Stephenson, *Goethe's Conception of Knowledge and Science* (Edinburgh: Edinburgh University Press, 1995), pp. 47–63

STOLZENBURG, ANDREAS, 'Jakob Philipp Hackert in Paestum und Sizilien (1777)', in *Jakob Philipp Hackert: Europas Landschaftsmaler der Goethezeit*, ed. by Hubertus Gaßner and Ernst-Gerhard Güse (Ostfildern: Hatje, 2008), pp. 164–81

—— 'Jakob Philipp Hackert in Rom und in der Campagna Romana (1768–1782)', in *Jakob Philipp Hackert: Europas Landschaftsmaler der Goethezeit*, ed. by Hubertus Gaßner and Ernst-Gerhard Güse (Ostfildern: Hatje, 2008), pp. 138–63

—— 'Die *Zehn Aussichten von dem Landhaus des Horaz*, 1780', in *Jakob Philipp Hackert: Europas Landschaftsmaler der Goethezeit*, ed. by Hubertus Gaßner and Ernst-Gerhard Güse (Ostfildern: Hatje, 2008), pp. 312–25

STOPPARD, TOM, *Arcadia* (London: Faber, 1993)

STRIEHL, GEORG, *Der Zeichner Christoph Heinrich Kniep (1755–1825): Landschaftsauffassung und Antikenrezeption* (Hildesheim: Olms, 1998)

TANTILLO, ASTRIDA ORLE, *The Will to Create: Goethe's Philosophy of Nature* (Pittsburgh: University of Pittsburgh Press, 2002)

—— *Goethe's Modernisms* (New York: Continuum, 2010)

TASSO, TORQUATO, *Discourses on the Heroic Poem*, trans. by Mariella Cavalchini and Irene Samuel (Oxford: Clarendon Press, 1973)

—— *The Liberation of Jerusalem (Gerusalemme liberate)*, trans. by Max Wickert (Oxford: Oxford University Press, 2009)

THOMSON, JAMES, *The Complete Poetical Works*, ed. by J. Logie Robertson (London: Oxford University Press, 1961)

TRAEGER, JÖRG, 'Goethes Kunstwelten: Vom Landschaftsgarten zum lebenden Bild', in *Johann Wolfgang Goethe zum 250. Geburtstag: Vorträge im Frankfurter Römer (April–Juli 1999)*, ed. by Jean-Marie Valentin (Paris: Didier Erudition, 1999), pp. 123–44

TRAUZETTEL, LUDWIG, 'Wörlitz: England in Germany', *Garden History*, 24.2 (1996), 221–36

TREVELYAN, HUMPHRY, *Goethe and the Greeks* (New York: Octagon, 1942; repr. 1972)

TRIMPI, WESLEY, 'The Meaning of Horace's Ut Pictura Poesis', *Journal of the Warburg and Courtauld Institutes*, 36 (1973), 1–34

TRUNZ, ERICH, 'Goethes Entwurf *Landschaftliche Malerei*', in Erich Trunz, *Weimarer Goethe-Studien* (Weimar: Böhlau, 1980), pp. 156–202

TURNER, TOM, *European Gardens: History, Philosophy and Design* (London: Routledge, 2011)
UEDING, GERT, 'Goethes Reden und Ansprachen', in *Goethe-Handbuch*, ed. by Bernd Witte and others, eds, 4 vols (Stuttgart: Metzler, 2004), III, 820–32
VAGET, HANS RUDOLF, 'The "Augenmensch" and the Failure of Vision: Goethe and the Trauma of Dilettantism', *Deutsche Vierteljahrsschrift für Literaturwissenschaft und Geistesgeschichte*, 75 (2001), 15–26
VALÉRY, PAUL, 'About Corot', in *Collected Works of Paul Valéry*, ed. by Jackson Matthews, 15 vols (New York: Pantheon, 1956–75), XII, trans. by David Paul (1960), pp. 134–54
VARENNE, GASTON, 'Goethe et Claude Lorrain', *Revue de littérature comparée*, 12 (1932), 5–30
VIRGIL, *The Aeneid*, trans. by Robert Fagles (New York: Viking, 2006)
WALPOLE, HORACE, 'On Modern Gardening', in Horace Walpole, *Anecdotes of Painting in England; with some Account of the Principal Artists and Incidental Notes on Other Arts* (Strawberry-Hill: Thomas Kirgate, 1771), pp. 117–51
WATKINS, CHARLES, and BEN COWELL, *Uvedale Price (1747–1829): Decoding the Picturesque* (Woodbridge: Boydell, 2012)
WEGNER, REINHARD, 'Von Klapp-Bildern und Kipp-Figuren: "Tournez s'il vous plait" — ein Schlüsselmotiv in Goethes *Wahlverwandtschaften*', in *Goethe 'Wahlverwandtschaften': Werk und Forschung*, ed. by Helmut Hühn (Berlin: de Gruyter, 2010), pp. 219–36
WEIDNER, THOMAS, *Jakob Philipp Hackert: Landschaftsmaler im 18. Jahrhundert* (Berlin: Deutscher Verlag für Kunstwissenschaft, 1998)
—— 'Philipp Hackert', in *Goethe-Handbuch: Supplemente*, 3 vols (Stuttgart: Metzler, 2008–12), III: *Kunst*, ed. by Andreas Beyer and Ernst Osterkamp (2011), pp. 395–403
WENZEL, MANFRED, 'Natur — Kunst — Geschichte: Goethes Farbenlehre als universale Weltschau', *Goethe-Jahrbuch*, 124 (2007), 115–25
WERCHE, BETTINA, 'Jakob Philipp Hackert als königlicher Hofmaler in Neapel und Caserta (1782–1806)', in *Jakob Philipp Hackert: Europas Landschaftsmaler der Goethezeit*, ed. by Hubertus Gaßner and Ernst-Gerhard Güse (Ostfildern: Hatje, 2008), pp. 182–221
WHATELY, THOMAS, *Observations on Modern Gardening* [3rd edn, 1771] (Woodbridge: Boydell, 2016)
WHITFIELD, CLOVIS, 'A Programme for "Erminia and the Shephherds" by G. B. Agucchi', *Storia dell'arte*, 19 (1973), 217–29
WIELAND, CHRISTOPH MARTIN, *Wielands Briefwechsel*, 20 vols (Berlin: Akademie-Verlag, 1963–2013)
WILLIAMS, CHARLES, 'James Thomson's "Summer" and Three of Goethe's Poems', *Journal of English and Germanic Philology*, 47.1 (1948), 1–13
WILLOUGHBY, L. A., 'The Image of the "Wanderer" and the "Hut" in Goethe's Poetry', *Etudes Germaniques*, 3/4 (1951), 207–19
WINE, HUMPHREY, *Claude: The Poetic Landscape* (London: National Gallery, 1994)
WITTE, ARNOLD A., *The Artful Hermitage: The Palazzetto Farnese as a Counter-Reformation 'Diaeta'* (Rome: 'L'Erma' di Bretschneider, 2008)
WITTE, BERND, and OTHERS, eds, *Goethe-Handbuch*, 4 vols (Stuttgart: Metzler, 2004)
WOLF, NORBERT CHRISTIAN, 'Einfache Nachahmung der Natur, Manier, Stil', in *Goethe-Handbuch: Supplemente*, 3 vols (Stuttgart: Metzler, 2008–12), III: *Kunst*, ed. by Andreas Beyer and Ernst Osterkamp (2011), pp. 303–17
WORTON, MICHAEL, 'Introduction', *Paragraph*, 19.3 (2010), 175–78
WYDER, MARGRIT, '"Ein unbegreiflicher Zauber, ein Zufall oder Verhängniß": Meyer und Goethes Farbenlehre', in *Johann Heinrich Meyer: Kunst und Wissen im klassischen Weimar*, ed. by Alexander Rosenbaum and others (Göttingen: Wallstein, 2013), pp. 49–72
ZATTI, SERGIO, 'Epic in the Age of Dissimulation: Tasso's *Gerusalemme liberate*', in *Renaissance Transactions: Ariosto and Tasso*, ed. by Valeria Finucci (Durham: Duke University Press, 1999), pp. 115–45

ZIOLKOWSKI, THEODORE, 'Die Natur als Nachahmung der Kunst bei Goethe', in *Wissen aus Erfahrungen: Werkbegriff und Interpretation heute: Festschrift für Herman Meyer zum 65. Geburtstag*, ed. by Alexander von Bormann (Tübingen: Niemeyer, 1976), pp. 242–55
—— 'Ich und die Vögel: Subjekt und Raum in vier Gedichten', *German Quarterly*, 87 (2014), 33–48

INDEX

(The Appendix with Goethe's Lorrain Collection, pp. 222–25, is not indexed.)

Addison, Joseph 163
Agucchi, Giovanni Battista 8, 42–44, 47 n. 44, 48 n. 61
   Impresa per dipingere l'Historia de Erminia 8, 42–43
Ahn(d)ung see hazy realization
Aldobrandini, see *The Aldobrandini Wedding*
allegory 15, 49–50, 70, 75, 200, 208
'anschauen' 11, 14, 27–28, 99, 100, 131, 194–95
Antiquity 2, 9, 14, 52, 55–56, 75, 80, 81, 82, 85, 86, 90, 113, 121, 137, 144, 156, 205
Apel, Friedmar 7
Arcadia 2, 39, 42–43, 45, 65, 111, 114–24, 137, 140–41, 159, 164, 172, 196, 202, 212
archetypal phenomenon (Urphänomen) 10–11, 100, 189
Aristotle 110, 132
   Poetics 110
Auge des Geistes (spiritual eye), see eye
Auge des Leibes (physical eye), see eye

background, see receding planes
Baldinucci, Filippo 20, 23
Barbault, Jean 52
Barocci, Federico:
   Madonna del Popolo 188
Barrell, John 177 n. 11
Beethoven, Ludwig van 219
Bellori, Gian Pietro 25, 47 n. 44
Bending, Stephen 18
Bible 14, 21, 94, 118, 153, 182, 196–97
Boehm, Gottfried 7
Borchardt, Rudolf 136
Bowring, Edgar Alfred 81
Bril, Paul 35
Brown, Lancelot 'Capability' 2, 150–53, 154, 162, 173
bunt (mottled), see colour
Burke, Edmund 20, 55, 210
   A Philosophical Enquiry into the Origin of our Ideas of the Sublime and Beautiful 9, 136, 142–43
Byrne, William:
   Evening 76
Byron, Lord 120, 123–24

camera obscura 24, 25, 145, 168
Canaletto 35
cangianti mode 187, 191

Caravaggio 85
Carl August, Duke of Saxe-Weimar-Eisenach 89–90
Carracci, Annibale (circle of):
   Erminia Takes Refuge with the Shepherds 43, 44
Carracci, Ludovico 42
Carus, Carl Gustav 17, 45 n. 10
Catel, Franz Ludwig:
   Gulf of Naples 86
chiaroscuro 96, 155, 157, 161, 182, 187, 194
Cicero 54–55, 144
Claude glass 149–50, 158, 166, 167
cognition 7, 28, 53, 69, 85, 90, 91, 95, 195, 201
coincidentia oppositorum 4, 17, 117, 147, 164
Coleridge, Samuel Taylor:
   'suspension of disbelief' 7–8, 43, 123
colore school of painting 92, 132
colour(s):
   circle of 10, 124, 131, 193, 194
   coloured shadows (farbige Schatten) 184, 189, 190–91, 195
   colouring 10, 32, 97–98, 109, 132, 153, 168, 183, 184, 186–88, 191, 194, 192–93
   formation of 10, 11, 182–83, 186, 189, 194, 196–98, 221 n. 41
   harmony of 2, 10, 31, 32, 34, 94, 176, 184, 187, 188, 190, 192–93
   hue 23, 91, 62, 121, 138, 141, 149, 153, 184, 185–86, 187, 188, 189, 190, 191, 213, 214
   local 43, 98, 185, 188, 193
   Mediterranean 108, 183–86
   misty transparency (Trübe) 11, 24–25, 32, 36, 85, 91, 93, 183, 184, 185–86, 189–90, 192–93, 196–97
   mottled (bunt) 34, 37–38, 183–84, 213
   tone 5, 23, 24–25, 30–31, 71, 91, 92–93, 94, 97–98, 108, 111, 181, 183–84, 188, 192–93
   saturation 181, 185, 187, 191
   see also cangianti mode, fresco, perspective (aerial)
contour (Kontur, Umriss) 2, 19, 22, 24, 31, 32–33, 34, 92–94, 96, 105, 106, 111, 129, 133 n. 5, 140, 161, 181, 182, 194, 203, 210, 211
Corot, Jean-Baptiste-Camille 181
Cortona, Pietro da 187–88
   The Triumph of Divine Providence 187
Currie, Pamela 186, 188

Index 243

disegno school of painting 92, 132
dissimulatio artis 149, 156–57, 159–60, 163–66, 175–76
Ditner, David 13 n. 31, 106
Domenichino:
   Dying Narcissus 179 n. 84
Dryden, John 138
Dufrenne, Mikel 26
Du Fresnoy, Charles-Alphonse 138
Dughet, Gaspard, *see* Poussin, Gaspard

Earlom, Richard:
   Liber Veritatis [...] 16, 138, 183
Eckermann, Johann Peter 6, 10, 16–17, 147, 175, 176, 206–09, 219
Egle, Steffen 7, 18 n. 20
ekphrasis 5, 7, 8–9, 16, 39, 40, 44, 47 n. 44, 53, 55, 57–63, 68, 69, 70, 72, 75, 86, 87 n. 16, 95, 112, 119, 120, 122, 123, 140, 145, 163, 192–93, 196, 203
English Garden 2, 9–10, 24, 45, 124, 133, 136–76, 176 n. 3, 201, 205, 209
   Downton Castle 153
   Genius of the Place 147–49, 151
   Hagley 140, 153
   'ha-ha' (sunk fence) 163
   Painshill 144, 164
   'picture gallery' 147
   'regulated wild' 160, 164, 173
   Stourhead 138–40, 155
   Stowe 147–49, 154–55, 164
   Twickenham 133, 145, 153
   Woburn Farm 147
   Wörlitz 148, 155–56, 157
   see also Brown, *dissimulatio artis*, Hirschfeld, Ilmpark (Weimar), Kent, Repton, Rousseau, Walpole, Wörlitz
Euripides 2
eye:
   painterly (*malerisches Auge*) 23, 144, 147, 149, 203
   reciprocity of perception (physical eye) and production (spiritual eye) 14, 54–55, 65, 193–97, 204–05
   see also 'anschauen', colour (formation)

Falconet, Etienne-Maurice 71
farbige Schatten (coloured shadows), *see* colour
Femmel, Gerhard 7
Fernow, Carl Ludwig 17
Förster, Eckart 54–55, 194, 220 n. 37
foreground, *see* receding planes
French Garden 9–10, 148, 157, 164, 165, 166–67, 176
   see also Le Nôtre
fresco 4, 10, 101, 187–88, 191, 215, 217–18
Friedländer, Max J. 20
Friedrich, Caspar David 45 n. 10, 208–09
Füssli, Johann Heinrich 63
Fuseli, Henry, *see* Füssli Johann Heinrich

Gauthier, David 145
Gessner, Salomon 63–73, 75, 87 n. 22
   Idylls 63–64, 75
   'Letter [...] on Landscape Painting' 63–64
Gilpin, William 149–51, 178 n. 31
   An Essay on Prints [...] 178 n. 32
   Observations on Several Parts of the Counties of Cambridge [...] 178 n. 33
   see also Claude glass, picturesque
Goethe, Cornelia Friederica Christiana, *see* Schlosser, Cornelia Friederica Christiana
Goethe:
   as draughtsman (sketcher) and painter 7, 90, 91–92, 93, 96, 102, 203
   works of:
      'Amor ein Landschaftsmaler' 9, 19, 91, 124–33, 134 n. 37, 148–49, 157
      'Anschauende Urteilskraft' 220 n. 37
      'Antepirrhema' 64–65
      'Antikritik' 196–97
      'Auf dem See' 94
      'Bedenken und Ergebung' 18
      Beiträge zur Optik 185–86
      Der Triumph der Empfindsamkeit 158–59, 160, 167, 175
      'Der Wandrer' 9, 37, 75–86, 162, 196
      Dichtung und Wahrheit 51–52, 68, 71
      Die Leiden des jungen Werthers 2, 15–16, 53, 90, 96, 159–60
      'Die Natur: Fragment' 56
      Die Wahlverwandtschaften 9, 150, 166–72, 175
      'Einfache Nachahmung der Natur Manier, Styl' 9, 101–11, 203
      'Ein Gleiches' 220 n. 27
      'Einleitung in die *Propyläen*' 215
      Ephemerides 52, 53, 68, 71
      'Epirrhema' 204–05
      Faust 9, 10, 28, 53, 62, 99, 111, 114–24, 137, 159, 165–66, 172–75, 176, 185, 191, 195, 201, 209–19
      'Im Gegenwärtigen Vergangenes' 205
      Iphigenie auf Tauris 2, 212
      Italienische Reise 9, 36–37, 89–101, 113, 132, 161, 201, 205–06, 210, 217
      'Künstlerische Behandlung landschaftlicher Gegenstände' 5–6, 35–36, 48 n. 56
      'Künstlers Apotheose' 121
      'Louisenfest' 157–58
      'Mailied' 25, 66
      Maximen und Reflexionen 6, 200
      'Mignon' 160, 182, 184
      'Nach Falkonet und über Falkonet' 71
      Nausikaa 9, 36, 111–14, 212, 219
      Philipp Hackert: Biographische Skizze, meist nach dessen eigenen Aussagen entworfen 19–20
      Prometheus (dramatic fragment) 74

'Prometheus' (ode) 74
Reviews in the *Frankfurter Gelehrte Anzeigen*:
  Engraving after Caravaggio's *Three Apostles* 85
  Falconet, *Observations on the Statue [...]* 71
  Gessner, *Idylls* n. 23 64–67
  Sulzer, *Theory of Fine Arts* 67
  Two Engravings after Lorrain 49–53, 57–63, 203
'Ruysdael als Dichter' 10, 65, 199–206
Torquato Tasso 8, 36–40, 44–45
'Über den Dilettantismus' 160, 175
'Über Wahrheit und Wahrscheinlichkeit der Kunstwerke: Ein Gespräch' 4, 215
'Versuch einer Witterungslehre' 213–14
'Von deutscher Baukunst' 54, 56
'Wandrers Sturmlied' 66, 73–75
West-östlicher Divan 182
'Wiederfinden' 182–83
Wilhelm Meisters Lehrjahre 91
  Wilhelm Meisters Wanderjahre 34, 182, 192–93, 197
Zahme Xenien 189, 220 n. 41
Zur Farbenlehre 10–11, 27, 32, 51, 55, 93, 96, 110, 131–32, 176, 182, 184–93, 195, 196–97, 199
Golden Age 37–39, 42, 141, 167, 168, 170
Gombrich, Ernst Hans 13 n. 31, 18
Goya, Francisco José de 181
Graham, Richard 138
Guarini, Giovanni Battista 37

Hackert, Jakob Philipp 8, 18–36, 46 n. 30, 47 n. 49, 90, 97–101, 107, 149
  Destruction of the Turkish Fleet in the Battle of Chesme 21
  Ten Views from Horace's Villa 26
  The Arno Valley near Florence n. 49
  The Eruption of Mount Vesuvius in 1774 21
  'Über die Landschaftsmahlerey' 20–28, 97–99
  View of the Tiber and the Milvian Bridge 47 n. 49
  View of the Tiber Valley with the Sabine Mountains 29–32, 34–36, 47 n. 49
  see also Goethe (works of): *Philipp Hackert [...]*

Hagedorn, Christian Ludwig 17, 45 n. 10
Hagstrum, Jean H. 12 n. 2, 150
Haller, Albrecht von 68
Haltung, see perspective (aerial)
Hamilton, Charles 144
Harrison, Robert Pogue 174
hazy realization (Ahn(d)ung) 53, 56, 72, 73, 75
heiter see serene
Herder, Johann Gottfried 69–70
heroic landscape painting 21, 35, 43
Hesiod 37
Hirsch, Edward 57
Hirschfeld, Christian Cay Lorenz 153
  Theory of Garden Art 153
history painting 35, 43, 186, 187–88

Homer 2, 9, 57, 68, 94–96, 108, 110, 111–13
  The Iliad 57
  The Odyssey 9, 57, 95, 111–13
Horace 8, 9, 14, 21, 25–26, 31, 42, 53, 68–72, 133, 145, 201
  Ars Poetica:
    prodesse et delectare 201
    ut pictura poesis 8, 9, 14, 31, 53, 68–72, 133, 145
Howard, Luke 215
hue, *see* colour
Hutchings, W. B. 70

idyll 9, 37, 64, 65–67, 75, 82–83, 84, 162, 165, 167, 196
  idyllic landscape (painting) 2, 8, 21, 28, 43, 185, 212
Ilmpark (Weimar) 2, 147, 148, 156–58, 160–62
imitation of nature (Nachahmung der Natur) 9, 19, 25, 30–31, 63–64, 67, 101–02, 104–05, 203
intuition 11, 14, 20, 28, 53, 69, 70, 72, 82, 99, 100, 147, 194, 195, 200, 201, 205, 220 n. 37
  see also perception

Kant, Immanuel 20, 25, 55, 56, 134 n. 17
Kauffmann, Angelika 90
Keats, John 5, 12 n. 14
Kent, William 154–55, 173
Klemm, Christian 185
Klopstock, Friedrich Gottlieb 53
Kniep, Christoph Heinrich 32–33, 92, 108–10, 123, 218
  Bocca di Capri 108–10, 218
Knight, Richard Payne 150–53
  An Analytical Inquiry into the Principles of Taste 150
  Expedition into Sicily 153
  The Landscape (poem) 150–53
'Kolorit' 186
Kontur, see contour
Kramer, Olaf 53–54

Lagerlöf, Margaretha Rossholm 56–57
landscape park, *see* English Garden, French Garden
laterna magica 124, 176
Le Nôtre, André 148
Leonardo da Vinci 94, 190
Leopold III, Duke of Anhalt-Dessau 155
Le Rider, Jacques 185
Lessing, Gotthold Ephraim 8, 52, 63, 67, 68–72, 132, 143
  Laocoön: An Essay on the Limits of Painting and Poetry 8, 52, 68–72
light:
  and darkness (shade, shadow) 39, 43, 62, 75, 129, 132, 143, 149, 157, 181–83, 185–86, 193–94, 196–97, 210
  iridescent (schillernd) 39, 184, 190, 191, 192
  reflected (Widerschein) 203–04
  source of 10, 181, 183, 188
  see also colour, Mediterranean

INDEX 245

Linnaeus, Carl 23, 166
    Systema naturae 166
Longinus 28, 54, 55–56, 57, 60, 69, 72, 208, 215
    On the Sublime 55–56
Lorrain (works of):
    Apollo and the Muses on Mount Helicon 91, 97, 154
    A View of the Campagna from Tivoli 21, 22
    Coast View 2–4
    Coast View of Delphi with a Procession 139, 140
    Coast View of Naxos with Ariadne and Bacchus 134 n. 25
    Coast View with Acis and Galatea 9, 118–22, 173, 210
    Coast View with Apollo and the Cumaean Sibyl 86
    Landscape with Abraham Expelling Hagar and Ishmael 4–5
    Landscape with Apollo Guarding the Herds of Admetus and Mercury Stealing Them 91
    Landscape with Dancing Figures 9, 19, 127, 128, 129, 134 n. 37, 157
    Landscape with Erminia and the Shepherd 8, 40, 41, 43–44
    Landscape with Jacob, Rachel, and Leah at the Well 188
    Landscape with Jacob Wrestling with the Angel 188
    Landscape with Mercury and Battus 56–57
    Landscape with Narcissus and Echo 10, 168, 170–72
    Landscape with Psyche outside the Palace of Amor 5, 6
    Landscape with Rural Dance 2
    Landscape with St Mary of Cervello 10, 215, 216–18, 221 n. 53
    Landscape with St Onuphrius 215, 216–18, 221 n. 53
    Landscape with the Father of Psyche Sacrificing at the Milesian Temple of Apollo 91
    Landscape with the Nymph Egeria Mourning over Numa 97
    Landscape with the Rest on the Flight into Egypt 97, 188
    Landscape with the Three Heliads Searching for the Dead Phaeton 2, 12 n. 7
    Landscape with Tobias and the Angel 7, 10, 185, 188–94
    Liber Veritatis 16, 138, 183, 215
    Parnassus see Apollo and the Muses on Mount Helicon
    Parnassus with Minerva Visiting the Muses 97
    Pastoral Landscape (1641) 97
    Pastoral Landscape (1677) 97
    Pastoral Landscape (*Landscape with a Temple of Bacchus*) 75
    Pastoral Landscape with Castel Gandolfo 91
    Pastoral Landscape with the Arch of Titus 52
    Pastoral Landscape with the Flight into Egypt 97
    Pastoral Landscape with the Ponte Molle 29, 33, 34–36
    Pastoral with the Arch of Constantine 2, 3
    Seacoast with the Landing of Aeneas in Latium 52
    Seaport 2
    Seaport with the Embarkation of St Ursula 4
    Seaport with the Embarkation of Ulysses from the Phaeacians 9, 111, 112
    Seaport with Ulysses Restituting Chryseis to her Father Chryses 12 n. 10
    Sun Setting 76–77
    The Herdsman 16
    Ulysses Introduced to Alcinous by Nausicaa 134 n. 25
    View of Carthage with Dido, Aeneas and Their Suite Leaving for the Hunt 97, 142
    View of La Crescenza 153
    View of Tivoli at Sunset 137
Louise Auguste, Duchess of Saxe-Weimar-Eisenach 157
    see also Goethe (works of): 'Louisenfest'

Magna Graecia 21, 114, 153
    see also Mediterranean, Naples, Sicily
Maisak, Petra 17
'malerisch' 22, 23, 26, 157–58
    see also eye
Magritte, René 150
Mason, James:
    The Landing of Aeneas in Italy: The Allegorical Morning of the Roman Empire 49–51
    Sun Setting 76–77
Mason, William:
    The English Garden (poem) 137–38, 153
McCormick, Edward Allen 18, 177 n. 11
Mediterranean:
    light 9, 24, 91, 113, 184, 185–86, 189, 212, 219
    nature 2, 9, 36, 37, 42, 90, 91, 92, 96, 113, 184, 185–86, 199, 213, 219
    see also colour, Magna Graecia, Naples, Roman Campagna, Sicily
Merck, Johann Heinrich 156
Meyer, Johann Heinrich 186–88
    'Die *Aldobrandinische Hochzeit* von Seiten der Kunst betrachtet' 187
    'Geschichte des Kolorits seit der Wiederherstellung der Kunst' 186–88
middle ground, *see* receding planes
Milton 142, 147
misty transparency (Trübe), *see* colour
Mitchell, W. J. T. 17
Möser, Justus 179 n. 60
Momper, Jodocus [Joos[t]] de [the Younger] 32–33, 47 n. 52
Moritz, Karl Philipp 17, 92, 106, 162, 175, 201, 205
    Über die bildende Nachahmung des Schönen 17, 92, 106, 201, 205–06, 208
mottled (bunt), *see* colour
Müller-Wolff, Susanne 156
myth 57, 63, 96, 118–23, 138, 142, 157, 162, 174, 192, 217
    see also Antiquity, Arcadia, Golden Age, Bible, Homer, Ovid, Virgil

Nachahmung der Natur see imitation of nature
Naples 18, 21, 86, 89–90, 92, 93, 97, 108, 110–11, 183–84
neoclassicism 8, 92, 106, 150, 153, 155, 162, 176 n. 3, 188

Newton, Isaac 186, 196–97
Nicholson, Francis:
  Rural Scenery at Stourhead 138, 140
Nietzsche, Friedrich 86

Oeser, Adam Friedrich 72, 157
Oeser, Friederike 72
offenes Geheimnis, see open secret
open secret (offenes Geheimnis) 6, 8, 13 n. 36, 34–35, 185, 195, 204, 205
Osterkamp, Ernst 7, 13 n. 25
Ovid 21, 42, 118–19, 124
  Galatea and Polyphemus 118–19
  Narcissus and Echo 170–71
oxymoron 5, 13 n. 36, 17, 35, 84, 93, 110, 113, 129, 131, 132, 147, 163, 164, 188, 205, 218–19

Palladio, Andrea 94, 162
Panini, Paolo 35
paradox 5, 6, 7, 17, 18, 28, 34, 100, 102, 109, 113, 123, 163, 164, 182, 185
perception 1, 5, 7, 10, 14, 18, 20, 21, 70, 73, 91, 93, 94, 95, 100, 102, 105, 132, 141–42, 156, 176, 186, 193–95, 201
  intuitive 11, 37, 100, 195, 220 n. 37
perspective:
  aerial (Haltung) 2, 19, 23, 32, 40, 85, 91, 129, 147, 156, 171, 183, 184, 189, 201, 219
  linear 23, 189
Philip IV, King of Spain 215
physical eye (Auges des Leibes), *see* eye
picturesque 9, 22, 136, 142, 143–44, 145, 149–53, 154, 157–60, 162, 166, 167–68, 171, 172, 177 n. 17, 178 n. 31, 178 n. 55
  see also Claude glass, Gilpin, Price
Pindar 56, 62, 67, 73, 74–75
Plato 65–66, 132, 175, 219
Plutarch 69
'polarity and intensification' (Polarität und Steigerung) 6, 10, 100, 107, 149, 192, 194, 212, 219
Ponzi, Mauro 62
Pope, Alexander 140, 145–49, 154, 162–64
  Epistle to Burlington 147–49, 164
  The Temple of Fame: A Vision 145–46
  Windsor-Forest 146–47
Poussin, Gaspard 35, 97, 141–42, 165
  Landscape with Abraham and Isaac Approaching the Place of Sacrifice 97
Poussin, Nicholas 14, 23, 35, 89–90, 97, 99, 157, 207
  Tancred and Erminia 40
  The Arcadian Shepherds 39, 118–19
  The Crossing of the Red Sea 14
Price, Uvedale 9, 136, 142, 143–44, 163–64
  An Essay on the Picturesque [...] 9, 136, 143–44, 163–64
primordial landscape (Urlandschaft) 9, 10, 11, 91, 97, 100

primordial plant (Urpflanze) 9, 97, 100

Quintilian 53, 54–55, 176

rainbow 62, 143, 185, 197, 213–14, 220 n. 12
Raphael 94, 100–01
  Mass at Bolsena 100–01
  The Liberation of St Peter 100–01
  The Parnassus 100–01
  The Triumph of Galatea 134 n. 34
  Sibyls 100–01
receding planes (foreground, middle ground, background) 4, 22, 31, 34, 40, 42–43, 76, 91, 96, 114, 119, 129, 147, 149, 189, 193, 203, 217
Rembrandt 157, 181
  Adoration of the Shepherds (with the Lamp) 71
Renaissance (Italy) 2, 4, 24, 92, 132, 160–62, 164, 165–66
  landscape painting 36–45
Repton, Humphry 165, 169
  Observations on the Theory and Practice of Landscape Gardening 165, 168
  Red Books 168–69
  Sketches and Hints on Landscape Gardening 168
rhetoric 7, 8–9, 21, 28, 31, 52, 53–75, 84, 91, 99, 104, 113, 117–18, 128–29, 130, 131, 132, 143, 156, 163–64, 168, 176, 186, 201, 208, 218–19
  see also Cicero, ekphrasis, Longinus, oxymoron, paradox, Quintilian, sublime
Riemer, Friedrich Wilhelm 107
Rilke, Rainer Maria 85–86, 95
Roethlisberger, Marcel 52, 62
Rogger, André 169, 177 n. 17
Roman Campagna 2, 21, 22, 29–30, 90
Romantic movement 2, 8, 45 n. 10, 121, 123, 124, 153, 158, 185, 188, 208
Rosa, Salvator 97, 141–42, 165, 210, 212
Rousseau, Jean-Jacques 28, 165–66, 167, 173, 175, 209
  Julie; or, the New Heloise 167, 209
  Reveries of a Solitary Walker 28
Rubens, Peter Paul 10, 143–44, 188, 199, 206–07
  The Peasants' Return from the Fields 10, 206–07
Ruisdael, Jacob van 7, 10, 199–206
  The Jewish Cemetery 199, 201–02
  The Monastery 199, 202–04
  Waterfall with Castle on a Mountain 198, 199

Sadoletus, Jacob 70
Sandrart, Joachim von 20, 21, 23, 24
saturation, *see* colour
Schein, *see* semblance
Schick, Gottlieb 188
Schiller, Friedrich von 17, 175, 181, 188, 190, 193
schillernd (iridescent), *see* light
Schlegel, Friedrich 206
Schlosser, Cornelia Friederica Christiana 144

Schneider, Helmut J. 166
Schöne, Wolfgang 181
Scholz, Bernhard 54, 55
Schopenhauer, Arthur 186, 195
semblance (Schein) 10, 43, 67, 85, 93, 123, 130, 163–64, 166, 175, 176, 204, 205, 208, 209
serene (heiter) 1, 2, 25, 35–36, 64, 71, 90, 95, 118, 123, 157, 183, 186–88, 189, 192, 193
sfumato mode 32, 94, 190
Shaftesbury, 3rd Earl of 148
Sicily 21, 36, 89–90, 92–97, 100, 108–10, 111–23
Southcote, Philip 147
Spence, Joseph 147
spiritual eye (Auges des Geistes), *see* eye
staffage 4, 14, 21, 23, 40, 43, 60, 64, 65, 66, 98, 113, 119, 120, 123, 130, 131, 132, 192–93, 195, 203, 210–11, 215, 217
Stein, Charlotte von 155, 183
Steinbach, Erwin 54
Stoppard, Tom:
  Arcadia 2
Striehl, Georg 134 n. 22
sublation 7–8, 17, 34, 104, 122, 123, 124, 188, 200, 203, 208, 219
sublime 9, 20, 33, 54, 55, 62, 63–64, 83, 84, 96, 136, 142, 210, 215
  Burke 9, 20, 56, 142–43, 210
  Goethe 20, 33, 54, 55, 56, 100, 113, 175, 209–10, 215
  Hackert 21, 97
  Kant 20, 56
  Longinus 55–56, 60, 72, 208, 215
  Price 143, 144
  rhetorical 21, 28
  Sulzer 21
Sulzer, Johann Georg:
  General Theory of the Fine Arts 21, 32, 67
'suspension of disbelief', *see* Coleridge
symbol 11, 15, 33–34, 42, 52, 62, 64, 70–71, 75, 85–86, 90, 100, 107, 117, 121, 131, 185, 187, 191, 197, 200, 203, 205, 207–09, 210–11, 213–14, 218

tableau vivant 9, 60, 63, 106, 128–29, 130, 131
Tantillo, Astrida Orle 194
Tasso, Torquato 8, 36, 37, 41, 42, 43–44, 164, 165, 206, 217
  Aminta 37
  Discourses on the Heroic Poem 43–44
  The Liberation of Jerusalem 8, 40–42, 44, 164, 165
The Aldobrandini Wedding 10, 187
theatricality 5, 9, 57, 63, 132, 147, 149, 150, 155, 157, 163
Theocritus 43
Thomson, James 9, 70, 140–42, 153, 160–61
  Liberty 141
  The Castle of Indolence 141

The Seasons 70, 140
  'Autumn' 164
  'Spring' 140–41
  'Summer' 160–61
Tieck, Ludwig 181
Tischbein, Johann Heinrich Wilhelm 2, 92
  Goethe in the Roman Campagna 2
Titian 188
Tobiesen, Ludolph Hermann 197
Tobit, Book of 195–96
Tobler, Georg Christoph:
  'Die Natur: Fragment' 56
tone, *see* colour
Trübe (misty transparency), *see* colour
Turner, J. M. W. 138–40, 163
  Crossing the Brook 140
  Pope's Villa at Twickenham 145
  Thomson's Aeolian Harp 138

Umriss (graphic outline), *see* contour
Urlandschaft see primordial landscape
Urpflanze see primordial plant
Urphänomen see archetypal phenomenon
ut pictura poesis see Horace

Valéry, Paul 181, 182
veduta 35
Veronese, Paolo 43, 94, 186–88
  The Family of Darius before Alexander 43, 187
viewing culture (black-and-white / colour) 51–52, 181–83
Virgil 2, 21, 36, 42
  The Aeneid 84, 148
  Aeneas 49, 50, 51, 52, 58, 59, 60, 62, 73, 75, 83, 84, 97, 142, 148
Voltaire 66, 153
  Letters Concerning the English Nation 153

Walpole, Horace 153, 154–55, 163
  On Modern Gardening 154–55
Wals, Gottfried 21
Whately, Thomas:
  Observations on Modern Gardening 153
Widerschein (reflected light), *see* light
Wieland, Christoph Martin 157
William VIII, Landgrave of Hesse-Kassel 188
Winckelmann, Johann Joachim 71–72, 92, 154
Wine, Humphrey 44, 143
Wolff, Caspar Friedrich 54–55
Woollett, William:
  Roman Edifices in Ruins: The Allegorical Evening of the Roman Empire 49, 50

Young, Edward 53

www.ingramcontent.com/pod-product-compliance
Lightning Source LLC
Chambersburg PA
CBHW082244220526
45469CB00009B/2869